Justus Möser and the
German Enlightenment

# Justus Möser and the German Enlightenment

JONATHAN B. KNUDSEN
*Wellesley College*

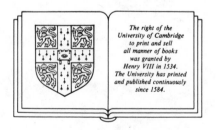

The right of the
University of Cambridge
to print and sell
all manner of books
was granted by
Henry VIII in 1534.
The University has printed
and published continuously
since 1584.

Cambridge University Press

Cambridge

London   New York   New Rochelle

Melbourne   Sydney

Published by the Press Syndicate of the University of Cambridge
The Pitt Building, Trumpington Street, Cambridge CB2 1RP
32 East 57th Street, New York, NY 10022, USA
10 Stamford Road, Oakleigh, Melbourne 3166, Australia

© Cambridge University Press 1986

First published 1986

Printed in the United States of America

*Library of Congress Cataloging-in-Publication Data*
Knudsen, Jonathan B.
Justus Möser and the German Enlightenment.
Bibliography: p.
Includes index.
1. Möser, Justus, 1720–1794.   2. Historians – Germany –
Biography.   3. Enlightenment.   4. Germany – Intellectual
life.   I. Title.
DD192.M6K58   1986   943'.053'0924   86–2269

*British Library Cataloguing in Publication Data*
Knudsen, Jonathan B.
Justus Möser and the German Enlightenment.
1. Möser, Justus
I. Title
943'.053'0924   DD192.M6

ISBN 0 521 32011 9

To the memory of my mother and father

# Contents

# *Preface*

I was led by a deep sympathy with the emigres and misfits of German society to study a figure who belonged to its mainstream. My attachment to twentieth-century culture took me back to its eighteenth-century foundations, and my involvement with the course of European socialism brought me to an ancestor of modern conservatism. The choice I made – to study Justus Möser's place in the German Enlightenment – was a scholarly one, and has remained so over the years this work has taken. I admit that Möser has often fascinated me, but I have never grown comfortable in his world or come to accept his values. But if the reader will find no apologia for *Gemeinschaft* or German paternalism here, neither will he or she find a simple condemnation of Möser's views or reform efforts. Instead, I have tried to present a broadly conceived intellectual biography that describes the problems facing German reformers in the later eighteenth century, but that provides no easy answers to the question: What could have been done?

Justus Möser (1720–94) was one of the pivotal figures in the German Enlightenment. He was an unusual commoner in a political world dominated by the German nobility, and he had broad political and administrative power in his northwest German state, the bishopric of Osnabrück; furthermore, he combined this power with a distinguished career as journalist, historian, and man of letters. His attraction for later readers rests in the numerous essays he wrote on politics, public morals, society, and the economy – essays that he collected as the *Patriotic Phantasies* – and in his pathbreaking *Osnabrück History*. He gained renown among his contemporaries as one of Germany's finest prose stylists and as one of its most articulate political writers. His was a genuinely critical intelligence that stood against the commonplaces of the age, and he has survived with those few writers from the German Enlightenment – Kant, Lessing, Mendelssohn, Lichtenberg – who have continued to be read by later generations.

But Möser's importance in the German Enlightenment goes beyond his political and literary achievements. His critical stance toward his age has encouraged later generations of historians to identify him as the first to break with the Enlightenment's "narrow rationalism." He has been viewed as the father of German conservatism, as the first modern historian to follow historicist principles, and as a founder of counter-Enlightenment irrationalism. He has been used, in other words, to substantiate popularly held views concerning Germany's separate cultural development in the modern era. Yet Möser's critical intelligence did not simply make him into a figure of intellectual revolt. As one friendly with major personalities of the German Enlightenment and as a contributor to its important journals, he must be placed within the movement itself. This is not an easy matter, since the German Enlightenment was ambiguous in its ideals and plans for reform. The predominant interpretation of Möser as a carrier of the counter-Enlightenment has emerged, I argue, from deep misconceptions about the varied impulses in the German movement.

We are now at a crossroads in our understanding of Germany in the age of the Enlightenment. The scholarly neglect of the eighteenth century within the German-speaking world has begun to alter in the last decade or so, but major work in social and economic history still must be completed before our understanding of German developments approaches that of other Western centers of the Enlightenment. The conservative and nationalist rejection of Enlightenment culture that predominated in the German historical profession in the late nineteenth and early twentieth centuries occasioned the scholarly neglect, and the revival of interest during the Weimar Republic was all too brief, being halted by National Socialist rule. Recovery in the post-Hitler era, moreover, has taken far longer than would at first seem reasonable, but clearly it has fallen to the post–World War II generation of historians to write contemporary history – to explain Nazism and to locate its continuities within the Second Empire and the Weimar Republic.

There are also inherent difficulties connected with describing the ebb and flow of the Enlightenment in German society. Germany was strongly decentralized in this period; lacking a single urban center like London or Paris, its society and culture remained heterogeneous and provincial, spread out over a wide geographical area and marked by strong local differences in religion and political organization. These difficulties are part of the reason we lack a biography combining a detailed knowledge of Möser's local conditions with an awareness of the wider culture of eighteenth-century Germany. There are various ways of approaching this matter, but I have tried to conceive of the Enlightenment less as the pure history of ideas and more as a response of Möser and his generation to concrete problems and societal constraints. Once we locate these problems, we can begin to speak of a variety of reform strategies, some of which could be implemented immediately, whereas others remained part of the agenda for the nineteenth century. By setting Justus Möser within the German Enlightenment, I have also sought to reconstitute some portion of the cultural diversity of the later eighteenth century. This approach has allowed me to develop historical models of competing

Enlightenment traditions and to place Möser within a German tradition of corporatist or estatist Enlightenment.

Justus Möser's published and unpublished writings, his essays and histories, memoranda, anonymous pamphlets, and legal briefs also make possible a kind of "total history" of Osnabrück in the later eighteenth century. This is a main source of his fascination. He allows us to study broadly and in depth the political, social, and economic organization of one of the many small ecclesiastical and secular states that formed the German Empire in the period, and to understand how these local conditions affected the reception of Enlightenment culture. Thus I have tried in this book to reconstruct, historically and through his eyes, the structures of meaningfully lived experience in Möser's world and the links connecting social consciousness to work and thought. The methodological concerns have sprung from a deep interest in problems of the sociology of knowledge, but I have also chosen to examine Justus Möser in the belief that his thought and work together clarify specific features of the European Enlightenment in its German setting.

As a whole, this study focuses on the uneven reception and development of Enlightenment values and reform ideas in German society, examining in turn the restructuring and consolidation of traditional elite roles; the Enlightenment perception of political and social change; the emergence of a specifically historical mode of explanation emancipated from church and state; the Enlightenment's limited program of social and economic reform; its science of society and theory of community; and the political components and consequences of its ethical theory. Such problems are of clear interest to readers not normally preoccupied with the culture and society of later eighteenth-century Germany. Thus in each of the study's key chapters, I explore how central Enlightenment concerns intersect with the most significant moments in Justus Möser's thought and career.

In Chapter 1, I seek to orient the reader by characterizing the German Enlightenment as a whole and placing Justus Möser within the it. Chapter 2 describes the environment of the urban notable in Westphalia and establishes the field of social and cultural interest. Chapter 3 explores the immobile political world of Westphalia, Möser's institutional universe, and analyzes his institutional commitment to the world of the Estates. Chapter 4 considers Möser as a historian and traces the inversion of cosmopolitan ideals in his *Osnabrück History*. Chapter 5 examines society and economy in Osnabrück as they are reflected in Möser's reform proposals and considers to what extent he, the "conservative," belongs to the movement of enlightened reform. Chapter 6 examines the fusion of corporatism and Enlightenment in his social theory as it expresses the value system of his generation. Chapter 7 explores what remains more or less implicit in Möser's understanding, the corporatist component in his ethical theory. It is this ethical attitude, as it crystallized in his debate over theory and practice with Kant and others, that tacitly underlies Möser's corporate world.

# Acknowledgments

I have developed many ties of friendship and have learned much through conversation and criticism over the years. The book was originally a dissertation written at the University of California-Berkeley under the direction of Hans Rosenberg. Every person who has had the fortune to attend his classes, listen to him formulate problems, and encourage his students to think with commitment and passion understands that the intellectual bonds are deep and yet difficult to express, since he sends us off into the world to work alone and to write our own books. Though the manuscript has been almost completley rewritten, sections of it still reflect discussions with Wolfgang Sauer and Martin Malia. Of my Berkeley companions, special thanks to Peter Augenthaler, Peter Bergmann, Cornelus Gispen, and Robert Waterman for the criticism of earlier drafts and for being in Berkeley during those years of our discontent. I wrote much of this book in Göttingen at the Max Planck Institut für Geschichte, having spent the year 1971–2 there and a number of summers since then. I owe much to its marvelous facilities and to its spirit of critical and open inquiry. Many thanks to a year of conversations with Ernst Hinrichs in 1971–2 and to continuing discussions with Hans Erich Bödeker, Horst Dippel, Hans Medick, David Sabean, and Jürgen Schlumbohm. Rudolf Vierhaus must be singled out especially for giving of his time and wide knowledge and for continuing to encourage me in this project. Of my Wellesley colleagues, Katharine Park read the manuscript with care and great sensitivity.

I also want to thank the following foundations for research funds granted to me over the years: the Deutscher Akademischer Austauschdienst, Ford Foundation, National Endowment for the Humanities, Wellesley College, and the Max Planck Gesellschaft.

# Abbreviations

| | |
|---|---|
| *AHR* | *American Historical Review.* |
| *CEH* | *Central European History.* |
| *CSSH* | *Comparative Studies in Society and History.* |
| *DVLG* | *Deutsche Vierteljahrsschrift für Literaturwissenschaft und Geistesgeschichte* |
| *FBPG* | *Forschungen zur Brandenburgischen und Preußischen Geschichte.* |
| Klöntrup, Handbuch | J. Aegidius Klöntrup. *Alphabetisches Handbuch der besonderen Rechte und Gewohnheiten des Hochstifts Osnabrücks mit Rücksicht auf die benachbarten westfälischen Provinzen.* 3 vols. Osnabrück, 1798–1800. |
| *HZ* | *Historische Zeitschrift.* |
| *JEH* | *Journal of Economic History.* |
| *JHI* | *Journal of the History of Ideas.* |
| *JMH* | *Journal of Modern History.* |
| Möser, *Briefe* | Justus Möser, *Briefe.* Edited by Ernst Beins and Werner Pleister. In *Veröffentlichungen der Historischen Kommission für Hannover, Oldenburg, Braunschweig, Schaumburg-Lippe und Bremen*, vol. 21. Osnabrück, 1939. |
| Möser, *SW* | Justus Möser, *Justus Mösers sämtliche Werke. Historische-kritische Ausgabe.* Edited by Eberhard Crusius, Paul Göttsching, Werner Kohlschmidt, and Ludwig Schirmeyer. vols. 1, 2, 4–10, 12/1–2, 13–14/1. Oldenburg, 1943–1981 to date. |
| Möser, *W* | Justus Möser, *Justus Mösers sämmtliche Werke.* Edited by Bernhard R. Abeken. 2nd ed. 10 vols. Berlin, 1858 [1842–3]. |
| *Osn. Mitt.* | *Mitteilungen des Historischen Vereins zu Osnabrück.* |
| *PSQ* | *Political Science Quarterly.* |
| *VSWG* | *Vierteljahrschrift für Sozial- und Wirtschaftsgeschichte.* |

| | |
|---|---|
| ZBLG | *Zeitschrift für bayerische Landesgeschichte.* |
| ZHF | *Zeitschrift für historische Forschung.* |
| ZSRG (germ) | *Zeitschrift der Savigny-Stiftung für Rechtsgeschichte. Germanistische Abteilung.* |

# 1

# *Justus Möser in the German Enlightenment*

For more than three decades, Justus Möser was the dominant cultural, political, and administrative figure in the bishopric of Osnabrück. Made secretary to the noble Estate (the *Ritterschaft*) in 1742, while still a student, he began to gather offices and incomes in the fashion typical of institutional life in the old regime: he was appointed *advocatus patriae*, the government's legal representative in foreign and domestic affairs (in 1747); syndic of the *Ritterschaft* (in 1755); justiciary in the criminal court (in 1756); and chief local administrator of the bishopric, its *Geheim Referendar*, during the absentee regency of its English bishop, Frederick of York (de facto in 1763 and formally in 1768). He was thus responsible – in fact, if not always in name – for Osnabrück's economic recovery after the Seven Years War and for its continued social and economic stability in the era before the French Revolution. [1]

Möser could enjoy such political and administrative preeminence because the prince-bishopric (*Fürstbistum*) of Osnabrück, like a number of other small ecclesiastical states in northwestern Germany, had neither a resident prince-bishop nor a resident court, and this gave its administrators significant power. Through his numerous offices, Möser mediated between the semiautonomous Estates – nobility, towns, and cathedral chapter – and the Hanoverian chancellery in Hanover and London. Accepting the political system, he attempted to reconcile the various entrenched interests and pasted over areas of real and potential conflict. In the process, he gave new life to Osnabrück's moribund institutions and brought about reforms in the spirit of the European Enlightenment.

Normally, such a figure would remain the stuff of local history. What made Möser, then and now, of more than parochial interest were his literary skills and his original synthesis of administrative practice and Enlightenment that emerged in his essays, memoranda, and history of Osnabrück. In these works he reflected on the economic origins of the political system of Estates, described agrarian

---

[1] See Chapter 2.

1

society with an unusual wealth of detail and insight, and analyzed the varied demographic and economic pressures that threatened Osnabrück's survival. Moreover, he did not present his views in a straightforward manner, nor did he usually make clear recommendations in his own voice. His many offices provided him entry into Osnabrück's institutions at different and often antagonistic points, and he expressed these various perspectives by becoming, in turn, the advocate for one or another of the numerous entrenched interests – sovereign, nobility, legal notability, peasantry, artisanate. This perspectivism emerged as fundamental to his character. He became a spokesman for the coexistence of opposites, a political foe of administrative centralization, the advocate of social and economic "facts," and the skeptical critic of all systems.

Möser's significance in the German Enlightenment rests in his years of political primacy in Osnabrück, his enormous economic and legal expertise, and his intellectual resistance to all dogmatic solutions. These in combination with unusual gifts as a writer ensured his appeal to many different audiences – to the ruling interests in Osnabrück and the absentee powers in London and Hanover, to his enlightened contemporaries, to the young Turks of the *Sturm und Drang*, and to reform-minded conservatives and classical liberals in the early nineteenth century. As we will see, his broad appeal was rooted in the conscious ambiguity of his prose – an ambiguity that made it possible to assimilate his views to a variety of intellectual positions. Such ambiguity mirrored the conflicting impulses in the German Enlightenment after midcentury. As the configuration of the German Enlightenment altered over the last half of the eighteenth century, so too did Möser's appeal. The social and political crisis of the 1780s and 1790s caused ideas and values from the earlier decades to become more inflexibly attached to particular ideological positions. Enlightenment became more readily associated with revolution and antirevolutionary attitudes with anti-Enlightenment. The Enlightenment and the figures of Möser's generation came, retrospectively, to acquire a more strictly dogmatic meaning that closed off essential dimensions of the movement. Yet the historical Enlightenment of the earlier period was in fact far murkier, since it comprised both the latent and manifest tendencies common to every complex cultural movement. In other words, it still remained open to an indeterminate future.

Justus Möser is significant to the historian of this entire period because, although his earlier career and writings reflect the reform aspirations of the midcentury Enlightenment, he lived until 1794, long enough to participate in the changing public mood of the 1780s and 1790s. Indeed, in these later years he reexamined his beliefs to such an extent that he became linked to the counter-Enlightenment. Our basic purpose in this study, then, must be to consider how the antiphonal structure of Möser's own thought recapitulated that of the wider culture. In this chapter, however, we must emphasize certain cultural particularities of the German Enlightenment after midcentury if we are to appreciate Möser's place in the developments.

## CORPORATIST ENLIGHTENMENT

Though many aspects of eighteenth-century German social and economic history remain to be explored, the contours of the German Enlightenment as an intellectual movement have become increasingly clear. Among other points, we see that its course paralleled intellectual developments elsewhere on the continent and in England. Similar ideals, values, and cultural institutions emerged in Germany at approximately the same time as elsewhere.[2] For this reason, we should resist efforts to see Germany's "break with the West" as originating in uniquely German ideas developed during these years.[3] As evidence, we can point to Gottfried Leibniz, Samuel Pufendorf, Christian Thomasius, Christian Wolff, Johann Gottsched, Georg Lichtenberg, Gotthold Lessing, and Moses Mendelssohn – each of whom was a figure of European significance within the broader history of the Enlightenment.

[2] On the general pattern of the Enlightenment in Germany, see the remarks by Werner Krauss in "Zur Konstellation der deutschen Aufklärung," in his *Perspektiven und Probleme* (Neuwied, 1965), 143–65. Other useful interpretive essays are two on the Protestant and Catholic Enlightenments by Joachim Whaley and T. C. W. Blanning in *The Enlightenment in National Context*, ed. Roy Porter and Mikuláš Teich (Cambridge, 1981), 106–26. For recent work with valuable bibliographies, see Rolf Grimminger, ed., *Deutsche Aufklärung bis zur Französischen Revolution 1680–1789*, vol. 3 in 2 parts of *Hansers Sozialgeschichte der deutschen Literatur* (Munich, 1980), and Franklin Kopitzsch, ed., *Aufklärung, Absolutismus und Bürgertum in Deutschland* (Munich, 1976). Of the older general works, still valuable are Hermann Hettner, *Geschichte der deutschen Literatur im achtzehnten Jahrhundert*, 4 vols. in 1 (Leipzig, 1928); Rudolf Unger, *Hamann und die deutsche Aufklärung* 2 vols. (4th ed.; Darmstadt, 1968), 1:4–111; Fritz Valjavec, *Die Entstehung der politischen Strömungen in Deutschland*, afterword by Jörn Garber (reprint 1951 ed.; Düsseldorf, 1978), 1–145; Frederick Hertz, *The Development of the German Public Mind*, vol. 2: *The Age of the Enlightenment* (New York, 1962); Leo Balet and E. Gerhard, *Die Verbürgerlichung der deutschen Kunst, Literatur und Musik im 18. Jahrhundert* (reprint 1936 ed.; Frankfurt, 1972); Hans M. Wolff, *Die Weltanschauung der deutschen Aufklärung in geschichtlicher Entwicklung* (2nd ed.; Bern and Munich, 1963); Henri Brunschwig, *Enlightenment and Romanticism in Eighteenth-Century Prussia*, trans. Frank Jellinek (Chicago, 1974), 5–98. Regarding the early Enlightenment, Eduard Winter corrects Krauss's views and generally writes with greater subtlety on the pluralistic social origins of the German Enlightenment; see his *Frühaufklärung* (Berlin, 1966), 47–106. Also relevant is the more specialized study of Herbert Schöffler, *Deutsches Geistesleben zwischen Reformation und Aufklärung* (2nd ed.; Frankfurt, 1956). For a discussion of the Catholic regions, see Max Braubach, "Träger und Vermittler romanischer Kultur in Deutschland des 18. Jahrhunderts," reprinted in his *Diplomatie und geistiges Leben im 17. und 18. Jahrhundert*, in *Bonner Historische Forschungen*, 33 (Bonn, 1969), 519–29; also Richard van Dülmen, "Zum Strukturwandel der Aufklärung in Bayern," *ZBLG*, 36 (1973):662–79, and Ludwig Hammermeyer, "Die Aufklärung in Wissenschaft und Gesellschaft," *Handbuch der bayerischen Geschichte*, ed. Max Spindler, 4 vols. in 6 (Munich, 1966–75), 2, esp. 986–8.

[3] The older view is summarized, with literature, in T. C. W. Blanning, *Reform and Revolution in Mainz 1743–1803* (Cambridge, 1974), 15–21. Against Blanning's belief that "in political philosophy at least the breach had occurred a great deal earlier" (p. 15), see the essay by Hans Thieme, "Die Zeit des späteren Naturrechts. Eine privatrechtsgeschichtliche Studie," *ZSRG (germ)*, 56 (1936):208 and throughout. See also the important works by Diethelm Klippel, *Politische Freiheit und Freiheitsrechte im deutschen Naturrecht des 18. Jahrhunderts*, in *Rechts- und Staatswissenschaftliche Veröffentlichungen der Görres-Gesellschaft*, n.s., 23 (Paderborn, 1976); Gerd Kleinheyer, *Staat und Bürger im Recht. Die Vorträge des Carl Gottlieb Svarez vor dem preußischen Kronprinz (1791–2)*, in *Bonner Rechtswissenschaftliche Abhandlungen*, 47 (Bonn, 1959), esp. 21–51, 143–51; Jürgen Schlumbohm, *Freiheit. Die Anfänge des bürgerlichen Emanzipationsbewegung in Deutschland im Spiegel ihres Leitwortes*, in *Geschichte und Gesellschaft*, 12 (Düsseldorf, 1975), 86–146.

Because the German Enlightenment was well integrated into the European movement, we should also resist the recent tendency to adopt Germanisms such as *Aufklärung* (Enlightenment) and *Aufklärer* (enlightener) to distance the German movement from that of Western Europe.[4] The features that distinguished the German Enlightenment from other national variants rested not so much in the ideas produced as in the ideas not produced and in the social and political context of enlightened culture. Though it is possible to find individuals who held radical views,[5] the German Enlightenment lacked the extremes – of materialism, atheism, radical republicanism, and utopian socialism. This was because its corporate institutions remained relatively vital and because its intellectuals were not concentrated in a few urban centers but were spread throughout the large land mass of the Empire. Both factors muted the cultural impact of Enlightenment ideas and forced Germany's intellectuals into a far greater compromise with the aristocratically dominated social and political order. The German Enlightenment expressed this compromise as a form of corporatist or estatist Enlightenment (*ständische Aufklärung*), and it is in this context that Möser is significant.

The Enlightenment had begun chiefly as a reaction of educated Europeans to the bloodshed and persecution of the wars of the seventeenth century. The configuration of ideas that had emerged – of tolerance, individual rights, public order, work, and self-discipline – had gathered strength earliest in England and the Netherlands, partly because political events had made it possible for minorities to survive in these countries and partly because sufficient numbers of humanists were able to support themselves in London, Amsterdam, and Rotterdam. In these cities educated men and women were first able to discuss views, influence policy, and even set the public tone. Although similar ideas of religious toleration, public right, and ethical asceticism developed almost simultaneously in Central Europe, there was no equivalent urban setting where German humanists could gather.[6] With their intelligentsia spread among more than seventy-two urban sites in the late seventeenth and eighteenth centuries, Germans were never able

---

[4] Thus, I resist adopting this stylistic tendency that, it seems to me, abandons the eighteenth-century dialogue among national and regional variants and becomes committed to national uniqueness. For examples, see the otherwise different works by T. C. W. Blanning, *Reform and Revolution in Mainz*, e.g., 34–7, and Peter Hanns Reill, *The German Enlightenment and the Rise of Historicism* (Berkeley, 1975), 1–3 and throughout for his reasoning.

[5] Fritz Mauthner, *Der Atheismus und seine Geschichte im Abendland*, 4 vols (Berlin, 1920–3), 3:161–390, 4:1–86; Valjavec, *Entstehung der politischen Strömungen*, 135–46; A. W. Gulyga, *Der deutsche Materialismus am Ausgang des 18. Jahrhunderts*, trans. from Russian by Ileana Bauer and Gertraud Korf (Berlin, 1966); Gerhard Steiner, *Franz Heinrich Ziegenhagen und seine Verhältnislehre* (Berlin, 1962); Emil Adler, *Herder und die deutsche Aufklärung*, trans. from Polish by Irena Fischer (Vienna, 1968), 238–50.

[6] Winter, *Frühaufklärung*, 47–106. See also Carl Hinrichs, *Preußentum und Pietismus* (Göttingen, 1971), 352–441; Gerhard Oestreich, *Neostoicism and the Early Modern State*, ed. Brigitta Oestreich and H. G. Koenigsberger, trans. David McLintock (Cambridge, 1982), 1–9, 135–54; Wolff, *Weltanschauung der deutschen Aufklärung*, 13–96; Marc Raeff, *The Well-Ordered Police State* (New Haven, Conn.: 1983), 11–42.

to reproduce the same intellectual subculture.[7] Thus, although Germans felt an intellectual kinship with the Enlightenment as it unfolded in England, in the Netherlands, and later in France, they remained relatively more isolated and were forced to maintain intellectual ties through extensive correspondence and to write for a much more widely dispersed audience.[8]

This situation resulted from the regional nature of Germany's development in the hundred years after the Treaty of Westphalia.[9] The Westphalian Peace had guaranteed political and religious pluralism: the secular and ecclesiastical small states, free cities, and class of imperial knights had largely survived absorption or secularization in 1648, achieving political parity at the expense of a central monarchy, strong central institutions, and the creation of a capital city that might have acted as a magnet for intellectual life. The three major religious denominations – Reformed Protestantism, Evangelical Protestantism, and Roman Catholicism – had also been guaranteed their legal existence in the Empire, thus bringing the open warfare of the Reformation and Counter-Reformation to a close.

Both decisions contributed to Germany's uneven recovery from the effects of the Thirty Years War. The lack of a strong central monarchy and effective central institutions left economic recovery exclusively to the individual states and to the relatively ineffective regional institutions of the empire, the imperial circles, which were often in economic competition with one another. This lengthened the time it took to develop the necessary entrepreneurial energy in the regions and urban areas to carry the new secular movement. The religious guarantees further contributed to the cultural fragmentation and fostered a watchful and suspicious attitude by the ecclesiastical and secular authorities toward the intellectuals, thus inhibiting the emergence of new ideas, particularly in Catholic areas such as electoral Bavaria.[10] In this environment the traditional educational institutions, the Latin schools and the universities, continued to organize and control intellectual life. The Germans were slow to break with the older Latin curriculum. Although publication of books in the vernacular had passed that of

[7] For the problem of urbanization and the unfolding of the Enlightenment, see Roger Emerson, "The Enlightenment and Social Structures," in *City and Society in the 18th Century*, ed. Paul Fritz and David Williams (Toronto, 1973), 99–124. For Germany, see Reiner Wild, "Stadtkultur, Bildungswesen und Aufklärungsgesellschaften," in Grimminger, ed., *Hansers Sozialgeschichte der deutschen Literatur*, 3/1:103–32; also the introduction and literature cited by Kopitzsch in his *Aufklärung, Absolutismus und Bürgertum in Deutschland*, esp. 27–41, 61–2.

[8] Erich Trunz, "Der deutsche Späthumanismus als Standeskultur," *Deutsche Barockforschung*, ed. Richard Alewyn (Cologne, 1965), 147–81.

[9] See the balanced account, with literature, by Rudolf Vierhaus, *Deutschland im Zeitalter des Absolutismus* (Göttingen, 1978), 12–36. The older essay by Hans Erich Feine, "Zur Verfassungsentwicklung des Heil. Röm. Reiches seit dem Westfälischen Friedens," *ZSRG (germ)*, 52 (1932):67–70, 79–83, 91, is also valuable, as are Karl Otmar Freiherr von Aretin, *Heiliges Römisches Reich 1786–1806*, 2 vols., in *Veröffentlichungen des Instituts für europäische Geschichte Mainz*, 38 (Wiesbaden, 1967), 1:26–31, 105, and Oestreich, *Neostoicism and the Modern State*, 241–57.

[10] See, for instance, Richard van Dülmen, "Antijesuitismus und katholische Aufklärung in Deutschland," *Historisches Jahrbuch*, 89 (1969):54–64.

books in Latin by the end of the seventeenth century, Latin remained the dominant language of scholarly discourse until the mid-eighteenth century.[11] Latin humanism remained the principal framework within which Enlightenment ideas were assimilated even as Germans increasingly wrote in the vernacular; this pattern is particularly apparent in areas like law, philosophy, theology, and history, where the Enlightenment began to penetrate with particular vigor after the mid-eighteenth century.[12]

These conditions promoted a certain intellectual eclecticism in Germany. The large number of princely courts, where aristocratic culture fell under the sway of foreign patrons – the Dutch, English, French, or the Catholic Church – left German culture open to diverse influences from other areas of Europe. One of the special characteristics of the German Enlightenment was its tendency to absorb and assimilate. This was Germany's intellectual strength, as is clear from the number of foreign works read, commented upon, and translated during the eighteenth century.[13] But it also meant that the Germans developed an eclectic and syncretistic attitude toward the various traditions and tendencies in the wider Enlightenment.

Indeed, though Leibniz, Thomasius, Wolff, and Gottsched each had a significant influence on intellectual tastes during the first half of the eighteenth century, no single strand within the Enlightenment dominated in Germany during Justus Möser's lifetime.[14] As a result, it is difficult to date with any

---

[11]  Albert Ward, *Book Production, Fiction and the German Reading Public 1740–1800* (Oxford, 1974), 30–4, 164–5. Ward's book is based on the valuable older study by Rudolf Jentzsch, *Der deutschlateinische Büchermarkt nach den Leipziger Ostermeß-Katalogen von 1740, 1770 und 1800 in seiner Gliederung und Wandlung* (Leipzig, 1912).

[12]  See, for example, Notker Hammerstein, "Zur Geschichte der deutschen Universität im Zeitalter der Aufklärung," in *Universität und Gelehrtenstand, 1400–1800*, ed. Hellmuth Rössler and Günther Franz (Limburg/Lahn, 1970), 145–82; and the same author's *Jus und Historie* (Göttingen, 1972), 17–42; Hans Maier, "Die Lehre der Politik an den älteren deutschen Universitäten," in his *Politische Wissenschaft in Deutschland* (Munich, 1969), 15–52. For statistics regarding continued scholarly publication in Latin, see Ward, *Book Production, Fiction and the German Reading Public*, 164–5.

[13]  Translations from French and English predominated, though works were also translated from Dutch, Italian, Spanish, Greek, and Latin; for a detailed analysis by language, see the tables in Helmut Kiesel and Paul Münch, *Gesellschaft und Literatur im 18. Jahrhundert* (Munich, 1977), 193–99; Ward, *Book Production, Fiction and the German Reading Public*, 37, 86; Kenneth Carpenter, *Dialogues in Political Economy. Translations from and into German in the 18th Century* (Boston, 1977); Bernhard Fabian, "English Books and their Eighteenth-Century German Readers," in Paul Korshin, ed., *The Widening Circle: Essays on the Circulation of Literature in Eighteenth-Century Europe* (Philadelphia, 1969), 117–96.

[14]  For an overview, see Lewis White Beck, *Early German Philosophy* (Cambridge, 1969), 196–339, and Max Wundt, *Die deutsche Schulphilosophie im Zeitalter der Aufklärung*, in *Heidelberger Abhandlungen zur Philosophie und ihrer Geschichte*, 32 (Tübingen, 1945). Leibniz's relations to the German Enlightenment were complex, based on the late publication of basic texts, the reworking by Gottsched and Wolff of basic ideas, and the consequent recovery later in the century by Lessing, Herder, and Fichte. On Leibniz, see Kurt Huber, *Leibniz* (Munich, 1951), 12, 283–97, and brief remarks in Hans Heinz Holz, *Leibniz* (Stuttgart, 1958), 133–7. On Thomasius, see Ernst Bloch, "Christian Thomasius, ein deutscher Gelehrte ohne Misere," reprinted in his *Naturrecht und menschliche Würde* (Frankfurt/Main, 1961); Hinrich Rüping, *Die Naturrechtslehre des Christian Thomasius und ihre Fortbildung in der Thomasius Schule* (Ph.D. diss., Bonn, 1968); Max

precision the diffusion of the Enlightenment in Germany. We can only speak of gradual expansion, modest fermentation, and relatively rapid contraction over the period from the 1740s through the 1790s. There was a general but apolitical spread of enlightened ideas through the end of the Seven Years War; in this phase the Enlightenment was active in the areas of pedagogy, domestic ethics as expressed in the moral weeklies, and natural science as supported by the various academies. After peace was made in 1763, the pace of public life quickened. These years saw substantial changes in public taste – as, for example, in the slow death of the moral weekly after 1760 or in the works of imaginative literature that began to flood the book market. They also saw an enormous increase in the number of books printed and of magazines and journals started. Furthermore, the Enlightenment spread into areas of social, economic, and religious life that had remained off limits until then. Most of the reform plans for the economy and society in these years were triggered by the depredations of the Seven Years War and the fiscal crisis brought on by the inflationary war economy. In the Catholic areas of Germany there was, in addition, intensified agitation for and against the Jesuit order that resulted in Clement IV's dissolution decree in 1773. The increasingly secular and mildly radical tone of the postwar years continued until the 1780s, when a religious and political counteroffensive began to splinter the common front. In the Austrian core lands the counteroffensive was launched by the Josephinian reforms; in Bavaria it was started by the elector's ban on the Illuminati; and in Prussia it can be said to have begun with the death of Friedrich II in 1786.[15]

Fleischmann, *Christian Thomasius. Leben und Lebenswerk* (Halle, 1931); and Rüping, "Thomasius und seine Schüler im brandenburgischen Staat," in *Humanismus und Naturrecht in Berlin-Brandenburg-Preußen,* in *Veröffentlichungen der Historischen Kommission zu Berlin,* 48 (Berlin, 1979), 76–89. On Wolff and his influence, see the contemporary account by Carl Günther Ludovici, *Ausführlicher Entwurf einer vollständigen Historie der Wolffischen Philosophie,* 3 vols. (Leipzig, 1737–8); Wundt, *Deutsche Schulphilosophie,* 122–99; the essays by Notker Hammerstein and Norbert Hinske in the recent collection *Christian Wolff 1679–1754,* ed. Werner Schneiders, in *Studien zum achzehnten Jahrhundert,* 4 (Hamburg, 1983), 266–306; and the brief comments on Wolff's language in Eric A. Blackall, *The Emergence of German as a Literary Language* (Cambridge, 1959), 19–48. On Gottsched see Werner Rieck, *Johann Christoph Gottsched. Eine kritische Würdigung seines Werkes* (Berlin, 1972).
[15] For various attempts to delineate phases within the German Enlightenment using political criteria, see Rudolf Vierhaus, "Politisches Bewußtsein in Deutschland vor 1789," *Der Staat,* 6 (1967):175–96; Fritz Valjavec, "Die Entstehung des europäischen Konservatismus," in his *Ausgewählte Aufsätze,* ed. Karl August Fischer and Mathias Bernath (Munich, 1963), 343–62; Richard van Dülmen, *Der Geheimbund der Illuminaten* (Stuttgart, 1975), 15–21; Schlumbohm, *Freiheit,* 39–42. Using criteria internal to Catholic Germany, see Richard van Dülmen, "Antijesuitismus und katholische Aufklärung in Deutschland," 54, 78–9; also idem, "Der Geheimbund der Illuminaten," *ZBLG,* 36 (1973):793–833; and idem, "Die Aufklärungsgesellschaften in Deutschland als Forschungsproblem," *Francia,* 5 (1977):251–75. For the Austrian core lands, see the excellent work by Leslie Bodi, *Tauwetter in Wein. Zur Prosa der österreichischen Aufklärung* (Frankfurt, 1977), esp. 34–116. For dating in terms of book production and the spread of literature, see Wolfgang von Ungern-Sternberg, "Schriftsteller und literarischer Markt," in Grimminger, ed., *Hansers Sozialgeschichte der deutschen Literatur,* 3/1:133–85; see similar arguments in Ward, *Book Production, Fiction and the German Reading Public.* For dating in terms of the development of philosophy, see Wundt, ibid., 1–18.

Thus the Enlightenment appears to have developed in a slower and less homogeneous fashion in Germany than among its neighbors to the West. As a broad cultural front, it emerged only in the 1760s and was faced with significant resistance by the early 1780s. In the years after 1763 the German Enlightenment received its special character from its conciliatory and even defensive relation to the established order. After midcentury the German public continuously searched for the ethical and political limits to their beliefs; they sought to define norms, establish the limits of social criticism, and locate boundaries between thought and social practice. Of course, this statement can be applied to varying degrees to every European society, since the number of those willing to compromise was everywhere in the majority, and there were also more radical movements in Germany during these years such as the Illuminati (suppressed in 1785). But, in general, the German situation differed from that elsewhere in Western Europe because the legal, social, and political institutions of the Estates remained largely intact. Estatist or corporatist language continued to predominate in the 1760s and 1770s, whereas the legal and political vision of the Enlightenment began to be articulated only in the late 1780s and 1790s. Thus the great legal codifications of the German Enlightenment, begun at midcentury in Prussia, the Austrian core lands, and Bavaria, gathered force only in the 1780s and 1790s.[16] Moreover, except for Hamburg, there was no large city like London or Amsterdam to erode the economic domination of the landed aristocracy or to cause rapid demographic and material change.[17] For these reasons, the language and material relations that we associate with the terms "civil society" and "representative government" were assimilated only very slowly, even at the level of thought.[18] As a consequence, when the Germans began to discuss political life,

[16] The Bavarian legal codification and commentaries were completed between 1751 and 1771 by Freiherr von Kreittmayr, but this summary in the service of bureaucratic centralization and the older erudite tradition of law did not occur in the spirit of the Enlightenment; nor did those codifications begun by Samuel von Cocceji in Prussia between 1749 and 1751 or those begun under Maria Theresa in the Austrian core lands. Reform, as carried by enlightened legal reformers, did not begin in Prussia or Austria until the 1780s and 1790s. See the brief comments by Ludwig Hammermeyer, "Staatliche Herrschaftsordnung und altständische Repräsentation," *Handbuch der bayerischen Geschichte*, 2:1074–5; and for a longer overview, see Franz Wieacker, *Privatrechtsgeschichte der Neuzeit* (2nd ed.; Göttingen, 1967), 322–47, and Reinhart Koselleck, *Preußen zwischen Reform und Revolution* (2nd ed.; Stuttgart, 1975), 23–51, as well as the older study by R. Stintzing and Ernst Landsberg, *Geschichte der deutschen Rechtswissenschaft*, vol. 2 in 2 parts (Munich, 1898), 2/1:214–27, 465–76, 519–28.

[17] See the comments by Kopitzsch in his edited volume *Aufklärung, Absolutismus und Bürgertum in Deutschland*, 27–41. See also the author's *Grundzüge einer Sozialgeschichte der Aufklärung in Hamburg und Altona* (Ph.D. diss., Hamburg, 1978), 22–39; and Percy Ernst Schramm, *Neun Generationen*, 2 vols. (Göttingen, 1963–4), 1:74–348. Compare to the English case, as described in E. A. Wrigley, "A Simple Model of London's Importance in Changing English Society and Economy 1650–1750," *Past and Present*, no. 37 (1967):44–70.

[18] Ursula A. J. Becher, *Politische Gesellschaft. Studien zur Genese bürgerlicher Oeffentlichkeit in Deutschland*, in *Veröffentlichungen des Max-Planck-Instituts für Geschichte*, 59 (Göttingen, 1978), 11–28, 146–52; also Diethild Meyring, *Politische Weltweisheit. Studien zur deutschen politischen Philosophie des 18. Jahrhunderts* (Ph.D. diss., Münster, 1965); and Schlumbohm, *Freiheit*, 42–57, 67–82.

they tended to treat questions in an abstract ethical language that never became as fully political as it did in Anglo-America or France, or they still continued to argue in the language of corporatism and the Estates. There was almost no concrete political and organizational writing in the press during these years. It is typical of political argument in the Germanies that neither the political pamphlet literature of the American war of independence nor the constitutions themselves were translated and printed before the outbreak of the French Revolution.[19]

To understand the German Enlightenment and Möser's place in it, we must realize that the distinctive shift from estate to civil society, which we so often associate with the historical model of Enlightenment, did not mark the Enlightenment in Germany during these years. I mean by this shift the move toward a juridical or de facto separation of church and state, the replacement of corporatism as a social system by the open, competitive model of civil society, and the replacement of aristocratic monarchic autocracy by a constitutional system of representative government. It is no exaggeration to say that until the 1780s the German Enlightenment was still readying itself to discuss categories that elsewhere had been long articulated and to some extent made concrete. Thus the German Enlightenment remained archaic from the perspective of modern political ideologies and incomplete with regard to an Anglo-French model of Enlightenment. In E. J. Hobsbawm's terms, the German Enlightenment stayed a traditional or "prepolitical" movement in the period before the outbreak of the French Revolution.[20] The majority of enlightened philosophers, publicists, and administrators in Germany were caught between stools, since they believed in a limited, evolutionary reform that would not disrupt the oligarchic institutions of estate society.

Any of a number of texts from these years might be used to illustrate the balance between the corporate order and the Enlightenment — from the commentaries to the Bavarian legal code by Freiherr von Kreittmayr to the essays on "true" and "false" Enlightenment written in the 1770s, 1780s, and 1790s.[21] I have chosen the noted essay on the Enlightenment (1784) by Möser's contemporary, Moses Mendelssohn (1729–86), because it reveals the pattern of restraint, conciliation, and self-discipline with exceptional clarity. "What does it mean to enlighten?" he asked.

---

[19] Horst Dippel, *Germany and the American Revolution, 1770–1800* (Chapel Hill, N.C., 1977), 28–9, 35–7.

[20] E. J. Hobsbawm, *Primitive Rebels* (New York, 1959), 2–3; see also Valjavec, *Entstehung der politischen Strömungen*, 7–11.

[21] See the thoughtful work by Werner Schneiders, *Die wahre Aufklärung* (Freiburg, 1974); also the interpretive essays by Gerhard Sauder, "Verhältnismäßige Aufklärung. Zur bürgerlichen Ideologie am Ende des 18. Jahrhunderts," *Jahrbuch der Jean Paul Gesellschaft*, 9 (1974):102–26; idem, "Aufklärung des Vorurteils – Vorurteil der Aufklärung," *DVLG*, 57 (1983):esp. 264–73; Dieter Narr, "Fragen der Volksbildung in der späteren Aufklärung," reprinted in his *Studien zur Spätaufklärung im deutschen Südwesten*, in *Veröffentlichungen der Kommission für geschichtliche Landeskunde in Baden-Württemberg*, series B research, 93 (Stuttgart, 1979), 182–208.

The words Enlightenment, Culture, and Cultivation [*Aufklärung, Kultur,* and *Bildung*] are new arrivals in our language. They belong clearly to the language of books. . . . Cultivation divides itself into culture and Enlightenment. The former appears to be more directed toward the Practical. . . . Enlightenment, on the other hand, appears to be more directed toward the Theoretical − toward intelligent perception (objective) and experience in intelligent reflection (subj[ective]) about the concerns of human life according to their significance and influence in determining man's nature and purpose. . . . Enlightenment is related to Culture as Theory is to Practice; Epistemology to Morality; Criticism to Virtuosity.[22]

Mendelssohn's definition presupposed the traditional philosophical division between theoretical and practical knowledge, and in this essay he argued without hesitation that Enlightenment emphasized theoretical reflection on man's nature and purpose. The division between Enlightenment and Culture was grounded in a twofold division in man's essential being. Man has both a spiritual and a social or institutional side; thus one must consider both his needs as man and his needs as citizen. "The Enlightenment which concerns man as man is *universal,*" he wrote, "without regard to differences of estate; [however,] the Enlightenment of man when he is viewed as a citizen modifies itself according to *estate* and *occupation.*"[23] Mendelssohn never went beyond this formulation to criticize corporate society or its institutions. Like others in the German Enlightenment he accepted the social barriers separating the orders and suborders of society. It was also typical of his gradualist spirit that he did not establish, as did Kant or Rousseau, the relation between intellect and institutions as one of necessary opposition and unremitting struggle.[24] Instead he expressed the regret of the unarmed prophet: though it may happen that "individual Enlightenment and Enlightenment of the citizen can come into conflict," at those points one can only

22  Mendelssohn, "Uber die Frage: was heiβt aufklären?" *Berlinische Monatsschrift,* 4 (1784):193−4, readily available in Erhard Bahr, ed., *Was ist Aufklärung?* (Stuttgart, 1974), 6 − all references to this edition. See also the excellent essays by Alexander Altmann, "Moses Mendelssohn über Naturrecht und Naturzustand," in *Ich handle mit Vernunft,* ed. Norbert Hinske (Hamburg, 1981), 45−84; and his *Prinzipien politischer Theorie bei Mendelssohn und Kant,* in *Trierer Universitätsreden,* 9 (Trier, 1981).

23  Mendelssohn, "Was heiβt aufklären?", 7. The same ideas appear in Johann Ludwig Ewald, *Ueber Volksaufklärung; Ihre Gränzen und Vortheile* (Berlin, 1790), 14, 18, 23. See the works cited in footnote 21 and Wolfgang Ruppert, "Volksaufklärung im späten 18. Jahrhundert," in *Hansers Sozialgeschichte der deutschen Literatur* 3/1:341−61. In France these views were commonplace; see Harry Payne, *The Philosophes and the People* (New Haven, Conn., 1976); and Harvey Chisick, *The Limits of Reform in the Enlightenment* (Princeton, N.J., 1980).

24  Though Mendelssohn had translated the *Second Discourse on Inequality* in 1756, he did not adopt Rousseau's interpretation of this antagonism in order to show how estate and occupation constricted individual enlightenment. Nor did he refer optimistically, as did Kant, to man's "unsociable sociability" as the mainspring of culture and progress. See Mendelssohn's criticism of Rousseau in the public letter addressed to Lessing published with the 1756 translation: "Sendschreiben an den Herrn Magister Lessing in Leipzig," in Mendelssohn, *Gesammelte Schriften. Jubiläums Ausgabe,* ed. Fritz Bamberger et al. (Berlin, 1929− ), 2:83−109. Compare with Immanuel Kant, "Idea for a Universal History with a Cosmopolitan Purpose," *Political Writings,* ed. Hans Reiss and trans. H. B. Nisbet (Cambridge, 1970), 44−5; German ed., Kant, *Werke,* ed. Wilhelm Weischedel, 6 vols. (Darmstadt, 1966−70), 6:37−9.

retreat, since "the ethically committed man of Enlightenment must proceed with care and caution and rather tolerate prejudice than also drive away the truth concealed with it."[25] Mendelssohn concluded his essay on Enlightenment in the spirit of restraint, warning that "abuse of Enlightenment weakens moral sense, and leads to rigidity, egoism, irreligion, and anarchy."[26]

Mendelssohn's hesitation to render political judgments may well have sprung from his isolation as a Jewish philosopher within a readily hostile Christian society and from fear of being distracted from his self-chosen task of mediating between the two cultures. Nevertheless, his essay reveals the ideas common to the prevalent style of thought: the division between the theoretical and the practical correlated with Enlightenment and social change, the emphasis on the Enlightenment as a theoretical movement, and the tendency to protect corporate institutions and values from the full force of enlightened criticism.

In essence, then, the German advocacy of Enlightenment ethical, religious, and pedagogic ideals remained confined within the institutions of the old regime, and the German Enlightenment of this period retained its special character because of this fact. I have called this phenomenon "corporatist" or "estatist" Enlightenment – an English translation of the more readily understandable phrase *ständische Aufklärung*[27] – in order to draw attention to the careful balancing act practiced by Möser and his contemporaries. The term refers to the political and social values of the Enlightenment thinkers active between midcentury and the outbreak of the French Revolution. The pairing of corporatism and Enlightenment reflects both the legal and social reality of the order of estates and the fact that this reality continued to be preserved within the thought of the German Enlightenment. Indeed, we can distinguish political, economic, and social sub-

---

[25] Mendelssohn, "Was heißt aufklären?", 7.

[26] Ibid.

[27] In using the terms "estatism" or "corporatism," I am rendering into English the German term *Stand* to refer to the social and political system of estates as it flourished in the *Ständestaat* from the sixteenth through the nineteenth centuries. I do not use the term statically, since it is clear that corporatism and the system of Estates changed substantially in these centuries. But it is also clear that for the eighteenth century the historian must treat this phenomenon as more than a survival of anachronistic institutions and values. For a conceptual orientation, see Ferdinand Tönnies, "Estates and Classes," in Reinhard Bendix and Seymour Martin Lipset, eds., *Class, Status and Power* (Glencoe, Ill., 1953), 49–63; Max Weber, *Wirtschaft und Gesellschaft*, 2 vols. (Cologne, 1964), 2:809–31; Heinz Reif, *Westfälischer Adel 1770–1860*, in *Kritische Studien zur Geschichtswissenschaft* 35 (Göttingen, 1979), 24–40. For a historical orientation, see Robert R. Palmer, *The Age of the Democratic Revolution*, 2 vols. (Princeton, N.J., 1959–64), 1:27–82; C. B. A. Behrens, "Government and Society," in *The Cambridge Economic History*, 7 vols. in 9 (2nd ed.; London, 1966–78), 5:549–60; Otto Brunner, "Die Freiheitsrechte in der altständischen Gesellschaft," in his *Neue Wege der Verfassungs- und Sozialgeschichte* (2nd rev. ed.; Göttingen, 1968), 187–98; and Dietrich Gerhard, "Regionalismus und ständisches Wesen als ein Grundthema europäischer Geschichte," in his *Alte und neue Welt in vergleichender Geschichtsbetrachtung*, in *Veröffentlichungen des Max-Planck-Instituts für Geschichte*, 10 (Göttingen, 1962), 13–39; Gerhard Oestreich, *Neostoicism and the Early Modern State*, 166–98; and, with I. Auerbach, the same author's "Ständische Verfassung," in *Sowjetsystem und Demokratische Gesellschaft*, ed. C. D. Kernig, 6 vols (Freiburg, 1966–72), 6:211–35.

elements, locating for each the institutional network and its resonance in the patterns of German Enlightenment thought.

The first component of corporatist or estatist Enlightenment is political paternalism accompanied by an allegiance to the political institutions of the old regime. This paternalism was not as extreme as the full-blown patriarchalism of Haller in the Restoration period, or of the seventeenth-century Englishman Robert Filmer, whose *Patriarcha* is classic for fusing biblicism with a defense of authority; such a point of view was rarely in evidence in eighteenth-century Germany and was certainly unacceptable in the enlightened republic of letters.[28] Even so, the model of the family remained primary, shaping all political argument. This paternalist element in German thought was reinforced by the hereditary primacy of the nobility and it patrimonal powers in the countryside, by the patronage system in the bureaucracy, and by the very ideal of a natural aristocracy of the educated and well-to-do. Though certain of these ideas were current elsewhere in Europe, paternalism was central to German enlightened thought. Politically, such paternalism entailed a defense either of the corporate bodies as a form of aristocratic republicanism or of absolute government; socially, it called for the primacy of paternal power in the family and defended the legitimacy of the master–servant relationship; culturally, it raised the ideal of an aristocracy of letters with "naturally" superior corporate rights and privileges.

The relative stagnation and underdevelopment of the German economy ran parallel to, and partly determined, the survival of paternalism in the social and political system of estates. This pattern is related, in turn, to the second component of corporatist Enlightenment – the survival of the older moral economy and the continued preeminence of the agrarian state, which slowed systematic efforts at social and economic reform.[29] The process of economic innovation continued to be dominated by the aristocratic, monarchic, and urban oligarchic carriers of the old order. The paternalistic fiction that the ruler was the ethical embodiment of the good, the economy an extension of the household, and the social product justly divided among the various orders and status groups according to the watchful beneficence of the ruler still survived in the later eighteenth century and influenced the attitudes of Möser's generation as it linked paternalistic

[28] See, for instance, the section on "patrimonial feudalism" in Hartwig Brandt, *Landständische Repräsentation im deutschen Vormärz: Politisches Denken im Einflußfeld des monarchischen Prinzips* (Neuwied am Rhein, 1968), 59; also the useful introduction by Peter Laslett to his edition of Robert Filmer, *Patriarcha* (Oxford, 1949), 11–43; Gordon J. Schochet, *Patriarchalism in Political Thought* (New York, 1975), esp. 1–18 and 244–81; and Martin Seliger, *The Liberal Politics of John Locke* (New York, 1968), 209–30. Also important is Dieter Schwab, "Die Familie als Vertragsgesellschaft im Naturrecht der Aufklärung," *Quaderni fiorentini per la storia del pensiero giuridico moderno*, 1 (1972):357–76.

[29] The classic formulation of the conceptual distinction between the older economic system and modern capitalism remains Otto Brunner, "Das 'ganze Haus' und die alteuropäische 'Oekonomik'," in his *Neue Wege der Verfassungs- und Sozialgeschichte*, 103–27. See also E. P. Thompson, "The Moral Economy of the English Crowd in the Eighteenth Century," *Past and Present*, no. 50 (1971):76–136; and the same author's "Eighteenth-Century English Society: Class Struggle without Class?" *Social History*, 3/2 (1978):133–65.

ethical norms to the economy. Just as Mendelssohn separated political change from personal Enlightenment, so, too, did Möser and his contemporaries divorce enlightened political and constitutional theory from social and economic life. The only exception proved to be the question of peasant emancipation, where a large literature emerged in the 1770s, 1780s, and 1790s to argue for the abolition of serfdom.[30] In other areas, the separation between theory and practice was mirrored in the treatment of the economy; it left an enormous ethical domain within the economy to manipulation by the state.[31]

It is not that enlightened economic thought was unimportant in later eighteenth-century Germany; rather, it was distanced from its individualist underpinnings by the burgeoning state apparatus. In the eighteenth century territorial rulers had begun to require special university training for officials in order to improve revenues and the exploitation of human and material resources. They were aided by enlightened reformers who saw university education as the means to effect significant change. At the turn of the century, publicists such as Leibniz and Thomasius had fought for the creation of university chairs of administration, finance, and statistics as a way to reform the scholastic curriculum and to discipline an arbitrary and corrupt administration. The German equivalent of political economy, "cameralism," was born of state usurpation of the private economic sphere and represents in this area as well the fusion of corporatism and Enlightenment. Friedrich Wilhelm I of Prussia established chairs for the "cameral sciences" (*die Kameralwissenschaften*) in Halle and Frankfurt/Oder in 1727. The next such chair was instituted in Vienna in 1752, and after the Seven Years War similar chairs were founded at universities throughout the Germanies: Prague and Leipzig (1763); Würzburg (1764); Freiburg, Klagenfürth, and Innsbrück (1768); Göttingen (1775); and Ingolstadt (1780).[32]

Thus during Möser's lifetime the older Aristotelian tradition of practical philosophy gave way at the university to the newer cameral sciences. The Aristotelian triad of politics, ethics, and economics still so apparent in the Scottish moral philosophy of Hume, Smith, and Ferguson was replaced not by a socioeconomic theory of possessive individualism but by a renewed corporatism spearheaded by the "state." Private economy was subordinated to territorial economy (*Landesökonomie*) as systematic theories of state finance and administration, state economic planning, social welfare, and domestic control came to predominate. It is indicative of the continuities with princely paternalism that the new cameral sciences were subsumed juridically under the policing powers of the sovereign and often called *Polizeiwissenschaft*.[33]

---

[30] For a summary with literature see Schlumbohm, *Freiheit*, 95–101.

[31] Hans Maier, "Die Lehre der Politik," 19–24; Blanning, *Reform and Revolution in Mainz*, 8–10.

[32] W. Lexis, "Kammeralwissenschaft," J. Conrad, et al., eds., *Handwörterbuch der Staatswissenschaften* (3rd. ed.; Jena, 1909), 751–2; Wilhelm Roscher, *Geschichte der Nationalökonomik in Deutschland* (Munich, 1874).

[33] Maier, *Die Aeltere deutsche Staats- und Verwaltungslehre (Polizeiwissenschaft)* (Neuwied am Rhein, 1966); Marc Raeff, "The Well-Ordered Police State and the Development of Modernity in Sev-

In this way, the princely state sought to monopolize the entire domain of the practical. It depressed the growth of a market-oriented private realm and in so doing managed to distort the discussion of material change. It is from this perspective that we must look at the various efforts at social and economic reform within the German Enlightenment. Although attempts to rationalize the economy and overhaul archaic institutions broadened during these years, coalescing into a general reform program for the old regime, the political boundaries Mendelssohn had not wanted to cross became increasingly apparent, since administrators and the princely state were the carriers of that reform.

If England and Scotland often supplied political models to the continental Enlightenment, it was the social and economic crisis in France that provided the language of material reform. In France attempts to reform fiscal and economic abuse were of long standing. From the late seventeenth century on, reform had been carried forward by the king's ministers and intendents in the name of law and absolute government, but in the half-century or more of paralysis by royal ministers who could not implement internal reforms they well understood, the initiative gradually shifted from them to the world of the salons and the French intelligentsia. The depth and profundity of the administrative problems, in addition, brought forth an expertise in the public realm that undermined the claims to omnicompetence and moral leadership by the French monarchy. From midcentury on, the Encyclopedists began to transform the general discontent into a systematic, detailed program of domestic reform. To a great extent, their views summarized and made concrete the proposals of previous generations: elimination of archaic offices and institutions; competition by merit; an impartial system of justice; tax reform; rationalization of agriculture; abolition of the real and symbolic vestiges of feudal exploitation; and separation of church and state. Their programs, though hardly monolithic – witness the struggles between fiscalists, physiocrats, and the followers of Gournay such as Turgot – gathered adherents and a practical urgency as the fiscal crisis of the French monarchy deepened in the years after the Seven Years War.[34]

After midcentury reformers in the German states analyzed German retardation in much the same way as their French counterparts. In the light of the legal, economic, and social reform literature that flowed into the Germanies, German conditions seemed qualitatively similar but, if anything, even more backward.[35]

enteenth- and Eighteenth-Century Europe," *AHR*, 80 (1975):1239–43, and the same author's *Well-Ordered Police State*, 43–179; Oestreich, "*Neostoicism and the Early Modern State*, 135–54.

[34] Of this large literature, see the recent survey with bibliography by C. B. A. Behrens, "Government and Society," 549–620, 676–80, and the excellent review essay by Rolf Reichardt, "Bevölkerung und Gesellschaft Frankreichs im 18. Jahrhundert: Neue Wege und Ergebnisse der sozialhistorischen Forschung 1950–1976," *ZHF*, 4 (1977):154–221. In addition, see Lionel Rothkrug, *Opposition to Louis XIV* (Princeton, N.J., 1965); Kingsley Martin, *French Liberal Thought in the Eighteenth Century* (New York, 1962); Douglas Dakin, *Turgot and the Ancien Regime in France* (New York, 1972); and John Lough, *The Philosophes and Post-Revolutionary France* (Oxford, 1982), esp. 8–133.

[35] Whether German conditions were everywhere more backward, even if they were often perceived

Like the French, German reformers lamented the archaic judicial system; administrative corruption and duplication of functions; inefficient agriculture; intolerable burdens, both real and spiritual, on the peasantry; inadequate waterways, postal services, and roads; and constraints on capital accumulation and entrepreneurial innovation. As in France, these years saw in Germany the intensification of reform, particularly in the countries and regions devastated by war – Westphalia, Hanover, the Hohenzollern domains, Saxony, and the Habsburg core lands. The recovery period after the Seven Years War gave birth in Saxony to the remarkable reforms led by Thomas Freiherr von Fritsch; in the Hohenzollern domains, to the fiscalism associated with Friedrich II's *Akzise* system and the legal codification in the *Allgemeines Landrecht* (General Legal Code); in the Habsburg domains, to the administrative reorganization begun under Maria Theresa and continued by Joseph II; in tiny Osnabrück, to the reforms of Justus Möser. In Saxony-Weimar, the electorate of Cologne, Baden, and the Habsburg domains, systematic and far-reaching reform efforts continued into the 1770s and 1780s, culminating in the Baden emancipation decrees of 1783 and the Josephinian reforms in the years that followed.[36] In the small Catholic states – Bavaria, Mainz, Trier, Münster – the reform movement also gathered the momentum that led to the expulsion of the Jesuit order and the passage of major economic and administrative decrees.[37]

But in Germany there was no equivalent to intense crisis or agitation for reform at the center. The fiscal crisis of one state could not easily threaten the political existence of the others, nor, conversely, could reforms made in one state have the same societal impact (the exception perhaps were the aborted Josephinian reforms). The institutions of the old regime in Germany simply were not under

to have been, is not easily judged. But clearly, certain regions of Germany had a level of well-being far beyond that of the poorer regions of France; moreover, the division in Germany was not always between the Protestant and Catholic regions. For two comparative studies, the first dealing with peasant burdens and the second with literacy levels, see Eberhard Weis, "Ergebnisse eines Vergleichs der grundherrschaftlichen Strukturen Deutschlands und Frankreichs vom 13. bis zum Ausgang des 18. Jahrhunderts," *VSWG*, 57 (1970):1–14; and Etienne François, "Die Volksbildung am Mittelrhein im ausgehenden 18. Jahrhundert," *Jahrbuch für westdeutsche Landesgeschichte*, 3 (1977):277–304. See also F. G. Dreyfus, *Sociétés et Mentalités à Mayence dans la second moitié du dix-huitième siècle* (Paris, 1968), 83–120, 158–92.

[36] See the recent survey of literature and problems in Eberhard Weis, "Absolute Monarchie und Reform in Deutschland des späteren 18. und des frühen 19. Jahrhunderts," reprinted in Kopitzsch, ed., *Aufklärung, Absolutismus und Bürgertum*, 192–219. Also see Horst Schlechte, *Die Staatsreform in Kursachsens 1762–63* (Berlin, 1958); Helen Liebel, *Enlightened Bureaucracy versus Enlightened Despotism in Baden, 1750–1790* (Philadelphia, 1965); Paul von Mitrofanov, *Joseph II. Seine politische und kulturelle Tätigkeit*, 2 vols. (Vienna, 1910), esp. 2:235–665; Gerhard Ritter, *Stein* (3rd ed.; Stuttgart, 1958), 37–120.

[37] Van Dülmen, "Antijesuitismus und katholisches Reich," 52–80; Blanning, *Reform and Revolution in Mainz*, 96–209; Dreyfus, *Sociétés et Mentalités à Mayence*, 127–57; Braubach, "Die kirchliche Aufklärung im katholischen Deutschland im Spiegel des 'Journal von und für Deutschland' (1784–1792)," in his *Diplomatie und geistiges Leben*, 563–659; the same author's *Kurköln. Gestalten und Ereignisse aus zwei Jahrhunderten rheinischer Geschichte* (Münster, 1949), 335–501.

the same intense fiscal pressure as in France, nor was the pace of economic and social change as accelerated as in Britain.[38] As a consequence, the debate over economic reform did not generally leave the realm of men attached to the state, as it had in France. In Germany state officials continued to monopolize the reform literature, and hence the practical assimilation of enlightened reform ideas went forward at a slower pace and with far greater eclecticism. Everywhere economic reform, as carried by the state and its administrators, stopped before the institutions of the old regime. In the institutional world of the Germanies there were no ready answers to its social, political, and economic problems; above all, in the absence of crisis there was no lever to compel change, because reform in the individual states would quickly have gone beyond state boundaries to involve a general reform of the institutions of the Empire and a restructuring of aristocratic and monarchic power. The practical impossibility of such a reform, as well as its perceived threat to individual "liberties," shaped the intellectual and emotional compromises of Möser's generation with the old order. We see such attitudes of acceptance particularly among the legal theorists who taught imperial public law; the servility of Johann S. Pütter was well known to his contemporaries in these matters, but not even the radical pietist Friedrich Karl von Moser was willing to conceive a restructuring of the political order at the imperial level.[39]

The eclecticism of Möser and his contemporaries was rooted in the political limits to substantial economic and social reform. Thus a third component of corporatist Enlightenment is related to the first and involves the difficulty of reforming the imperial system in the later eighteenth century.[40] Widespread

---

[38] Vierhaus, "Politisches Bewußtsein in Deutschland vor 1789," 194–6. That the German states also suffered a weaker version of this fiscal crisis cannot be denied. Balet and Gerhard, for example, trace the radical decline of courtly patronage during the second half of the century; see their *Die Verbürgerlichung der deutschen Kunst, Literatur und Musik im 18. Jahrhundert*, 5–89. See the literature in footnotes 35 and 36, and a summary of the crisis in agriculture and aristocratic landholding in Hanna Schissler, *Preußische Agrargesellschaft im Wandel*, in *Kritische Studien zur Geschichtswissenschaft*, 33 (Göttingen, 1978), esp. 34–71; and Reif, *Westfälischer Adel*, 176–86, 213–40.

[39] See Moser's laments about the Empire in his *Von dem deutschen Nationalgeist* (n.p., 1765), 5–12, 28–39. For his political ideas, see Notker Hammerstein, "Das politische Denken Friedrich Carl von Moser," *HZ*, 212 (1971):335–6. For views of Pütter and Pütter's views, see Arnold Berney, "August Ludwig von Schlözer's Staatsauffassung," *HZ*, 132 (1925):46, 65; and Ulrich Schlie, *Johann Stephen Pütters Reichsbegriff*, in *Göttinger Rechtswissenschaftliche Studien*, 38 (Göttingen, 1961), 4–6, 41–51. For Johann Jakob Moser's views, see Reinhard Rürup, *Johann Jakob Moser*, in *Veröffentlichungen des Instituts für europäische Geschichte Mainz*, 35 (Wiesbaden, 1968), 141–52; and Mack Walker, *Johann Jakob Moser and the Holy Roman Empire of the German Nation* (Chapel Hill, N.C., 1981), 289–309. For an overview of the relations between public law and the imperial constitution, see Hanns Gross, *Empire and Sovereignty. A History of the Public Law Literature 1599–1804* (Chicago, 1973), 382–480; Ernst Rudolf Huber, "Reich, Volk und Staat in der Reichsrechtswissenschaft des 17. und 18. Jahrhunderts," *Zeitschrift für die gesamte Staatswissenschaft*, 102 (1942):621–7; and Wolfgang Zorn, "Reichs- und Freiheitsgedanken in der Publizistik des ausgehenden 18. Jahrhunderts (1763–1792)," *Darstellungen und Quellen zur Geschichte der deutschen Einheitsbewegung*, 2 (1959):11–66.

[40] I find largely unpersuasive the recent effort to revise our estimates of the institutional effectiveness of the Holy Roman Empire from the end of the Thirty Years War to the mid-eighteenth century. See the review essay by Gerald Strauss, "The Holy Roman Empire Revisited," *CEH*, 11 (1978):290–301. In this revisionist tradition, see James Vann, *The Swabian Kreis: Institutional*

reform threatened the precarious balance achieved in 1648 and tested in the wars of the eighteenth century. It was especially disturbing to the small states that rejected Habsburg or Hohenzollern domination and that were the carriers of the imperial ideal. In these years, enlightened reformers explored the various institutions, political strata, and organized interest groups within the individual states and the empire, betting on one and then the other to alter the status quo. The political impasse fostered, on one side, the enthusiasm for monarchic autocracy, for "enlightened absolutism," as the only force capable of breaking the power of the Estates and aristocratic self-interest.[41] On the other side, it encouraged the particularist attempt to revivify corporate institutions in the service of enlightened reform; indeed, the second half of the century witnessed a Renaissance among the Estates – in Württemberg, Hanover, Saxony, the Mecklenburg duchies, Cologne, Münster, and Bavaria.[42] It also promoted the populism and anarchism of the *Sturm und Drang* generation, their turning back to the

*Growth in the Holy Roman Empire* (Brussels, 1975); the collection of essays edited by him and Steven Rowan, *The Old Reich: Essays on German Political Institutions 1495–1806* (Brussels, 1974); Gerhard Benecke, *Society and Politics in Germany 1500–1750* (London, 1974); and John Gagliardo, *Reich and Nation* (Bloomington, Ind., 1980), vii–xiv, for his assumptions.

    These works argue that the Holy Roman Empire, especially the imperial circles (*Kreisverfassungen*), performed valuable integrative functions, particularly in defending the regions against hostile armies. For Benecke there are ready analogies between Germany after 1648 and after 1945 (see esp. pp. 23–38). Unfortunately, these works are institutional histories that do not treat matters of economic, social, or demographic change. Furthermore, the work of Vann and Benecke stops in the early eighteenth century or earlier, before the Austro-Prussian dualism and the rapid economic expansion of France, the Netherlands, and Great Britain had made itself felt. Gagliardo's work, on the other hand, chiefly focuses on the early nineteenth century, when the Empire was caught in the wars of the French Revolution. These works also provide few objective criteria for measuring success, except the longevity of the imperial system. That the Holy Roman Empire survived until the wars of the French Revolution, however, is not a persuasive argument for its vitality, nor does it demonstrate that from the 1740s on it was effective at times of crisis such as the Seven Years War, the economic crisis of the 1770s, or the French Revolution. All the evidence, not to mention the dissolution of the Empire in the French revolutionary wars, points in the opposite direction. In the spirit of my comments, see the older judgment of von Aretin, *Heiliges Römisches Reich*, 1:75, 94–6, 105.

[41] For a judicious overview, see Rudolf Vierhaus, "Absolutism" in *Marxism, Communism and Western Society*, ed. C. D. Kernig, 8 vols. (New York, 1972–73), 1:1–12; the introduction by Karl Otmar von Aretin and the collection of essays in his *Der aufgeklärte Absolutismus*, in *Neue Wissenschaftliche Bibliothek*, 67 (Cologne, 1974); and also Geraint Parry, "Enlightened Government and Its Critics in Eighteenth-Century Germany," *Historical Journal*, 6 (1963):181–5. In the dispute concerning how "enlightened" absolutist rule was, I follow the line of argument taken by Hans Rosenberg and Georges Lefebvre in Aretin's *Der aufgeklärte Absolutismus*. See also Ingrid Mittenzwei, "Ueber das Problem des aufgeklärten Absolutismus," *Zeitschrift für Geschichte*, 17 (1970):1162–4, where she links enlightened absolutism to the political language of the French Enlightenment and to issues of economic underdevelopment.

[42] Rudolf Vierhaus, "Ständewesen und Staatsverwaltung in Deutschland im späteren 18. Jahrhundert," *Dauer und Wandel der Geschichte. Festgabe für Kurt von Raumer*, ed. Rudolf Vierhaus and Manfred Botzenhart (Münster, 1966), 337–60; as well as Vierhaus's "Land, Staat und Reich in der politischen Vorstellungswelt deutscher Landstände im 18. Jahrhundert," *HZ*, 223 (1976):40–60; also the excellent introduction and essays in *Ständische Vertretungen in Europa im 17. und 18. Jahrhundert*, ed. Dietrich Gerhard, in *Veröffentlichungen des Max-Planck-Instituts für Geschichte*, 27 (Göttingen, 1969).

sixteenth and seventeenth centuries for political models of individual struggle and corporate freedom.[43] Alternatively, it gave rise to the legal struggle of Möser's enlightened contemporaries – their efforts to separate the civil from the political, the public from the private – that actually abandoned the political realm to aristocracy and monarchy in the hope that judicial limits would inhibit arbitrary attacks on the property and freedom of the individual. This legal struggle was immensely significant in formulating legal and political relations in the language of natural rights, but in these years it meant that enlightened reform still focused on the institutions of the old regime and could not emancipate itself from estatist language or values.[44] Consequently, most administrators concentrated on administrative adjustments of the technical kind and on those areas of public education and influence of the powerful that were preparatory to substantial reform. As we will see, part of Justus Möser's significance as a publicist resided in his support of reforms that would not disturb the political balance.

For the Germanies, finally, the link between corporatism and Enlightenment meant, as I have already indicated, that the entire arena of civil society remained diffuse. The consequences were not wholly negative. In the 1780s, for example, Friedrich Nicolai argued that urban pluralism prevented intellectual tyranny and raised the level of Enlightenment throughout the Germanies.[45] Recent work on the French provincial academies has confirmed Nicolai's view by showing how Paris drained the regions of intellectual vitality.[46] A rich provincial life in the Germanies meant, however, that the intellectual subculture was less autonomous, making it more difficult for a free intelligentsia and a literary underground to emerge. Nicolai himself, as publisher and career manager, novelist and autodidactic philosopher, came as close to the ideal of independence as anyone in Germany, and he was a lone and often resented exception. Thus it was more difficult for the heterodox views at the fringes of the Enlightenment to take hold in the German language area. There was no well-established "low" Enlightenment: there were relatively few Spinozists and materialists, and few popular writers who undermined the established authority in chapbooks, calendars, and breviaries.[47]

Within German culture, then, the German counterpart to the French *philosophe* and the English man of letters continued to be more completely defined and bounded by corporate institutions. It is difficult to generalize about what this

---

[43]  Roy Pascal, "The 'Sturm und Drang' Movement," *Modern Language Review*, 47 (1952):131–6; also the same author's *The German Sturm und Drang* (2nd ed.; Manchester, 1959), esp. chap. 3; Isaiah Berlin, *Vico and Herder* (New York, 1976), 156–86.

[44]  Wieacker, *Privatrechtsgeschichte der Neuzeit*, 272.

[45]  Friedrich Nicolai, *Beschreibung einer Reise durch Deutschland und die Schweiz im Jahre 1781*, 12 vols. (Berlin and Stettin, 1783–96), 4:926–8.

[46]  Daniel Roche, *Le Siècle des lumières en Province*, 2 vols. (Paris, 1978).

[47]  Hans-Jürgen Haferkorn, "Der freie Schriftsteller. Eine literatursoziologische Studie über seine Entstehung und Lage in Deutschland zwischen 1750–1800," *Archiv für Geschichte des Buchwesens*, 5 (1964):523–712. For France see Robert Darnton, "The High Enlightenment and the Low-Life of Literature in Pre-Revolutionary France," *Past and Present*, no. 51 (1971):81–115.

difference meant in quantitative terms – in the size of the German intelligentsia, the range of incomes, degree of mobility, size of markets and readership – since the social history of the educated classes in the Germanies during this period is still in its beginnings.[48] But even though the number of individual critics grew after midcentury and the number of professional and popular societies climbed dramatically, the new intellectual ideal had relatively less social impact on the older forms of intellectual life. The intellectual, accordingly, continued to be more completely defined by the received set of social and economic relations. He was forced everywhere to make some professional and pecuniary compromise with the urban government, court, university, or clerical establishment and to attach himself to the corporate specialists who continued to perform the intellectual functions for each institutionalized social group. Intellectuality was thus only one factor among the many that composed his group characteristics, his sense of personal place, his particular social consciousness, in short, his *Standesbewußtsein* or corporate ethos. In this context, birth, status, and legal privilege remained the significant determinants of intellectual life, and emancipation according to enlightened principles still a goal for the distant future.[49]

The constellation of corporatist Enlightenment, in sum, describes a series of disjunctures: intellectual intention, political vision, and social reality often stood in contradiction to each other, largely because the German Enlightenment remained in an arrested state of political and socioeconomic development – both theoretically and practically – in the decades before the French Revolution. Political immobility and the diffuseness of enlightened culture also affected the pattern of intellectual change. The new ideals were not able to take deep root and set the cultural tone. Rather, various Enlightenment intellectual generations managed to survive and coexist as reified constituencies that were nurtured by the cultural pluralism and institutional stalemate of the Empire. Such real historical pluralism, where residues and archaisms predominate, defies simple efforts at developmental reconstruction.[50] Linking corporatism and Enlightenment in the phrase "corporatist Enlightenment" thus describes less the *movement* and more the social and political *matrix* beneath the dynamic of change in the emancipatory language of the German Enlightenment.

---

[48] See the summary in Kopitzasch, ed., *Aufklärung, Absolutismus und Bürgertum in Deutschland*, 41–95; and von Ungern-Sternberg, "Schriftsteller und literarischer Markt," 133–85; Hans Gerth, *Bürgerliche Intelligenz um 1800*, in *Kritische Studien zur Geschichtswissenschaft*, 19 (Göttingen, 1976).

[49] Again, even in countries such as England or France, where there may have been greater mobility and career chances for the gifted and lucky, conditions similar to those in Germany still continued to prevail. For the general problem, see the literature cited in footnote 6. For France see Alan Kors, *D'Holbach's Coterie: An Enlightenment in Paris* (Princeton, N.J., 1976); and the work by John Lough, *The Encyclopédie* (New York, 1971). For similar problems in Scotland, see John Clive, "The Social Background of the Scottish Renaissance," in *Scotland in the Age of Improvement*, ed. N. T. Phillipson and Rosalind Mitchison (Edinburgh, 1970), 227–30; N. T. Phillipson, "Culture and Society in the 18th-Century Province: The Case of Edinburgh and the Scottish Enlightenment," in *The University in Society*, ed. Lawrence Stone, 2 vols. (Princeton, N.J., 1974), 2: 407–48.

[50] Schramm, *Neun Generationen*, 1:7 for similar methodological conclusions.

## MÖSER AS PUBLICIST

German culture thus retained its traditional and syncretistic character and its links with established corporate institutions well into the last quarter of the eighteenth century. All these factors acted together to blur distinctions that emerged in other countries between generations or between starkly contrasted ideological positions. For this reason, it is difficult to define the points of disjuncture between the older Latin humanism, Enlightenment ideas, and the reactionary strain of thought often associated with Justus Möser and usually characterized as anti-Enlightenment or counter-Enlightenment. Furthermore, particular individuals identified themselves with the cultural ideals of the Enlightenment to varying degrees, and their allegiances often shifted as they and the movements developed and changed. It is important to keep such distinctions before us as we begin to consider just how Justus Möser fit into the German Enlightenment – what cultural needs were answered by his writing, how the ambiguities in his thought were common to the culture, and in what ways he may have remained the outsider.

Among the factors that particularly complicated Möser's relationship to German culture in his lifetime was the matter of audience. Because German culture resided in the regions, the Enlightenment could only constitute itself nationally – in the sense of a linguistic nation – as a movement of readers and writers. Friedrich Nicolai, for example, understood this fact clearly when in founding the *Allgemeine Deutsche Bibliothek* (*Universal German Library*) he proposed that his journal might forge the intellectual consensus that Germany lacked. In this sense, the notion of a public realm of letters was critical to the German Enlightenment.[51] Writers saw themselves as members of an intellectual elite who, in the interest of a reforming humanism, stood above regions and corporate constraints. Their essays, consequently, were coded to appeal to a local or regional audience, which was likely to know the author intimately, and to a widely dispersed readership, for which impersonal considerations of genre and style were far more important.

What made Möser's works exceptional in this respect was the way in which the ambiguous structure of his prose reinforced the plurality of interpretive contexts. Most of Möser's essays, including the *Osnabrück History*, were written to explain specific legal relationships and potential or pending legislation – the decrees that reformed the textile trade, banned peddlers from the countryside, regulated peasant fees and obligations, and established religious liberties in a local village. But Möser almost always concealed his own views, particularly in his occasional essays, assuming instead the voices of the various social interests involved. Furthermore, in order to test local resistance, he often presented the worst possible case, and he always seemed to conclude that the less done the

[51] Jürgen Habermas, *Strukturwandel der Oeffentlichkeit* (4th ed.; Frankfurt, 1969).

better. Life is too complex for simple answers, he would argue; even the best reforms may have unwanted consequences; we must recognize that our ancestors may not have been so stupid; it is better to proceed with caution than to act precipitously; and so forth. His Osnabrück readers were able to penetrate such masks and locate the concrete interests and pressures shaping legislation. Adopting the voices of various local interests deflected attention away from Möser's personality and political commitments; further, it enhanced his political effectiveness by placing administrative decisions within an artificially constructed public realm.

But concealment also made it difficult for readers outside the bishopric to know what Möser thought. This was particularly true for those who read his essays as collected for republication in the *Patriotische Phantasien (Patriotic Phantasies)*. There Möser hid his own views even more completely, dissociating them from specific issues in the bishopric. He made no attempt, for instance, to tell his readers about the original occasion for the essays; he disregarded dates of composition and even disrupted the thematic continuity from essay to essay.[52] The resulting kaleidoscope of views suppressed context and personality. For this reason, Möser's friend and first biographer, Friedrich Nicolai, felt compelled to emphasize Möser's actual importance in Osnabrück and to remind his readers of Möser's habit of ironic concealment.[53] Möser himself, in his preface to the *Patriotic Phantasies*, acknowledged the confusions created by the shifts in audience: "The strangest [fact]," he wrote, "is, however, that at home I am considered the greatest enemy of serfdom and on the outside as the most eager defender of the same. . . . The distracted readers of a sermon judge completely differently than the audience."[54]

The problems a distant reader might have faced in interpreting Möser's works did not end there. His essays first appeared in newspapers and editions scarcely available outside Westphalia and the Hanoverian domains. The larger German public discovered him only through the republication of his works in the 1770s when, with the rapid expansion of the publishing trade, writers of Möser's literary ability were eagerly being sought. By that time, he was already an experienced publicist past his fiftieth year, and any understanding of his intellectual development had been obscured. He had the fortune to sell for the second time views gathered years earlier.

Möser's publishing history lets us see concretely how this happened. Within a few years of his entry into local government in Osnabrück, he began a series of short-lived moral weeklies: *Versuch einiger Gemälde von den Sitten unsrer Zeit (Attempt at Various Portraits of Our Contemporary Morals)* (1746); *Die deutsche Zuschauerin (The Female Spectator)* (1747); *Osnabrückisches Journal* (1754). Like all

---

[52] See the perceptive discussion of this issue in Brigitte Lorenzen, *Justus Mösers Patriotische Phantasien. Studien zur Erzählkunst* (Ph.D. diss., Göttingen, 1956), 10–17.
[53] Möser, *W*, 10:5.
[54] Möser, *SW*, 6:10.

German journals of the period, they were closely patterned after their English precursors, [55] and, like most, they assumed a local audience – in this case, the one confined to Hanover and Osnabrück. Though typical of the local notable culture of these years, the journals were not especially significant and were never reprinted in Möser's lifetime; they did, however, train him for the regular newspaper he started at the end of the Seven Years War. The newspaper was published into the 1780s under varying mastheads: *Wöchentliche Osnabrückische Anzeigen (Weekly Osnabrück Advertiser)* (1766–7); *Nützlicher Beylage zum Osnabrückischen Intelligenz-Blat (Useful Supplement to the Osnabrück Intelligencer)* (1768–72); *Westfälische Beyträge zun Nutzen und Vergnügen (Westphalian Contributions for Utility and Pleasure)* (1773–83). Möser was almost entirely responsible for the newspaper until 1783, when he suspended his active support and began to contribute sporadically to more prestigious Enlightenment journals – the *Berlinische Monatsschrift (Berlin Monthly)* of Gedicke and Biester; Schlözer's *Staatsanzeigen*; and other local periodicals, including the *Westfälisches Journal* of Peter Weddigen.

From the beginning Möser's newspaper abandoned the form of the moral weekly for that of a modern newspaper.[56] Möser contributed regular essays of varying length that dealt almost solely with local and provincial affairs. The whole range of Westphalian economy, history, folklore, and geography was paraded before his readers, and now and again philosophical or aesthetic issues also appeared in Westphalian garb. As Goethe said of Möser's essays in his *Dichtung und Wahrheit (Poetry and Truth)*, "Everything occurring in the civil and moral world would have to be enumerated were the subjects he treated to be exhausted."[57] Since these newspapers had a very restricted readership, Möser began to collect and arrange many of his essays in additional volumes under his daughter's general editorship. These appeared in the 1770s and 1780s as the *Patriotic Phantasies*, and it is by their publication that we can date Möser's entry into the wider world of the German Enlightenment.[58]

During the earlier part of his career, Möser had also written other, longer essays, as well as his history of Osnabrück, and pieces of imaginative literature that were issued separately in small editions. These included a letter to Voltaire (1750); a treatise on ethics, *Der Wert wohlgewogener Neigungen und Leidenschaften (The Value of Well-Inclined Intentions and Passions)* (1756); an essay on comedy, *Harlekin oder Verteidigung des Groteske-Komischen (Harlequin, or the Defense of the Grotesque-Comical)* (1761); a critical letter to Rousseau, *Schreiben an den Herrn*

---

[55] Wolfgang Martens, *Die Botschaft der Tugend. Die Aufklärung im Spiegel der deutschen moralischen Wochenschriften* (Stuttgart, 1971), 22–3; Gerhard Sauder, "Moralische Wochenschriften," in Grimminger, ed., *Hansers Sozialgeschichte der deutschen Literatur*, 3/1:267–9.

[56] Margot Lindemann, *Deutsche Presse bis 1815* (Berlin, 1969), 248–55.

[57] Goethe, *Dichtung und Wahrheit*, in *Werke*, 16 vols. (Leipzig, 1912–20), 3:634.

[58] The *Patriotic Phantasies* were published in four volumes in 1774, 1775, 1778, and 1786. They are issued as Volumes 4 through 7 of the collected works; Volumes 8 and 9 contain the rest of the known essays that, for a variety of reasons, Möser chose not to have collected and published in book form.

*Vicar in Savoyen (Letter to the Vicar of Savoy)* (1762); and the "General Introduction" to his *Osnabrück History* (1765).[59] Since most of these works were also occasional pieces with small printings, few were read beyond the borders of Westphalia and Hanover.

The exception proved to be *Harlequin*, Möser's defense of the *commedia dell'arte*. Favorably reviewed by Lessing, it brought Möser into contact with the Berlin Enlightenment. He became friends with the young philosophers Thomas Abbt and Friedrich Nicolai at this time and established looser ties with Lessing. Nicolai's lifelong friendship and encouragement were responsible for the eventual publication of the *Patriotic Phantasies*, and Nicolai also afforded Möser ready access to major Enlightenment journals, particularly the *Berlinische Monatsschrift*. Though very different in temperament, these two friends shared basic utilitarian and commonsense prejudices about life and letters and similar beliefs concerning practical social and economic reform. They eventually became allies in Nicolai's anti-Kantian writings of the 1790s, and thereby both entered into the history of anti-Kantianism at the end of the century.

Möser's mounting administrative and political responsibilities in the years immediately following the end of the Seven Years War caused him to turn to serious historical scholarship, and these studies were the source of appeal to yet another audience. About 1763 he conceived the idea of composing a history of Osnabrück, and this scholarly ambition stayed with him until his death. He first published the "General Introduction" to his *Osnabrück History* in a limited edition of two hundred copies (1765), then issued it as a separate work (1768), and finally published it (1780) as part of an incomplete two-volume history of the bishopric from its settlement until the mid-thirteenth century.[60] In 1773 this work, too, assumed a separate life, for in that year Johann G. Herder published the "General Introduction" in abbreviated form, along with essays by Goethe and himself, in *Von deutscher Art und Kunst (Of German Manners and Art)*, the literary manifesto of the young *Sturm und Drang* movement.[61]

Thus Justus Möser's popularity grew in the 1770s and 1780s, simultaneously with the rapid expansion and moderate radicalization of public life. As noted, these decades marked the first years of relatively open political discussion, when

---

[59] Except for the letter to Rousseau, all of these essays are collected in Volume 2 of the collected works; the letter to Rousseau is still available only in volume 5 of the Abeken edition, 230–51. Despite minor errors, the most complete bibliography of Möser's works, listing each item chronologically and according to place of publication, remains Wolfgang Hollman, *Justus Mösers Zeitungsidee und ihre Verwirklichung*, in *Zeitung und Leben*, 40 (Munich, 1937).

[60] Only in 1824 were the fragmentary sections of the planned third volume published from Möser's papers by C. B. Stüve. See Paul Göttsching, "Editor's Foreward," Möser, *SW*, 12/1:22. The *Osnabrück History* has been reissued in its various eighteenth-century editions as Volumes 12 through 14 of the collected works.

[61] Hermann August Korff, *Geist der Goethezeit*, 1: *Sturm und Drang* (4th ed.; Leipzig, 1958); Roy Pascal, "The German 'Sturm und Drang' Movement," 129–51; Pascal, *The German Sturm und Drang*; Edna Purdie, "Introduction," *Von deutscher Art und Kunst* (Oxford, 1924), 6–41; Hans Dietrich Irmscher, ed., "Nachwort," *Von deutscher Art und Kunst* (Stuttgart, 1968), 163–96.

the German public began to constitute itself as a secular moral and political community. They also saw the beginning of the cultural and political counterattack by those groups and political bodies – pietists, Jesuits, spokesmen of Protestant orthodoxy, nobles – who became increasingly threatened by the growing autonomy of burgher society. Until the outbreak of the French Revolution, however, the lines were not clearly drawn; Möser thus became a major link between the corporatist Enlightenment and the young critics of "absolutism" and "shallow rationalism." He gained even more prestige as a defender of German letters against the critical essay of Friedrich II of Prussia, *De la littérature allemande*.[62] This mediating role continued into the 1790s when, at the end of his life, he began to publish in the *Berlinische Monatsschrift* a series of critical essays dealing with the course and legitimacy of the French Revolution. At that moment, however, Möser's political and cultural views became caught up in the significance of the revolution in France. His critique of absolutism, defense of corporate institutions, praise of the ancient German commonalty, and appeal to "freedom and property" against the institutions of civil society – all these suddenly appeared as part and parcel of an antiquated corporatism that denied men the power to alter their institutions. In this way, his rationalistic but antirevolutionary position became reconstituted as an aspect of counter-Enlightenment. But even then, Möser's counter-Enlightenment position retained a complex admixture of Enlightenment values.

Integral to Möser's ability to intersect and partially to bridge the intensifying generational struggle during these years was his image as a politically powerful intellectual, or – to speak in the language of the day – as a political "servant" who was also a "patriot" and "writer." Like Turgot or Friedrich II, Möser embodied for his readers the union of intellectual pursuits with an active political life; but like the publicists of reform after the Seven Years War, he also consciously employed the language of reform in his essays.[63] He thus fulfilled the vocational aspirations of the man of letters and the *philosophe* in the Anglo-American and continental Enlightenment. But Möser also fit in with the new public temper coalescing in these years, since he fulfilled many of the ideas of self-cultivation that emerged with the *Sturm und Drang* movement and formed the educational vision of German idealism.[64]

Möser's public appeal in the decades between the Seven Years War and the French Revolution thus went beyond his successful career. What made him and his work so important to his readers was not a sense of his everyday life and world. Unlike Lessing, Goethe, Nicolai, or Wieland, whose disagreements, loves, and sorrows were public fare, Möser remained a disembodied journalistic voice, not a multidimensional personality. What appealed to the public was his im-

---

[62] See the recent critical edition of Friedrich der Große, *De la littérature allemande*, ed. Christoph Gutknecht and Peter Kerner (Hamburg, 1969).

[63] Rudolf Vierhaus, "Politisches Bewuβtsein in Deutschland vor 1789," 175–96; Hans Wolf Jäger, *Politische Kategorien im Poetik und Rhetorik der zweiten Hälfte des 18. Jahrhunderts* (Stuttgart, 1970), 35, 37, 44; Krauss, "Zur Konstellation der deutschen Aufklärung," 149–72.

[64] Hans Weil, *Die Entstehung des deutschen Bildungprinzips* (2nd ed.; Bonn, 1967).

aginative and diverse reconstruction of corporate society. Möser created socio-political and moral archetypes in his many essays, and these slippery and idealized images were felt to articulate fundamental features of German social and political life. "In his lecture style," Goethe wrote, "we also thought we could discover ourselves; but who could hope to master such a rich subject matter and to handle the most intractable subjects with so much freedom?"[65]

For the historian, then, Justus Möser's place in the German Enlightenment was shaped by the separation between his local political career and his role as journalist in the larger world of German letters.[66] He functioned in the emerging public sector as a source for political education of a particular corporate variety. His superior literary talents allowed him at the moment of political radicalization to keep alive the link between corporatism and Enlightenment that formed the everyday political understanding of the midcentury generation.

### MÖSER, CORPORATIST ENLIGHTENMENT, AND COUNTER-ENLIGHTENMENT

Let us now focus with greater care upon these links between Möser's Enlightenment ideas and his corporate values. What held the German Enlightenment together was not a specifically articulated commitment to the views of one powerful thinker, but rather a loose attachment to the traditions of rationalism and secular humanism. The latent struggle between Protestantism and Catholicism also meant that religious questions stayed close to the surface, manifesting themselves in that intensely ethical attitude we associate with the German Enlightenment. Beyond this, the Germans shared those basic assumptions that linked them to the European movement. They, too, blended a rational, individualistic epistemology with an appeal to experience, a Newtonian conception of the world, and a belief that nature could be mastered and manipulated rationally in the service of humanity. They were also committed to the older and more

---

[65] Goethe, *Dichtung und Wahrheit*, in *Werke*, 3:635. In his notes concerning art and antiquity, Goethe wrote even more directly: "I gladly mention this admirable man [who] . . . has had a very great influence on my education. He was the very embodiment of human understanding, worthy to be a contemporary of Lessing, who represented the critical spirit. . . . The utterances of such a spirit and character, like grains of gold and gold dust, have the same value as bars of pure gold and even a higher value than the minted product." Quoted in William F. Sheldon, *The Intellectual Development of Justus Möser: The Growth of a German Patriot*, in *Osnabrücker Geschichtsquellen und Forschungen*, 15 (1970), 123. See also Ludwig Bäte, *Justus Möser* (Frankfurt am Main, 1961), 170. The Goethe quotations became part of the Möser mythology almost from their publication. As Möser fell into relative insignificance in the nineteenth century, his ties to Goethe helped to recall his importance. These pages from *Dichtung und Wahrheit* were appended to Nicolai's biography of Möser by Abeken in the 1843 edition; see Möser, *W*, 10:104.

[66] Renger minimized this point in his valuable study of Osnabrück's local government in the eighteenth century, *Landesherr und landstände im Hochstift Osnabrück in der Mitte des 18. Jahrhunderts*, in *Veröffentlichungen des Max-Planck- Instituts für Geschichte*, 19 (Göttingen, 1968).

recent traditions of natural rights, to broad religious toleration, and to reducing to some extent the power of the established church and the hereditary aristocracy.[67] In general terms, Möser shared the secular humanist impulse of the Enlightenment, with its anticlerical and antiaristocratic sensibility; he believed in the broadest religious freedom and, with it, the separation of church and state. He adopted the rationalist categories of the Enlightenment; he agreed with its eudaemonistic and utilitarian ideal; and he, too, was concerned with public understanding and popular education. But even as the German Enlightenment was shaped by its compromise with the social and political system of Estates, so in Möser this compromise manifested itself in characteristic fashion.

The first area of compromise resided in Möser's practical bias. Möser was an administrator with substantial political power, who participated in the civic humanist's disdain for the university scholar. Consequently, he did not acknowledge the claims of theory even to the extent Mendelssohn did. Instead he dealt in a world of details and interests, refusing to see the particular as the accidental instance of a general theory. He was content to achieve limited reforms, because deeds were more important to him than words. "Möser lived in the real world," his friend Nicolai wrote, "and sought to be effective in it."[68] His practical bias, of course, reflected the growing worldly reform efforts we have touched upon, but because of the cultural domination by the universities, his sensibilities were atypical in German letters and more akin to those of the schools of empiricism in England and to the commonsense philosophical attitude of the Scottish and American Enlightenments. "I know . . . of nothing better," he wrote, "than to advance the following historical truths; conclusions are often better drawn from actual events than from too lofty presuppositions."[69] His essays, as a consequence, were always specifically concerned with local problems, with necessary individual reforms, in short, with what was termed "local patriotism" (*Lokalpatriotismus*). His political and technical expertise allowed him to examine rural and urban life in a manner freed from the ethically tinged theoretical language of his generation. Social life became its own autonomous realm of interdependent facts, with its own necessity and descriptive complexity. But more was involved than this: by stressing the practical, he also argued for the limited capacity of rationally oriented behavior to alter life. Thus he supplied much needed information to public debate while reversing the priorities of the philosophical movement. What concerned

---

[67] Franklin Ford redefined the European Enlightenment in these terms by isolating four assumptions that underlay national and regional diversity. These were, first, a belief in secular humanism; second, the acceptance of an analytical method; third, an attitude toward the control of change; and, fourth, a belief in history as progressive human liberation. See Franklin Ford, "The Enlightenment: Towards a Useful Redefinition," in R. F. Brissenden, ed., *Studies in the Eighteenth Century* (Toronto, 1968), 17–29. See also the comments by Klippel, *Politische Freiheit*, 19–30; and those by Lucien Goldmann, *Der christliche Bürger in der Aufklärung* (Neuwied, 1968), 55–88.

[68] Nicolai, *Leben Justus Mösers*, in Möser, *W*, 10:47.

[69] Möser, "Ueber Theorie und Praxis," *SW*, 10:152; Karl Brandi, "Justus Möser, *Ausgewählte Aufsätze* (Oldenburg, 1938), 554.

him was how the world of the practical determined the scope of political Enlightenment.

This reversal of priorities had much in common with that skeptical, anxious form of Western rationalism that had crystallized in early English liberalism. We find in Möser, as in Locke, the recognition that human rationality was but a limited tool of change, and alongside this the secular assumption that "meaning" itself resided in the "facts" of human experience.[70] In the absence of political conflict and options, this skeptical attachment to the world of facts often stayed politically neutral, leading to the emancipation of social science from law and epistemology and helping to foster a heightened sense of the everyday at the center of the European Enlightenment. But in moments of political crisis, when untempered by an attachment to natural rights or a commitment to the ideals of representative government, this form of rationalism proved, in the minds of men like Möser, to be politically conservative in the defense of interest and inegalitarian in its understanding of rights. Thus it abandoned the ideal of individual freedom and offered no ethical foundation for political life, as did the natural rights tradition. Kant emphasized this danger in his late writings, and we must face these issues in evaluating the cogency of Möser's views.

The corollary to Möser's practical bias was his fully developed corporatist view of society, a view rooted in an explicit anti-individualism. For Möser there was no "self" – neither the hypothetical "possessive individual" postulated by rationalism nor the confessional, self-critical self of pietism, sectarian Protestantism, or Jansenism. The minute self-examination of Johann Jakob Moser's multi-volumed autobiography, of Karl Phillip Moritz's marvelous autobiographical novel, *Anton Reiser*, of G. F. Lichtenberg's *Südelbücher*, or of J. G. Herder's correspondence never appears in Möser's work. His was a self tied to the human community by categories of place, birth, estate, and occupation. All that was perceived and experienced was, to Möser, objectively given, and in this sense was a mirror of that self-in-the-world. In spite of his burgher pride, his sensibility was actually a hybrid of aristocratic and corporatist elements, articulated in vigorous response to the idea of the subjectivity of human nature that he saw in the epistemology and ethics of the Enlightenment. There was, consequently, an implicit ideological component to his own self-understanding: he denied selfhood in favor of history and society.

Möser's denial of a subjective self linked his personality, the way he perceived himself, and his ties to his environment. If he tells us little about his internal world, we learn much about Westphalian culture and society. He saw this external, public world in particular terms, as a world not living from the present to the future but as one in which the present was the most recent moment in a millennium of human history.[71] His attitude toward that historical Osnabrück

---

[70] Sheldon Wolin, *Politics and Vision* (Boston, 1960), chaps. 8–9, esp. 293–4, 315; Seliger, *John Locke*, 17–30.

[71] Nicolai saw that Möser tended to blend together the various historical pasts into his own present,

appears in the secondary literature as an emancipation from the narrowness of the Enlightenment; yet we can better attribute it to an older corporate understanding of self and world. This understanding had its roots in both the political pluralism and economic backwardness of his home and his long administrative experience with its problems. The sacrifice of Möser's own inner world is one indication that for him individuals and particular events were subordinated to social, political, and economic structures that were necessary and determining.

Möser examined his world in its historical necessity, it seems, in conscious opposition to the Enlightenment emphasis on human emancipation. His turn to the study of history was part of an implicit ideological reflex against change and the threat of change. He was certainly not alone: Montesquieu, Hume, and Winckelmann also explored the historical world from this direction. But where Montesquieu examined the general relations between political virtues and political systems, Möser studied the particular case – the relations between the ancient Saxon political world, traces of which were still present in Westphalia, and the political virtue idealized by Tacitus. Where Hume explored the tenacious irrationality of custom and its hold over reason, Möser analyzed custom's higher rationality in its relation to abstract reason. Where Wincklemann created a world of noble, pagan Hellenes that in its aesthetic intent served the emerging ideals of classicism, Möser envisaged a flourishing world of free Saxon soldier-farmers, a vision that later fueled the delusions of romantic conservatives.

In this way, Möser managed to employ the older Latin humanism and the history of his bishopric to stand outside certain tendencies in his own time. As a historian, he stayed, for instance, free from certain myths of early Enlightenment liberalism.[72] In marked contrast to Möser, most Enlightenment historians understood their world to be infused with greater individual freedom. Deeply influenced

and he described this propensity when discussing Möser's defense of serfdom: "Diesem Menschenfreunde war zwar, es ist nicht zu leugnen, durch die besondere osnabrücksche Verfassung, welche er beständig nicht nur im gemeinen Leben, sondern auch im Geschäftskreise vor Augen hatte, der Begriff der Leibeigenschaft gewöhnlicher geworden; und nachdem sein Scharfsinn aus der Geschichte die Entstehung entwickelt hatte, lebte er in Gedanken mehr in der alten Zeit, wo Hörigkeit und und Leibeigentum noch wohl überwiegende Vortheile waren, und der Besitz des Grundes allein die Nation formirte. Er konnte daher von *Heloten* und *Leibeigenen* welche notwendig in die Brüche fallen müssten, wenn sie keine *Actie* in der Gesellschaft, die das Land unter sich theilte, hätten erlangen können, mit mehr Gleichgültigkeit reden, als in der jetzigen Lage der Dinge eigentlich schicklich sein möchte, wo das, was eine Nation bildet, noch auf andern Gegenständen beruhet als auf der ursprüngliche Theilung des Bodens, und wo man nicht mehr als ein Wehr in den Krieg ziehet" (Nicolai's emphasis throughout). From Nicolai, *Leben Justus Mösers*, in Möser, *W*, 10:50.

[72] In this way I accept that a coherent system of liberal ideas existed within the European Enlightenment before there was a fully formed liberalism. For the prehistory of nineteenth-century liberalism, see Harold J. Laski, *The Rise of European Liberalism* (London, 1947); Guido de Ruggiero, *The History of European Liberalism*, trans. R. G. Collingwood (Boston, 1959), 1–90; the same author's "Positivism," *Encyclopedia of the Social Sciences*, 12 (New York, 1934), 260–5. For individual countries, see J. R. Pole, *Political Representation in England and the Origins of the American Republic* (Berkeley, 1966); Seliger, *John Locke*; Kingsley Martin, *French Liberal Thought in the Eighteenth Century*; Valjavec, *Entstehung der politischen Strömungen*.

by natural rights theory and various strands of epistemological individualism, they created a particular myth of the state and civil society. The state became the place in which the common good was created and regulated: it became the isolated political sphere in which a free-floating representative system functioned; and in order to demonstrate their historical necessity, the law and the legal progression of humankind to liberty or the history of "civil society" were traced over the centuries. "We must always concentrate our attention on civil constitutions, their laws, and the mutual relations among states," Kant stated in the "Ideal for a Universal History," "and notice how these factors, by virtue of the good they contained, served for a time to elevate and glorify nations (and with them the arts and sciences). Conversely we should observe how their inherent defects led to their overthrow, but in such a way that enlightenment always survived, developing further with each revolution, and prepared the way for a subsequent higher level of improvement."[73] For Möser, on the other hand, the history of Osnabrück taught constraint and, over the centuries, the inevitable deterioration of freedom.

Equally, Möser stood outside the mainstream development toward nineteenth-century historicism (*Historismus*), which Meinecke saw as rooted in the new spiritual inwardness that had begun with pietism and culminated in the cultural ideal of German classicism.[74] (In attaching Möser to the origins of historicism, Meinecke was affirming the nineteenth-century rejection of the Enlightenment and obscuring the eighteenth-century contribution to social, demographic, and economic history.) Paradoxically, Möser's historical sense seems much closer to our own than that of other eighteenth-century historians precisely because it was not rooted in philosophical individualism. His so-called emancipation from enlightened ideals was in fact freedom from a set of intellectual assumptions that he never fully appropriated and thus from a journey he never fully commenced.

Thus if corporatist Enlightenment corresponded to the particular historical moment of German society between the Seven Years War and the French Revolution, there was also no clear break between this form of the Enlightenment and the antirevolutionary counter-Enlightenment that grew from the 1780s on. Möser is an especially significant figure, because he revealed the typical contours of this society with atypical acuity. Northwestern Germany became for him the source for a myth of landholding, economic scarcity, and limited rights. His sense of a contingent world rested on the distance between the modernizing values of the Enlightenment and the corporate institutions of Osnabrück. Standing firmly in this corporate world of institutionalized inequality, where the fundamental patterns had been frozen by the Treaty of Westphalia, he struggled with the disintegrative possibilities of change. His response was twofold. He sought, first, to revive and reform Osnabrück's institutions and economy in order to preserve them. Second, he reinterpreted his corporate world in an unadorned

---

[73] Kant, *Political Writings*, 52; or Kante, *Werke*, 6:48–9.
[74] Friedrich Meinecke, *Zur Philosophie der Geschichte* (Stuttgart, 1959), 217–20.

language suitable to the Enlightenment. By describing the practical difficulties in implementing vague programs of political reform, he both offered a commonsense realism to public discussion and used his ecclesiastical state as a testing ground for the modest reforms supported by many of his enlightened contemporaries.

Thus Möser participated dialectically in the Enlightenment debate concerning necessity and freedom, the constraining power of custom, and the transforming potential of reason. He shared Hume's skeptical view of reason and proposed to study the rationality of human customs in a similar manner. In the 1780s and 1790s, his defense of experience was mobilized in the increasingly bitter struggle over the meaning of Enlightenment. He became part of the anti-Kantian wave launched by Kant's attacks on fundamental Enlightenment assumptions. Furthermore, once a radical reform movement emerged under the impress of the French Revolution, his support of limited reform transformed itself readily into a defense of the threatened corporate order. At this point, his type of corporate Enlightenment – a fusion of empiricism, skepticism about the future, and praise of common sense – could no longer be viewed as progressive, nor could corporatist Enlightenment survive much longer in that form. Instead it became part of the wider movements of inegalitarian liberalism and reform conservatism that developed within the new political movements of the nineteenth century.[75]

This great watershed, however, occurred in the years after Möser's death in 1794. As a consequence, this study ends in the twilight world of the Estates, in the decade before the collapse of the Westphalian settlement and the secularization of Möser's Osnabrück. It begins in the social universe of Osnabrück's ruling elite at midcentury.

[75] See Brandt, *Landständische Repräsentation*; Lothar Gall, *Benjamin Constant. Seine politische Ideenwelt und der deutsche Vormärz*, in Veröffentlichungen des Instituts für europäische Geschichte Mainz, 30 (Wiesbaden, 1963); Koselleck, *Preußen zwischen Reform und Revolution*, 23–152; Theodor Schieder, "Partikularismus und nationales Bewußtsein im Denken des Vormärz," in *Staat und Gesellschaft im deutschen Vormärz*, ed. Werner Conze (Stuttgart, 1962), 9–38; James Sheehan, "Liberalism and the City in Nineteenth-Century Germany," *Past and Present*, 51 (1971):119–20; Lothar Gall, "Liberalismus und 'bürgerliche Gesellschaft'," *HZ*, 220 (1975):324–56; Karl-Georg Faber, "Strukturprobleme des deutschen Liberalismus im 19. Jahrhundert," *Der Staat*, 14 (1975):201–28.

# 2

*Möser's social universe: urban notability and Enlightenment intelligentsia*

Except for two years of university study in Jena and Göttingen (1741–3), one six-month diplomatic trip to England (1763–4), and regular journeys to Hanover and the neighboring spa at Pyrmont, Justus Möser never left Osnabrück. It is not that he was forced to remain there but that, apparently, he lacked the desire to leave. On one known occasion (1753) he rejected an offer of advancement in the Hanoverian chancellery in order to remain in Osnabrück. In his polite letter to the privy councillor, Strube, Möser gave no clues to his personal motivations for staying; rather he couched his refusal in terms of local politcs. Were he to leave his Osnabrück posts, a Catholic secretary would have to be appointed as his replacement: "on this account various patrons and particularly a few from the evangelical *Ritterschaft* have made objections which have brought honor but also even more obligations."[1] Of his trip to England, we feel none of the profound regret that characterized Lichtenberg's sense of exile in Göttingen. "The English are slaves to freedom," Möser wrote shortly after his return. "[T]hey pay too dearly for it with a large portion of their peace and their wealth. Their phantasy, however, remains unaffected in the way they portray the law of other countries so that it will best contrast with their own freedom. Looking abroad there is nothing but Hell itself. . . . [T]heir ignorance about this is so great, that they view it as a fairy tale whenever someone tells them that the same freedom exists in the best states of Germany, that the laws and taxes are voted upon by the Estates, that the ruler has only the executive power, and that on that account not much about freedom is made, because, like our daily bread, it is had without much cost."[2]

We do not know why Möser stayed content with Osnabrück's narrower horizons, although perhaps his real sentiments are contained in advice he once gave to his younger friend, the philosopher and publicist Thomas Abbt: "I would choose that place everytime, where there was hope of more comforts and better

---

[1] Möser, *Briefe*, 80.
[2] Ibid., 147.

career chances."[3] The fact is that by remaining in Osnabrück, Möser became the chief administrator there during the twenty-year regency (1763–83) of the non-resident bishop, the Duke of York, and he continued to be involved in the everyday workings of the Osnabrück administration almost until the day of his death in January 1794.

It was not unusual in early modern society for a man to spend his professional life in the place he was born, and certainly such a fact would not normally hamper historical interpretation. With Möser, however, it is always difficult to define precisely the ties between his environment and his intellectual world. The main source of this interpretive difficulty is the paucity of surviving detail concerning his private and inner life. We possess only two extremely short autobiographical fragments, one volume of mostly impersonal letters, a biography written by his friend and publisher Nicolai in the elegiac style common to the century, and bits and pieces of daily life revealed in notes and random comments written by his daughter, friends, and admiring acquaintances.[4] What these fragments reveal seems curiously monochromatic and inarticulate. The details do not bring life to our subject; obliterating motivations and passions, they force us to describe indirectly what we would like to explain directly. "You would like me to describe my life," Möser once wrote, "and indeed in a manner that will do me honor. But you simply haven't realized that a man experiences little of whom it is said, he sits and writes; and when he takes an oath to carry everything entrusted to him to the grave, he has even less to say."[5]

Therefore it is wholly appropriate to begin Möser's biography by examining his social environment and intellectual predispositions as shaped by that environment. Möser belonged to the social world of Osnabrück's legally trained notables. Early modern historians have done much in recent years to trace a rich

---

[3] Ibid., 201.

[4] Möser's autobiographical statements and fragments have been collected in both the Abeken edition and the modern edition, still incomplete, published under the auspices of the Göttingen Academy of Sciences. It is a demonstration of the scarcity of biographical detail that editors have let such comments remain scattered throughout the collected works. See Möser, *SW*, 2:201–10; 10:214. The personal letters and those with biographical evidence of Möser's development are collected in Möser, *Briefe*. The administrative correspondence remains as yet largely unpublished, but is being edited by William Sheldon as part of a new two-volume edition of Möser's correspondence; the editor kindly shared his research with me in the summer of 1979. Of the biographical accounts written in Möser's lifetime, C. F. Nicolai, *Leben Justus Mösers*, reprinted in Möser, *W*, 10:3–85, has remained the only one of value, despite obvious weaknesses; on this work, see Horst Möller, *Aufklärung in Preußen*, in *Veröffentlichungen der Historischen Kommission zu Berlin*, 15 (Berlin, 1974), 161–72; and the critical remarks by Bruno Krusch, "Justus Möser und die Osnabrücker Gesellschaft." *Osn. Mitt.*, 34 (1910):271–81. For another contemporary biography, see Winhold Stühle, *Ueber Möser und dessen Verdienste ums Vaterland, nebst verschiedenen Bemerkungen über Staats-Verfassung* (Osnabrück, 1798); see also the brief portrait of Möser at Bad Pyrmont by Johanna Schopenhauer, *Jugendleben und Wanderjahre*, I (Braunschweig, 1839). Otherwise there are random comments about Möser in various correspondences, but these add little to our overall knowledge of his life; see especially the introduction by Ulrike and William Sheldon in their *Im Geist der Empfindsamkeit. Freundschaftsbriefe der Mösertochter Jenny von Voights und die Fürstin Luise von Anhalt-Dessau, 1780–1808*, in *Osnabrücker Geschichtsquellen und Forschungen*, 17 (Osnabrück 1971).

[5] Quoted in Nicolai's biography, Möser, *W*, 10:5; reprinted in *SW*, 2:201.

portrait of this legal culture, particularly in France, in terms of social and political structure and values.[6] These works have contributed substantially to our understanding of the shape of the French bourgeoisie, its links to the aristocracy and to the state.[7] For the purpose of this chapter, they have also opened up new perspectives on lawyers and jurists by examining their basic commitments to the institutions and mores of old regime France.[8] The example of Möser lets us draw, with variations, similar conclusions. Like most French notables with legal training, Möser did not resist or resent the inherited structure of institutions and power. On the contrary, he accepted social privilege and exceptional political status as a natural birthright. Indeed, his attitudes to the German Enlightenment were formed by his total commitment to the traditions of oligarchic rule. He retained, as a result, a basic antagonism to the Enlightenment ideal of knowledge free from social interest and corporate privilege. Instead of an equality of the spirit, he assimilated the inegalitarian tendencies in the Enlightenment, taking from them the cultural ideal of the gentleman of letters that was a typical subcurrent in the European and German Enlightenments. He also rejected natural rights theory in law, maintaining instead the commitment to precedent, case law, and history that his contemporaries found so striking.

[6] Especially relevant for understanding Möser's situation, the descriptions of career chances and social antagonisms between notaries, procurators, advocates, and judges, are Philip Dawson, "The *Bourgeoisie de Robe* in 1789," *French Historical Studies*, 4 (1965):1–21; idem, *Provincial Magistrates and Revolutionary Politics in France 1789–1795* (Cambridge, Mass., 1972); Lenard R. Berlanstein, *The Barristers of Toulouse in the Eighteenth Century (1740–1793)* (Baltimore, 1975); Richard Kagan, "Law Students and Legal Careers in Eighteenth-Century France," *Past and Present*, no. 68 (1975):38–72.

The situation of the legal profession in England was far different, given the decline of university education and the abandonment by the gentry of legal study. Though ending in 1730, see the excellent introduction, with literature, by Geoffrey Holmes, "The Lawyers and Society in Augustan England," in his *Augustan England. Professions, State and Society 1680–1730* (London, 1982), 115–65, 302–8. Also suggestive is Robert Robson, *The Attorney in Eighteenth Century England* (Cambridge, 1959). The essays by Paul Lucas show the decline of legal study at the Inns of Court and efforts by reformers such as Blackstone to make the career a gentleman's profession by excluding the less wealthy. See his "Blackstone and the Reform of the Legal Profession," *English Historical Review*, 77 (1962):456–89; and idem, "A Collective Biography of Students and Barristers of Lincoln's Inn, 1680–1804," *JMH*, 46 (1974):227–61.

[7] Dawson, *Provincial Magistrates and Revolutionary Politics*, 1–27, 66–128; Kagan, "Law Students and Legal Careers," 51–61; George V. Taylor, "Noncapitalist Wealth and the Origins of the French Revolution," *AHR*, 72 (1966–7):469–96; Colin Lucas, "Nobles, Bourgeois, and the Origins of the French Revolution," *Past and Present*, no. 60 (1973), reprinted in *French Society and the Revolution*, ed. Douglas Johnson (Cambridge, 1976), 88–131.

[8] Since Edmund Burke's remark that the revolutionary movement was carried by "provincial advocates" and "country attorneys," who indeed comprised nearly a fourth of the Constituent Assembly, historians have been concerned with the degree of political radicalism of the legal community in the last years of the old regime and the first years of the revolution. Dawson's work is very suggestive for describing the political differences between "aristocrats" and "patriots" within the legal community as that between judges and procurators on the one side and notaries and attorneys on the other. See Dawson, "*Bourgeoisie de Robe*," 20–1; idem, *Provincial Magistrates and Revolutionary Politics*, 334–43. Also essentially supporting this view is Lucas, "Nobles, Bourgeois, and the Origins of the French Revolution," 108–18. In disagreement are Berlanstein, *Barristers of Toulouse*, 148–82; and Kagan, "Law Students and Legal Careers," 67–8.

Let us examine more closely in what ways Möser's family history and position within the Osnabrück notability formed his attitudes and social ethos. The chapter moves from a description of the notability in Osnabrück – its structure, place within the political system, marriage and career patterns – to a discussion of Möser's own family history. It ends by considering how the social historical moment shaped Möser's cultural ideal and created basic patterns in his thought that were mirrored elsewhere in the European Enlightenment.

### OSNABRÜCK AND ITS LEGAL NOTABLES

Northwestern Germany – Westphalia – in the eighteenth century was a political and economic hinterland even with respect to the retarded conditions prevailing almost everywhere in Germany. Aside from the cottage textile industry, it lacked major economic resources, and it was, along with Swabia, Franconia, and the southern areas along the Rhine, politically one of the most fragmented regions in Germany. More than thirty sovereign units constituted Westphalia from the end of the Thirty Years War until secularization in 1803. The prince-bishopric of Münster, the most substantial state, encompassed an area of approximately 180 square miles; the smallest states were sovereign latifundia of less than one square mile; and Osnabrück, with an area of about fifty square miles, was among the five largest states. In this case fragmentation ensured stagnation,[9] and for this reason northwestern Germany remained literally and figuratively on the periphery of the forces causing change in the eighteenth century.[10]

In addition, more than two-thirds of the Westphalian territories were either Protestant or Catholic ecclesiastical states. Even though elements of the rural nobility, the peasantry, and the urban population had converted to Protestantism, the Catholic Church and the institutions of ecclesiastical polities had resisted secularization until the end of the Thirty Years War, when the Peace of Westphalia established religious parity and integrated the ecclesiastical states into the constitution of the Empire. Cologne, Münster, Osnabrück, Paderborn, Hildesheim, and the abbey of Corvey had all resisted efforts at secularization. The survival of these polities had fundamental consequences that converged with those

---

[9] It did not always follow in the eighteenth century that political fragmentation produced economic stagnation; see the provocative works by Herbert Kisch, "The Textile Industries in Silesia and the Rhineland: A Comparative Study in Industrialization," *JEH*, 19 (1959):541–64; idem, *Prussian Mercantilism and the Rise of the Krefeld Silk Industry: Variations Upon an Eighteenth-Century Theme*, in *Transactions of the American Philosophical Association*, n.s. 58/7 (1968); and the expanded German edition *Die Hausindustriellen Textilgewerbe am Niederrhein vor der Industriellen Revolution*, in *Veröffentlichungen des Max-Planck-Instituts für Geschichte*, 65 (Göttingen, 1981).

[10] Rudolfine Freiin von Oer, "Landständische Verfassungen in den geistlichen Fürstentümern Nordwestdeutschlands," in *Ständische Vertretungen in Europa im 17. und 18. Jahrhundert*, ed. Dietrich Gerhard (Göttingen, 1969), 94–119; Rudolf Vierhaus, "Die Landstände in Nordwestdeutschland," in the same, 72–93; Albert K. Hömberg, *Westfälische Landesgeschichte* (Münster, 1967), 133–67; Paul Casser, "Der Neiderrheinisch-Westfälische Reichskreis," in *Der Raum Westfalen*, ed. Hermann Aubin, 4 vols. (Münster, 1931–58), 2/2:40.

brought about by political fragmentation. One result was that the elected prince-bishops, who only served their terms of office and had no right to bequeath these domains to their issue, most often lacked the incentive to begin long-range improvements. A second was that the political Estates survived in the eighteenth century as the carriers of legal and social continuity. A third was that the peace perpetuated confessional issues in Westphalia, and these remained central to intellectual, social, and political life in the eighteenth century.[11]

Osnabrück was the embodiment of confessional politics. The Reformation had been successful in the city, but the Protestant party has not been able to conquer and hold the state.[12] The Peace of Westphalia recognized that neither Protestant nor Catholic fortunes predominated; more than that, it left Osnabrück an ecclesiastical state but strictly enforced an alternating Evangelical-Catholic episcopal succession. Osnabrück thus shared with other ecclesiastical states the mixture of secular and religious authority represented in the figure of the prince-bishop; it was unique in that it became partly a hereditary possession of the house of Hanover (at first Braunschweig-Lüneburg) and partly an electoral Catholic bishopric. When it was a Catholic possession, church and state were embodied in the prince-bishop; when a Protestant state, the bishop was purely a secular prince, the religious powers of the Catholic bishop falling to the metropolitan in Cologne. Osnabrück was thus a half-secularized ecclesiastical state in the period after 1648 – a juridical anomaly within both Protestant and Catholic legal traditions.[13]

The Westphalian settlement was nonetheless of critical significance to Osnabrück, just as it was for other small states in the Empire, for it guaranteed its independence against future assimilation by a territorial ruler and placed the bishopric in the web of imperial institutions. Furthermore it gave to Osnabrück a charter of fundamental rights and privileges that allowed the political Estates – nobility, cathedral chapter, cities – to retain a vital role. Religious quotas for each confession had been reached at the peace settlement through a negotiated compromise that made the year 1624 the "normal year." In the eighteenth century, as a result, Osnabrück had a mixed religious population spread throughout the noble, servile, and urban social orders. Sometimes there was physical separation, but in many cases Evangelical and Catholic parishes lay side by side. Each political Estate had the important function in the post-1648 period of defending its coreligionists. This meant that membership in the cathedral chapter was legally fixed – to twenty-two Catholic and three Protestant canons – so that the Westphalian Catholic nobility would always predominate, whereas the Estate

[11] Karl Otmar von Aretin, *Heiliges Römisches Reich 1776–1806. Reichsverfassung and Staatssouveränität*, 2 vols. (Wiesbaden, 1967), 1:7–9.

[12] Franz Flaskamp, "Reformation und Gegenreformation im Hochstift Osnabrück," *Westfälische Forschungen*, 11 (1958):68–71; Johannes Freckmann, "Die *capitulatio perpetua* und ihre verfassungsgeschichtliche Bedeutung für das Hochstift Osnabrück (1648–50)," *Osn. Mitt.*, 31 (1906):129–55.

[13] Reinhard Renger, *Landesherr und Landstände im Hochstift Osnabrück*, in *Veröffentlichungen des Max-Planck-Instituts für Geschichte*, 19 (Göttingen, 1968), 19–31.

of the landed nobility and the Estate of cities, dominated by the city of Osnabrück, retained their Protestant majorities.

Thus in Osnabrück the political Estates retained political clout because the confessional struggle was played out there. They also remained active due to the constitutional constraints placed on hereditary succession to episcopal office. The cathedral chapter in Osnabrück always felt itself to be the most important political Estate, since it elected each new Catholic bishop and became the princely authority during periods of episcopal vacancy.[14] This electoral power was exploited at times of election for the personal enrichment of the canons. In fact, the elections were more apparent than real in the post-Reformation era, when the Catholic Church in northwestern Germany was careful to seek political support from the Catholic south and Bavaria. From 1583 to 1761 the Cologne see was continuously in the possession of the Wittelsbach family, and often the same individual occupied more than one episcopal office in the area. Clemens August, archbishop of Osnabrück while Möser was coming of age, occupied five sees: Osnabrück, Cologne, Paderborn, Münster, and Hildesheim. The canons in the cathedral chapter retained their collective power within the bishopric, however, because of capitularies agreed to at the time of election. Absentee bishops such as Clemens August also needed the support of the chapter to enforce the policies executed by his privy councillors. These tendencies, for example, also prevailed in neighboring Münster.[15]

At times of Protestant ascendancy the noble Estate, the *Ritterschaft*, formulated legislation in conjunction with the Estate of the cities and the prince-bishop. In Osnabrück the noble Estate had shrunk dramatically in size because of the aristocratic *Ahnenprobe*, the enforced demonstration of sixteen noble ancestors before a noble had rights of personal representation in the Estate. This meant that of sixty-nine landed estates eligible for the *Ritterschaft*, only fifty were in noble hands; of these only thirty-five fulfilled the qualifications for membership, and of these only eight to fifteen nobles regularly attended meetings.[16]

Political fragmentation, confessional politics in the form of religious quotas and struggle between the Estates, and the political system of the estates with absentee rule by the prince-bishop created the institutional framework that allowed commoners in Osnabrück to have extensive social and political rights. The city of Osnabrück, where the Möser family had lived since the mid-seventeenth century, was the main guarantor of burgher rights in the bishopric. Within the

[14] Von Oer, "Landständische Verfassungen," 95–9; Alfred Hartlieb von Wallthor, "Die Verfassung in Altwestfalen als Quelle moderner Selbstverwaltung," *Westfälische Forschungen*, 9 (1956):31–2; Renger, *Landesherr und Landstände*, 63–5; Max Bär, *Abriß einer Verwaltungsgeschichte des Regierungsbezirks Osnabrück* (Hanover, 1901), 44–5. Of the contemporary views on the power of the chapter, see Johann Eberhard Stüve, *Beschreibung und Geschichte des Hochstifts und Fürstenthums Osnabrück* (Osnabrück, 1789), 589.

[15] Friedrich Keinemann, *Das Domkapitel zu Münster im 18. Jahrhundert*, in *Geschichtliche Arbeiten zur Westfälische Landesforschung*, 11 (1967):60–82.

[16] Renger, *Landesherr und Landstände*, 83–5.

Estate of cities, it dominated the lesser towns of Quackenbrück, Wiedenbrück, and Fürstenau, and seven of its council members, along with its syndic and clerk, controlled the twelve-member Estate. Osnabrück also acquired greater preeminence during the periods of Protestant rule, but it was in many ways insulated from the powers of the bishop and the other two Estates. Although never an imperial city, Osnabrück had since the fourteenth century possessed almost legal autonomy in managing its internal affairs, and this de facto autonomy was confirmed in the Westphalian Peace.[17] Möser idealized the city's immunity and freedom in this way:

> I know of no city where each person fulfills his office or pursues his occupation in such peace and self-satisfaction as here. The magistracy, which consists of sixteen good citizens, expires yearly and is chosen anew. . . . This occurs in the following manner: usually the same ones are reelected, although he who is not, does not have the right to question why he was not reelected. [In the margin for insertion here:] No patriciate; each artisan is eligible for office.
>
> None of the sixteen is paid, because it is the duty (*Reheipflicht*) of the citizen to serve his fellows (*Bürgerschaft*). Only those with special official duties receive honorable compensation for their services. Princely confirmation has not occurred in many hundreds of years, and, consequently, there are not [persons with particular] titles among the sixteen. The city's judge (*Stadtrichter*) has his office for life in order to make him independent of his fellow citizens' favors.
>
> The magistracy has the police powers. However, because the princely servants are not under its power and because the sections of the city (*Freiheiten*) under episcopal control are also exempted, everything must take care of itself and each person must hold himself within limits. Thus neither censorship nor the suppression of books occurs here. The printer prints, the bookseller sells, and the reader reads what he wants without ever having heard a thing about suppression.[18]

The chief beneficiary of the city's autonomy, however, was not the discriminating reader or the eligible artisan, who may indeed have voted but certainly did not influence elections or occupy important offices. Instead it was the small number of families who comprised Osnabrück's ruling notability (*Honoratiorentum*). In Osnabrück as elsewhere among the independent or semiindependent cities of northwestern Germany, the notability monopolized the urban power apparatus and set the cultural tone. Although not enjoying the castelike privileges

---

17 See, for instance, the entire struggle for the city's legal independence discussed in J. Aegidius Klöntrup, "Osnabrück," in his *Handbuch*, 3:43–7. Klöntrup points out that "Der Magistrat [of Osnabrück] verlangt auch, daß der fürstliche Obergograf als Gograf der Stadt Osnabrück ihm schwören." (44); "Der Gerichtbarkeit über Fremde ist auch zwischen dem Magistrate und dem Obergografen streitig. . . . [D]ie Stadt hat eine eigene Policey-Ordnung vom Jahre 1734" (46). See also the older study by Bär, *Abriß einer Verwaltungsgeschichte*, 61–3, and the more recent valuable study by Olaf Spechter, *Die Osnabrücker Oberschicht im 17. und 18. Jahrhundert, in Osnabrücker Geschichtsquellen und Forschungen*, 20 (Osnabrück, 1975), 5–14.

18 Abeken dated this fragment in the 1780s: Möser, *W*, 5:116–17; Möser, *SW*, 10:210–11. See also Klöntrup, "Osnabrück," 3:35.

of a formal patriciate, these families still ran a very closed operation.[19] Their elevated position was increasingly based upon wealth. But the mere possession of wealth was not enough: men became members of the notability only when their respectability received outward recognition. Acceptance into the city council, acquisition of an important title, appointment to an honorary office, or marriage into a notable family were necessary visible signs. In the German language of the period, this constellation was expressed in one surviving meaning of the word *Vermögen*, wherein capacity, income, and status are still fused together.

Since the urban revival of the High Middle Ages, the ruling groups in German urban society had sought to increase the odds in favor of their self-perpetuation by attempting to limit severely participation in the electoral process and access to offices. They also sought to transfer aristocratic notions of order, privilege, and estate to urban life and thereby to undermine the egalitarian ethos that was central to the urban corporate ideal. Among other measures of domination, they passed sumptuary laws that – often beginning as isolated prohibitions to preserve public propriety – gradually were transformed into ornate codes of behavior. These laws divided urban society into numerous substates and regulated each subgroup's dress and rights of public display. By the seventeenth century, when aristocratic ideals finally did come to choke the "free air" of the city, the *Bürgermeister*, council, and juridical elite came to define themselves in these sumptuary laws as the first order, one separate and distinct from a middle group of common citizenry, who were further distinguished from the majority of disenfranchised laborers and the poor.

The hierarchic ideal is explicit in almost all early modern sumptuary codes, sometimes expressed with great elaborateness: the Strasbourg Sumptuary Decree of 1660, for instance, divided the population into 256 occupations within six estates and their suborders.[20] Osnabrück's sumptuary code, though far less complex, was similar in hierarchical spirit. First codified in 1618, amended and reprinted in 1648, it was renewed throughout the eighteenth century and was

[19] Contemporaries used the term "patriciate" in the precise sense of a formal urban nobility. In the article "Patricien," for instance, Klöntrup wrote: "Mir sind aber weder in der Stadt noch im Hochstifte Osnabrück Patricien bekannt; wenigstens ist in der Hauptstadt Osnabrück jeder Bürger ratsfähig. Indessen steht nicht zu leugnen: daβ auβer der jetzigen Adel viele Familien ritterbürtig gewesen sind, und noch jetzt theils ihre eigne, theils die Wapen derjenigen Familien führen, mit denen sie einerley Namen haben." In Klöntrup, *Handbuch*, 3:56. For conceptual points see Dieter Koch, *Das Göttinger Honoratiorentum vom 17. bis zur Mitte des 19. Jahrhunderts* (Göttingen, 1958), 1–3; Max Weber, *Wirtschaft und Gesellschaft*, 2 vols. (Cologne, 1964), 2:683–9, 781–94; Friedrich von Klocke, *Patriziatsproblem und Werler Erbsälzer* (Münster, 1965), 45–6; Joachim Lampe, *Aristokratie, Hofadel und Staatspatriziat in Kurhannover*, 2 vols. (Göttingen, 1963), 1:70–6, 213–365.

[20] Concerning the Strasbourg decree, see Lisolette C. Eisenbart, *Kleiderordnungen der deutschen Städten zwischen 1350 und 1770* (Göttingen, 1962), 31–3 and throughout. For a general discussion of corporatism and aristocracy in urban life, see Gene Brucker, *The Civic World of Early Renaissance Florence* (Princeton, N.J., 1977), 14–39. On urban rigidification in sixteenth-century Germany, see Bernd Moeller, *Reichstadt und Reformation*, in *Schriften des Vereins für Reformationsgeschichte*, 180 (1962):67–76; also Fritz Rörig, *Die europäische Stadt und die Kultur des Bürgertums im Mittelalter* (4th ed.; Göttingen, 1964), 121–5, and "Die Stadt in der deutschen Geschichte," in his *Wirtschaftskräfte im Mittelalter* (Cologne, 1959).

only permitted to lapse in 1788 when another, more general marriage and mourning code was enacted. In Möser's lifetime the sumptuary law of 1648 was republished for public posting and reading in church in 1724 and again in 1734.

Is it significant that the decrees of these years only refer to the 1648 sumptuary law and do not reproduce the seventeenth-century divisions? We cannot know for certain, but most likely such a tactic indicates some blurring of specific social boundaries within the city even as the inegalitarian sensibility survived in the council. In any case, the 1648 law had divided Osnabrück's population into four suborders: (1) "the [two] *Bürgermeister*, titled doctors licentiates, and members of the city council; along with them the clergy, secretaries, and guild masters"; (2) "the citizens of the guilds, the militia and those with moveable property (*habselige Bürger*) and their children, as well as those magistrates of the council, members of the curia, and school; (3) "the common citizenry in offices and among the militia officials and those with goods valued at 500 Taler"; and (4) "day laborers, male and female servants."[21] By the later eighteenth century the regulations regarding the types and quality of appropriate dress, the size of wedding parties, the proper period of public mourning, and so forth appear to have become difficult to enforce. Möser wrote an anonymous article concerning mourning dress in the quasi-official *Osnabrück Intelligencer* (1766) that stated the problem directly:

Where a distinction is made between the various estates and something is allowed to the one that is forbidden to the other, such a law can seldom be fulfilled exactly. . . . Birth and positions of honor are not insignificant. Yet whoever has wealth also does not want to be forgotten.[22]

Thus the notability or first order in Osnabrück still saw itself in the later eighteenth century in close relation to the city's officialdom. If the nobility, Roman Catholic clergy, and administrators of the bishopric were excluded from the city's sumptuary law because they lay outside the council's control,[23] it is significant to see in the list of members of the first estate – *Bürgermeister*, titled doctors, members of the city council, clergy, secretaries and guild masters – how central the formally educated members of Osnabrück's population had become to the self-definition of the notability. In Protestant Osnabrück, indeed, the city's notability was composed overwhelmingly of lawyers – the politically and socially most important category of doctors – whose families intermarried with the surviving merchant elite and the local and regional Protestant clergy.

---

[21] Osnabrück's sumptuary laws are located in Sta Osn, Dep. 3b VI, Nr. 5. The archive has decrees from 1648, 1734, and 1788. The substates in the city are listed in the 1648 decree, 18. See also the discussion in Spechter, *Osnabrücker Oberschicht*, 46–59.

[22] "Vereinigung zwischen einem H. Domcapittel und der H. Ritterschaft wegen der Trauer," *Wöchentliche Osn. Anzeigen* (Nov. 29, 1766), coll. 137–8; reprinted in Möser, *SW*, 8:56–7.

[23] Important in this connection are the head tax lists drawn up by the city in 1759 to exact "contributions" demanded by the invading English army. From these we can see how the resident noble canons, the Catholic clergy, and the episcopal officials blended together with the city's first families. Among them birth and confessional differences predominated over public display. See Sta Osn, Dep 58d A XLVI, Nr. 324.

Though lawyers formed a subgroup of fundamental importance in each of the small territories of the region, their predominance in Osnabrück derived from the institutional peculiarities connected with the alternating Protestant–Catholic episcopal succession. A juridically closed patriciate, if it had ever formally existed, had long since disappeared from the life of the city. Möser had made note of this distinction in the quoted fragment: "No patriciate; each artisan is eligible." Even so, the city had been more visibly run by large textile merchants and the entrepreneurs who had controlled the guilds in the sixteenth and seventeenth centuries during the heyday of the Osnabrück linen trade. But by the end of the seventeenth century the city's economic life was no longer flourishing, and from then on the physical autonomy of the bishopric was based not on its wealth but on the legal settlement of the Treaty of Westphalia, which prevented the city and the bishopric from being absorbed by a more powerful ruler. In the context of narrowed economic activity, juridical training and university degrees structured to an even greater extent the values and career aspirations of the city's notability. Throughout the eighteenth century, much of its power was based upon its function as a legal and administrative caste.

From the early eighteenth century on, the size and importance of the legal profession in Osnabrück provoked commentary, complaint, and administrative efforts to control abuse and overcrowding. A chancellery report from the year 1716, for instance, recommended that the number of lawyers (*Advokaten*) practicing in Osnabrück be reduced at once from fifty to forty-two and that no new lawyers be admitted until the number had dropped to twenty-four. Similarly, the procurators (*Prokuratoren*), the underclass of legal clerks who acted as proxies, were to be reduced in number to twelve. By 1723 the number of registered lawyers had indeed dropped to thirty-three, twenty-five Evangelical and eight Catholic, and of these only nineteen, thirteen and six, respectively, actually practiced. The stance of the chancellery was reflected further in the large number of eighteenth-century decrees, collected in the *Codex Constitutionum Osnabrugensium* (1783), that sought to prevent unlicensed legal practice, especially in the countryside among gullible and contentious serfs. Continuous legislative effort throughout the century, however, indicates the failure to control the size of the legal profession. In 1773, for example, during Möser's tenure in power, the number of registered lawyers had again risen to thirty-three and the number of *Prokuratoren* to twenty-two. The archivalist Krusch noted that this meant almost one lawyer or *Prokurator* for every hundred inhabitants.[24]

Eighteenth-century travel accounts almost always commented on the size of Osnabrück's legal class. An anonymous critic wrote in the *Deutsches Museum* (1784)

---

[24] See Klöntrup, "Advocat," in his *Handbuch*, 1:49; decrees of 1734 and 1744 dictated that "[o]hne eines legalen Procuratoren oder bewehrten Advocatus Unterschrift soll keine Bittschrift bey den Gerichten angenomenen werden." See the decrees regulating the legal profession collected in Sta Osn, Dep 58d A XLVI. Also Bruno Krusch, "Justus Möser und die Osnabrücker Gesellschaft," *Osn. Mitt..*, 34 (1910):258–62. The city's population, according to the 1801 census, was 6,558 persons: Bär, *Abriß einer Verwaltungsgeschichte*, 70.

that "another branch of the city's economy is the many courts. There are between seventy and eighty lawyers and *Prokuratoren* in Osnabrück alone. Only the Lord knows how they all support themselves. However, live they do and apparently not from wind."[25] Pastor Hoche (1800) maintained that the surplus of lawyers was one critical reason why the "more efficient" Prussian domains of Westphalia were preferable places in which to live. In his travels through the region, he reported a conversation with a supposed Osnabrück "peasant." " 'It would be good,' he [the peasant] said, 'if the lawyers and the *Prokuratoren* were restricted. . . . The doctors, that is what lawyers here are called – and the *Prokuratoren* take the money and live from the discord of man.' " Hoche, filled with a sense of deep injustice but without visible statistical proof, assessed the number of *Prokuratoren* in Osnabrück at close to one hundred.[26] Möser's god-child, Justus Gruner, also complained of the large number of lawyers, notaries, and *Prokuratoren* in the bishopric.[27]

The juridical bias of Osnabrück's notability, the competition and overcrowding in the legal profession, only accentuated tendencies observable elsewhere.[28] In early modern urban society, formal education had become increasingly the key to upward social mobility as well as economic gain. From at least the sixteenth century on, the possession of professional degrees – and even advanced educational training without degrees – had begun to create new tensions within the orders of urban society. Previously, men of property and men of education had existed, theoretically and often practically, on two completely distinct and incomparable social levels. Thereafter this situation began slowly to alter, largely because, with regard to education, the growing professionalization of urban administration had consequences similar to those accompanying the administrative bureaucratization of the ambitious state-building monarchies.[29] The partial professionalization of urban government profoundly affected the structure and career patterns of the urban councillor elite.[30] An outgrowth of the mounting overall importance of

[25] Anon. [Frhr. v. R.], "Briefe über Westphalen," *Deutsches Museum*, 1 (1784):240.

[26] J. G. Hoche, *Reise durch Osnabrück und Neidermünster in das Saterland, Ostfriesland und Groningen* (Bremen, 1800), 60, 63.

[27] Justus Gruner, *Meine Wallfahrt zur Ruhe und Hoffnung oder Schilderung der sittlichen und bürgerlichen Zustandes Westphalens am Ende des 18. Jahrhunderts*, 2 vols. (Frankfurt, 1802–3), 2:524–7.

[28] In Italy the importance of legally trained syndics was already apparent in the thirteenth century; Germany was more than a century behind in this respect. See William Bouwsma, "Lawyers and Early Modern Culture," *AHR*, 78 (1973):310; Lauro Martines, *Lawyers and Statecraft in Renaissance Florence* (Princeton, N.J., 1968), esp. 54–7, 62–112. For the eighteenth century these pressures are particularly well documented for France; see, for instance, Kagan, "Law Students and Legal Careers," 63–7.

[29] Of this large literature, see particularly Hans Rosenberg, *Bureaucracy, Aristocracy, and Autocracy: The Prussian Experience, 1660–1815* (Boston, 1966), 1–74. Though written from the perspective of the early nineteenth century, also valuable are the comments by Bernd Wunder, "Die Entstehung des modernen Staates und des Berufsbeamentums in Deutschland im frühen 19. Jahrhundert," *Leviathan*, 4 (1974):458–78, esp. 461–4, 468–9.

[30] Heinrich Kramm, "Besitzschichten und Bildungsschichten der mitteldeutschen Städte im 16. Jahrhundert," *VSWG*, 51 (1964):476, 482, 489; Franz Wieacker, *Privatrechtsgeschichte der Neuzeit* (2nd ed.; Göttingen, 1967), 130, 152–89.

university education was the long-protracted push by the gifted and less wealthy into the legal profession as a means of economic gain and elevation in social prestige.[31]

Eventually, a distinct group of notable professionals emerged within the cities. It was made up of men who, in possession of some legal training and expertise as holders of prominent positions in the urban administrative apparatus, moved into the recognized social notability alongside, or in place of, the old established families, whose members were seen, in comparison, as patricians. Not strictly a legally defined class, this fluid group of educated professionals attempted to perpetuate its power in two typical ways. It sought the hereditary monopolization of council offices and incomes, and attempted to marry into the inner leadership of the upper economic strata of the city. Gradually, then, the originally amorphous group of educated professionals began to merge with the prosperous propertied, mercantile, or otherwise economically active families. Together they ultimately formed the stable inner core of urban ruling groups. However, even though the new and old notabilities shared the inegalitarian values of estate society, the monopolization of offices and intermarriage only rarely resulted in legal closure; other mechanisms, such as sumptuary laws and restrictive residence requirements, were applied to exclude and coerce. Throughout the seventeenth and eighteenth centuries, as a consequence, education and the legal profession remained an open though controlled avenue of continuous recruitment for the local ruling groups.[32] Education, in other words, remained a constant element in the consolidation and perpetuation of the urban councillor elite.

It is significant that higher education in law, medicine, and teaching did not have the ideal of a free intellectuality that would become a central component of the educational ideal of the Enlightenment. Rarely an end in itself, higher education was often necessary to maintain the family's social rise; alternatively, it was a beginning or transitional point for further social and economic advancement into the urban notability or state administration. Sometimes it served as a resting point in a path of downward decline. Heinrich Kramm's important regional study of urban mobility in the early modern period has demonstrated how education created three general patterns of social advancement: (1) grammar or secondary teacher to a legal career in city administration (clerk, syndic) and then to council member; (2) grammar or secondary teacher to deacon, minister, and eventually superintendent; and (3) grammar or secondary teacher to medical

---

[31] See the excellent study by Bernd Wunder, "Die Sozialstruktur der Geheimratskollegien in den süddeutschen protestantischen Fürstentümern (1660–1720). Zum Verhältnis von sozialer Mobilität und Briefadel im Absolutismus," *VSWG*, 58 (1971):145–220; for this point, see especially 145–62; also useful is the older study by Hans Liermann, "Die rechtsgelehrten Beamten der fränkischen Fürstentümer Ansbach und Bayreuth im 18. Jahrhundert. Ein Beitrag zur Geschichte des deutschen Beamtentums," *Jahrbuch für fränkische Landesforschung*, 8–9 (1943):258–64. For comparison with France, see Kagan, "Law Students and Legal Careers," 65–7; and Berlanstein, *Lawyers of Toulouse*, 32–42.

[32] See the general observations by Lawrence Stone, "Social Mobility in England 1500–1700," *Past and Present*, no. 33 (1966):16–21, 36–7.

doctor and natural scientist. In addition, such career patterns were often made more complex by simultaneous activity in other fields as men sought to combine honorary with profit-making offices.[33] Thus when Enlightenment ideas began to make their way into northwestern Germany, they were adapted to these pre-existing career patterns and were employed in their perpetuation.

## THE MÖSER FAMILY

The details of Möser's family history are few, but the little we know confirms the pattern of mobility just described. For at least three generations, and for perhaps as many as five, the avenues of higher education and marriage into the Osnabrück ruling elite appear to have been the means by which the family consolidated its social position and continued its economic improvement. From the mid-sixteenth century on, the male line of the Möser family moved from the craft guilds into teaching opportunities in the blossoming Latin schools, from there into the ministry, and thence into the legal profession, which solidified the family's membership within the Osnabrück notability.

Although genealogical lists for the Möser family extend back to the twelfth century, reliable biographical information, as recorded in the family Bible, begins only with Justus Möser's great-grandfather, the patriarch of the male line.[34] This Zacharias Möser (1601–82) was a Latin school headmaster (*Rektor*) who taught first in Kiel and then in Hamburg at the *Johanneum*. His son Johann (1663–99) became the first minister of the *Marienkirche* in Osnabrück, and by marrying Anna Maria Münnich he attached the Möser family to the small group of inter-related families of the city's councillor elite. Her parents, Dr. Johann Gerhard Münnich and Regina Maria von Lengerke, were members of two important lines. The von Lengerkes had provided members to the city council and the regional administration from the early seventeenth century on. The Münnich family was equally distinguished: Anna Maria's uncle, Dr. Kasper Franz Münnich, was *Bürgermeister* of the city from the 1660s to his death in 1688, and her brothers and cousins also became city councillors and *Bürgermeister*. The son of Johann and Anna Maria, Johann Zacharias (1690–1758), Justus's father, received the

---

[33] Kramm, "Besitzschichten und Bildungsschichten," 460–1; Koch, *Göttinger Honoratiorentum*, 27–48.

[34] Nicolai, *Leben Justus Mösers*, in Möser, *W*, 10:6–9; Krusch, "Justus Möser und die Osnabrück Gesellschaft," 266–8.; Otto Hatzig, *Justus Möser als Staatsmann und Publizist*, in *Quellen und Darstellungen zur Geschichte Niedersachsens*, 27 (Hanover, 1909); H. Banniza von Bazan, "Ahnenliste von Justus Möser," *Osn. Mitt.*, 66 (1954):181–96; R. Gösling and Harold Schoeller, "Zur Ahnenliste Justus Mösers. Ergänzungen," *Osn. Mitt.*, 68 (1959):391–7; Karl-Egbert Schultze, "Zur Ahnenlist Justus Mösers. Ergänzungen," *Osn. Mitt.*, 69 (1960):127–8; Roland Seeberg-Elverfeld, "Zur Ahnenliste Justus Mösers. Ergänzungen," *Osn. Mitt.*, 69 (1960):128–9. The most recent interpretations of the genealogical context are two important works already cited: Lampe, *Aristokratie, Hofadel und Staatspatriziat*, and Spechter, *Osnabrücker Oberschicht*. Also quite suggestive is the essay by Clements Steinbicker, "Das Beamtentum in den geistlichen Fürstentümern Nordwestdeutschlands," *Beamtentum und Pfarrerstand*, ed. G. Franz (Limburg/Lahn, 1972), 126–9, 138–40.

doctor of law degree in Gelderland at Harderwijk and remained in Osnabrück to practice. He, too, advanced the family a step farther within the inner core of ruling families by his marriage to Regina Gertrud Elverfeld. Like the Münnich and von Lengerke families, the Elverfeld family had been prominent among the legally trained notability since the seventeenth century. Regina Gertrud's grandfather, H. Justus Elverfeld, was a notary and procurator who had left sizable holdings to his family. Her father, Dr. Justus Itle Elverfeld, had been elected to the city council numerous times (1699–1702, 1708, 1714) and had also been second *Bürgermeister* for two years (1700–2).

The marriage of Justus Möser's parents marked a new phase of family consolidation within the urban notability and the beginning of a different sort of advancement for the father outside the confines of the city within the episcopal administration. Johann Zacharias Möser was a member of the church council of the *Marienkirche*, where his father had been minister; but, more important, he was first named as episcopal magistrate (*Gograf*) of the district of Iburg during the reign of Ernst August II; then appointed a member of the chief secular and ecclesiastical administrative bodies, the chancellery and the consistorial council; and finally named director of the chancellery.

The success of Johann Zacharias Möser largely eliminated any career pressures on Justus Möser. One sign of this difference is that Justus did not depend on excelling in his formal education at the Latin school and the university for his own professional advancement. Although he was sent to Jena and Göttingen from 1741 to 1743 to prepare himself for a legal career in his father's and maternal grandfather's footsteps, he never completed his university education, and his years spent there do not have the imprint of serious study. We have little evidence of the enormous commitment that characterized not only the poorer of his contemporaries such as Winckelmann and Lessing, as well as his fellow Hanoverian of the next generation, Ernst Brandes, but even his own historically obscurer classmates from Osnabrück, Bertling and Lodtmann. Möser drew this conclusion himself in an autobiographical remark written in the third person: "His industriousness does not deserve praise; he was able to learn many things more easily than others; and the little that he knew he was able to use more beneficially than others. Moreover, he believes that both his friends from early childhood, the eventual Helmstadt professor Lodtmann and the superintendent Bertling, were considerably more industrious."[35]

Recent attempts to analyze Möser's notebooks from these years, though quite valuable for understanding the chronology of his interests, seem to exaggerate their importance as signs of deep application.[36] At most the notebooks establish his early love for Tacitus and the history of the ancient Germanic peoples. Only later in his forties, when, upon the death of Bishop Clemens August, he wrote a series of anonymous pamphlets in defense of a Hanoverian minority succession,

[35] Quoted in Nicolai, *Leben Justus Mösers*, in Möser, *W*, 10:7.
[36] Peter Schmidt, *Studien über Justus Möser als Historiker* (Göppingen, 1975), 1–11.

would he acquire and display the juridical knowledge that made him such an expert within the Empire on ecclesiastical administrative law. Until then, literary contacts appear to have been far more valuable to him. In Göttingen he became acquainted with the Swiss scientist and poet Albrecht von Haller, whose epic poem "The Alps," with its idealistic descriptions of the Swiss landscape and the free Swiss peasant communities, may have served as an impetus to his own studies of Westphalia. He also came into contact during the Göttingen years with Gottsched and the beginnings of the German literary revival, and this influence, not his legal studies, is most apparent in his first publications after his return to Osnabrück.[37]

The extant sources are not adequate to show precisely why Justus never completed his university education. Except for a few letters from these years, the notebooks (thematically organized *collectanea* he used for excerpting quotations from his reading), glimpses of his participation in the Göttingen literary society, hints at alchemical studies, and a few belabored poems, we know little of the outlines of his intellectual life during these years and, as I have indicated, nothing about the personal motives shaping it.[38] A surviving letter from his father, written while Justus was still in Göttingen, records displeasure that his son might not complete his law degree.[39] Nonetheless, his father removed the administrative obstacles to a career in Osnabrück, just as he was later to do for Justus's brother, Johann Zacharias (1726–67). Justus was named secretary to the *Ritterschaft*, while still a student and before he became a licensed advocate. And since his father was a member of the decisive licensing bodies, Justus was admitted to the local ranks of lawyers, as was his brother, without completing the usual legal degree.[40] Significantly, of twenty-five registered lawyers in 1761, only three others besides Justus and his brother lacked degrees.[41]

Möser's multiple office holding both mirrors the patterns sketched earlier and follows the model of his father's own career. It is safe to conclude that Justus Möser's early advancement resulted from a combination of political obligations owed to his father and the special place of the Möser family within the local notability. His appointments as secretary, *advocatus patriae*, syndic, and justitiary

---

[37] The best summary remains Werner Kohlschmidt, "Neuere Möser-Literatur," *Göttingsche Gelehrten Anzeigen*, 102 (1940):229–47. For the debate concerning Möser's education, see Heinrich Schierbaum, "Justus Mösers Stellung in den deutschen Literaturströmungen während der ersten Hälfte des 18. Jahrhunderts," *Osn. Mitt.*, 33 (1908):174–6, 180; Peter Klassen, *Justus Möser*, in *Studien zur Geschichte des Staats- und Nationalgedankens*, 2 (Frankfurt an Main, 1936), 11–20; 427–8, n. 17; 429, n. 45. Werner Pleister, "Die geistige Entwicklung Justus Mösers," *Osn. Mitt.*, 50 (1929):1–89; Ludwig Schirmeyer, "Das Möserbild nach neuen Briefen," *Osn. Mitt.*, 59 (1939):57–98.

[38] The early poems and essays are collected in Möser, *SW*, 2; see also Pleister, "Die geistige Entwicklung."

[39] Möser, *Briefe*, 10–11.

[40] See, for instance, Klöntrup, "Advocat," in his *Handbuch*, 1:48: "Die Erlaubniβ zu advociren wird beym geheimen Rathe nachgesucht, das Examen aber und die Immatriculation oder Reception des Candidaten von der Land- und Justizcanzley verfügt."

[41] Krusch, "Justus Möser und die Osnabrücker Gesellschaft," 263, 277.

are to be viewed in this light. Once these offices were in the Möser family, they stayed there. When his brother Johann Zacharias died, Justus requested and received his position as actuary to the criminal court, a post that had been dispensed originally at his father's request.

Continuing the marriage practices of the Möser family, Justus improved his fortunes in 1746 by marrying Regina Juliana Elisabeth Bruning, the daughter of Privy Secretary Karl Wilhelm Bruning and Maria Elisabeth von Lengerke. The von Lengerke family had already appeared in the generation of Möser's paternal grandparents; this branch of the von Lengerke family had moved from the Osnabrück councillor elite into the administrative world of Hanover. The Bruning family history was similar.[42] One of the most important mercantile families in Osnabrück that had been active since the early seventeenth century in the city administration as councillors and *Bürgermeister*, it had largely given up commerce to enter the educated professions. Regina's grandfather, Johann Wilhelm Bruning, a doctor of law, had been traveling companion to Bishop Ernst August II on his journeys to Italy and was made magistrate to the district of Groneberg in the bishopric. Her father was privy secretary in Osnabrück during the reign of Ernst August II, and after the succession of Clemens August in 1728, he moved to Hanover and occupied the important post of privy secretary to the German Chancellery until his death in 1736.

In Justus Möser's marriage and early accumulation of offices, we can observe the power and prestige available to the urban notability within the city proper. His family history also shows how the legally trained notables of the city spilled over into the entire administration of the bishopric and became the main providers of personnel for the executive offices in the political apparatus as a whole. Within the episcopal administration these men became the magistrates, judges, and *advocatus fisci*. Their emergence signified as well the growing professionalization of the ecclesiastical administration, whereby only legally certified members from the city came to be employed in the administration of the prince-bishop, the cathedral chapter, and the *Ritterschaft*.[43]

In Osnabrück as elsewhere throughout northwestern Germany, families like the Möser family came to form a semihomogeneous subgroup of secretarial families that has been labeled an "aristocracy of secretaries."[44] The Möser, Pagensticker, Frederici, and later the Lodtmann families constituted the Osnabrück variant of

---

[42] Christine Rohde, *Beamtenschaft und Territorialstaat. Behördenentwicklung und Sozialstruktur der Beamtenschaft im Hochstift Osnabrück 1550–1800*, 2 parts (Ph.D. diss.; Bochum, 1982), 252.

[43] Wunder shows similar patterns of mobility in the Protestant states of southern Germany in the previous generations (1660–1720). See Wunder, "Sozialstruktur der Geheimratskollegien," 176–85.

[44] For Osnabrück see particularly Spechter, *Osnabrücker Oberschicht*, 117–30; for the Hanoverian lands, see Ernst von Meier, *Hannoversche Verfassungs- und Verwaltungsgeschichte, 1680–1866*, 2 vols. (Leipzig, 1898–9), 1:495–6; Lampe, *Aristokratie, Hofadel und Staatspatriziat*, 1:215–365, esp. 238–275; Carl Haase, *Ernst Brandes*, 2 vols. (Hildesheim, 1973–4), 1–6; Gerhard Ritter, *Stein* (3rd ed.; Stuttgart, 1958), 99–120.

interrelated secretarial families who had emerged from original positions of power within the city's councillor elite. Their efforts to maintain social and professional control through marriages, alliances, and nepotism are a reminder that career mobility appears, from the study of regional genealogies, to have rigidified greatly by the later eighteenth century. By then, social accommodation had been made with the process of academic professionalization, at least in its corporatist form, so that the patterns of mobility previously described for earlier centuries were far less common among the ruling families of the bishopric. Osnabrück, in fact – Möser's rosy portrait to the contrary – appears to have been as narrowly oligarchic as the Nuremberg Nicolai attacked in his writings.[45] Certainly offices and careers within the administration of the city and the bishopric were tightly controlled by particular families of each religious confession. The careers within the Möser family were only one example. As far as is known, this condition existed in all cities throughout northwestern Germany and parallels the growing ossification of office holding by the local Catholic and Protestant nobility.[46]

Although one historian has called such oligarchic patterns of office holding a "regime of uncles,"[47] contemporaries labeled it "cousin economy" (*Vetternwirtschaft*), and Möser summed it up in the apt phrase, "no promotions according to merit." In a short piece of the same title addressed to an unnamed officer, he wrote: "I, at least, would never stay in a state, whether rewarded or not, wherein it had become a rule to receive distinction (*Ehre*) only according to merit. . . . Believe me, it is better that birth and age determine the order of rank in the world."[48] Accordingly, he did his best to advance his own relatives within the episcopal administration. As his father had aided him, he aided his son-in-law, Just Gerlach von Voigts, his god-child, Justus Gruner, and his wife's cousin,

[45] Nicolai, "Einige Nachrichten über Nürnberg," *Berlin Monatsschrift*, 1 (1783):76–96; and his *Beschreibung einer Reise durch Deutschland und die Schweiz im Jahre 1781*, 12 vols. (Berlin and Stettin, 1783–96), 1:201–33, esp. 222–7 For an overview see Reinhard Hildebrandt, "Die Verfassungskonflikete in den Reichsstädten des 17. und 18. Jahrhunderts," *Zeitschrift für Stadtgeschichte, Stadtsoziologie und Denkmalpflege*, 1 (1974):221–41, esp. 228–30; and Otto Borst, "Zur Verfassung und Staatlichkeit oberdeutscher Reichsstädte am Ende des Alten Reiches," *Esslinger Studien*, 10 (1964):106–94.

[46] For Westphalian examples, see the history of the Timmerscheidt family, summarized in von Oer, "Landständische Verfassungen," 108–9; Heinz Reif, *Westfälischer Adel, 1770–1860*, in *Kritische Studien zur Geschichtswissenschaft*, 35 (Göttingen, 1979), 67–73; Keinemann, *Das Domkapitel zu Münster*, esp. 31–50. For Osnabrück see the contemporary reports of political life at the end of the eighteenth century in Carl Betram Stüve, *Heinrich David Stüve, Doktor der Rechte und Bürgermeister der Stadt Osnabrück* (Jena, 1827), 7–29, and Gruner, *Meine Wallfahrt*, 2:518–40. As Renger notes, Krusch exaggerated and sensationalized the evidence of a patriciate in Osnabrück, but Renger tends to ignore the evidence of ossification in an effort to make Osnabrück appear institutionally viable in the decades before the French Revolution; see Renger, *Landesherr und Landstände*, 89n.

[47] Mack Walker takes a curious position regarding the realities of oligarchical rule in his provocative book, *German Home Towns* (Ithaca, N.Y., 1971). Because in Part One he projects community back into the seventeenth and eighteenth centuries, he overlooks the oligarchical nature of urban political life. The phrase is used on p. 57. See the sharply critical review by Wolfgang Zorn in the *HZ*, 216 (1973):175–7.

[48] Möser, "Keine Beförderung nach Verdiensten," *SW*, 5:161.

J. F. A. Lodtmann. The latter actually followed in Möser's own footsteps and led the administration until secularization in 1803.[49]

But it should be noted that in comparison to the test of ancestry (*Ahnenprobe*) practiced by the regional nobility, offices within the city and state administration remained open to limited competition. It is clear, for instance, that Justus's brother, Johann Zacharias, received only one office within the local administration. Though such an office was the starting point for the accumulation of more offices, hard work, if not always honest work, was required of the nonnoble administrator, since the bulk of the day-to-day business fell to him. If his father was also responsible for Justus's first posts, nonetheless it attests to his diligence and ability that he managed to rise to the top. For those, like the younger Johann Zacharias, the family black sheep who went to Tripoli as secretary to the Dutch ambassador, tried to make his fortune speculating in pirated goods, and eventually had to be brought home in disgrace, this type of carefully managed and manipulated advancement seems to have been impossible.[50]

Career patterns like those within the Möser family are clearly part of the hierarchical administrative system of the old regime. The nonnoble administrators victimized those below them, and they were victimized in turn by an aristocratic system in which it was not suitable to a noble's rank for him to work like a commoner, either as hard, or as long, or for similar remuneration.[51] As a consequence, the aristocracy of secretaries that developed in the Hanoverian domains had actual administrative power while lacking the highest titles. It became a rule within these domains, and hence within Osnabrück, that only aristocrats could be given the highest title of privy councillor (*Geheim Rat*).[52] These fine distinctions in rank were made at a time when the publicist Friedrich Karl von Moser complained: "the trade in titles has so completely inundated a councillor-craving Germany with Privy Councillors that the confusion would be boundless if all of these people were to council."[53] Thus, although Möser was given the honorary title of *Geheimer Justizrat* in 1786, he held the lesser title of *Referendar* during his chief reform period of the late 1760s and 1770s. (This situation partly resulted from Möser's own decision to refuse a higher title and ennoblement.) Not only was Möser's workload heavier than that of a noble *Geheimer Rat*, his income was less. During the regency, at the height of his administrative power when the two *Geheim Räte* served as administrative figureheads, it is estimated

---

[49] Rohde, *Beamtenschaft und Territorialstaat*, 300–1; Krusch, "Justus Möser und die Osnabrücker Gesellschaft," 302–24. See also the unsubstantiated reports of meddling in the appointments process by Frau Möser in Stüve, *Heinrich David Stüve*, 7. Traces of Möser's efforts to find suitable posts for his relatives appear in his correspondence; see *Briefe*, 308–9, 318–19, 373–5, 400–1.

[50] Möser, W, 1:44–5; Krusch, "Justus Möser und die Osnabrücker Gesellschaft," 287.

[51] Rosenberg, *Bureaucracy, Aristocracy, and Autocracy*, 54–5; Wunder, "Sozialstruktur der Geheimratskollegien," 185–90. For Osnabrück, see Rohde, *Beamtenschaft und Territorialstaat*, 367–8, 400–2.

[52] Wunder shows somewhat greater mobility at the beginning of the eighteenth century; see ibid., 160–70.

[53] Friedrich Karl Frhr. von Moser, *Der Herr und der Diener* (Frankfurt, 1762 [1758]), 228–9.

that Möser's yearly income from his various offices was a more than respectable 1,875 Taler. When he died he left to his only daughter, Jenny, an estate of houses, stables, and gardens valued at more than 75,000 Taler. Yet his income could not compete with that of the two noble *Geheim Räte* above him, which was set at 3,700 Taler plus free lodging in the Osnabrück *Schloβ*.[54]

On one side, then, the political activities of the notables were restricted by the aristocracy. Aristocrats were placed at the top of all administrative hierarchies outside the city administration, although the city itself remained the domain of the traditional notability, and the highest posts were dispensed with great care in order to maintain both the confessional balance and the existing ties to the most important ruling dynasties in Germany, the Habsburgs, the Hohenzollerns, and the Wittelsbachs. It is this exclusion by those at the top that strengthened the special "burgher pride" of the nonnoble notability. The political and institutional restraints within German society stifled the individual development of the many but also shaped and reinforced the intellectual independence of the few. There was, indeed, a certain feeling shared by these men of affairs that the social boundaries nurtured and reinforced.

Since these notables were actually urban aristocrats without letters of patent, one way to advance political careers otherwise closed was to enter the nobility. Over two to four generations of a family's career pattern, the teaching profession ultimately could lead upward to the nobility and to a status of *Briefadel* (noble by letters of patent). In the electoral bishopric of Cologne, and sometimes in Hanover, such a *noblesse de robe* did emerge.[55] However, given the rigid proof of blood and breeding required throughout Westphalia, and by the cathedral chapter and the *Ritterschaft* of Osnabrück, ennoblement was a rare phenomenon. Even in those exceptional cases, such as the von Voigts family into which Möser's daughter

---

[54] See Hatzig, *Justus Möser als Staatsmann und Publizist*, 20, 194. Hatzig details Möser's income from his various offices as follows (194):

| | |
|---|---|
| Ritterschaftlicher Syndikus | 90 Taler |
| advocatus patriae | 100 Taler |
| ad dies vitae | 200 Taler |
| Kriminal justitiar | 535 Taler |
| Konsulent | 600 Taler |
| Referendar | 350 Taler |
| | 1,875 Taler |

This yearly income does not include the private income from his legal practice. See also Sheldon and Sheldon, *Geist der Empfindsamkeit*, 3; Krusch, "Justus Möser und die Osnabrücker Gesellschaft," 294–6; Spechter, *Osnabrücker Oberschicht*, 74.

[55] For Osnabrück see Rohde, *Beamtenschaft und Territorialstaat*, 396n. For the Westphalian region see Steinbicker, "Beamtentum in den geistlichen Fürstentümern," 121–48. The development of a service nobility has been much better studied for Prussia; see Rosenberg, *Bureaucracy, Aristocracy and Autocracy*, 182–92; Henning von Bonin, "Adel und Bürgertum in der höheren Beamtenschaft der preußischen Monarchie 1794–1806," *Jahrbuch für die Geschichte Mittel- und Ostdeutschlands*, 15 (1966):139–74; John R. Gillis, "Aristocracy and Bureaucracy in Nineteenth Century Prussia," *Past and Present*, no. 41 (1968):109–12. For southern Germany see Wunder, "Sozialstruktur der Geheimratskollegien," 145–220.

Jenny married, it is doubtful that such a promotion in social rank provided the social entrance into the nobility that might have seemed likely, especially since the local Hanoverian nobility refused to recognize such titles.[56] For this reason, many like Möser preferred to remain firmly within the boundaries of the Third Estate. Möser seems to have been considered for ennoblement at the time of his appointment as *Referendar*. Then he wrote dryly of his desire to remain a commoner, requesting that Minister von Behr "would please spare me the title and the horns, since I do not want for that to forego the right to crawl through a hedge."[57]

Thus, though the hereditary distinctions were strictly enforced in the later eighteenth century, it is difficult to draw clear conclusions regarding the way the social divisions functioned in practice. The everyday social boundary separating the local nobility from the legal notables had already become somewhat indistinct. Yet in a provincial place such as Osnabrück, the erosion of such boundaries most likely tended to remain private and individual. For example, it was not until 1793 – thus decades later than elsewhere in Germany – that a social club was founded, the so-called *Großer Klub*, where administrators, nobles, and commoners could meet as social equals. During Möser's lifetime the spa at Bad Pyrmont fulfilled the function of bringing the aristocracy and nonnoble elite together on neutral ground.[58]

Möser's example was most likely still exceptional. He not only represented the nobility in his various daily administrative tasks as secretary to the *Ritterschaft*, but he also served individual noblemen privately as their legal agent and entered into business ventures with them. The most complete surviving group of Möser's letters are those between Möser and Klamor von dem Bussche-Hünnefeld in the 1740s and 1750s.[59] They show us how intimately versed he was in the affairs of the von dem Bussche-Hünnefeld family and the routine financial operations concerning the estate. Möser also lent money to the local nobility: his account book for 1793, the year before his death, listed outstanding loans to the local

[56] Much contemporary evidence for this conclusion is cited by Lampe, *Aristokratie, Hofadel und Patriziat* 1:276–86; for Westphalia see also the comments by Reif, *Westfälischer Adel*, 48–56, 176–86. Wunder draws similar conclusions for southern Germany in ibid., esp. 213–20.

[57] Quoted in Nicolai, *Leben Justus Mösers*, in *W*, 10:24; Krusch, "Justus Möser und die Osnabrücker Gesellschaft," 295.

[58] For comments on Osnabrück's *Großer Klub*, see Rohde, *Beamtenschaft und Territorialstaat*, 403–5. Regarding the function of such clubs in the late Enlightenment, see Richard van Dülmen, *Geheimbund der Illuminaten* (Stuttgart, 1975), 15–20, 107–12, and Thomas Nipperdey, "Verein als Sozialstruktur im späten 18. und frühen 19. Jahrhundert," in *Geschichtswissenschaft und Vereinswesen im 19. Jahrhundert*, ed. Hartmut Boockmann et al., in *Veröffentlichungen des Max-Planck-Instituts für Geschichte*, 1 (Göttingen, 1972), 1–45. For Bad Pyrmont see the contemporary history by Heinrich Matthias Marcard, *Beschreibung von Pyrmont*, 2 vols. (Leipzig, 1784–5), 1, esp. 84–107 for Marcard's attacks on aristocratic arrogance at Pyrmont. See also Reinhold P. Kuhnert, *Urbanität auf dem Lande. Badereisen nach Pyrmont im 18. Jahrhundert*, in *Veröffentlichungen des Max-Planck-Instituts für Geschichte*, 77 (Göttingen, 1984).

[59] These letters have been transcribed and are being edited for publication by William Sheldon and the Herzog August Library in Wolfenbüttel; see footnote 4.

nobility totaling some 34,000 Taler.[60] Similarly, a list of signatories to a local mining venture undertaken by Möser and his son-in-law, Just Gerlach von Voigts, included the nobles von Münster-Langelage, von Bar-Bärenau, von Bar-Osnabrück, von Schele, von Vincke, and von der Horst zu Hollewinke. Sometimes these business ties also bespoke personal attachments as well. Möser's ethical treatise on friendship, for example, was composed in the memory of Johann Friedrich von dem Bussche-Hünnefeld, and Möser was executor for the surviving children.[61] Finally, nowhere in Möser's correspondence do we note the servile attitude in his relations to the nobility that marked the work of his younger, equally famous contemporary, the legal philosopher and historian Stephan Pütter.[62]

The inherent ambiguity in the Möser family ties to the local nobility is illustrated by the difference between women's and men's marital and social functions. In a culture where marital strategies were so important, the women were used to bring new male blood into the families of the notability through marriage to promising lawyers, educators, or clergymen, or they were used to link the familiy to the regional nobility. All the sisters of Justus Möser's wife, Regina Juliana Bruning, married clergymen. Justus Möser's maternal aunt, Ernestine Juliana Elverfeld, entered the nobility with her marriage to Karl Klamor von Grothaus zu Kritenstein in 1746. He was apparently poor enough to force the newlyweds to live in her father's Osnabrück house, and they were one of the families owing money to Justus Möser at his death. We gather from a letter by Justus Möser's wife, which describes a macabre scene of betrothal at the deathbed of Möser's father, that Justus Möser and his father pushed the marriage of his only daughter, Jenny, to the nobleman Just Gerlach von Voigts (1768).[63] The von Voigts family had been among the few families of the Hanoverian administrative elite to have been raised to the nobility in the previous generation, so that the marriage of Jenny Möser and Just Gerlach von Voigts occurred at the social boundary between the nobility of the robe and the nonnobility.

These two marriages, both by women of the notability, were the only two within Möser's extended family where members entered the local nobility, and they were among the few "mixed marriages" between the local nobility and the city's first families. Yet such a marriage with the local nobility would appear to have been far less acceptable for a male. The fragmentary evidence is, however, somewhat contradictory. The correspondence reveals that Möser interceded in

[60] Spechter, *Osnabrücker Oberschicht*, 74n.

[61] Möser, *W*, 9:3–54.

[62] Johann Stephen Pütter, *Selbstbiographie zur dankbaren Jubelfeier Seiner 50 jährigen Professorstelle zu Göttingen*. 2 vols. (Göttingen, 1798).

[63] In a letter shortly after the wedding, Frau Möser wrote: "Mein Künftiger Schwieger Sohn der H. v. Voigt, dem meine Janne mit ihrer eltern genehmhaltung und auf ausdrückliches verlangen meines sel. Schwieger Vatters zwey Tage vor dessen absterben ihr ja Wort gegeben." Quoted in Sheldon and Sheldon, *Geist der Empfindsamkeit*, 12. The von Voigts family genealogy appears in Lampe, *Aristokratie, Hofadel und Staatspatriziat*, 2:456–7.

the intimate family affairs of George Ludwig von Bar to aid the daughter when she fell in love with a nonnoble secretary, her "Trueworth."[64] But when the young Thomas Abbt was considering leaving his university post to enter the service of the Duke of Schaumburg-Lippe, Möser advised strongly against it. His words to Abbt have even greater weight if we can accept Jenny Möser's statement that she and Thomas Abbt had wanted to marry. (Abbt was to die two years later of a virulent fever, some months before Jenny's engagement.) Möser wrote at that time: "Digestion is not easy at court; vegetables which I have to swallow while standing do not become me as well as when I have the freedom to have my elbows on the table. I only hope your soul will not suffer."[65]

What we see, then, is that Osnabrück's notables lived in their own subuniverse within corporate society, and that the lawyers, as another professional subgroup among the nonnobility, had a special existence among and between the aristocracy, the notability, and the professional administration. Moreover, as the sumptuary laws and the oligarchic patterns of office holding indicate, the social boundaries between nobles and commoners did not prevent them from sharing the inegalitarian values common to estate society. Since closure was partly informal, a combination of wealth, birth, and education remained the critical factors in the maintenance of social rank from one generation to the next. Insofar as they did not marry into wealthy families, the children of the educated professionals were forced to perpetuate their social positions through continuing activity in a profession based upon, and consolidated by, degrees and university training.

### EMANCIPATION AND THE OLD ELITES

Intellectual change within complex and geographically diffuse movements like the Enlightenment is normally neither clear-cut nor uniform, even in closely related branches of knowledge or in those sharing common assumptions; therefore, as a matter of course, the historian of ideas must always confront a varied contemporaneous pattern of intellectual resistance and alteration. Beyond this, increased professionalization in Western life has long affected the composition and transmission of intellectual systems. From the late medieval period on, such professionalization had had two social functions within urban society: it acted as a leavening agent within the ruling elite, and it formed new criteria for estab-

---

[64] Schirmeyer, "Georg Ludwig von Bar, 'der beste französische Dichters Deutschlands,' ein Vorbild Wielands und Freund Mösers," *Osn. Mitt.*, 32 (1907):1–71.

[65] Möser, *Briefe*, 217. Abbt's decision prompted a serious debate between Nicolai, Mendelssohn, and Abbt over his loss of "honor from too much sustained contact with the nobility." For this exchange see Thomas Abbt, *Vermischte Schriften*, 6 vols. (Frankfurt and Leipzig, 1783), 5:181–4, 189–91. Möser expressed this concern in other places in the letters; see Möser, *Briefe*, 205, 211, 229. Of the secondary literature, see the anti-Semitic dissertation by Gertrud Brück, *Die Bedeutung Justus Mösers für das Leben und Denken Thomas Abbts* (Munich, 1937), 8–15. To understand Abbt's motivations, see the insightful study by Hans Erich Bödeker, "Thomas Abbt: Patriot, Bürger und bürgerliches Bewußtsein," in *Bürger und Bürgerlichkeit im Zeitalter der Aufklärung*, ed. Rudolf Vierhaus (Heidelberg, 1981), esp. 239–44, 247–9.

lishing and maintaining social hierarchies. The rhythmic movement of upward mobility, consolidation, and eventual ossification was only incompletely affected by the Enlightenment because educational reform was, and is, a circumscribed process — only grafted onto other processes that by itself can affect only to a limited degree a complexly ordered social system.[66]

Consequently, the cry for education (*Bildung* or *Erziehung*) at the center of the German Enlightenment, the Horatian *"sapere aude"* ("dare to know"), remained socially contradictory. Although hoping that education would abolish estatist distinctions, many contemporaries overlooked or accepted the way in which it also created hierarchical principles that, although different, overlapped and buttressed the corporate order. Diderot was one of the exceptional figures in the late eighteenth century who had understood this dialectical process. He formulated it as a social aporia in his then unpublished dialogue, *Rameau's Nephew*, where *Lui* is made to accuse *Moi*, the philosopher, of social hypocrisy, of supporting the Enlightenment to further his own social ascent. Society is essentially parasitical, *Lui* proposes; each member is one of numerous types of "social parasites" with their own special languages or "trade idioms." Though *Moi* attempts to dispute with *Lui* by denying *Lui*'s grounds and belittling his itinerant life, he is not able to shake *Lui*'s conclusion that the so-called Enlightenment ideals are simply trade idioms in the service of a new social caste.

The social historian of Germany in the late eighteenth century must set aside the rhetoric of emancipation and follow Diderot's lead by exploring in what ways the emancipatory claims of education could become — and indeed did become — a powerful ideology in the service of a refurbished corporatism. If examining this question in any detail takes us far beyond the framework of Möser's biography, still the attitude we adopt is critical for analyzing the boundaries between social roles, systems of ideas, and the dynamic of change. The questions involve matters of both structure and function. We must move from an understanding of the corporate order in the eighteenth century and how the Enlightenment functioned within that order to an understanding of the transformation of both the Enlightenment and social roles in the hybrid structure of nineteenth-century society, where corporate and class values comingled.

Such an analysis is not easy because the dominant Enlightenment social and intellectual ideal merely substituted one inegalitarian order for another — that of a meritocracy for an aristocracy of birth. How differently are ideas and roles

---

[66] Like most nineteenth-century thinkers, Pareto thought in terms of the replacement of elites, not in terms of accommodation; in his stark formulation: "the history of man is the history of the continuous replacement of certain elites: as one ascends, another declines." See Vilfredo Pareto, *The Rise and Fall of the Elites* (Totowa, N.J., 1968), 36. For a discussion of the social process whereby old and new elites adapt to each other, see the general comments by Lawrence Stone, "Literacy and Education in England 1640–1900," *Past and Present*, no. 42 (1969):70, 74; also the reflections by Konrad Jarausch, *Students, Society and Politics in Imperial Germany* (Princeton, N.J., 1982), 70–90; and for Germany in the later eighteenth century, Hans Weil, *Die Entstehung des deutschen Bildungsprinzips* (2nd ed.; Bonn, 1967), and Ulrich K. Preuβ, "Bildung und Bürokratie," *Der Staat*, 14 (1975):371–96.

embedded in the two value systems of corporatism and Enlightenment?[67] I believe there are significant differences, but we must analyze without illusion how meritocracies have attempted to perpetuate themselves and how informal closure in an "open" society can resemble the formal systems of exclusion in a corporate society. These questions have been central for the history of the Germanies since the Prussian educational reforms in the early nineteenth century fused a meritocratic educational system with the military-aristocratic state; it is important to realize that these reforms are continuous with Enlightenment thought and practice.[68]

How much do we exaggerate lived reality by setting Klopstock's corporate ideal of a *Gelehrtenrepublik*, with its infinite gradations and arcane ideal of intellectual life, next to the social closure practiced at the nineteenth-century German university?[69] The intervening revolutionary wars and restoration must make us cautious about blanket comparisons. Nonetheless the survival, both institutional and personal, of corporatism and an inegalitarian humanist ideal cannot be overlooked. Such survivals are doubly significant in the Germanies because the chances for careers outside or at the periphery of the state and its institutions were almost nonexistent. Until after the revolutions of 1848, the history of Germany's "free-floating" intelligentsia remained one of emigration and exile.

### ENLIGHTENMENT IN OSNABRÜCK

These reflections about changing intellectual ideals and the pace of change into the nineteenth century keep us from false expectations about Möser's Germany. The weight of the past, the sense of social and intellectual options as foreclosed by custom, predominated, whether one lived at court, in an urban setting, or in the countryside. In the provincial towns and cities of northwestern Germany, such as Osnabrück, which lagged behind in terms of social and economic change throughout the eighteenth and nineteenth centuries, Enlightenment culture had even more limited social consequences. Whatever its social ideal, whether egalitarian, meritocratic, or corporatist, Enlightenment culture in the society of Osnabrück was far more readily assimilated to the hegemonic values of the urban notability. Even so, this assimilation was not a simple matter: Just as the notability lived in its own social universe between the common citizenry and the aristocracy, so too did its intellectual universe express this complex mediation.

---

[67] See the historical models of educational alternatives in Detlef K. Müller, *Sozialstruktur und Schulsystem. Aspekte zum Strukturwandel des Schulwesens im 19. Jahrhundert* (Göttingen, 1977), 90–153.

[68] See, for example, Fritz Ringer, *Education and Society in Modern Europe* (Bloomington, Ind., 1979), 70–90; Charles E. McClelland, *State, Society and University in Germany 1700–1914* (Cambridge, 1980), 101–49; Lenore O'Boyle, "Klassische Bildung und Sozialstruktur in Deutschland zwischen 1800 und 1848," *HZ*, 207 (1968):584–608.

[69] See Ulrich Dzwonek et. al., " 'Bürgerliche Oppositionsliteratur zwischen Revolution und Reformismus.' " F. G. Klopstocks *Deutsche Gelehrtenrepublik und Bardendichtung als Dokument der bürgerlichen Emanzipationsbewegung in der zweiten Hälfte des 18. Jahrhunderts,* in *Deutsches Bürgertum und literarische Intelligenz 1750–1800,* ed. Bernd Lutz (Stuttgart, 1974), 286–301.

The social habits of the notability, shaping as they did the forms of intellectual discourse, comprised the substratum that linked corporate, urban culture to the European Enlightenment. The following chapters examine the forms this mediation took and the ways in which material limitations and social habit shaped Justus Möser's intellectual universe. Thus it is important to conclude this chapter by describing how such corporatist intellectual habits structured and bounded Möser's own life work.

In Osnabrück, as I have stressed, social and intellectual life was tied together by the religious divisions between Catholic and Protestant; by carefully controlled marriages and careers; and by sumptuary laws that continued to link dress with birth, wealth, occupation, and, by extension, with thought itself. It is difficult to discern how confining and, in this sense, "provincial" everyday discourse was. But it is clear, for instance, that the formal education of children in the city was as yet little affected by modern ideas. Only toward the end of the century did Enlightenment pedagogical ideas begin to affect the structure of the *Gymnasium* system in Osnabrück, with reforms beginning at the *Ratsgymnasium* after 1770 and at the Catholic *Carolinum* after 1798. Far-reaching reforms had to wait for the French occupation of Osnabrück and the administration of *Bürgermeister* Heinrich David Stüve. In Möser's day the educational system was still strictly confessional and estatist in tone. The city council sponsored the *Ratsgymnasium* for Protestant students, and the cathedral chapter, under the zealous stewardship of the Jesuits and then, after their expulsion in 1773, the Franciscans, supported the other *Gymnasium*, the *Carolinum*. It is significant for confessionally divided Osnabrück that theologians were the only teachers to enjoy modest fame inside and outside the bishopric during the eighteenth century. Moreover, if the negative reminiscences of contemporaries are accurate, secondary education, based on a traditional curriculum of Latin, rhetoric, and religious orthodoxy, was not of very high quality.[70] Möser's remarks about the intellectual narrowness of at least one teacher at the *Ratsgymnasium* indicate as much:

The future Senior Bertling in Danzig, the Helmstadt Professor Lodtmann and I had founded in our twelfth year a scholarly society in which sundry essays were read aloud each week. The real value [of these written essays] consisted in the fact that they had been composed in our own invented language. We had not advanced much farther than the preliminary phase of creating a grammar and dictionary and, as is in the nature of things, of having begun a scholarly journal in the language. At this point we left the

---

[70] Julius Jaeger, *Die Schola Carolina Osnabrugensis* (Osnabrück, 1904); Friedrich Runge, *Geschichte des Ratsgymnasiums zu Osnabrück* (Osnabrück, 1895), 51–91 and attached supplementary study plans from 1732, 1764, and 1800. See also the remarks by Stüve concerning the 1770s in *Heinrich David Stüve*, 4–8; and remarks from the same period by B. R. Abeken, the tutor of Schiller's children and editor of Möser's works, in "Erinnerungen B. R. Abeken," *Festschrift zur dreihundertjährigen Jubelfeier des Ratsgymnasium zu Osnabrück 1895*, ed. A. Heuermann (Osnabrück, 1895), 13–18. For the pattern of educational reform at the secondary level in Westphalia and Osnabrück, see A. H. von Wallthor, "Die höheren Schulen Westfalens," *Westfälische Forschungen*, 11 (1958):43–51.

class of the Cantor who had not disturbed us in our play. But our next teacher, who managed to get a copy of my autobiography which I had written in this language, forced us, with blows, to return to our mother tongue. Often afterward I have wished that he had channeled our energies and, since we only wanted to learn something special, had encouraged us to learn Arabic or Hebrew. Instead he tortured us with Latin poetry and became angered when we immediately translated his prose assignments into verse and read them aloud, in order to convince him to challenge us with something else. But nothing helped. We were consigned with blows to write the exercises first in prose. Yet he was the best teacher for slow minds.[71]

For these and similar reasons, the fundamental educational experience prior to the few years spent at a university occurred in the home under the guidance of parents and private tutors.[72] (Möser had a private tutor, of whom we only know that he was sent to bring home his charge when at the age of fourteen Justus set off for three days to make his fortune.)[73] Furthermore, in the homes of notable families, the bilingual French-German courtly ideal remained of the highest importance, since such language skills were a distinctive badge of social standing. Möser's family environment was typically French speaking. He conversed with his mother in French and took as his literary models French playwrights and novelists (Marivaux, St. Evremond, Voltaire). He later perpetuated a similar bilingual environment in his own home. His wife, it seems, was even more accomplished in French letters than he, and most of her surviving correspondence was conducted in French. At one time, according to Möser, she "wanted to become a writer," and two of her translations were actually published. Their daughter, Jenny, who reached maturity when Osnabrück had become effectively an English-Hanoverian domain, was never able to read English authors in the original but was apparently as fluent in French as her mother.[74]

The French-German bilingual ideal deserves special emphasis both because it provided an important link in the post-Latin era after midcentury to the cosmopolitan ideal of the Enlightenment and because it presupposed a degree of personal autonomy and social exclusiveness. As an implicit cultural code that fused style and subject matter, the bilingual ideal reproduced the forms of political, cultural, and economic antagonism within the Germanies. These antagonisms were reflected in the ambivalent appeal of French culture and the French Enlightenment throughout the century. The comparison between cultures is significant. The social type underlying the French intellectual ideal resulted from the fusion of an aristocratic code with a meritocratic ideal. Contacts between the aristocracy and the nonnobility in Parisian salon culture had created an enlightened culture in which, though the tensions between aristocracy and nonnobility were never resolved, the social code was still more emancipated from moral

[71] Möser, *SW*, 10:240–1.
[72] Lampe, *Aristokratie, Hofadel und Staatspatriziat*, 1:288–91.
[73] Möser, *SW*, 2:204.
[74] Möser, *Briefe*, 65, 319; Sheldon and Sheldon, *Geist der Empfindsamkeit*, 4.

constraint, social *ressentiment*, and *Standesdünkel*.[75] In addition, unlike the warring gentry and mercantile ideals at the base of English Augustan life, the French ideal was urban, residential in distinction to mercantile, and representational in outlook. This form of the French Enlightenment, though quintessentially high bourgeois, was adopted more onesidedly by the German courts and aristocracy as "Epicureanism" or "libertinism."

It is fair, in fact, to speak of the cultivation of bourgeois individuals at the German courts but a suppression of the burgher dimension. The values of Friedrich II were exceptional in this regard, for he threatened to undermine the aristocratic code by assimilating the ascetic materialism and radical religious criticism of the French Enlightenment. This is a key to the importance of the Prussian Academy of Sciences; through the Academy, Friedrich II made French Enlightenment ideals serve the social values of the Hohenzollern dynasty and thereby deflected its critical potential away from the court and the Prussian state.[76]

This appropriation by the German aristocracy of the French Enlightenment created natural social boundaries for its reception in Germany.[77] Anti-French feeling had appeared periodically since the beginning of the seventeenth century. A fresh wave developed among the German nonnobility in the later eighteenth century, expressing both criticism of aristocratic excesses and narrower social horizons, a greater ethical inwardness, and a more emotionally cramped life. The case of Rousseau, his ostracism in Paris and more powerful appeal among the nonnobility east of the Rhine, is one indication of the differences in cultural style between France and Germany.

But to reduce burgher attitudes toward the French Enlightenment to cultural *ressentiment* does not tell the whole story, for some Germans attempted throughout the seventeenth and eighteenth centuries to emulate the bourgeois intellectual ideal. The young Christian Thomasius, for instance, had scandalized the professorate at the University of Leipzig by lecturing (1696) in German on Gracian's *Oracle*.[78] In those lectures he tried to interpret in a German context the meaning of *l'homme honnête*. The "honest man" was for Thomasius the social ideal of the free intellectual, found in France but not in Germany. His dress was freed from

[75] See, for instance, Norbert Elias, *Ueber den Prozess der Zivilisation*, 2 vols. (2nd ed.; Frankfurt am Main, 1978), 1:7–50; Robert Darnton, "The High Enlightenment and the Low-Life of Literature in Pre-Revolutionary France," *Past and Present*, no. 51 (1971):90–3; Alan Kors, *D'Holbach's Coterie* (Princeton, N.J., 1976), 184–222.

[76] Ingrid Mittenzwei, *Friedrich II. von Preussen* (Cologne, 1980), 97–100, 163–6; Franz Mehring, *Die Lessing Legende*, in *Gesammelte Schriften*, ed. Thomas Höhle et. al., 9 (Berlin, 1963), 230–34.

[77] Fritz Brüggemann, "Der Kampf um die bürgerlichen Welt- und Lebensanschauung," *DVLG*, 3 (1925):94–127.

[78] Concerning Balthasar Gracian, see Karl Borinski, *Baltasar Gracian und die Hofliteratur in Deutschland* (Halle a. S., 1894), and Werner Krauss, *Gracians Lebenslehre* (Frankfurt am Main, 1947). Concerning Thomasius, see Ernst Bloch, "Christian Thomasius. Ein deutscher Gelehrter ohne Misere," in his *Naturrecht und menschliche Würde* (Frankfurt am Main, 1961), 315–56; Carl Hinrichs, "Das Bild des Bürgers in der Auseinandersetzung zwischen Christian Thomasius und August Hermann Francke," *Preußentum und Pietismus* (Göttingen, 1971), 352–87; Hans Wolff, *Die Weltanschauung der deutschen Aufklärung in geschichtlicher Entwicklung* (2nd ed.; Bern, 1963), 27–45.

sumptuary laws; he wrote and spoke a language emancipated from corporate jargon; he lived in a polity where there were clear boundaries to public coercion; and his intellect opened up to him the realm of social and political action. Thomasius argued against the prevailing academic Francophobia: French values were to be imitated because the comparison would serve German intellectual emancipation.[79] His view of French mores as the model and arena of free spirituality continued to inspire German intellectuals throughout the following century — witness Gottsched's efforts in Leipzig and Lessing's phase of cavalier dress and his boundless affection for Diderot's bourgeois dramatic ideal.[80] In spite of this, however, attitudes toward the French remained brittle and were easily undermined.

Notable culture reflected the German ambivalence toward French culture and the intellectual concerns of the French Enlightenment. But since the notability formed the peak of one social pyramid, it reproduced, on a provincial scale, the more emancipated conditions of French high bourgeois culture. Möser, for example, was far more like a French *philosophe* than many of his contemporaries: he was neither burdened by an inward, self-critical Protestantism nor disenfranchised by the local aristocracy. Furthermore, his attitude toward French culture held no social rancor. Throughout his life, in fact, he retained an unadulterated pleasure in things French. French letters formed his taste and judgment on aesthetic questions and the writing of clear, forceful prose. Indeed, many of his printed works from the 1740s and 1750s, like Thomasius's early essays, concerned the adoption of French cultural styles in Germany. His moral weeklies, open letters to Voltaire and Rousseau, and the treatise *The Value of Well-Disposed Inclinations and Passions* all had these concerns at their center.

Yet, Möser's contribution to the broad effort to formulate a particular burgher *Weltanschauung* or life-style was more complex than the simple absorption and translation of French cultural values. Although French mores formed one dominant comparative resource, English values, as portrayed in the novel and other forms of popular literature, were also significant. Questions of social habit and public propriety, for instance, figured prominently in the German moral weeklies that had become increasingly modish during the 1730s and 1740s. These weeklies differed substantially from handbooks like Gracian's *Oracle*, which were socially subversive guides for the court schemer and man on the make. Such handbooks were akin in cultural function to the novel — for example, to Defoe's *Moll Flanders* or Richardson's *Pamela*. The general purpose of the weeklies, on the other hand, was not to undermine by showing how to succeed but rather to describe the

---

[79] Christian Thomasius, "Discours welcher Gestalt man denen Frantzosen in gemeinem Leben und Wandel nachahmen soll," easily accessible in his *Deutsche Schriften*, ed. Peter von Düffel (Stuttgart, 1970), 7–49.

[80] Fritz Brüggemann, "Die Entwicklung der Psychologie im bürgerlichen Drama Lessings und seiner Zeit," *Euphorion*, 26 (1925):376–88; idem, "Lessings Bürgerdramen und der Subjektivismus als Problem. Psychogenetische Untersuchungen," *Jahrbuch des Freien Deutschen Hochstifts* (1926):69–110; Werner Rieck, *Johann Christoph Gottsched* (Berlin, 1972), esp. 170–81.

boundaries between social universes in order to establish acceptable rules of decorum.[81]

In these years Möser's weeklies, issued from 1746 on for the small circle of readers in Hanover and Osnabrück, typified the search for propriety. They mark his early efforts to link linguistic and other cultural codes with particular social types and to pinpoint the particular ethos appropriate for each type. Möser's weekly essays most often had a narrow social horizon, focusing on the circle of his peers. They began with the representation of manners, moving to a description of the morally responsible agent and then to the domain of personal integrity. The September 1746 issue is quite representative of his early style. Structured in two parts and filled with commonplaces, Möser's essay starts with general reflections about human psychology and ends in a series of tales – moral metamorphoses, to be exact – that illustrate the principles. Man is a creature of passions that may take good and evil forms, Möser notes, and these "passions are like the waves which bring the honest and the deceitful into port with the same force and speed." Reason, however, makes the control of passion possible, and man, when he is fortunate, learns to understand himself and virtue, eschewing passion for the "middle road" of virtue. Then follow the moral tales that illustrate the views of the twenty-six-year-old Möser.[82]

But Möser's middle road is not necessarily one of Christian virtue and capitalist frugality. In this sense, his weeklies do not show the "embourgeoisment" of aristocratic mores that occurred in similar periodicals, such as the influential Hamburg weekly, the *Patriot*.[83] They remain more purely representational in their concern to display an ethical attitude of gentlemanly restraint and womanly propriety. They also lack the cultural tension of the best examples of the genre and in this way reflect Osnabrück's more static universe.

In addition to the moral weeklies, the most sustained essay of Möser's early years to clarify his cultural attitudes was his essay on the inclinations and the passions that was occasioned by the death of his aristocratic patron, Johann Friedrich von dem Bussche-Hünnefeld (written in 1746, published in 1756). Composed as a monologue to Philocles, who is taken to have known the deceased, the essay commented on Shaftesbury's *Moralist*, a dialogue between the characters Philocles and Palemon.[84] Möser's main concern in this work, beyond honoring the memory of his sponsor and friend, was to defend the natural goodness of the

[81] Wolfgang Martens, *Die Botschaft der Tugend* (Stuttgart, 1971), 171–84; Wolff, *Weltanschauung der deutschen Aufklärung*, 61–74; Rieck, *Gottsched*, 76–8; Bernhard Fabian, "English Books and their Eighteenth-Century German Readers," in *The Widening Circle*, ed. Paul Korshin (Philadelphia, 1976), 169–71.

[82] Möser, *SW*, 1:209–10.

[83] Martens, "Bürgerlichkeit in der deutschen Aufklärung," in Kopitzsch, ed., *Aufklärung, Absolutismus und Bürgertum*, 347–63.

[84] Möser, *W*, 4:6; also *SW*, 2. Concerning the importance of Shaftesbury, see Henry Sidgwick, *Outlines of the History of Ethics* (London, 1886), 180–8; Leslie Stephens, *History of English Thought in the Eighteenth Century*, 2 vols. (reprint 3rd ed.; New York, 1962), 2:15–33; Christian Friedrich Weiser, *Shaftesbury und das deutsche Geistesleben* (Leipzig, 1916).

emotions. Like Shaftesbury, Möser wished to salvage moral feelings from the charge of both base egoism and cultural arbitrariness. "If one were to go so far and to negate the entire power of the best inclination or to allow everything to reside in the arbitrary choice of the soul, then I fear that we truly will begin a dangerous trade, giving away the certain without retaining the better but uncertain."[85]

In several ways, this treatise recapitulated the debates of the English deists; Möser repeated the argument from design, a belief in a harmonious order, and an antidogmatic stance on revealed religion, while suppressing the question of radical evil. But Möser, like Shaftesbury, was concerned less with the epistemological and ontological bases of ethics than with the social instincts toward obedience and duty. It is in this realm that he saw the charge of egoism as most pernicious. His treatise on well-inclined passions and emotions thus defended the *utility* of virtue as a necessity for every social system. But more than that, in the key middle sections, Möser committed himself strongly to the *representation* of virtue. The word "representation" bears emphasis, for Shaftebury's great appeal in the German eighteenth century was based on this: he articulated a vision of moderation, fortitude, generosity, and gentlemanly mastery – in his language "virtuousity" – that could serve as a personal model for the gentleman humanist. In one key passage, Möser linked inclination to representation while revealing the modest analytical power he was able to display in this work:

Yet there was never revealed in him [Bussche-Hünnefeld] the rough defender of the good cause, before which his own friends reddened or took affront; nor the stiff pride which causes regard to decline in the eyes of princes and which makes freedom into a goddess in order to laugh at monarchs from her lap. No: a natural feeling for order, a delicate sensitivity for peace let him judge intelligently the value of a noble dependency. And as hateful to him as violent or legal (*gnädig*) oppression was, he was able with the aid of his innate delicacy to translate this natural hatred, this primordial outpouring of Nature, into pleasing forms. His candor, this nerve of honest inclinations, gained him high esteem, his kindness love, and the judgment of his cultivated pride the affection of all those, whom he knew how to place over himself by a decorous affability.[86]

Most important in this treatise, social virtue justified the world as given: "Nothing was more agreeable to him than when each person fulfilled his appropriate sphere and by his part thereby helped to support the perfection of the whole system."[87]

If Möser's cultural ideal reflected the need of the urban notability for propriety and noble bearing, it also illustrated his own need to display professional erudition as a member of the councillor elite.[88] At midcentury such erudition was largely

[85] Möser, *W*, 9:6.
[86] Ibid., 34–5.
[87] Ibid., 30.
[88] Hanna Gray, "Renaissance Humanism: The Pursuit of Eloquence," in *Renaissance Essays*, ed. Paul O. Kristeller and Philip P. Wiener (New York, 1968), 199–216; Erich Trunz, "Der deutsche Späthumanismus um 1600 als Standeskultur," in *Deutsche Barockforschung*, ed. Richard Alewyn

historical, as befit lawyers who studied case law, and it was still based on Latin culture, even as the actual demand for publication in Latin was waning. It is typical that Möser's surviving Latin compositions are letters, written from Jena to his father and childhood companion Lodtmann, and an essay, from the same period, on popular religion among the ancient Germans. The letters announced to his father and closest friend his arrival in the learned world, and the essay tackled one of the popular areas of cultural speculation to emerge from a Latin education.

Far more important than the survival of Latin as the language of learned discourse was the prehistorical or archaeological bias to German culture that the study of Latin transmitted. Reading Tacitus, Caeser, and Agricola (the assigned fare in the Latin schools) focused inordinate attention on the history of contacts between the Germanic peoples and Roman civilization. This meant, for instance, that works of legal history, such as those by G. Mascov and J. P. Ludewig, concentrated on the earliest period of German history by studying Caesar, Tacitus, and the establishment of the Carolingian Empire. Such attention encouraged an effort, which grew even more powerful in the nineteenth century, to describe a primordial Germanic culture free from Roman and Christian influences. These intimations of a cultural racialism were less significant in the eighteenth century than the more politically restricted use of the confrontation between Germanic, Roman, and Christian cultures as a metaphor for the struggle between church, aristocracy, and commonalty.

These themes also expressed the widespread Francophobia in German letters of the eighteenth century. This Francophobia, too, could serve both antiaristo- cratic and anticosmopolitan views. It is difficult to disentangle the ways in which historical erudition concealed secular, antiaristocratic attitudes, but clearly the rediscovery of the ancient Germanic peoples could also take the form of a regressive utopia divested of the legal prerogatives of aristocracy and church. Möser's abiding concern with the earliest German history followed exactly in this notable tra- dition, and his *Osnabrück History* contains all these elements. It is traditional in archaeological focus, erudite, secular, and antiabsolutist in intention. Still it marks a watershed in German historical writing because it is written in a modern prose that makes the judgments of this Latin legal-historical tradition accessible to the general world of letters.

Thus we can use the discussion of Möser's family, professional, and estate ethos to understand his cultural function within the German Enlightenment. As a lawyer, member of the Osnabrück notability, and one of corporate society's professional intellectuals, Möser lived and worked within the traditional insti- tutions, attempting to adapt Enlightenment values to that world. The intellectual product remained necessarily ambivalent. The German Enlightenment had a

(Cologne, 1965), 151–5; Hermann Forst, "Die Geschichtschreibung im Bistum Osnabrück bis zum Ende des XVII. Jahrhunderts," *Deutsche Geschichtsblätter*, 5 (1904):117–27.

certain intellectual radicalism from the 1760s on because of its growing commitment to the ideal of a free, secular individualism. Such beliefs posed great
difficulties for writers enmeshed in corporate institutions that, though no longer
thriving, were not yet moribund. Two possible visions of compromise both led
backward in time. The first was urban: the recovery of a particularly German
burgher constitutional ideal that rested in the past glories of the independent
cities. The second vision paralleled the myth of the English yeomanry and postulated a golden age of rural freedom and property before aristocratic enslavement.
Both idealized portraits were clearly prevalent among the youthful members of
the *Sturm und Drang* and can be read especially in the plays of Klinger, Wagner,
Goethe, and Schiller. The second was more exclusively Möser's solution. In both
cases, however, the appeal was to an unrecoverable past, not an achievable future.
Furthermore, the impulse to go backward in time was in important ways fundamentally reactionary and profoundly unlike the speculative philosophy of history or natural rights theories that represented other mainstream Enlightenment
tendencies; the work of popular philosophers like Immanuel Kant, Issak Iselin,
and Christian Garve or natural rights jurists like Carl G. Svarez or Ferdinand
Ernst Klein aimed at reforming the present and rationally constructing the
future.[89]

   Thus a person like Möser was important to the German Enlightenment because
he mediated between a forward-looking Enlightenment culture and an ideal
Germanic past. As a lawyer he was especially qualified to recover that historic
past, display it in his essays and *Osnabrück History*, and encourage the public
examination of its significance in an enlightened future. His contribution to
sociopolitical theory in the German Enlightenment was for this reason contradictory and ambiguous: he was the ancient who was also the modern, the theorist
from a politically peripheral and institutionally stagnant area of Germany who
attempted to see the utility of those institutions if modestly reformed. His
education merged with his corporate culture and yet emancipated him from its
narrow strictures, allowing him to be at once the most provincial and the most
cosmopolitan of observers.

   In holding such values Möser was not unique, either in Germany or elsewhere
in Europe. His example is a reminder of the essentially moderate to conservative
impulses of most jurists in the period.[90] Historians of France have noted the

---

[89] Ulrich Im Hof, *Issak Iselin*, 2 vols. (Basel, 1947), 2:290–358, esp. 351–8; Michael Stolleis, *Die
    Moral in der Politik bei Christian Garve* (Ph.D. diss., Munich, 1967); Zwi Batscha, *Studien zur
    politischen Theorie des deutschen Frühliberalismus* (Frankfurt am Main, 1981), 43–65; Erik Wolf,
    "Carl Gottlieb Svarez," *Große Rechtsdenker* (4th ed.; Tübingen, 1963), 424–66; Diethelm Klippel,
    *Politische Freiheit und Freiheitsrechte im deutschen Naturrecht des 18. Jahrhunderts* (Paderborn, 1976),
    135–90.

[90] See the literature cited in footnotes 6 and 8; also significant are the comments by Wieacker, who
    noted, first, that natural law codifications in Germany were carried out by teachers of law or
    trusted agents of the regents and not by practicing lawyers, who were often hostile; and, second,
    that the sense of justice of the codifiers was nurtured by the study of philosophy. See his *Priva-
    trechtsgeschichte der Neuzeit*, 324–5.

open conflict between practicing lawyers and magistrates and enlightened publicists.[91] Like Möser, most magistrates of the *bailliage* courts and most lawyers (barristers and procurators) of the various *parlements* held onto the received corpus of French law and defended existing legal institutions as a bulwark of natural liberties against the claims of unlimited monarchy.[92] Publicists, on the other hand, were more likely to be French followers of Christian Wolff, Emer de Vattel, and J. J. Burlamaqui; they were far more committed to natural law traditions, to fundamental legal reform, and to an alliance with the crown against the aristocracy and the courts.[93]

As he grew older, Möser, too, came to uphold the legal traditions of Osnabrück against natural rights philosophy, but the antagonisms cannot be so easily cast in terms of jurists versus enlightened publicists for two main reasons. First, the philosophy of natural rights was broadly represented in the German universities, thanks to the teachings of Christian Wolff and students such as Johann Cramer, Joachim Darjes, and Johann Adam Ickstatt, who lectured to two generations of jurists and administrators.[94] As a result, ideas of natural rights became an increasingly accepted part of the training of Germany's officials. Second, natural rights philosophy was also assimilated by German monarchs, who under Friedrich Wilhelm I in Prussia already saw that legal codification under the principles of natural rights could be used to blunt, if not break, the power of entrenched interests.[95] By the 1770s, such efforts at legal codification – in Bavaria, Brandenburg-Prussia, and the Austrian core lands – were much further advanced than in France. Hence reconceptualizing rights and obligations in the language of natural rights could in itself be a radical intellectual act, but one that also supported monarchical autocracy.[96] As a consequence, Germany witnessed a somewhat different constellation: resisting natural rights philosophy in its varied forms was often seen by enlightened publicists, especially those living in the small states, as a rejection of autocracy in favor of local freedoms. As we will see in the next chapters, Möser became known for holding this position within the German Enlightenment.

[91] William F. Church, "The Decline of the French Jurists as Political Theorists, 1660–1789," *French Historical Studies*, 5 (1967):26–40.

[92] Berlanstein, 104–5. In his article on the *"Bourgeoisie de Robe,"* Philip Dawson showed through a study of the *cahiers de doléances* in 1789, that the legal community formulated more than two hundred different grievances. Those regarding reform of the law were chiefly five in number, the most significant requesting abolition of venality of office. The second and third most important demands were to limit the *parlements* to a more strictly appellate function and to require decentralization of the legal system. See his *"Bourgeoisie de Robe,"* 16–20.

[93] Alfred Dufour, "Die Ecole romande du droit naturel – ihre deutsche Wurzeln," in *Humanismus und Naturrecht in Berlin-Brandenburg-Preußen*, ed. Hans Thieme (Berlin, 1979), 133–43.

[94] Ernst Landsberg and R. Stintzing, *Geschichte der deutschen Rechtswissenschaft*, 3 vols in 4 (Munich, 1880–1910), 3/1:198–206, 272–85; Wieacker, *Privatrechtsgeschichte der Neuzeit*, 318–22.

[95] Wieacker, ibid., 277; Hans von Voltelini, "Die naturrechtlichen Lehren und die Reformen des 18. Jahrhunderts," *HZ*, 105 (1910):65–104.

[96] Wieacker, ibid., 272; Reinart Koselleck, *Preußen zwischen Reform und Revolution*, in *Industrielle Welt*, 7 (2nd ed.; Stuttgart, 1975), 23–34.

Scotland also produced a similar conservative defense of legal traditions by its lawyers, but that defense was complicated by union with England.[97] In Edinburgh the "law lords" Kames, Mackenzie, and Monboddo contributed to that curious Scots parochialism among its jurists that evokes so strongly Möser's attitudes. But Möser came to reject natural law in favor of Germanic case law and historical precedent, whereas the Scots upheld local tradition against English law by supporting Roman law and the older natural rights theories of Grotius and Pufendorf.[98] Thus, with essentially similar motivations, Möser came to resist juridical modes of thought that the Scots upheld.

As we well know, the Enlightenment had an imperialistic impulse that tended to mask compromises with received traditions. When the various systems of ideas we associate with the Enlightenment entered the different cultures, they were assimilated to existing relationships of power and privilege. In particular, natural rights philosophy had both egalitarian and inegalitarian dimensions, and these could be adapted in the service of established antagonisms such as those between the centralizing monarchies and the traditional corporate orders and political Estates. Hence it is not enough to understand the content of certain beliefs; it is also necessary to know how such ideas functioned in the various cultures where the Enlightenment unfolded. Möser was a significant figure in the German Enlightenment because he attempted to adapt the inegalitarian world of Osnabrück's notables to the new secular values.

[97] Concerning the Enlightenment in Scotland, see John Clive, "The Social Background of the Scottish Renaissance," in *Scotland in the Age of Improvement*, ed. N. T. Phillipson and R. Mitchison (Edinburgh, 1970), 227–34. With respect to the special perceptions of its lawyers, see Phillipson, "Culture and Society in the Eighteenth-Century Province: The Case of Edinburgh and the Scottish Enlightenment," in *The University in Society*, ed. Lawrence Stone, 2 vols. (Princeton, N.J. 1974), 2:407–48, esp. 435–48.

[98] Peter Stein, "Legal Thought in Eighteenth-Century Scotland," *Juridical Review*, 1 (1957), 1–20; idem, "Law and Society in Eighteenth Century Scottish Thought," in *Scotland in the Age of Improvement*, 148–68; T. B. Smith, "Scots Law and Roman-Dutch Law," *Judicial Review*, 6 n.s. (1963):32–52.

# 3

## Möser's political universe: secular politics in a confessional state

In Chapter 2 I presented the social assumptions, commitments, and obligations that shaped Möser's mind and career. The extant material is simply too skimpy for a more careful chronological reconstruction. Above all we lack details concerning his twenties and thirties, the typical decades of revolt and reconciliation. What survives does not hint at any private search or crisis; like most of the biographical evidence, it stays at the surface of everyday life, revealing in this instance only the settled habits of a young and preferred advocate among the local notability. The brief glimpse of a fourteen-year-old running away from home is not repeated. Family and work, friendships, personal cultivation, and scholarship seem to extend themselves uneventfully. Möser's life, then, as far as we can reconstruct it, was not shaped by internal turmoil, rebellion of another kind, or religious conversion. The formative moments came from events in the life of the bishopric: the lengthy crisis of the Seven Years War, the change in political allegiance to Protestant Hanover in the midst of the war, and his expanded responsibilities in the episcopal administration. These substantially altered his intellectual character.

In this chapter, I describe the ways in which the confessional struggle and ecclesiastical institutions affected Justus Möser. Accordingly, the chapter enters the political world of the small states in far greater detail. It shows from the perspective of Osnabrück why the small states were the carriers of German "liberties," why at the same time the institutional stalemate at the imperial level promoted the image of constitutional ineffectuality that has survived, and why, as a result, certain enlightened critics thought the future of Germany lay with the large states absorbing the smaller ones.[1] In addition, if we consider the matter of confessional politics carefully, we will see that Germany in the 1760s was as yet untouched by the liberal–conservative split that had become clear by the end

---

[1]  Hans Erich Feine, "Zur Feine, "Zur Verfassungsentwicklung des Heiligen Römischen Reiches seit dem Westfälischen Friedens," *ZSRG* (*germ*), 52 (1932):84.

of the century.[2] Möser's example illustrates well that politics was still largely conducted in confessional terms. He emerged in the 1760s as a political reformer who came to power with the Protestant Party and carried its enlightened impulses to limit the secular influence of the church. In an ecclesiastical state, he advocated the separation of church and state and sought to introduce religious toleration that would go beyond the legal parity of the Westphalian Peace. Yet there were several limitations to secularizing an ecclesiastical state. This chapter explores, finally, the substantial hindrances to political modernization in the small states without a simultaneous attack on the constitutional system of the Empire. In disentangling the matters particular to Osnabrück, therefore, we must move to wider reflections about the ways enlightened legal and political theorists conceived of political change within the constitutional realities of the Empire.

## CONSTITUTIONAL CRISIS DURING THE SEVEN YEARS WAR

The new set of political factors altering life in the bishopric were occasioned by the Seven Years War and the death of Archbishop Clemens August in 1761. These events threatened the confessional balance and Osnabück's independence as an ecclesiastical state. At the same time, they made possible Möser's position of administrative power in the years after the war. We must examine their significance from both points of view.

For Britain as for France, the Seven Years War was both a colonial and a continental war. It was in particular the first European war where the struggle for colonial hegemony determined military strategy on the continent and also brought about a reevaluation of the commitment to the continental balance of power.[3] William Pitt conducted the first year of the war under the assumption that the British Crown's Hanoverian domains should be left to their own devices in exchange for colonial monopoly. It is true that he altered this view radically in the following years, allocating far greater sums to the armies of northwestern Germany, but his change of heart was not due to a greater commitment – contractual, cultural, or sentimental – to the continent. He undertook the war on the continent, rather, for the tactical purpose of dividing French forces. Other concerns remained secondary: expanding the crown's Hanoverian domains, weakening the alliance against Prussia, or preventing its political dismemberment and the concomitant growth of Habsburg power. This meant that northwestern

---

[2] Karl Otmar Aretin, "Die Konfessionen als politische Kräfte am Ausgang des alten Reiches," in *Festgabe Joseph Lortz*, ed. Peter Mans and Erwin Iserloh, 2 vols. (Baden-Baden, 1958), 2:181–241.

[3] The clearest overview of the Seven Years War remains Walter Dorn, *Competition for Empire 1740–1763* (rev. ed; New York, 1963), 318–20; 357; and, with literature, the brief discussion by Rudolf Vierhaus, *Deutschland im Zeitalter des Absolutismus* (Göttingen, 1978), 182–9, 209; useful from the Catholic perspective is the discussion in Heribert Raab, *Clemens Wenzeslaus von Sachsen und seine Zeit (1739–1812)*, 1 vol. to date (Freiburg, 1962), 112–77; concerning Osnabrück during the war, see Alfred Frankenfeld, *Justus Möser als Staatsmann und Publizist im Siebenjährigen Kriege und am englischchen Hofe* (Ph.D. diss., Göttingen, 1922).

Germany was treated as a stepchild in the British war effort. The French position was similar. Though finally more committed to the continent than to its overseas empire, France, too, came to view northwestern Germany as significant chiefly as a source of plunder.

The Seven Years War was a severe crisis for the Empire. Military struggle between the Habsburgs and Prussia, on the one hand, and between France and England, on the other, meant that the Empire was involved in a civil war controlled by foreign belligerents.[4] This was especially clear for Osnabrück and the other small states of Westphalia. The region was a major staging area of the war in Germany, the ecclesiastical states being allied with the emperor against neighboring Hanover, Prussia, Hessia, and Braunschweig (tiny Gotha was also in revolt against the Empire). Yet unfortunately for Osnabrück and the small states of the region, the defense of Westphalia was never a French–Habsburg military priority: troops committed to conquer Hanoverian and Prussian territory were not risked in defense of the ecclesiastical states.[5] The damage to the small states in the ebb and flow of war lay not so much in actual physical destruction – though this occurred, too, – as in material exhaustion by the armies of occupation. Given the system of supply and requisition in eighteenth-century warfare, demands for draught animals, foodstuffs, housing, and cash contributions impoverished every state where the armies fought, camped, or wintered over. Osnabrück was no exception. Almost the only phrases of the passionate despair in Möser's entire correspondence come in the letters of these years, which paint Westphalia's economic and social collapse.

In practical terms, the warfare of these years temporarily set aside the constitution of the Empire. It also caused the reawakening of the local dynastic ambitions and religious animosities that had been placed in abeyance by the Treaty of Westphalia.[6] Support for the war was determined by confession. In the case of Osnabrück, the Protestant *Ritterschaft* and the city had resisted involvement from the beginning of the conflict and had sought to maintain Osnabrück's neutrality; but Archbishop Clemens August committed Osnabrück, along with the other Catholic ecclesiastical states under his sovereignty, to the emperor's war against Hanover and Prussia. He was supported in the alliance by the cathedral chapter. Once the Seven Years War broke out, in fact, the long stalemate appeared near its end as plans were hatched among both confessions to unmake the treaty.[7]

[4] John Gagliardo, *Reich and Nation* (Bloomington, Ind., 1980), 49–55. Feine argues persuasively that the large autonomous or semiautonomous states – Prussia, Saxony, Hanover, Sweden, Austria – had in practical terms emancipated themselves from the Empire, and this fact motivated much of the political rhetoric by publicists in the later eighteenth century. See Feine, "Zur Verfassungsentwicklung des Heiligen Römischen Reiches," 79–83.

[5] See the analysis by Alwin Hanschmidt, *Franz von Fürstenberg als Staatsmann*, in *Veröffentlichungen der Historischen Kommission Westfalens*, 18 [*Westfälische Biographien*, 5] (Münster, 1969), 15–22.

[6] Leo Körholz, *Die Wahl des Prinzen Friedrich von York zum Bischof von Osnabrück und die Regierung des Stiftes während seiner Minderjährigkeit* (Ph.D. diss., Münster, 1908), 1–8; Raab, *Clemens Wenzelslaus*, 121–8.

[7] For this point and the narrative in the following pages of this section, I largely follow Körholz,

At the beginning of the war, for instance, the Osnabrück cathedral chapter sent memoranda to Clemens August referring to victory as an opportunity to eliminate the Protestant presence and permanently recatholicize the bishopric – a sign that the Westphalian Peace had not promoted religious toleration among the cathedral canons, who retained the spirit of the Counter-Reformation.

At the same time, the Hanoverian Crown and its ruling body of German chancellery in London and *Kollegium* in Hanover developed their own plans. Understandably, these focused less on England's overseas struggle and more on expansion within northwestern Germany. Such plans were a potential source of political difference between crown and cabinet; this became clear at war's end. But while the war lasted, Osnabrück was an important symbol in any expansion because the partial secularization of the bishopric has been Hanover's only material acquisition in the Westphalian Peace, representing, in fact, a partial foreign policy defeat that military victory could again set aright. Hanover and Prussia held various discussions throughout the war that touched on the joint secularization of the bishoprics of northwestern Germany. One such scheme was based on giving Münster and Osnabrück to the English Crown in exchange for the Prussian appropriation of Hildesheim. In this way, the belligerents on both sides fought to press their advantage and were less than committed to the hundred-year constitutional settlement.

The dreams of a Catholic reconquest by the Osnabrück cathedral chapter were cut short by the death of Archbishop Clemens August in the midst of the war (February 6, 1761). With his death Osnabrück lost its status as a Catholic bishopric, becoming once again a Hanoverian possession, according to the formula of alternate succession. Hanoverian rule could not begin de jure, however, until the cathedral chapter invested the new bishop with his office. Until then, the princely administration existed in the twilight of legality: it had inherited the right to rule, but could not rule in fact before the cathedral chapter transferred power. In the interim, the cathedral chapter was the legal head of the government, collecting the episcopal revenues, issuing decrees for the bishopric, and controlling the system of justice. Thus, the chapter naturally wished to extend the vacancy, whereas Hanover wanted to seize immediately the domains it enjoyed only intermittently.

The war now gave Hanover an opportunity to end the alternating succession and secularize the bishopric. Though the secularization plans were secret, the general intention soon became clear to all. The cathedral chapter, now on the defensive and concerned with its political and financial future, tried to prevent secularization by promptly investing a new bishop from the house of Braunschweig-Lüneburg. The English Crown and its Hanoverian agents, by the same

---

*Wahl des Prinzen*, 3–36. Körholz's careful archival account loses sight of British foreign policy and the tensions between the continental plans and the needs of the overseas empire; moreover, he argues the position of the cathedral chapter.

token, sought to postpone any and all proceedings so that appropriation could take its natural course unencumbered by oaths of office and agreements with the Estates. The complicated maneuvers that ensued over the next years do not need to be followed in detail. It is enough to know that, until the death of Clemens August, the Catholic party had been at war with Hanover and was therefore in a weak bargaining position; that the English Crown did not readily have anyone to assume the episcopal post and hence sought delay; and that, finally, the crown viewed the bishopric in purely secular terms and consequently had no compunctions about integrating it permanently into the Hanoverian kingdom. For the time being, then, Britain–Hanover simply occupied the bishopric with troops and enforced its will militarily upon the cathedral chapter with the acquiescence of the Protestant population.

George II had also died in the middle of the war, and George III had acceded to the throne in late 1760. Osnabrück's constitutional difficulties thus coincided with the first years of the new reign. The change of monarchs brought about the eventual fall of Pitt in 1762, the building of a more conciliatory war cabinet under Lord Bute, gradual abandonment of the plans to secularize the ecclesiastical states of northwestern Germany, and for Osnabrück the decision by the British Crown in the midst of peace negotiations to resolve the impasse by investing the newborn (August 16, 1763) second son of George III, Frederick of York, as bishop of Osnabrück.

If the question of secularization was thereby abandoned in favor of constitutional practice established in the Westphalian Peace, it opened at the same time another set of constitutional issues surrounding a prospective twenty-year regency until the future bishop came of legal age to assume the duties of office. The constitutional struggle over secularization, in sum, was transformed into a struggle over the structure and formal powers of the regency. So important did this issue seem to the confessional balance within the Empire that in 1765 and 1766 the constitutional struggle in Osnabrück eventually occupied the Imperial Diet for more than a session while a compromise was sought. Möser was swept along by the crises of these years, his career rising with that of the Protestant party. As syndic to the *Ritterschaft* he was one of the men who negotiated terms with the various armies of occupation, and he assumed more influence as his skills became apparent. After the death of Clemens August, Möser also began to be drawn into the English plans for the bishopric. With the end of the war, it fell to him to travel to London and negotiate directly with the English government over debts and reparations and, further, to advise the crown on the impasse surrounding the succession. Due to his careful handling of these negotiations and his willingness to serve English interests as an advocate of questionable constitutional positions, he became the trusted agent of both the crown and the *Ritterschaft*, and this trust made possible his preeminence in the regency that followed.

If we analyze Möser's political career in greater detail, the critical point is that his position in the new Protestant administration was never constitutionally clear because the unique Westphalian settlement prevented Osnabrück's administration from being clearly defined. In resolving the case of Osnabrück, the peacemakers at the end of the Thirty Years War had created an asymmetrical system. Critical from Hanover's perspective was that sovereignty never fully accrued to the territorial prince, even when the bishopric became a Hanoverian possession, because he was strictly bound by the constitutional provisions imposed at the end of the Thirty Years War. The asymmetry was most aggravating to Hanover in material terms; when rule fell to the Catholic party, so the crown's agents argued, its valuable resources were drained away by profligate, gouging, nonresident Catholic bishops, who had no long-term interest in the well-being of the bishopric. To protect its interests, consequently, Hanover had begun even before the Seven Years War to erode the legal dualism of alternate sovereignty by attaching an extralegal Hanoverian representative to the bishopric. This gradual confrontation at the princely level also affected the administrative boundaries between church, prince, and the Estates.

Thus, any tampering with the succession had potentially serious consequences for the system of Estates. For this reason, the occupation by Hanover in 1761 was seen by all three Estates as illegal; it was protested as such in a common memorandum, drafted by Möser, that presented the seizure as the last in a series of steadily escalating attempts by both Protestant and Catholic prince-bishops to undermine Osnabrück's political system. Möser's first legal briefs as secretary to the *Ritterschaft*, in fact, had been directed toward the incursion of absolutist behavior into Osnabrück's institutional life and called for continuous consultation with the Estates before legislation could be made into law. When George III assumed control of the bishopric, this struggle was still before the courts. The issue of consultation was now raised once again in the complaints of all three Estates.[8]

It is important to keep this state of constitutional and confessional conflict in mind, because it underlines the ambivalence of Möser's administrative position from the moment he began to gather the reins of government about him. Even while he was drafting the complaint of the Estates, he was also working privately with the crown's administrative agent, Privy Councillor Albrecht von Lenthe, to develop a formula that would avoid constitutional protest by the Estates. He expressed the following doubts to von Lenthe (December 14, 1762) in a letter comparing present Hanoverian actions to forcible rule from 1633 to 1648 by the occupying Swedish army:

I do not know whether your Royal Majesty wants to go so far. However, I doubt whether the future administration can be constituted without the Estates rendering an oath of

---

[8] Reinhard Renger, "Justus Mösers amtlicher Wirkungskreis," *Osn. Mitt.* 77 (1970):4–5; Otto Hatzig, *Justus Mözer als Staatsmann und Publizist*, in *Quellen und Darstellungen zur Geschichte Niedersachsens*, 27 (Hanover, 1909), 5–12.

allegiance, or at least by a special command of his Royal Majesty being referred to the future administration, [or] without the officials and servants swearing an oath to his Royal Majesty as *administratori* who now are bound by oath and responsibility to the cathedral chapter. [I] fear difficulties if the latter steps are taken, [for they] cannot be overcome by leniency and goodness. Also the papers of previous administrations will most likely not be given up without a show of force, and it will not be a pleasant matter to attempt to keep the secretaries, *Referendarien, Cancellisten*, and *Pedellen*, or thereafter to dismiss them."[9]

But a week later (December 19, 1762), still before the official protest by the Estates, Möser again wrote to von Lenthe, analyzing local officials by name and detailing how to proceed with the administrative takeover: how to address an edict and, in particular, how to make legal relations within the bishopric an internal affair. "If notification occurs in this manner," he wrote, "then it will be indifferent what the cathedral chapter answers."[10]

From what we can decipher, in other words, Möser's attitude toward the gradual consolidation of Hanoverian power was twofold: he was fundamentally in favor of a Protestant administration, and he was also in favor of the constitutional system of Estates. As long as the principle of consultation with the Estates was confirmed, he was willing to accept illegal activity vis-à-vis the cathedral chapter. He reconciled this inconsistency with his legal scruples because he viewed the cathedral chapter strictly as a clerical body, albeit one filled with the unregenerate spirit of political Catholicism. Thus in September 1763, nine months after advising von Lenthe on the procedures for consolidating Hanoverian control, he complained to an unnamed privy councillor of what he termed the *"esprit de chapitre et de catholicisme."* "The best chapter," he wrote, "is [to be treated] like the woman who wants to be ravished, in order to have her conscience free and to be able to damn another. Honorable canons have said more than once, 'Why doesn't the king take it, if he wants it?' . . . If the king wants to complete matters it must occur on the basis of might (*harte maiori*), *ex opinione Catholicorum*. They must be allowed *protestater et applellativ pro liberanda conscientia*; and then they will learn to derive advantage from necessity."[11]

Möser expressed such views even before the election of the infant Frederick of York was an openly discussed option. In fall 1763, therefore, his function remained that of mediator: he stood between the crown's plans for secularization and the Protestant bodies in Osnabrück that would have to support the seizure. He was certainly compromised by his commitment to Hanoverian interests, but, not having taken a royal oath of office, he still remained officially outside the Hanoverian administration.

In this period of uncertainty when much remained to be done to restore basic supplies and services in the bishopric, Möser left Osnabrück for a five-month

---

[9] Möser, *Briefe*, 122.
[10] William Sheldon, ed., forthcoming collection of Möser's correspondence: see Chapter 2, footnote 4.
[11] Ibid.

period in London (November 1763 to April 1764) to negotiate for the *Ritterschaft* the unresolved financial matters of the war and the impending transfer of power. This period was critical for deepening his comparative insights into Osnabrück's history, but it was nonetheless a frustrating time, as the surviving London letters show. He spent much of the time waiting among the petitioners at the court and the German chancellery. There was to be no movement on indebtedness, he communicated to von Lenthe, until the crown "received a good report from the elections there;"[12] until then, he was to remain one hanger-on among the rest. Indeed, once the cathedral canons agreed to accept Frederick of York as heir to the episcopal post and duly elected him (February 28, 1764), Möser was able to wrap up his business rapidly in London and return to Osnabrück.[13]

During the months of delay in London, Möser's administrative position gradually crystallized. He continued to believe that the new administration would not be able to proceed legally with the cathedral chapter. In a letter to von Lenthe (February 3, 1764), we see him once again recommend that the king act on the basis of might and "afterward let negotiations continue until they fall to sleep by themselves. Because it is simply not to be believed that the cathedral chapter will admit formally and in writing what can occur de facto or that it will give in enough to his Royal Majesty to satisfy the requirements of law."[14] Such views clearly identified Möser as an agent of Hanoverian interests, and it is little wonder that the pressure mounted for him officially to enter Hanoverian service. Von Lenthe had made such an offer informally before Möser's departure from Osnabrück, and Burghard Christian von Behr, head of the German chancellery in London and von Lenthe's brother-in-law, apparently repeated the offer on more than one occasion.[15] Möser responded to these repeated requests from London in a lengthy *Pro-Memoria* to von Lenthe (February 17, 1764).[16] He explained that he did not want to give up his other posts in the Osnabrück administration, arguing further that he would be a far more effective agent of Hanoverian interests were he also to remain an official of the Estates. He had already conveyed this decision privately to von Lenthe a couple of weeks earlier (January 30, 1764) in a letter remarkable for the openness with which it discussed his political and ethical situation:

In my view I retain more involvement and have more influence, spare the king a salary and all necessity to guarantee my future, when I keep my previous ties. The interests of the Estates has always been bound together with the interests of the Royal House, and if an unfortunate division were to begin against expectations, I retain a certain freedom

[12] Ibid.
[13] Körholz, *Wahl des Prinzen*, 57–78.
[14] Möser, *Briefe*, 138.
[15] Ibid., 136, 423.
[16] Möser, "Promemoria bzgl. seiner Stellen als Consulent der Regierung" (London, February 1764), in Sta Osn, Dep. 110 II, Nr. 37B.

to choose according to the circumstances and thus am more bound to my inclinations than to any necessity. This is a great comfort to me, and since I have served up to now with honorable zeal, Your Grace can also be assured for the future that I will never abuse a trust and that if a disagreement were to emerge between head and limbs I would remove myself with apologies from such incompatible responsibilities. Perhaps a one year trial can decide the matter better than anything else.[17]

Möser accepted the post of *Konsulent* or consultant to the government on this basis, taking an oath in June 1764 to defend Hanoverian interests "especially against the cathedral chapter" and agreeing that in cases of conflict between the royal family and the bishopric or the *Ritterschaft* he would not defend the latter against royal interests. He also accepted the restriction that as *Konsulent* he would advise the government but would not have a formal vote in the administration. This compromise solution, however, did not prove constitutionally adequate in the eyes of Hanover. By 1767 the Hanoverian government, through von Lenthe, asked Möser to accept the expanded post of *Referendar* and, along with it, the responsibility to attend all normal and extraordinary sessions of the government. After much wavering Möser accepted the new position (1768), although because he continued to retain his other offices he still was not given a formal vote. The post of *Referendar*, as noted in the previous chapter, remained his official position throughout the regency.[18]

If we pause to consider Möser's ascent in the Protestant administration, it is clear that his administrative power was based in the strong oligarchical tendencies of Osnabrück's political system, which tended to close ranks around the known and trusted few. Möser drew upon his network of family connections, now expanded by his client-friend relationships with von Lenthe – soon to go to Hanover as a minister – and von Behr in the London chancellery. This oligarchical structure dictated that Möser worked with very few administrators over the years. Of these he was the only nonnoble. In practice, moreover, Möser came to have the tie-breaking vote between the two resident privy councillors, and his written opinion always accompanied their reports to London. Beyond this, he exercised additional power within the bishopric both through the episcopal administration and through the Estates. As *Referendar* he prepared the agenda for the meeting of the Estates, and as syndic to the *Ritterschaft* he orchestrated the response. As *Justizrat* he dealt with criminal matters, and as *advocatus patriae* he concerned himself with the bishopric's finances and its borders.[19]

---

[17] Möser, *Briefe*, 136.

[18] For the description of Möser's negotiations with the English government, see Hatzig, *Justus Möser als Staatsmann*, 14–21.

[19] For a discussion of Möser's place in the Osnabrück government, see Christine Rohde, *Beamtenschaft und Territorialstaat. Behördenentwicklung und Sozialstruktur der Beamtenschaft im Hochstift Osnabrück 1550–1800*, 2 parts (Ph.D. diss.; Bochum, 1982), 287–97; Hatzig, ibid., 21–6; Renger, "Mösers amtlicher Wirkungskreis," 13–21.

## SECULARIZATION IN THE ENGLIGHTENMENT

The preceding discussion of Möser's administrative posts, like the entire excursion into political narrative, is necessary to clarify the domain of Protestant politics in which he operated. The confessional issue has remained unexplored in almost every study of Möser's life and thought, because religious matters appear only at the periphery of his published work. Yet since Möser was an administrative representative of Protestant interests in an ecclesiastical state, we need to restore the confessional context to the political struggles if we are to understand his attitude toward the institutions and history of the bishopric – indeed, if we are to appreciate how fundamental religious conflict was in the German Enlightenment. The account in the first section of this chapter has taken the narrative away from the succession crisis and somewhat further ahead into the regency; we must now retrace our steps in order to examine the aspirations buried in the succession crisis itself and its historical meaning. In this section, I discuss the limits of political reform in the German ecclesiastical states; this, in turn, is tied to one of the chief issues of the Enlightenment – the secularization of ecclesiastical institutions.

Consequential administrative reform in the eighteenth century logically presupposed the secularization of such institutions and their absorption into a large worldly territory.[20] Without this there was no lever to compel change in the ecclesiastical states. Until the reorganization schemes of Joseph II and Karl Theodor of the Palatinate in the 1770s and 1780s,[21] secularization had been almost entirely a Protestant goal, bound up with the ideals of the Reformation and the institutionalization of dependent territorial churches. Remarkably, the confiscation of church properties on the scale of the Netherlands or Britain had never occurred in Germany. The ecclesiastical states had, moreover, largely managed to survive the wave of confiscations in the decades of the Reformation. Though some territories had been secularized during the Thirty Years War (Bremen, Verden, Magdeburg, Halberstadt, Minden), even this movement had been halted by the Peace of Westphalia. The settlement consciously had created a new status quo that wove the established political bodies into the fabric of the

[20] See the judgment by Hanschmidt, *Franz von Fürstenberg*, 2. Of special value for understanding the internal problem of reform in the post-Westphalian period is the classic essay by Feine, "Zur Verfassungsentwicklung des Heiligen Römischen Reiches," 65–133; the survey by Vierhaus, *Deutschland im Zeitalter des Absolutismus*, 116–50; and Gagliardo, *Reich and Nation*, 49–113. For the ecclesiastical states in particular, the eighteenth-century compendium by Joseph von Sartori is filled with shrewd analytical comments; see Joseph von Sartori, *Geistliches und weltliches Staatsrecht der deutschen, catholischgeistlichen Erz- Hoch- und Ritterstifter*, only 2 of 3 parts printed in 6 vols. (Nürnberg, 1788–91), esp. 1/1:148–88; 1/2:10–23; 2/1: 260–71, 407–35; 2/2: 2, 10–34. Of the secondary literature, consult Rudolfine von Oer, "Landständische Verfassungen in den geistichen Fürstentümern Nordwestdeutschlands," in *Ständische Vertretungen im 17. und 18. Jahrhundert*, ed. Dietrich Gerhard (Göttingen, 1965), 94–119; and Peter Wende, *Die geistlichen Staaten und ihre Auflösung im Urteil der Zeitgenössischen Publizistik*, in *Historische Studien*, 396 (Lübeck, 1966).
[21] Karl Otmar von Aretin, *Bayerns Weg zum souveränen Staat. Landstände unde konstitutionelle Monarchie 1714–1818* (Munich, 1976), 64–119.

Empire. The ecclesiastical princes had gained most of all: the integrity of their territories was guaranteed from the time of the peace settlement, and they were given a formal vote in the Council of Princes.

This triumph of regional liberty and confessional parity created the political stalemate in the Empire that in the eighteenth century robbed its institutions of political élan and reconstituted political activity as a permanent defense of the equilibrium. Inevitably, politics was reduced to social stalemate. It was ritualized, transformed, and embedded in questions of family power and administrative and religious parity in the selection of office holders. Nowhere was this more the case than in the ecclesiastical states, and mixed-confessional Osnabrück was, if anything, an even more extreme example. The pattern of confessional office holding we saw among Osnabrück's notable families was spread throughout the political society of northwestern Germany in an ever-widening distributive network that reflected the expanded horizons of the cathedral canons and bishops. Clemens August, for example, as we have already seen, controlled five bishoprics at once, and according to a contemporary story, the pope was supposed to have asked him during his audience in Rome: "Are you the prince who wants to occupy all the bishoprics in Germany?"[22] The same pattern of social ossification was mirrored in the office holding of the regional Catholic nobility who supplied the personnel for the cathedral chapters. At this lower level the regional stranglehold was even more complete, since the Westphalian nobility were largely successful in excluding the group of Rhenish imperial knights from the Westphalian chapters even as they themselves were excluded from the Rhenish chapters.[23] Many canons also held multiple offices: at least 50 (from a sample of 110 out of a possible total of 137) of the Osnabrück canons during the seventeenth and eighteenth centuries possessed offices simultaneously in Münster, and a small number were members of three chapters – in Osnabrück, Münster, and Paderborn.[24]

When the Leipzig professor of law Christian Ernst Weiße (1766–1832) came to explore the history of secularization and its legal status in the eighteenth century (1798), he concluded that it remained much more an ideal of radical Protestantism than a political reality.[25] In the Reformation period, Lutheran theological teaching, the concern for political "hierarchy," the fear of social

---

[22] Von Sartori, ibid., 1/2:19.

[23] The difference in the social composition of the cathedral chapters began in electoral Cologne, which had imperial knights in its chapter; but even though Münster was held in personal union with Cologne, the Rhenish nobility was excluded from offices in Münster. See Max Braubach, *Maria Theresias Jüngster Sohn Max Franz. Letzter Kurfürst von Köln und Fürstbishof von Münster* (Vienna, 1961), 118; Hanschmidt, *Franz von Fürstenberg*, 11–12; T. C. W. Blanning, *Reform and Revolution in Mainz 1743–1803* (Cambridge, 1974), 49–64.

[24] The statistical analysis is from Friedrich von Klocke, "Westfälische Landesherren in ihrer Bodenverbundenheit," *Der Raum Westfalen*, ed. Hermann Aubin, 4 vols. (Münster, 1931–58), 2/1:53–4, 59–70, esp. 68–9.

[25] Christian Ernst Weiße, *Ueber die Säkularisation deutscher geistlicher Reichsländer in Rücksicht auf Geschichte und Staatsrecht* (Leipzig, 1798), 6–35.

unrest, and chance had all combined, he decided, to keep the ecclesiastical states intact. Once these were integrated into the constitution of the Empire, the idea of secularization had become progressively narrower. The radical act of a general expropriation of church properties "without concern for the consequences" had been reduced to a view of secularization as the legal transfer of authority to a worldly ruler or parliamentary body.[26] This process could appear as part of an accommodation with religious difference or as part of the slow triumph of the rule of law. But what Weiße had in mind was neither of these interpretations. Rather, he focused on the political consequences of the social stalemate just described. He was concerned with the sticky question of financial compensation to the regional Catholic nobility and the Catholic princely houses. Secularization in the eighteenth century, he argued, could not attack the wealth and social prerogatives of the group that provided the princes, bishops, and canons, were the backbone of the imperial idea, and were supported by the Catholic emperor against Protestant designs. A root and branch secularization of one or more or all of the ecclesiastical states, in sum, would attack the institutions and social network of the Empire at its center. Such an act could never be justified within the code of law; at most, he concluded, it would reflect the need of states to survive.[27] Any thought of secularization, accordingly, was forced to distinguish between secularization as a transfer of sovereignty and secularization as the social and political expropriation of land and income from the Catholic nobility.

Of course, the latter form of secularization in the ecclesiastical territories did occur during the wars of the French Revolution, and it was the discussion of this possibility in the 1790s that provoked Weiße's work. Then the principle of noncompensation was forced on the Catholic nobility by the Napoleonic armies and the larger territorial rulers, including the emperor, who deserted them for their own interests. This secularization did, in fact, bring with it the dissolution of the Empire as it had been known since the Treaty of Westphalia. But in the decades before the Revolution, an upheaval of this magnitude was unthinkable, and the talk of secularization halted before the practical difficulties.[28]

Nonetheless, even as the political reality of secularization receded in the eighteenth century, the ideal remained quite alive.[29] We have seen it caught up with

[26] Ibid., 3–4.

[27] Ibid., 159–65.

[28] See the summary and conclusions of Wende, *Geistliche Staaten*, 30–7; Rudolf Morsey, "Wirtschaftliche und soziale Auswirkungen der Säkularisation in Deutschland," in *Dauer und Wandel der Geschichte*, ed. Rudolf Vierhaus and Manfred Botzenhart (Munich, 1966), 361–83; Rudolfine Frein von Oer, "Der Eigentumsbegriff in der Säkularisationsdiskussion am Ende des Alten Reiches," in *Eigentum und Verfassung*, ed. Rudolf Vierhaus, in *Veröffentlichungen des Max-Planck-Instituts für Geschichte*, 37 (Göttingen, 1972), 193–228; Christof Dipper, "Probleme einer Wirtschafts - und Sozialgeschichte der Säkularisation in Deutschland (1803–1813), "in *Deutschland und Italien in Zeitalter Napoleons*, ed. A. von Reden-Dohna (Wiesbaden, 1979), 123–70; and Harm Klueting, "Die Folgen der Säkularisation," in *Deutschland Zwischen Revolution und Restauration*, ed. Helmut Berding and Peter Ullmann (Königstein/Ts., 1981), 184–207.

[29] This summary is based on the following contemporary sources: Christian Friedrich Menschenfreund, *Warum ist, oder war bisher der Wohlstand der Protestantischen Staaten so gar viel grösser als der Katholischen*

the annexationist plans of Hanover and Prussia in the Seven Years War. In the Catholic states – Mainz, Cologne, or Münster, for instance – it survived in the efforts by certain bishops and their chief administrators to secularize particular cloisters and monasteries in order to gain money for specific reforms.[30] We can also see it in the reform literature on the ecclesiastical states written in the next decades. How was secularization conceived by the authors of this literature? The basic ideal was to separate church and state, and this in turn would promote a greater rationality in administrative life and in the dispensation of justice. Often it was thought to be the precondition for immediate material improvement; only by appropriating church income could money be gathered for the common good that was otherwise squandered by the Catholic Church for its use and for the support of the papal court abroad. But beyond such specific legal reforms, the ideal of secularization was nurtured by the association of Protestantism with moral and cultural progress. In this sense, it was part of the intellectual baggage of the Enlightenment. It provided a philosophy of demystification, as in Hume's "Natural History of Religion," and intellectual criteria for the condemnation of clerical politics. Throughout the reform literature, as a result, there was a steady undertone of Protestant superiority leveled against the anachronistic clerical states.

We can best see how Protestantism and reform were brought together in Germany during these years in the work of Friederich Karl von Moser, and specifically in his contribution, written in 1787, to the debate on reform of the ecclesiastical states.[31] This study, like all of Möser's journalism, was zealous in its pietism and filled with a hatred of princely absolutism: according to him, the founding of the ecclesiastical states in the early Middle Ages everywhere revealed Christianity's loss of religious purpose; the secular power of the church confirmed the division of humanity into two classes of clergy and people; Catholic "hierarchy" "adulterated and mutilated the plain and simple teaching of Christianity," and "monasticism and hierarchy oppressed the people" until Luther gave "freedom of thought to all." If the princes appropriated church properties in these years, the people themselves had lost nothing, since they had had nothing before. But they had now "won everything in terms of freedom of thought, belief, and conscience." In Catholic lands, however, "every path to the light was even more carefully blocked and sealed up," and "ignorance, indolence of spirit,

---

(Vienna, 1782), 8–12; Joseph von Sartori, *Statistische Abhandlung über die Mängel in der Regierungsverfassung der geistlichen Wahlstaaten und von den Mitteln, solchen abzuhelfen* (Augsburg, 1787), 10–11, 20–22, 70; Friedrich Carl Moser, *Ueber die Regierung der geistlichen Staaten in Deutschland* (Frankfurt, 1787); Andreas Joseph Schnaubert, *Ueber des Freiherrn von Mosers Vorschläge zur Verbesserung der geistlichen Staaten in Deutschland* (Frankfurt, 1787), esp. 90–130; Ernst von Klenk, *Preisfrage . . .* (Frankfurt, 1787), 30–40.

[30] In the Catholic states, such limited acts of secularization usually occurred in order to improve the schools. See Blanning, *Reform and Revolution*, 117, 133–4, 166–8; Hanschmidt, *Franz von Fürstenberg*, 142–4; Braubach, *Max Franz*, 147–56.

[31] Cited in footnote 30. Such views are also apparent in Menschenfreund, *Warum ist, oder war bisher*, 6–8; also see von Klenk, *Preisfrage*, 16–17.

silence and blind belief [continued to] prevail." Furthermore, the only concern of the Westphalian Peace had been to prevent the erosion of the "hierarchical forces." For that reason alone, the "ecclesiastical princes were confirmed in all their powers . . . and most importantly they were thereby freed from any need to change or alter the future." And before Möser went on to make specific reform recommendations, he concluded this lamentation by stating that the spirit of hierarchy lived on in those lands, preventing serious reform, perpetuating poverty, and suppressing learning.[32]

### THE SUCCESSION CRISIS IN OSNABRÜCK

If the works of Weiße and Moser take us ahead into a more politicized public debate, we can still detect, in muted form, the same prejudices and limited hopes among the Protestant administrators in Osnabrück at the end of the Seven Years War. The self-conscious Protestant undertone is evident everywhere in the documents and the correspondence: the feeling of superiority that led Möser to speak of the *"esprit de chapitre et catholicisme,"* the belief that political Catholicism was incapable of progressive government, the fear that education and freedom of thought would be further stifled under extended Catholic rule. In the first phases of confrontation, this faith in a higher Protestant rationality was also expressed as a hope that a more impartial administration could be established that would separate the legal system from clerical influence and thereby control or abolish the church courts. Similarly, a small whiff of reform can be detected in the attitude toward the ecclesiastical revenues and in the opinion that the money previously granted to a nonresident Catholic bishop might be applied to the material recovery of the bishopric from the war and the neglect of Catholic rule. But the two-tiered view of secularization was also there from the beginning. The larger question of the constitutional conflict – secularization as the precondition for modernization – was reduced to a precise technical debate over the language in the *capitulatio perpetua* and the constitutional mechanisms by which power was transferred to Hanover and a Protestant administration created. Placed outside the discussion was the broader attack on Catholic privilege. Hanover, in fact, was willing throughout its negotiations to compensate the cathedral canons liberally for their loss of political power.

Here as in many places of our account, we must seek the large historical questions concealed in the most modest intimations and technical distinctions that in states like Osnabrück substituted for dramatic movement. From this point of view, the constitutional arguments in the Osnabrück conflict are a microcosm of the institutional conflict in Germany between 1648 and the French Revolution.[33] Hanover eventually decided not to expropriate Osnabrück and integrate it fully into its domains. From that point on, the ideal of secularization was confined to

---

[32] Moser, *Ueber die Regierung*, summary of 11–34.
[33] On this entire problem, see Körholz, *Wahl des Prinzen*, 79–132.

the type of administrative adjustment Weiße had described. The conflict in Osnabrück focused, first, on the two episcopal councillors in the government: did they have the constitutional power, in the name of the king as the father of the bishop to be, to initiate legislation and oversee the collection of taxes, or were they there as observers to protect Hanoverian interests? A second question concerned the right to vote in the Imperial Diet during the regency: did it belong to the cathedral chapter – since the bishop had been selected but not installed – or to the king as the paternal guardian? These technical questions stemmed ultimately from the unwillingness of George III and his Hanoverian advisers to abide by Article 33 of the *capitulatio perpetua*, which regulated a regency government. Unfortunately for the Hanoverian legal position, Article 33 was very specific:

Whenever and as often as a member of the princely house of Braunschweig-Lüneburg is made eligible or is proposed who is under 20 years of age, the government may indeed be led until the twentieth year by the cathedral chapter and by no other governor (*Stadthalter*) or administrator, whether of princes, *Herren*, counts, or by his male relatives; but it shall remain open to the *Postulatio minorenni* to place alongside such government one or two persons as Councillors, as well as for the duration of the regency (which will end after the twentieth year is reached and the *postulatus eo ipso pro maiorenni cum omni iure ac potestate* shall take place) 8000 Reichstaler in cash shall be paid and delivered to the *Postulatio minorenni* by the cathedral chapter and thus appointed government; and when beyond the mentioned 8000 Reichsthaler the usual salaries have been paid and deducted, then, after a proper accounting, the remaining *Residuum* shall be divided into two parts, and one half shall be dispersed with foreknowledge to the minor episcopal *Postulati* either remitted as part of the episcopal provisioning monies (*Tafelgüter*) or purchased anew or dispensed to the same as interests, while the other half shall be taken for the improvement of the cathedral churches and their buildings.[34]

The explicitness of the article's language did not dissuade Hanover: they had occupied the bishopric, taken control of the administration and taxes, and sought to turn their possession into a position of right. The negotiations with the cathedral chapter tried to develop a face-saving compromise that kept the crown in effective control. Hanover proposed, for instance, to build a regency government of four councillors, two from the Hanoverian side, two from the cathedral chapter; but it was to reserve the right to choose which two canons would enter the government, and, beyond that, it was to retain the decisive vote whenever the four councillors could not agree among themselves. In addition, the crown sought to prevent the cathedral chapter from casting the decisive vote at the Imperial Diet, and after much maneuvering the position was reached that the vote would not be cast by either party during the regency. Simultaneously, it offered financial incentives to the canons: salaries would be paid for offices now supernumerary, expense money would be granted for Catholic envoys to the

---

[34] *Codex Constitutionum Osnabrugensium*, 1/2 (Osnabrück, 1783), 79–80.

Imperial Diet, even though they would not cast votes or be required to attend, and so forth.

But in spite of the various compromise formulas, the cathedral chapter would not sacrifice its legal right to rule. The negotiations dissolved and it turned to the emperor, the imperial courts, the Imperial Diet, and the various courts of Europe to restore its rights. The all-out judicial warfare that broke out between late 1764 and 1767 loosed a flood of legal briefs and pamphlets.[35] The surviving documents are a fascinating introduction to the hectically active but institutionally immobile world of the Holy Roman Empire in the later eighteenth century. Hanover, for example, was able to get the Corpus Evangelicorum to vote unanimously for its position because it meant another Protestant vote in the Council of Princes. The cathedral chapter managed the same results for the same reason from the Corpus Catholicorum. The Habsburg court became favorably disposed to the Catholic position, though it tried to resolve matters privately, since it did not want to offend the British Crown over this relatively minor affair in the first years of the peace. Both sides also argued without result before the imperial courts.

Möser's role throughout the entire conflict, as his oath of office as *Konsulent* had dictated, was to defend Protestant interests against the cathedral chapter. But it is a sign of his sensitive position within the administration that he conducted this defense in a series of *anonymous* pamphlets and legal briefs.[36] His views in these documents are thoroughly secular in the spirit of the Enlightenment. They show how deeply he had immersed himself in Protestant and Catholic law to argue the Hanoverian position. But having said this, there is no need to develop his views chronologically because he laid far less weight on intellectual novelty than on a vigorous rejection of Catholic views in a number of pseudonymous perspectives.

In the flurry of responses, Möser's pamphlets all reveal Protestant prejudice. He held Catholic rule, for instance, responsible for an impoverished Osnabrück no longer capable of supporting the young bishop with "an income commensurate with his high estate."[37] He accused the cathedral chapter of moral arrogance in apparently forgetting that it had declared war on the Hanoverian Crown: "that the cathedral chapter of that moment did not let troops march against his Royal Majesty, had its good reasons, namely, because it did not have any. Still the monies for that purpose were approved, and because of this his Royal Majesty cannot be expected to turn the revenues from the domains over to the cathedral chapter as their rewards."[38] He further charged them in veiled language with

---

[35] Many of them were bound together by an unknown participant and are now located in Harvard's Widener Library; the call number is Ger 6915.5.10F.

[36] Six pamphlets are known to have been written by Möser. The titles are so long that the interested reader should consult the bibliography. Möser's authorship is established both in direct statements now in the Osnabrück archives and in the correspondence. See, for instance, *Briefe*, 164.

[37] [Möser], *Kurze und vorläufige Abfertigung*, 3–5.

[38] Ibid., 35.

indulgence to the detriment of the bishopric: Only Protestant rule was capable of abolishing frivolous spending habits and restoring the episcopal economy, for only the crown was willing to foreswear its income during the regency.[39]

The political attack on the competence and goodwill of the cathedral chapter is characteristic but remains secondary to Möser's constitutional position. In a letter to von Lenthe of September 28, 1764, he had already advised that the crown must pursue its rights on the basis of a consequential Protestant legal perspective: from that point of view, Osnabrück becomes a hereditary state, paternal power the mode of legal continuity, and the right of the father to act as regent a position of such "common and known right . . . that . . . [it] requires no higher confirmation."[40]

The pamphlets developed this position. Möser's chief purpose was to emphasize that Osnabrück was ruled by both a Protestant legal tradition that viewed the bishopric in worldly terms and a Catholic canon law that wedded together clerical and worldly authority. But, he argued, the Catholic view had been compromised by accepting the alternate succession. If the question of minority rule was critical in canon law because of the fusion of worldly and clerical powers, such was not the case under Protestant law and in the bishopric under Protestant rule. At the moment of Protestant succession Osnabrück was transformed, de facto, into a hereditary monarchy, and the pope and the metropolitan – in this case the archbishop of Cologne – were granted the sovereignty over the bishopric's Catholic religious life according to the *capitulatio perpetua*.[41] The appeal for Article 33 regulating the regency was therefore irrelevant. Secular functions were exercised from Protestant succession by the prince-bishop through his administrative agents. Thus, the cathedral chapter had confused its two roles "first as a corporation and clerical Estate . . . and thereafter as an appointed administration (*bestellte Regierung*)."[42] As a corporation it provided for continuity of rule during periods of Catholic domination; then only briefly in the six-month period before the new bishop was chosen did it assume both secular and ecclesiastical authority. Otherwise the chapter only exercised authority indirectly through the position of the bishop. During a Protestant reign, in other words, the cathedral chapter was only one of the Estates and did not have the right to raise itself above the others.[43]

Möser employed the same arguments to explain the legality of the Hanoverian regency in the name of George III. Since the alternation was inviolate, and this aspect of the conflict had not been thrown in doubt, so Möser claimed, sovereignty now fell to the house of Braunschweig-Lüneburg. There could be no doubt of the continuity of authority between George III and his son in Protestant terms.

---

[39] Ibid., 5–6, 30.
[40] Sheldon, ed., Möser's correspondence, forthcoming.
[41] [Möser], *Kurze und vorläufige Abfertigung*, 26–8.
[42] Ibid., 14–15.
[43] Ibid., 54–5.

"God, nature, and justice," he wrote in one place, upholds paternal power during a minority reign.[44] Thus, the crucial point became the exercise of that power. Möser pointed out in real terms that power was exercised through the agents of the crown, that is, through administrators who had taken an oath of office and acted in the crown's name. Recognizing the reality of absentee rule, he made a careful distinction between "rule" (*regieren*) that is direct and the "delegated exercise of power" (*Regierung führen*).[45] The reader can get a taste of Möser's polemical language in this partial summary of his position:

It is annoying to waste time with such transparent matters and to be forced to explain to the cathedral chapter the difference between an independent and a dependent government; and to have to derive from this [distinction] that it mixes together completely different matters, consequences, and concepts: that it [the cathedral chapter] is immediate *sede vacante* (when the seat is vacant) [but] a mediate Estate *sede plena* (when the seat is occupied); that these qualities of completely different governments cannot be confounded and a princely privy councillor equated with a ruling territorial prince. Either the cathedral chapter must assume the complete guardianship over its bishop, . . . or, since that is not the case, the elected bishop shall have no other head than his father and no other *personam standi in quovis judicio* (person of standing in any legal matter) than the same. The *Capitulary* . . . has recognized the legal right of friends and relatives to intervene *post quaestia regalia* (after the regalia have been acquired); and at least has said nothing of a new type of guardianship over a royal prince of blood: for this reason the father and guardian of an underaged bishop always remains the supplemental component of a full territorial prince and sovereign, and the Estates who are subordinate to an appointed bishop, whether they lead the government or not, always remain mediate Estates, who are, by definition, incapable of receiving and spending regalia in their own name.[46]

Who had the better case? It is unclear that it made a difference. As with so many other legal conflicts at the imperial level in the eighteenth century, the judicial process failed and a decision was never reached. The Protestant and Catholic factions in the Council of Princes agreed informally that Osnabrück was to suspend its vote during the regency. But since uttering any words at all might have prejudiced the unresolved legal issues, it was further agreed, after much negotiation, that no answer was to be given to the call for Osnabrück's vote and "vacat" was to be entered into the protocols of the Council of Princes. This decision halted the agitation at the imperial level and made it politically unnecessary for the courts to decide the legality of the regency. The cathedral chapter, however, never relented on the matter of principle, never rendered an oath of loyalty to the Hanoverian administration, and thus was excluded from corule. The offer of additional subsidies to the cathedral canons was also withdrawn, so that, as noted earlier, Osnabrück was ruled throughout the regency by Möser and two Hanoverian privy councillors. When it came time for Frederick

---

[44] [Möser], *Pro-Memoria der Chur-Braunsweigischen Gesandtschaft*, 19; similar language on 16.
[45] Ibid., 12–14; also *Kurze und vorläufige Abfertigung*, 21, 39.
[46] [Möser], *Kurze und vorläufige Abfertigung*, 23–4.

of York to assume the episcopal office in 1783, a complicated formula was worked out by which the cathedral chapter could protest against the regency again in writing, after which it duly invested the bishop in his office and rendered the oath of loyalty.

Thus the regency was a quasi-legal government throughout its twenty-year life, since only the two Protestant Estates gave oaths of loyalty to the king's administrators. This explains the ambiguity of Möser's position in the government. Constitutionally undisputed were only those offices independent of the crown; these made the regency more acceptable to the Estates and Möser more important to the crown. In addition, the failed compromise between crown and cathedral chapter rendered legal reform more or less impossible during the regency, since the tenuous working compromise gave little administrative leverage for substantial administrative reform. For that reason, reform occurred in the interstices of Osnabrück's ecclesiastical institutions, and in the postwar decades it was by nature piecemeal and inadequate. But whatever spirit of reform survived in this situation was necessarily carried by Justus Möser in his person and through the manipulation of offices at his disposal.

The quasi-legitimacy of Möser's position in the Osnabrück administration most likely reflects the inflexibility of the system of Estates in responding to the material crisis caused by the war. In the absence of constitutional change, Osnabrück needed a figure like Justus Möser who could manipulate the system while retaining the veneer of constitutional legitimacy. It is striking that Franz von Fürstenberg came to power in neighboring Münster during the same period (1762–80) when Münster was facing the same crisis and that he had a similarly contested constitutional position. A member of the cathedral chapter who served the bishopric during the war, he was named *Geheimer Konferenzrat* or chief minister for Münster by Archbishop Max Friedrich and was paid out of the Cologne treasury. Fürstenberg's position was unassailable because he served at the will of the archbishop and because he also sat as a member of both the *Ritterschaft* and the cathedral chapter. Thus he, like Justus Möser, combined the key political and administrative positions in his person, and as a noble he could, even more than Möser, attempt to force reforms on the increasingly resistant *Ritterschaft* and cathedral chapter. His fall from power in 1780 when Max Franz of Austria was elected coadjutor bishop reveals the great pressures toward institutional stalemate that existed in the ecclesiastical states.[47]

Clearly, therefore, to return to the question of reform aspirations and historical significance of the previous section, the succession crisis in Osnabrück was no more than a narrow oligarchical struggle, confessionally determined, between the regional Catholic nobility, on the one hand, and the crown, Protestant nobility, and cities, on the other. It bears all the technical narrowness Professor

---

[47] The 1780 capitulary with Max Franz contained the clause that no future minister who might come from the cathedral chapter or the *Ritterschaft* could appear at the diet as long as he held office. On this see Hanschmidt, *Franz von Fürstenberg*, 81–2.

Weiße still noted at the end of the century. Embedded in the institutional stalemate of the post-Westphalian period, its significance rests in the lack of serious institutional alternatives. But the Osnabrück experience can be generalized. When we examine the literature on the reform of the ecclesiastical states occasioned by the Herr von Bibra in the *Journal of and for Germany* (1786), the Osnabrück crisis acquires a somewhat different perspective. Justus Möser and Count Wallersdorf in Mainz were announced as judges of the 25-ducat prize. (Both later declined, and Carl Theodor von Dahlberg made the award.) Significantly, almost no author from among the large number of respondents drew from his criticisms the conclusion of far-reaching secularization. Almost all the writers, however, developed the same criticisms – admittedly in a more public and straightforward manner – that appear in Möser's writings of the succession crisis.

Two positions merit a brief comparative summary: the statistical analysis of Joseph von Sartori, since it won the first prize, and the work of Friedrich Carl von Moser, whose idiosyncratic political radicalism was as extreme a position as the debate produced. Von Sartori made most of the criticisms we have seen emerge in the Osnabrück crisis: the incapacity of ecclesiastical regents to govern their domains; their celibacy and advanced age, which made continuity of rule impossible; the impoverishment of the ecclesiastical states by the practice of nonresidency; the rigidity and inflexibility of the political system, which made reform impossible; and, above all, the irresponsible electioneering and political power of the cathedral chapters. To correct these problems, he recommended a modified absolutism: the cathedral chapters were to bind each new regent with the responsibility to seek the best for the land, and they were then to give him unlimited power to execute his task. He further argued that the administrators in ecclesiastical states should be better-trained professionals. In his view, most were incompetent because the posts had always been treated as sinecures and there were no incentives to improve the states they administered. The limits of von Sartori's criticisms are clear. Like almost all of the writers in the competition, he transformed the systemic criticism of the ecclesiastical states into a question of adequately trained administrators. "The general problem," as he stated it, "lies principally in the manner of government (*Regierungsart*)." He concluded that all reforms were possible with the proper administration and thereby without eliminating the "regent, the clergy . . . or the basic constitution."[48] His prize-winning essay, in sum, has that strict division between structure and function noted earlier in the chapter.

Until the military collapse of the Empire in the wars of the French Revolution, Friedrich Karl von Moser's *Concerning the Government of the Ecclesiastical States in Germany* (1787) was by far the most thorough critique of the ecclesiastical states. I have already mentioned this work for the Protestant view of history it unfolded.

---

[48] Von Sartori, *Statistische Abhandlung*, 21.

From Moser's anti-Catholic perspective, he made three serious suggestions for reform: separate church and state, for there could be no improvements until "prince and bishop" were separated from each other; eliminate the spirit of hierarchy by separating the ecclesiastical states from Rome; and transform the ecclesiastical states into worldly states. But along with this, Moser argued that the system of Estates as well as the electoral system should be retained. Moser called this latter reform "monarchical aristocracy" and argued that the ecclesiastical states should fight monarchical despotism by becoming hereditary electoral states.[49]

These two works represent the most enlightened opinion in Germany in the 1780s. If we use them as a yardstick, we can see that Möser's Osnabrück already satisfied most of their reform aspirations. Under Protestant rule Osnabrück was a hereditary state; during the regency, money was no longer drained away to the same extent; under Möser's administration and the activities of the other Hanoverians, the bishopric acquired highly competent professionals; suspending the rules requiring a Catholic regency created a certain possibility for the material improvement of the bishopric; and by its attachment to Britain–Hanover, Osnabrück became in essence the monarchical aristocracy Moser had called for. This comparison, in other words, gives us some sense of why Möser felt pride in his commitment to Osnabrück. Measured in the oligarchical terms of the late eighteenth century, the bishopric could be seen as among the most progressive of ecclesiastical states.

## MÖSER'S RELIGIOUS VIEWS

The consequences of war and the succession crisis for Möser's thought extend far into the regency. In Chapters 4, 5, and 6, we consider how they are reflected in the *Osnabrück History*, in the reforms of the postwar years, and in his social theory. In concluding Chapter 3, I examine the way in which the confessional stalemate shaped his response to more particularly ecclesiastical and religious questions.

Möser avoided discussing specific matters of religious doctrine in a society where, by definition, confessional issues were central. His public religious writings are few in number and without a trace of metaphysical introspection.[50] Even among his unpublished papers, we find almost no statements of religious awe or wonderment. The speculative sentence – "If the soul is material, then it cannot leave this world" – stands as an isolated fragment.[51] Möser seems instead to have had a functional attitude toward religion, which suppressed reflection, causing

[49] Moser, *Ueber die Regierung der geistlichen Staaten*, 160–76.
[50] Of the older literature concerning Möser's religious beliefs, see Heinrich Schierbaum, "Justus Mösers Stellung in der Literaturströmungen des 18. Jahrhunderts. II Teil," *Osn. Mitt.*, 34 (1909):1–12; also Ludwig Bäte, *Justus Möser*, 101, 169. Hatzig saw Möser as a confirmed Christian who believed in Christian salvation, but he brings forth little evidence for this view; see *Justus Möser als Staatsmann*, 9.
[51] Möser, *SW*, 9:216.

him to deal with religious matters only insofar as they had a social or political meaning for civil society.[52]

Now a functional or utilitarian attitude toward religion would seem to be naturally congenial to the administrator; but it was also a critical cultural step both in the gradual secularization of European society and in the development of religious toleration. Only by confining religion to its own realm – that is, from a secular perspective – could legal pluralism be instituted; legal pluralism, by the same token, would appear to be a prerequisite for religious toleration. Such was the perspective toward toleration we find in Möser's writings. Unfortunately, his views are not always easy to decipher. Here as elsewhere in his works, he stated his opinions in a curious and sometimes perverse manner, and it is in fact difficult for the general reader to understand that he was deeply committed to religious toleration. I begin, then, by discussing his literary essays dealing with this issue, which often conceal as much as enlighten, and then move on to discuss several far more significant documents, which describe the institutional structure of toleration within the bishopric. What we will uncover is a fundamental aspect of Möser's thought – one, however, that has received almost no attention because the confessional framework in which his life unfolded has been largely neglected.

Let us start with the open "Letter to the Vicar of Savoy," written in 1762 during the succession crisis.[53] This essay is characteristic of Möser's utilitarian attitude toward theological questions. Typically, he evaded the central metaphysical issues in the vicar's confession – the vicar's anti-Cartesian materialism, which still ended in radical dualism over the question of evil – and saw only that natural religion threatened to destroy public religious norms. That Möser attacked Rousseau from this one side is important to keep before us, because in order to find grounds for criticism, Möser defended positive Christianity with arguments that did not reflect his own beliefs. He argued, for instance, that "positive religion often comes into existence with civil societies," because humans are imperfect beings who cannot regulate themselves individually. For this reason, "lawmakers and founders of all states have found the norms of natural religion inadequate to establish and bind together civil society. Consequently, they have resorted to gods and other mechanisms or to positive religion" to enforce public order. Positive religion has these purposes: to make monarchs humble, elevate human dignity in the civil realm, and command the recalcitrant. "Religion is the politics of God in the kingdom of man."[54] It must be broadly cast, even awe-inspiring, in order to appeal to and retain its ethical power over different groups within the human community.

---

[52] Möser, *Briefe*, 166: "Jede gesetzte Religion, sie sey wahr oder falsch, wenn sie das beste der Gesellschaft befördert und nur die Einbildung beherrscht ist gleichgültig . . . ; die ganze Kunst is nur, die Lüge zu verbergen und so viel Blindwerk zu machen, dass nur einige Adepten ins gemein zweifeln."

[53] Möser, *W*, 5:230–51.

[54] Ibid., 235–6.

It is significant that Möser rejected out of hand the conventional distinction between a religion for the educated and one for the uneducated; on the contrary, he remarked that "religion is made for us rabble and not for the angels."[55] Here we arrive at the central point behind Möser's defense of positive Christianity: natural religion is dangerous precisely because it caters to the few, thus threatening to undermine the civil order. Civil society, as a consequence, cannot allow the individual to structure his own belief. Rather, he must accommodate to positive Christianity. This unequivocal conclusion does not accurately reflect Möser's personal views. Provisionally, however, we see him defending against Rousseau the claims society makes on the individual.

Möser championed the right of society to control religious life even more crudely in two other lengthy essays: the "Letter to Aaron Mendez de Costa, Chief Rabbi in Utrecht Concerning the Easy Conversion of the Pharasaical Sect" (1773) and "Concerning General Toleration; Letters from Virginia" (1787–9).[56] The "Letter to Aaron Mendez de Costa" is, in fact, a semiscurrilous attack on Judaism by a thoughtless official Christianity. The piece would appear from a note to have been provoked by Moses Mendelssohn's *Phaedon*. Möser sought to subvert Mendelssohn's views by showing how insubstantial were the theological differences that prevented Jews from converting to Christianity. Where they existed – with respect to the immortality of the soul, for example, – Möser thought he found intimations within Judaism that made accommodation possible. Unfortunately, he engaged in a bitter caricature of Judaic beliefs in the essay; the *ad hominem* comments on circumcision and other Old Testament customs seem strangely out of place in the works of one who did not shy away from the most sentimental description of Teutonic warriors. What we glimpse, in sum, is merely Möser's impatience with theological speculation and a willingness to ostracize Jews from German society for the sake of cultural homogeneity.

Möser also defended religious uniformity in his fictitious "Letters from Virginia." These trace the gradual dissolution of general religious toleration in Virginia as the colony struggled to achieve greater consensus. The parable's structure is transparent: the atheists are the first to be driven from the "list of honorable men," since their oaths have no otherworldly anchor; then the Christian majority, distrustful of religious difference, threatens to expel the religious minorities, bringing the colony close to civil war; finally, the colony decides to admit to the political society every male whose religious beliefs, codified in the form of written articles of faith, are judged to support the state. Those refusing to make such pledges are excluded from the protection of the colony's law and not permitted citizenship or the right to hold office.

[55] Ibid., 249.
[56] Ibid., 252–63, 293–315. It is chiefly due to the "Letter to Aaron Mendez de Costa" that the case for Möser's anti-Semitism was built by Gertrud Brück in *Die Bedeutung Justus Mösers für das Leben und Denken Thomas Abbts* (Ph.D. diss., Munich, 1937). There is a certain anti-Semitic undertone in the "Letter to Aaron Mendez de Costa"; however, it derives from a basic Christian intolerance of Judaism and was not "völkisch" as she understood it.

In these essays the threat to the established Christian order posed by natural religion, Judaism, or atheism seems far greater than intra-Christian animosities. But Protestant prejudice reemerged whenever Catholicism alone was Möser's subject. For example, he wrote a humorous response to one of the periodic pleas for reunification of the faiths by an anonymous Catholic priest. There he argued that the political difficulties of merger were far more complicated than any theological differences.[57] Protestant sovereigns would never abandon their control of church institutions, he noted; nor would Protestants accept Catholic prodigality in church life or surrender their intellectual freedom.

Möser's functional approach to religious life took yet another form, finally, in his "Celibacy of the Clergy Viewed from Its Political Perspective."[58] It was most likely occasioned by one of the arrangements of the Westphalian Peace that required three Evangelical canons to be added to the twenty-one Catholic canons of the cathedral chapter. The price the Evangelical party paid was that these canons, unlike those in other Protestant chapters (Minden, Halberstadt, Lübeck), were forced to remain celibate. In 1773 one of the Protestant canons tested this provision by announcing his intent to marry and retain his office. The usual pamphlet war and legal process began over the next two years, which the Protestant canon lost, forcing his resignation from the chapter. Interestingly, the *Ritterschaft* supported the cathedral chapter in rejecting his claim, since it feared that the prebends might become the hereditary property of the same Protestant families.[59]

Möser adopted the position of the *Ritterschaft* in the essay. He inverted Protestant dislike of priestly celibacy, tracing Catholic practice to an admirable political decision originally designed to preserve the effective boundaries between secular and religious authority. Were the Catholic clergy to marry and make their electoral offices into hereditary possessions, he argued, increasing competition by their impoverished offspring would dangerously erode political freedom. Celibacy was politically necessary because it assured the present political pluralism. For this reason, Möser came to the startling conclusion that concubinage and illegitimacy among the high clergy and canons must once again be publicly accepted as part of the political bargain.

What are we to make of the peculiar reasoning in this essay? Joseph von Sartori praised it for its acumen, and A. L. Schlözer thought enough of it to print it in the *Staatsanzeigen*.[60] If we believe that Möser was serious in calling for the public acceptance of concubines – and I cannot but feel he was playing with Protestant prejudice – we can see that he was once again stripping away the spiritual aura attached to religious matters. He translated the ethical questions connected with

[57] Möser, *W*, 5:264–73.
[58] Ibid., 275–85.
[59] Dr. Beckschäfer, "Evangelische Domherren in Osnabrücker Domkapitel," *Osn. Mitt.*, 52 (1930):192–4.
[60] Von Sartori, *Statistische Abhandlung*, 135. Möser's article was printed in Schlözer's *Staatsanzeigen*, 2 (1783): 401–11.

celibacy into ones that concerned the social and economic perpetuation of the regional nobility. His conclusions were surprising, for in order to maintain the stability of this hereditary caste, he was willing to revive principles of concubinage that were inconceivable in his own day. He wrote in defense of the social stalemate, since he was not willing to consider the expropriation of the Catholic nobility.

This sampling of Möser's essays gives us a good sense of the view of toleration that lay beneath his public posture. Möser refused to construct a pluralistic religious society on the basis of individual initiative. This explains his attack on natural religion and on the ideal of universal toleration, both of which were potentially subversive of the state. On the surface, this statism would appear to be politically reactionary. But in assessing Möser's views, we must not forget that religious parity was highly legalistic in the post-Westphalian era. It did not necessarily produce toleration of religious difference, nor did it functionally separate church and state. The major achievements of the peace were to neutralize religious conflict, subordinate church life to the state, and prevent the recurrence of civil war through tightly woven constitutional compromises, like the one that created confessionally divided Osnabrück. Möser agreed with the strategy of the Westphalian settlement and was clear about its significance. Thus he shared the widespread prejudice against enthusiasm so common to the Enlightenment in Germany and wherever else the religious wars had broken out – in France, England, and the Netherlands. His views concerning toleration, in other words, still reveal fears and conclusions already present generations earlier at the beginning of the Englightenment, when the concern had been to remove confessional issues from the civil realm. The need to segregate seems to be a preliminary phase to universal toleration and reflects the reality of deep religious differences.

Each of these essays I have discussed has its roots in this unstated situation. Möser believed that some broad Christian consensus was necessary to sustain the civil order, but beyond that he was equally concerned that each faith refrain from judging the other. Even the essay on celibacy should be read from this perspective, for though he shared the Protestant worry about the spirit of political Catholicism, as we have seen, he did not want Protestant values to subvert the fragile political settlement by an unreasoned attack on Catholic custom. More than this, Möser simply did not believe that toleration could exist in any form but that based on legal compromise. He fought against intellectual naiveté in these essays, but he was also willing to struggle for institutional toleration.

Two documents, both published anonymously, reveal Möser's real views with far less ambiguity. The first is a review of J. C. Maier's *Teutsches geistliches Staatsrecht (German Ecclesiastical Law),*[61] which was published in 1773 in the *Auserlesene Bibliothek der neuesten Literatur (Selected Library of the Most Recent German Literature.)*[62] In his work Maier considered ecclesiastical law from three perspec-

---

[61] Johann Christian Maier, *Teutsches Geistliches Staatsrecht abgetheilt in Reichs- und Landrecht* (Lemgo, 1773).

[62] Published in *Auserlesene Bibliothek der neusten Literatur,* 4 (Lemgo, 1773–6), 575–92.

tives: the origins of a communal religious sensibility in individuals inside and outside society; the establishment of a communal religious life in institutions and laws once these individuals decide to band together; and the legal integration of religious life within the civil order.

The individual retains freedom of conscience in the first historical era, according to Maier, but once he enters society, freedom of thought must end and the power to regulate must be transferred to the religious community. Civil society also possesses rights over individual conscience connected with the preservation of the civil order – rights that Maier analyzed in the third part of his study. This general perspective had been Möser's own in the "Letter to the Vicar of Savoy," and if that essay had in fact expressed Möser's true opinions, we should find him here in agreement with Professor Maier. Yet his review is written as a criticism of Maier's attack on freedom of conscience.

Maier's chief point in the second part of his work, which describes religious institutions and laws, was that there cannot be toleration from the perspective of the Catholic Church – that "the conception of an ecclesiastical (*kirchlichen*) toleration is contradictory and impossible."[63] Möser, however, defended freedom of conscience by showing that institutional compromise with other faiths was a matter of the historical record in the post-Westphalian era, and he adduced examples of such toleration. Thus he gave instances of confessional border areas at the time of the Westphalian Peace where Catholic and Protestant practices were since fused together – a church with a Lutheran sexton and a Catholic priest; a church with Lutheran hymns and Catholic sermons; a church that was required by law to lend its preacher and buildings to another faith; a church where the congregation voted to change its confession, and the minister from the old faith stayed on to care for them. Möser saw each of these as a mode of official toleration – a toleration he defended without equivocation: " . . . it is not as strange as it might seem at first glance that lands, courts, and dynastic families have a firm religion but that the people who live there should retain the freedom to believe what they will. The Westphalian Peace had cut through the knot by decree, but philosophy will find it hard to persuade the members of a church to sever all their ties with the [legal] change of their confession. The individual and the church member are lodged in the same skin with the citizen, and can be easily separated in *abstracto* but never in *concreto*."[64]

In this review, then, Möser defended religious toleration from the perspective of clerical institutions and actual ecclesiastical practice; but in addition, he wanted to show that toleration was indeed difficult, yet possible within the civil realm. In his book Maier had focused chiefly on the evolution of Protestant ecclesiastical law.[65] He described the limits of the imperial laws regulating religious life,

---

[63]   Maier, *Staatsrecht*, 26.
[64]   *Auserlesene Bibliothek*, 579.
[65]   Maier, *Staatsrecht*, esp. 102–17, 143–4.

demonstrating that, by tolerating three faiths, the Peace of Westphalia had created a system of official intolerance.[66] Yet the peace could not have done otherwise, he concluded, because the civil order needed to defend itself from tendencies within Protestantism toward division and sectarian struggle. A strictly limited pluralism was essential to prevent future political anarchy.

Möser basically accepted Maier's account. Expanding toleration was difficult, he commented, because there was a basic asymmetry within Catholic and Protestant legal traditions. Under Protestantism there was no superior court of appeal in matters of doctrine. Since Protestantism had emerged at the same historical moment as the territorial state, the tendency within Protestantism had been to solve this problem by allowing ecclesiastical power to accrue to the territorial princes. Such a concentration of power led, unfortunately, to a new orthodoxy and not to toleration.

But at this point, Möser took issue with Maier's analysis. He stressed the possibility that religious toleration might evolve further by permitting a legal existence to those confessions willing to "transform old articles of belief into mere ethical norms."[67] (Here we encounter the justification behind the extend parable in the "Letter from Virginia.") The possibility of expanding toleration rests in the Empire's religious laws, which are based on concrete contracts and compromises between sovereign and Estates; these, in turn, constitute the institutional life of the church. The old dualism was preferable in the legal evolution of toleration, for, according to Möser, it separated ecclesiastical and secular authority, shared power between the princes and the Estates, and made possible toleration based on contractual compromise. In Möser's words, "it appears not insignificant to a proper understanding of the various territorial laws and contracts, as well as to the preservation of civil (*bürgerlicher*) freedom and rights, [that] the old system [should] still be retained."[68] Thus, he rejected the fusion of secular and ecclesiastical authority in the territorial system of Protestant absolutism and praised the Westphalian Peace for creating the religious parity that elaborated in the "smallest possible instances the consequences of the religious settlement."[69] Lasting toleration, in other words, could always occur on this juridical basis, and such toleration would not disrupt the civil order, since rights and obligations would have been resolved on the basis of oath and contract. It was from this point of view that Möser had attacked the ideal of nonjuridical or philosophical toleration in the "Letters from Virginia." Now we can see that the justification lay in the religious wars and the Westphalian Peace.

It is important to ask what such a functional view of toleration meant for Osnabrück. A partial answer is given in one of Möser's last works, a folio-sized

---

[66] Ibid., 44–65.
[67] *Auserlesene Bibliothek*, 580–1.
[68] Ibid., 584.
[69] Ibid., 588–9.

pamphlet in which he described the failed efforts to introduce toleration into two parishes within the bishopric.[70] The reader should understand that though Osnabrück was a mixed confessional state, religious freedom did not exist everywhere in the bishopric. Confessional struggle had continued at the parish level, partly because the Westphalian settlement had been imperfect in solving the matter of financial compensation. This was especially true of the Parish of Schledehausen, which had had only one Catholic noble (*Erbmann*) in 1648 but which had had to return to Catholicism because the parish priest had still lived. The problem in the town of Fürstenau was somewhat different, since it had had a predominantly Evangelical population and had been fortunate to fall into Swedish hands in 1647. The peace settlement had freed the Evangelical majority from the control of Franz Wilhelm, the prince-bishop at the time of the settlement and one of the most "energetic" of all Catholic princes. Once peace had been concluded, however, Franz Wilhelm had reintroduced Catholic services into the parish, against the conditions of the treaty, which had stipulated Evangelical services only. This abuse had continued in Fürstenau until Möser's day. During years of Protestant rule, Catholic services were prohibited, only to be reintroduced during each successive Catholic reign.

The mix of Catholics and Protestants in each parish had not changed much since 1648. According to Möser, Schledehausen had a population of 2,342 in 1786, of which "not even 43" were Catholic. Fürstenau's population in the same year was 891, of which one-third was Catholic, two-thirds Evangelical. In Schledehausen, in other words, some 2,300 Protestants were ruled by a tiny Catholic minority. This meant that the Catholic Church in Schledehausen forbade public prayer by the Evangelical majority, only allowing individual families private worship behind locked doors. It also denied the majority the right to educate their children by hiring a private teacher at their expense. In Fürstenau, on the other hand, the problem was to achieve permanent religious rights for the substantial Catholic minority.

Under Möser's administration, so he tells us, a start was made to aid the two populations in each parish. Schledehausen was essentially a homogeneous Evangelical parish; there, accordingly, the basic issue concerned financial compensation of the much larger Evangelical population by the Catholic Church. But financial compensation was only one aspect of the problem in Fürstenau, because each confession was well represented. There the basic struggle of the Reformation was still being fought. Protestants especially were enormously resentful of the public life of the Catholic minority: the processions of wedding and burial, the frequent pealing of bells, feast and holy days that interrupted the rhythm of work. After much deliberation these issues were settled, and the community agreed to allow Catholic processions but to restrict them to the boundaries of their churchyards,

---

[70] Anon. [Justus Möser], *Darstellung der Gründe welche seine Königliche Hoheit den Herrn Herzog von York als Bischofen zu Osnabrück bewogen haben das Simultanum zu Fürstenau und Schledehausen einzuführen* . . . (Osnabrück, n.d. [c. 1790]); Osnabrück archive signature: OsA Fol. 2311c.

since such processions had "often been the occasion for disturbance of the public peace by both faiths and since such processions had been the major cause preventing the introduction of Catholicism in Evangelical areas." Yet the settlement as a whole had collapsed at the writing of the pamphlet, in spite of this accommodation, over a variety of other material issues. These Möser outlined in detail, and we can see by their enumeration what were the practical difficulties to negotiated religious toleration in Osnabrück. The matters of procession, bells, and burials were again opened up by the failure of the talks; awaiting resolution, in addition, were the issues of surplice fees, preservation of buildings, holidays, election of the magistracy, poor relief, and the tax-exempt status of the Catholic population.

The general purpose of Möser's pamphlet was to break through the religious stalemate in the two parishes by establishing the power of the bishop to legislate a compromise in the spirit of the Peace of Westphalia. If we do not follow the specific legal arguments, the point of Möser's position was to establish the authority of the prince-bishop to act as a neutral mediator in the interest of both confessions. In a confessional state, it was precisely this neutrality that was lacking. Thus we can see Möser attempting to move the bishopric to legislate impartially in the interest of the commonweal, without also destroying the careful political balance between the Estates and the prince-bishop.

The effort to secularize Osnabrück while maintaining political dualism is the thread that ran throughout Möser's career and ties together the various strands in this chapter. The pamphlet on toleration in the two villages, written a few short years before his death, shows us that confessional politics in the small states was a painstaking struggle for incremental change. Toleration had a concrete but never general meaning in this society because general meanings threatened the political stalemate. The Enlightenment and Justus Möser halted before this institutional reality, and it took the wars of the French Revolution to break the knot of the Westphalian settlement: this abolished the legal parity that had existed for more than 150 years, expropriated the prebends and chapter offices from the regional Catholic nobility, and brought about Osnabrück's assimilation into Protestant Hanover.

# 4

~~~~~~~~~~~~~~~~~~~~~~~~~~~~~~~~~~~~~~~~~~~~~~~~~~~~~~~~~~~~~~~~~~~~~~~~

## *Möser's historical universe: regional history and cosmopolitan history*

Justus Möser's historical vision, like his attitude toward Osnabrück's ecclesiastical institutions, was fully formed only in the crisis of the Seven Years War. But whereas ecclesiastical questions assumed a minor place in his work once the regency of Frederick of York was accepted, the historical problems surrounding the bishopric's institutions preoccupied him for the rest of his life. The result of these reflections was (except for certain minor studies) the multivolume *Osnabrück History*, on which his fame continues to rest.[1] In it he managed to combine a powerfully expressive German prose with humanist erudition – a remarkable achievement for the period. Furthermore he rejected conventional political narrative for multilayered social and economic explanation at the regional level; this was the intellectual innovation that inspired his contemporaries and historians throughout the nineteenth century and caused historians like Dilthey, Baron, Meinecke, and Moritz Ritter to link him with Winckelmann, Montesquieu, and Gibbon.[2]

---

[1] Both editions of the *Osnabrück History* are part of the *SW*, 12/1–2 and 13. Möser's minor historical essays, chiefly studies for the history of Osnabrück, are partly collected in *SW*, 14.

[2] For the impact of Möser on his contemporaries, see Ernst Hempel, "Justus Mösers Wirkung auf seine Zeitgenossen und auf die deutsche Geschichtsschreibung," *Osn. Mitt.*, 54 (1933):1–76.

For the judgments by the historians mentioned in the text, see Wilhelm Dilthey, "Das achtzehnte Jahrhundert und die geschichtliche Welt," in *Gesammelte Schriften*, ed. Paul Ritter, vol. 3 (4th ed.; Stuttgart, 1969), 210–268, esp. 247–57; Hans Baron, "Justus Mösers Individualitätsprinzip in seiner geistesgeschichtlichen Bedeutung," *HZ*, 130 (1924):31–57; Friedrich Meinecke, *Die Entstehung des Historismus*, ed. and intro. Carl Hinrichs (4th ed.; Munich, 1965), 303–54; and Moritz Ritter, *Die Entwicklung der Geschichtswissenschaft* (Berlin, 1919), 287–96.

Of the large literature dealing with Justus Möser's historical writings, the richest interpretation remains Friedrich Meinecke's account in *Die Entstehung des Historismus*. Important as a commentary to Meinecke is Joachim Streisand, *Geschichtliches Denken von der deutschen Frühaufklärung bis zur Klassik* (2nd ed.; Berlin, 1967); for Möser, 8, 67–72. Peter Schmidt's study is also significant, particularly for the author's careful efforts to trace the development of Möser's historical sensibility as revealed in his reading and educational experience; see his *Studien über Justus Möser als Historiker*, in *Göppinger Akademische Beiträge*, no. 93 (Göppingen, 1975). Of the older studies, also useful are Ulrike Brünauer, *Justus Möser* (Berlin, 1933); William J. Bossenbrook, "Justus Möser's Approach to History," in *Medieval and Historiographical Essays in Honor of James Westfall Thompson*, ed. James Lea Cate and Eugene N. Anderson (Chicago, 1938), 397–422; and two essays by Paul Göttsching,

Though recognizing Möser's achievement, we must be careful to avoid the Germanic nationalism that has accompanied most studies of Möser's historical writings. Friedrich Meinecke, the most subtle interpreter of Möser's historical work, epitomized the ideological view that emerged at the beginning of the twentieth century by treating Möser in the context of an emerging historicism that stood in dialectical opposition to the Enlightenment. According to Meinecke, Möser was the figure who first broke through the narrow rationalist mentality of Enlightenment historiography. He turned away from moralism in politics, discovered the individual in the social group, and developed the irrational as the significant aesthetic principle in historical explanation.[3] Thus, he was a major contributor to the new "inwardness" that led to historicism. Like Dilthey and Baron before him, Meinecke placed Möser almost exclusively in the context of the *Sturm und Drang* and the currents of counter-Enlightenment that gathered strength in the 1780s and 1790s. In Meinecke's florid intellectual shorthand, "[we see] with Möser the beginning in Germany of the conscious resistance of the earthy-irrational, the popular and the permanent (*des Erdhaften-Irrationalen, des Volkstümlichen und Bodenständigen*) to the rational, abstracting and generalizing spirit."[4]

Meinecke's historicist interpretation was possible because it took Möser out of his own intellectual context. Meinecke tended, in particular, to underestimate Möser's dependence on the older historiographical traditions of imperial reform (*Reichspublizistik*), imperial history (*Reichshistorie*), and Latin humanism. My concern in this chapter is to restore the Osnabrück context of Möser's history, showing how it produces a different reading of Möser's work. In the first section, I examine the genesis and political context of the *Osnabrück History*; in the second, I isolate the central interpretive themes from the 1760s, particularly Möser's defense of the Estates, and examine how these themes could be reformulated in the service of a developing historicism; and in the third, finally, I consider the broader importance of the *Osnabrück History* within Enlightenment historiography.

## GENESIS AND CONTEXT OF THE *OSNABRÜCK HISTORY*

Precisely when the themes of the *Osnabrück History* began to assume importance for Möser is not completely clear. We saw in Chapter 2 that the study of local

---

"Zwischen Historismus und politscher Geschichtsschreibung," *Osn. Mitt.*, 82 (1976):60–80, and "Geschichte und Gegenwart bei Justus Möser," *Osn. Mitt.*, 83 (1977):94–116. The Göttingen thesis by Fritz Rinck is mostly a collection of quotations; see his *Justus Mösers Geschichtsauffassung* (Erfurt, 1908).

The older literature is often flawed by ideological presuppositions and an inadequate understanding of historical writing in the eighteenth century: especially Hans Baron, previously cited in this note; Peter Klassen, *Justus Möser* (Frankfurt am Main, 1936); and Carlo Antoni, *Der Kampf Wider die Vernunft*, trans. Walter Goetz (Stuttgart, 1951), 103–58.

[3] Meinecke, *Entstehung des Historismus*, 316–18, 320–5.

[4] Friedrich Meinecke, *Zur Theorie und Philosophie der Geschichte*, ed. Eberhard Kessel (Stuttgart, 1959), 244.

history formed part of the education of Osnabrück's legal notability. Möser's own father participated in this tradition: he had written an extensive introduction to Osnabrück's ecclesiastical legal code as part of Gottfried Mascov's *Notitia Iuris et Iudicorum Brunsvico-Luneburgensicorum* (1738). Beginning in Latin school, Justus also showed particular interest in the classical sources of local history and pride: Tacitus's *Germania* and the Arminius legend. Later, while studying in Jena, he heard C. G. Buder's lectures on the art of history, and he attended in Göttingen the lectures of J. D. Köhler on German imperial history. He may well have heard other scholars in the field. In any case, we know that he possessed the works of B. G. Struve, the legal historian of the Empire, who died in Jena shortly before Möser's arrival there, as well as works by C. G. Buder, Köhler's and J. J. Schmauβ's introductions to German imperial history, and C. G. Gebauer's published lectures on Tacitus's *Germania*.[5] In the 1740s, the first fruits of his reading began to appear: a treatise on the religion of the ancient Germans and a play, *Arminius*, which survives only in part. Fragments from the 1750s show that he began to write the history of Osnabrück based on the narrative models of the imperial historians;[6] in this he was spurred on by the researches of his childhood friend, K. G. Lodtmann, who was writing a history of Osnabrück at the time of his premature death.[7]

Yet none of these early efforts led directly to the *Osnabrück History*. They served instead as intellectual resources for Möser's later attempts to interpret the transfer of authority to Protestant Hanover and the constitutional crisis over the regency. We know from Möser's letters that he began to formulate the ideas of the *Osnabrück History* during the Seven Years War, writing the early drafts on his trips to and from the camps of the occupying armies.[8] The Seven Years War underscored the political weakness of the Empire and the dependence of the Westphalian region on the outside warring powers. The succession crisis juxtaposed competing Catholic and Protestant explanations of political authority. The alternative allegiance to Hanover and the constitutional struggle in the Imperial Diet raised additional questions regarding the subordination of the region to the dynastic interests of the Empire. All these issues forced Möser to search for the origins of political authority and to examine the historical pattern of its evolution.

At some point between 1760 and 1763, the various interpretive strands of the *Osnabrück History* came together. We can feel Möser's sense of discovery in a letter he wrote to his patron, K. A. von dem Bussche-Hünnefeld, on the eve of his departure to London (October 1763). This document shows that his historical

---

[5] See the catalogue by Bernhard R. Abeken of that part of Möser's library that was intact in the 1840s: Sta Osn Dep. 58 d A LXXII. For a description of the difficulties of using Abeken's catalogue, see Schmidt, *Möser als Historiker*, 161–4; also Horst Meyer, "Bücher im Leben eines Verwaltungsjuristen. Justus Möser und seine Bibliothek," in *Sammler private und öffenfliche Bibliotheken im 18. Jahrhundert* (Heidelberg, 1979), 149–58.

[6] Möser, *SW*, 14/1:249–76. See also Schmidt, *Möser als Historiker*, 23–30, 59–60.

[7] See Möser's admission in the preface to the *Osnabrück History*, *SW*, 12/1:31.

[8] Ibid., 32; also Möser, *Briefe*, 241–2.

insights were newly won and were linked closely to the unresolved succession crisis. After sketching some of the momentary issues of the crisis, Möser revealed that Privy Councillor von Lenthe had offered him a prominent role in the new administration. He had decided to refuse the position, he explained, in order to find time to write a history of Osnabrück: "that is my main concern, because I have fallen in love with the history of the bishopric and have discovered a totally new, quite intriguing theory. In it I completely overturn all previous systems of imperial and regional history; restrict imper[ial] and territorial sov[ereign] rights from completely new principles; and restore to Germany the *nobles* and *commons* that have survived in England, Sweden, and Poland, by showing convincingly that, although the Franks suppressed both imperial Estates, they survived until the Westphalian Peace."[9]

Beyond this indication, however, the record of Möser's thoughts and "innumerable attempts," as he called them, have disappeared; what remains appears largely in the letters from 1764 and early 1765 that he wrote to his young friend Thomas Abbt after returning from England. Abbt had announced his intention to abandon philosophy for "philosophical history," and Möser was concerned with putting his friend's feet on the ground. The letters have a strong didactic tone; at the same time, they are fragmentary and analogical, confused in their metaphors, and less than concrete, and as semipublic statements they may have only roughly approximated his own intellectual procedures. Nonetheless, the letters give valuable insights into Möser's conceptualization of political power; they treat, in particular, the relative weight of political events in historical narrative and the historian's perception of legal, social, and economic continuities. In an often quoted passage, Möser admonished Abbt not to write dynastic history: "I desire a history of the people and its form of government and view the ruler as an accidental circumstance, who is merely essential in so far as he contributes a certain amount to the alteration of this or that. To this extent he also plays a part in the story; for the rest, however, he is only a mile marker which must stand at the side of the highway. You will gain a great deal . . . if you give *tableaux historiques des périodes* in such a manner and then drag the mile markers along afterward."[10]

Thus there were direct ties between the legal pamphlets of the succession crisis and the *Osnabrück History*. Both the pamphlets and the *History* were written in the mid–1760s, and both concerned the same problems. Yet they differed in genre and function. The pamphlets and briefs were partisan justifications for the political legitimacy of the ecclesiastical states within a Protestant Germany. As such they argued for the political and paternal rights of the Hanoverian Crown against the inappropriate claims of the cathedral chapter. The *Osnabrück History*, on the other hand, although adopting the Protestant premises of the tracts, went beyond political immediacy to reconceive the history of the bishopric in a far

[9] Möser, *Briefe*, 424.
[10] Ibid., 190

more substantial manner. But here too the purpose was to show the secular origins of political society and to argue in particular that the emergence of clerical power represented the loss of an original common freedom and that ecclesiastical centers of authority — bishop and cathedral chapter — were only individual constituents in the institutional world of the Estates. Indeed, Möser's intent was even more radical, for the first part of the *Osnabrück History*, the "Short Introduction to the Oldest Constitution," ends by showing the irrelevance of an ecclesiastical interpretation of Osnabrück's constitution.

In our bishopric [Möser wrote,] the bishop has a particular relationship to his cathedral chapter, a different one with his imperial vassals, another one with the nobility, who are bound with him to the administration of the local peace and some of whom in the course of time have been bound through oaths to him, as will emerge from the history. Yet all of these special relationships do not comprise institutions of the commonweal (*gemeine Landesversammlung*) which the bishop calls together as the invested judge — or duke — and whose true object is not the church books (*Kirchenorbar*), not the allode, not the benefice, but the common military system and its defense as part of the public burdens. That today the militia system (*Wehre*) is often separated from the estate and belongs to a seigneur of clerical, noble, or burgher origins, and that secondary ties have created three estates in the general collectivity are as much accidental occurrences as the fact that nobles [became] knights and only certain families [became] eligible to sit in the Diet. These three Estates have indeed existed for a long time, and each has its special context. In the common collectivity, however, they appeared merely, as in the march, as property holders for the militia; I will follow this strand throughout history.[11]

This quotation contains in compressed form Möser's explanation of the evolution of Osnabrück's political institutions. He assumed a secular, pre-Christian founding in the militia system and the settlement of the land; this was the historical, legal contract that still bound the present, legitimated the Estates in his own day and clarified contemporary rights and obligations. As we will see, the centrality of the militia system in Möser's interpretive framework reflects the strength of his ties to the tradition of humanist historiography. At this point, however, I must stress that most later readers, including Meinecke, have underestimated Möser's intellectual achievement in the *Osnabrück History*, because they have rarely, if ever, read the work in the context of the succession crisis. Only in this context can we appreciate Möser's conscious intention: to write the secular history of an *ecclesiastical* state. Clearly, a salvational history (*Heilsgeschichte*) of Osnabrück in the manner of Vico's *New Science* or Lessing's metahistorical speculations was not significant to a concrete historian like Möser; but even from the perspective of institutional history, Möser concluded that an ecclesiastical history of Osnabrück was not central to the bishopric's drama. His studied avoidance of ecclesiastical issues becomes even more apparent when we compare the *Osnabrück History* to another contemporary history of an ecclesiastical principality, Johann

---

[11] Möser, *SW*, 12/1:130.

Franz Thaddäus von Kleinmayr's *Staat von Salzburg* (1770).[12] Von Kleinmayr organized his account around the juridical history of ecclesiastical Salzburg and a description of the rights of the archbishop against Bavarian counterclaims. For obvious reasons, such an approach was closed to Möser. A Protestant account of Osnabrück, which accepted religious pluralism, the alternating succession, and corule with the Estates, had to be constructed on entirely different principles.

## PARTICULARISM AND THE DEFENSE OF THE ESTATES

Questioning the Catholic canonical position from the point of view of the Protestant Estates led Möser to search for broader patterns that might explain the evolution of authority. Ultimately, he came to idealize the institutional arrangements of the Saxon tribes prior to the Carolingian conquest. The period was critical, in his view, because "freedom and property" achieved institutional form in the militia system, and this cultural moment provided the necessary beginning point to motivate a historical narrative with its terminus in the stable world of the eighteenth-century Estates. But the reader unfamiliar with the *Osnabrück History* should be aware that Möser's broad interpretive schema was never completely traced out in empirical detail. As his researches grew, the small general introduction of 1765 became the volume of 1768; this edition was revised and expanded to become the two-volume edition of 1780; and he was working on a third volume at the time of his death. In spite of the expansion in size, the work never went beyond the mid-thirteenth century. Moreover there remained unintegrated explanatory layers in the *Osnabrück History* that reflected the various historiographical traditions Möser combined with his own substantial historical imagination. We can isolate at least three traditions that served as sources for Möser's work: the political Aristotelianism of the imperial reform literature (*Reichspublizistik*), the tradition of imperial history (*Reichshistorie*), and the older humanist historiography. None of these strains is completely distinct. We might add to them a fourth, indistinct interpretive tradition of "civic republicanisms" which Möser does not seem to have appropriated consciously but which emerges in muted form from the other interpretive traditions.

The *Reichspublizistik*, the literature concerning imperial reform, was generally written in terms of Aristotle's *Politics*.[13] This explanatory tradition had retained

[12] Johann Franz Thaddäus Kleinmayr, *Unpartheyische Abhandlung von dem Staate des hohen Erzstifts Salzburg und dessen Grundverfassung zur rechtlich- und geschichtsmäßigen Prüfung des sogenannten Iuris Regii der Herzoge in Baiern, entworfen, im Jahre 1765* ([Salzburg,] 1770).

[13] Concerning the Aristotelian political tradition in general, see Manfred Riedel, *Metaphysik und Metapolitik* (Frankfurt am Main, 1975), 109–66. Concerning the *Reichspublizistik*, see the valuable introduction by Harry Bresslau to his edition of Severinus von Monzambano (Samuel von Pufendorf), *Ueber die Verfassung des deutschen Reiches*, in *Klassiker der Politik*, ed. Friedrich Meinecke and Hermann Oncken, vol.3 (Berlin, 1922), 7*–53*; also E. R. Huber, "Reich, Volk und Staat in der Reichsrechtswissenschaft des 17. und 18. Jahrhunderts," *Zeitschrift der gesamten Staatswissenschaft*, 102 (1942):596–9; Erik Wolf, "Idee und Wirklichkeit des Reiches im deutschen Rechtsdenken des 16. und 17. Jahrhunderts," in *Reich und Recht in der deutschen Philosophie*, ed. Karl Larenz, 2 vols. (Berlin, 1943), 1:93–133.

its force for a number of reasons. It linked history and ethics by examining the fate of virtue in the moral community (the *koinonica politike* or *societas civilis*), and it provided rationalistic criteria for the analysis and criticism of public life. Furthermore, its Aristotelian language was loosely tied to the corporate social order in Germany. The pamphlet works of Pufendorf and Chemnitz, seventeenth-century polemics that were reprinted often in the eighteenth century, are good examples of this literature. Their central question concerned the form of the Empire. Was it aristocratic, monarchic, or democratic? What was the reason and purpose of each imperial Estate? Chemnitz and Pufendorf supplied differing answers, each of which was in its own way typical: Chemnitz sought to prove that the Empire was an aristocracy whose function had been usurped by the emperor; Pufendorf, on the other hand, described it as an "irregular, monster-like hybrid" doomed to remain in a "situation of permanent conflict."[14]

Given the institutional complexity of the German Empire, such taxonomic criticism did little to promote historical explanation. The legal historian H. E. Feine noted for this reason that whenever the Aristotelian language survived in enlightened thought, it was a sign of a basic hostility toward the hybrid institutions of the Empire.[15] By its very nature, moreover, political Aristotelianism was focused on the imperial center rather than on the constituent regions. Whatever the exact reasons, Möser avoided Aristotelian political categories in the *Osnabrück History*,[16] although he did adopt the critical perspective of the imperial reformers as, for example, when he lamented the legal confusion that reigned in eighteenth-century Germany, when he linked together virtue and form in the ancient Germanic community, and when he discussed the structure of the imperial nobility.

Otherwise, the language of the imperial reformers has little direct resonance in the *Osnabrück History*, because Möser's concern was with the evolution of local authority and not with taxonomy at the level of the Empire. Nonetheless, once we examine the political ideal of the ancient Germanic community in the *Osnabrück History*, we must qualify this statement. Then we can see that there was a deeper affinity to the Aristotelian *Reichspublizistik*. First, the Aristotelian analytical framework survived in Tacitus's description of *libertas* in the *Germania* to serve as the point of departure for Möser's ideas on freedom; second, the attempt to link political form to societal virtue also infused the language of

---

[14] [Pufendorf], *Ueber die Verfassung des deutschen Reiches*, ed. Bresslau, chap. 6, par. 9, 94. For a problem-oriented analysis, see also Wolfgang Sauer, "Das Problem des deutschen Nationalstaates," in *Moderne deutsche Sozialgeschichte*, ed. Hans Ulrich Wehler (Cologne, 1966), 410–15; Meinecke, *Die Idee der Staatsräson in der neueren Geschichte*, ed. Walther Hofer (3rd ed.; Munich, 1963), 264–86; Hanns Gross, "The Holy Roman Empire in Modern Times: Constitutional Reality and Legal Theory," in *The Old Reich*, ed. James Vann and Steven Rowan (Brussels, 1974), 3–29.

[15] Hans Erich Feine, "Zur Verfassungsentwicklung des Heiligen Römischen Reiches seit dem Westfälischen Frieden," *ZSRG (germ)*, 52 (1932):72–4, 84.

[16] We find it in only one place in his correspondence with Thomas Abbt when, as an echo of Polybius's cyclical theory of constitutional decay, he wrote that "freedom is youth and despotism old age." See Möser, *Briefe*, 198.

humanistic historiography.[17] Möser explored the virtue of the ancient Germanic commonwealth in the *Osnabrück History*; this was a chief question. But he also rejected the urban dimension, for the rural world of the ancient Germans became a mirror image of the polis and thus a countermyth to the urban republicanism that had emerged in early modern Europe from reflecting on the Aristotelian political tradition.

Much more directly significant to Möser was imperial history (*Reichshistorie*) as it was still written in his day.[18] Its central concerns were exactly those of Möser in the *Osnabrück History*: to discover the origins of German law in the pre-Carolingian past, to trace the evolution of the political community over time, to explore the discrepancy between the Germanic and Roman inheritances, and to examine the struggle between the regions and the central authority. The search for the origins of Germanic law, for instance, led continuously back to Tacitus and Caesar; commenting on these sources promoted the anthropological or broadly material perspective that often seems unique to Möser but that had intimations in the older *Reichshistorie* – in the works, for example, of N. H. Gundling (1708), J. J. Schmauβ (1720), Johann J. Mascov (2nd ed., 1750), and Burghard G. Struve (4th ed., 1747) contained in Möser's library.[19] These historians of the Empire also sought to solve the narrative problem posed by the enormous chronological sweep from Germanic beginnings to the post-Westphalian era by dividing imperial history into various ages or periods. Thus where Schmauβ's history had ten periods or Köhler's had nine, Möser proclaimed his explanatory superiority in reducing the number of periods to four.[20]

The periodization in these works was often based on dynastic changes and had little internal coherence; at times, however, the imperial historians were subtler,

[17] E. g., Möser, *SW*, 12/1:41–2. The *Germania* represented only one small part of Tacitus's significance in the early modern period; concerning the general problem, see Else-Lilly Etter, *Tacitus in der Geistesgeschichte des 16. und 17. Jahrhunderts*, in *Basler Beiträge zur Geschichtswissenschaft*, 103 (Basel, 1966), 5–26, 149–95.

[18] Of the large literature dealing with *Reichshistorie* and individual historians of the Empire, valuable are the general comments by Karl Otmar von Aretin, *Heiliges Römisches Reich 1776–1806*, 2 vols. (Wiesbaden, 1967), 1:94–6. Of the interpretive works, see especially Notker Hammerstein, *Jus und Historie* (Göttingen, 1972); Ernst Landsberg, *Geschichte der deutschen Rechtswissenschaft*, 3 vols. in 4 (Munich, 1880–1910); Reinhard Rürup, *Johann Jakob Moser* (Wiesbaden, 1965), 110–19, 141–52; Lotte Hiller, *Die Geschichtswissenschaft an der Universität Jena in der Zeit der Polyhistorie 1674–1763*, in *Zeitschrift des Vereins für Thüringische Geschichte und Altertumskunde*, n.s., suppl. 18 (Jena, 1937); Carlo Antoni, *Der Kampf wider die Vernunft*, 89–102. Of the works in English, Hanns Gross's is especially good for the period before 1750, and Mack Walker's study treats the internal logic of Johann Jakob Möser's views of history and the Empire. See Hanns Gross, *Empire and Sovereignty* (Chicago, 1973), esp. 427–65 for the period after 1750; and Mack Walker, *Johann Jakob Möser and the Holy Roman Empire of the German Nation* (Chapel Hill, N.C., 1981), 112–52, 283–309.

[19] N. H. Gundling, *Abriβ zu einer rechten Reichshistorie* (Halle, 1708); Johann Jakob Schmauβ, *Kurzter Begriff der Reichshistorie* (Leipzig, 1720); J. J. Mascov, *Geschichte der Teutschen bis zum Abgang der Merowingischen Könige in sechzehn Büchern verfasset*, 2 vols (2nd ed.; Leipzig, 1750); Burcard Gotthelf Struve, *Einleitung zur Teutschen Reichs-Historie* (4th ed.; Jena, 1747). See also footnote 5.

[20] Johann David Köhler, *Kurzgefaβte und gründliche Teutsche Reichshistorie* (Frankfurt, 1737), 21; Schmauβ, *Kurzter Begriff der Reichshistorie*, 3; Möser, *SW*,2/1:35.

arguing that chronology and structure were directly interrelated. Thus Schmauβ announced that his work was a great improvement on that of his predecessors, because it explained the relationships between events. "The business of war and peace," he wrote, "spiritual and worldy matters, and in a word, everything which makes its appearance in history have their movement, drive and motivation. Whoever isolates these matters one from another wrests the true causes from the narrative; and where these are lacking, history lacks soul and life."[21] Schmauβ's explanations, however, like those of the entire tradition of imperial history, remained focused on political narrative. Schmauβ told the reader of his *Kurzter Begriff der Reichshistorie* (*Short Outline of Imperial History*) (1720) that political events in a republic could be conceived from the point of view of either internal constitutional development or foreign policy. The historian must master both perspectives in a "manner which reveals their connections from the earliest to the most recent times, because each event precipitates the next." Only then can his work be called "pragmatic," because "only then does it reveal its usefulness to the *Jure publico* of an imperium, in that most materials are displayed simultaneously with their *rationes a priori*."[22] In order for a German imperial history to be pragmatic, Schmauβ concluded, "it must be written with a view toward the contemporary constitution and all of its parts, and the origins and alterations from one period to the next should be noted and conclusions drawn continuously with respect to the *Jus publicum*."[23]

Möser accepted the analytical ideal of the imperial historians in his *Osnabrück History*. He too wanted to write history that was "pragmatic" or explanatory, but he rejected the political and dynastic framework of imperial history. He had expressed this position in the correspondence with Abbt when he claimed that the ruler is an "accidental circumstance" in the history of a people and its form of government. Elsewhere he complained even more caustically to Abbt: "our German historians diddle with the genealogies of imperial officials [i.e., heads of regional dynasties] and believe in that to be producing a history of the nation."[24] He wrote in the same vein to Klamor v. d. Bussche-Hünnefeld that he wanted to study the bishopric's history from the perspective of the Estates rather than of the ruler: "my inclination has never been *pro principe*, but always *pro statibus*."[25]

Thus the enormous silence with respect to the church bounds only one side of the *Osnabrück History*; Möser refused equally strongly to make the history of the sovereignty of the episcopal center the focus of his account. Instead he adopted

---

[21] Schmauβ, *Kurzter Begriff der Reichshistorie*, 20.

[22] Ibid., 2–3 (parts 6 and 7).

[23] Ibid., 3 (part 8). See the similar conclusion in Johann Stephen Pütter, *Vollständiges Handbuch der Teutschen Reichshistorie* (Göttingen, 1726), 1, par. 1: "Die Teutsche Reichshistorie oder die Geschichte des Teutschen Reichs hat zu ihrem eigentlichen Gegenstande, daβ man diejenige Begebenheiten in ihrem Zusammenhange kennen lerne, welche dazu dienen, den heutigen Zustande des Teutschen Reichs aus seinen Gründen einzusehen."

[24] Möser, *Briefe*, 146.

[25] Ibid., 424.

the perspective of the Protestant Estates, especially that of the nobility, the *Ritterschaft*. For this reason, his history was rightly viewed by the young Herder as antiabsolutist in intent. Möser focused on the evolution of the military institutions among the ancient Saxons – their "national militia," as he called it – in order to show how the gradual militarization of their society in the wars with the Franks and thereafter led to the loss of "freedom and property." As he expressed it to his friend Nicolai years later,

People will believe that I prattle too much of militia (*Heerbann*) and professional military retainers (*Dienstmannschaft*), and yet this alone gives me the powerful [thread] – and for a small provincial history a far too powerful thread . . . . Our entire system of taxation and transportation, nobility and serfdom, in short everything which touches freedom and property in any way, evolved from this single thread; thus I am simply describing the physical history of a political structure (*Verfassung*). Every history must become the natural history of a nation's original contract through all its actual changes if, in the real sense, it is ever to be pragmatic.[26]

The explanatory intent of the *Osnabrück History*, in other words, was pacific. In place of a conquering dynasty, Möser studied the semiautonomous Estates and the other regional peculiarities that had prevented an all-powerful monarchy from dominating the region. The settlement of the land, the "natural," essentially peaceful evolution of the social estates, geography, trade, and productive life: these dominate the narrative, whereas powerful dynasties become the subversive carriers of political despotism, undermining the collective life of the region.

To Möser, then, particularism and its actual or potential destruction by centralizing monarchies became the powerful secular theme of German history. The "General Introduction" of 1768 begins with this assertion:

The history of Germany can hope to take an entirely new turn, in my estimation, if we examine through all their changes the common landed proprietors – if we construct the body from them and view the great and obscure servants of this nation as bad or good accidents of the body. We can then not only give to this history the unity, movement and power of an epic (*Epopee*), where territorial sovereignty and despotism ultimately take their place as either a fortunate or disastrous resolution; we can also develop with much greater clarity and order the progress and varied relations of the national character.[27]

What follows in the "Preface" is a highly compressed account of imperial history conceived in terms of the fate of "freedom and property." In the manner of the imperial historians, Möser sketched through four "ages" the transformation of local institutions. Möser began with the destruction of communal Saxon society during the years of war with Charlemagne and the period of continued struggle under the immediate heirs to the Carolingian conquest, the sons of Louis the Pious. He recorded the loss of political liberty and property rights as Frankish legal relations were gradually imposed on the conquered Saxon tribes. The social

[26] Ibid., 321. See also the introductory comments by Paul Göttsching in *SW*, 12/2:20.
[27] Möser, *SW*, 12/1:34.

and legal institutions of feudalism – the coercive apparatus created by a society organized for perpetual warfare – became for Möser the motor force of despotism, and, he argued, it was not until an effective territorial sovereignty (*Landeshoheit*) emerged in the fifteenth century as a counterweight to imperial pretensions that the era of imperial despotism began to wane. The appearance of the Estates and the confessional dualism ushered in by the Reformation created, in Möser's eyes, the institutional checks and balances needed to restrain arbitrary authority. Finally, the rigidification of this political world after the Thirty Years War became the guarantee of local political freedom.

Möser's dating in the sketch was quite imprecise: he found it far more important to use the broad political chronology of the four ages to structure the institutional pattern of political freedom than to offer an exact historical periodization. For Möser the evolution of political consciousness, interpreted in the accustomed mode as the link between virtue and institutions, was the deeper parallel account. Thus freedom also had four ages, and here also Möser's account lacks clarity; he is imprecise not only in his chronological boundaries but also in his use of the word "freedom" itself, which is at times contrasted to and at times identified with Germanic "honor." In the first or "golden" age, honor (*Ehre*) was the profounder communal virtue, whereas freedom meant only exclusion from the community. Honor existed for all within a community organized in equality and mutuality for aid and the common good. Each proprietor was dependent upon the other, and, according to Möser, "all freedom [was] hated as a disgraceful exception to the common defense." In the second period, starting with the Carolingian conquest, honor began to disappear. The commons (*Gemeine*), in the sense of both land and population, were squandered to the avarice of the clergy, royal servants, and imperial stewards (*Reichsvogte*). The local militia (*Wehre*) was suppressed and replaced by the imperial military system. In the following period, that of fully developed feudalism, "common honor" all but disappeared: "Lost was even the name and the true conception of property, and the entire imperial realm was transformed everywhere into feudal estates, leaseholds, copyholds, and peasant farms, as it pleased the head of the Empire and his vassals."[28]

As devastating to the commons as the growth of feudal militarism was the emergence of a "monied economy" spearheaded by the cities, "these anomalistic bodies which for so long the Saxons had not wanted to tolerate."[29] The urban economy altered relations of authority, so that "monied interests" outweighed landed property and distorted the original legal relations in response to the power of the cities. Honor was gradually replaced by newer notions of dependence; "freedom suffered uncommonly thereby, and the entire state opposed a new conception (*Verfassung*), wherein gradually every person was to be accepted as a citizen or legal peer, exactly as under the later Roman emperors, and his obligation

[28] Ibid., 36.
[29] Ibid., 38.

and duty was to be founded merely on his quality as subject."[30] From this struggle among the various factions emerged the fourth period, the period of "fortunate" territorial sovereignty. The imperial stewards, who eventually became the territorial sovereigns or *Landesherren*, created order and stability, effecting a lasting counterbalance to imperial arbitrariness. In the process, however, they also contributed to the disappearance of the older concepts of honor and property.

Meanwhile in this period, [Möser concluded,] the old concept of property completely lost its meaning; it was barely perceived that one must be a legal peer in order to have rightful property. The same [loss of meaning] occurred with respect to noble as well as to common honor. The first transformed itself almost completely into freedom; of the latter, *honore quiritario* [Roman honor], we have barely intimations, in spite of the fact that it was the spirit of the German constitution and should have remained forever. Religion and the sciences elevated man more and more over the citizen; the rights of mankind triumphed over all limited (*bedungene*) and judicated law. An easy philosophy supported conclusions from general principles better than those which could not be made without erudition and judgment.[31]

In this account we can see not only the framework of German *Reichshistorie*, but also the familiar elements of Latin humanist history in combination with the amorphous traditions of civic republicanism that pervaded seventeenth- and eighteenth-century constitutional debate. These last constitute a third historiographical cluster of themes that Möser drew upon in his *Osnabrück History*. Since a number of recent studies have explored these traditions,[32] I need only remind the reader of the structural elements appropriated by Möser: the myth of a free Germanic community composed of freeholders in arms; the sense of the reciprocal dependence of communal virtue on the bearing of arms; the feeling that landed property was the force of communal stability, whereas movable property was a source of instability; the explanation that electoral democracy and political freedom were "lost" through conquest and usurpation; the notion that some traces

---

[30] Ibid., 38.

[31] Ibid., 41.

[32] See especially J. G. A. Pocock, *The Machiavellian Moment* (Princeton, N. J., 1975), 3–86 and bibliography; also the same author's introduction to his edition of *The Political Works of James Harrington* (Cambridge, 1977), 15–76, 128–52. Pocock's influential and valuable work must be read with a certain care, since he is forced to write at a very high level of abstraction in order to demonstrate the coherence of the traditions of civic republicanism. As a result, he tends to ignore the historical phases of the tradition, especially the differing intellectual and political purposes to which the tradition was put. See the criticisms by Issac Kramnick, "Republican Revisionism Revisited," *AHR*, 87 (1982):630–4; and Horst Dippel, *Individuum und Gesellschaft. Soziales Denken zwischen Tradition und Revolution*, in *Veröffentlichungen des Max-Planck-Instituts für Geschichte*, 70 (Gottingen, 1981), part 1.

Also suggestive are the older works of Zera Fink, *The Classical Republicans*, in *Northwestern University Studies in the Humanities*, 9 (Evanston, Ill., 1945); and Christopher Hill, "The Norman Yoke," in his *Puritanism and Revolution* (New York, 1958), 50–122.

Concerning Germany, see the studies by Erwin Hölzle, *Die Idee einer altgermanischen Freiheit vor Montesquieu* (Munich, 1925), 1–11; Kurt von Raumer, "Absoluter Staat, korporative Libertät, persönliche Freiheit," *HZ*, 183 (1957):55–96; and Rudolf Vierhaus, "Montesquieu in Deutschland," in *Collegium Philosophicum*, ed. Ernst-Wolfgang Böckenförde et al. (Basel, 1965), 403–37.

of this freedom still survived in property law and in the politically organized intermediate bodies; the guiding idea that political life was to be interpreted within the framework of the mixed constitution; and the view that this mixed constitution was restored in Germany in the period after the Reformation, and especially after the Westphalian Peace. Möser used the political language of "court" and "country," in other words, to structure his account of Osnabrück's struggle between the imperial center and the regional nobility.

We find these elements in various combinations everywhere in the political and historical literature of Western Europe, from the Latin writings of Conring in Germany to Harrington's *Oceana* in England. Möser saw himself as writing in this tradition. He was a German Harrington, defending the agrarian state by adapting the general structure of agrarian republicanism to his own cultural setting. He consciously compared his work to English accounts of the Norman yoke and the balanced constitution, basing his own version of these English themes, like other German writers, on Tacitus. We can also glimpse something of his comparative intention in a letter written from England to Thomas Abbt: "In England I often diverted myself by untying the knots [at those places] where Hume made his ignorance known. I worked there," he explained to Abbt, "to compare the consequences of the institutions [founded by] William the Conqueror with those [founded by] Charlemagne and to find the causes of the differing results. Both were Franks, both conquerors, both instituted *comitatus* [counties] and other closed districts; yet in England there are *communes* and in Germany there are not. Hume falters here, as an Englishman who knows nothing outside his own country."[33] These reflections find their echo in paragraph 55 of the "Introduction to the Oldest Constitution," where Möser took Hume to task for not understanding the legal continuity of nobles and commons.[34]

But Möser's use of this tradition was very narrow. Indeed, the juridical framework that he assumed from the imperial historians and from the legal conflict of the succession crisis restricted his full appropriation of this tradition; it negated historical development and confined his perspective to a search for points of institutional and legal continuity with the distant past. This narrowing created a paradoxical movement in the *Osnabrück History*, for though the historical motivation lay in the present, Möser closed the present to change by shifting the justification for the present to far in the past. Consequently there was a rupture in explanation between past and present, even as he attempted to demonstrate continuity. In a typical humanist manner, he identified this rupture as much in philological as in substantive terms. He lamented in the "Preface," "What I felt most of all was this: that our language had become a traitor to [our] noble freedom (*edlen Freiheit*) and had lost the meaning which corresponded to my concepts."[35] In the next sentence, he expressed his dilemma as explicitly philological: "The oldest his-

[33] Möser, *Briefe*, 146.
[34] Möser, *SW*, 12/1:129n.
[35] Ibid., 33.

torians of Germany did not write in our language and consequently gave to the strong German constitution (*Körper*) a wholly alien coloration."[36]

These words remind us of Valla's recognition that "none of the words of Christ have come down to us, for Christ spoke in Hebrew and never wrote down anything";[37] in Möser's hands, however, their purpose was obfuscatory, because they allowed him to invert meanings and thereby to overcome the separation between present and past. He tried to recover ancient Germanic meanings for the militia system, freedom and unfreedom, lordship and bondage, honor and service. Accordingly, much of the argument he conducted in the footnotes took a philological form and involved the explanation of terms that, as his concern underlined, were clearly no longer readily comprehensible to his audience. This "recovery" of meanings had the general ideological function of demonstrating the restoration of the balance between nobles and commons in the period after the Westphalian Peace. Yet the sense of "commons" recovered by Möser proved not to be the commonalty as it existed in the eighteenth century but, from the perspective of the Empire, the property-holding aristocracy who were heirs on their estates to the original pre-Carolingian separation between nobles and commons. Similarly, the "nobles" were identified with the various rulers of the states and principalities of the Empire. Although this may not have been a historical misinterpretation in legal terms, its principal effect was to deny legitimacy to the struggle for rights by the eighteenth-century commons.

In searching for the political legitimacy of the world of the Estates, Möser was trapped by his narrow juridical framework. He could not allow for cultural change, for the evolution of society and the expansion of rights, since he upheld the exclusive right of the nobility to corule with the bishop. Thus his work was fundamentally regressive in character, because historical change was viewed only as the erosion of rights that had an arbitrary legitimacy in the original settlement of the Westphalian region. In the 1760s this antagonism to future political change could still be expressed in the language of the mixed constitution or of court and country; with its appeals to civic virtue and its attacks on corruption and movable wealth, moreover, it retained the radical rhetorical stance that marked its historical genesis in the seventeenth century.[38] By the later eighteenth century, however, its function had changed. Where the rhetoric of court and country survived in a form untouched by or hostile to natural rights theory, it began increasingly to be a sign of political conservatism.[39] The discussion of

---

[36] Ibid., 33–4.

[37] Quoted in Pocock, *Machiavellian Moment*, 61.

[38] These arguments have been best studied in their English context. See Perez Zagorin, *The Court and the Country* (New York, 1970), esp. 19–40, 198–250; Felix Raab, *The English Face of Machiavelli* (London, 1964); Fink, *Classical Republicans;* Issac Kramnick, *Bolingbroke and His Circle* (Cambridge, Mass., 1968).

[39] Again, these arguments have best been analyzed for England. See Kramnick's essay "Republican Revisionism Revisited," 630–1, 635–9, 661–4, which traces the revival of Lockean natural rights speculation and the corresponding transformation of republican ethical ideas into ones of political and class interest. Also valuable is the detailed political history of radical agitation for parliamentary

rights in the later eighteenth century simply could not be conducted without attacking the balanced constitution. In Germany this meant an attack on the institutional world of the Estates; in England, similarly, it meant an attack on the oligarchical nature of Commons or the powers of the monarchy. In order to argue for the expansion of rights in Germany, one had to extend either the power of the monnarchy with respect to the Estates or the idea of participation within the Estates themselves. Conversely, using the once progressive language of court and country to protect the Estates without change required one to place political and historical questions surrounding their continued legitimacy outside one's work. It became more and more difficult to use this language in the service of freedom and property while retaining any claim to universality; instead the rhetoric of court and country became the language of oligarchical self-interest. This defense of privilege, implicit in the *Osnabrück History*, became increasingly transparent in Möser's later political writings and, as we will see, provoked criticism by his more progressive contemporaries.

While criticizing the present in the language of the mixed constitution, Möser simultaneously shifted the problem of explaining it in two directions: on the one hand, as we have seen, he looked backward to the past to discover a political freedom incapable of expansion in the present; on the other, he appealed to the material life of the Westphalian region, to its topography, climate, and natural resources. In both the 1768 and 1780 editions of the *Osnabrück History*, Möser devoted the second part of the first volume to a "Brief Sketch of the Character of the Land." Like the shift backward in time, this description was crucial for justifying the present by rooting in impersonal forces the survival of the world of the Estates. This perspective too represented a survival from humanist historiography; Bruni's panegyric to Florence is a typical example of writing where geography served as the explanation for the greatness of the city-state.[40]

Like the earlier humanists, Möser did not always argue his case forcefully or harness his evidence systematically. We learn marvelously irrelevant details in the course of his description: petrified seashells are brought forth; etymologies are explained in physical terms. We learn that the English word "quake" (lower Saxon "Kuak") is derived from the sound of shifting earth in the moors, and we discover at the same time that the ancient Greeks had a lower Saxon pronunciation, whereas the Romans did not. Amazingly, salmon reached Osnabrück in 1764.

---

reform and the extension of the franchise by John Brewer, *Party Ideology and Popular Politics at the Accession of George III* (Cambridge, 1976).

[40] Leonardo Bruni, *Panegyric to the City of Florence*, trans. Benjamin G. Kohl, in *The Earthly Republic*, ed. Benjamin G. Kohl and Ronald G. Witt (Philadelphia, 1978), sec. 1, 135–49. Similar patterns can also be found in Leibniz's historical writings; see Günter Scheel, "Leibniz und die deutsche Geschichtswissenschaft um 1700," in *Historische Forschung im 18. Jahrhundert*, ed. Jurgen Voss and Karl Hammer (Bonn, 1976), 87–8. Given Möser's wide reading in the older Latin humanist historians, in other words, he did not have to read Montesquieu's *Spirit of the Laws* to pursue a geographical argument. On this issue see Peter Hanns Reill, *The German Enlightenment and the Rise of Historicism* (Berkeley, 1975), 136–45.

The best butter and cheese came from Ireland and Frisia.[41] In fact, Möser wrote the entire section from a traveler's perspective. He described the hills, moors, rivers, the plants and the crops, the villages and the peasant homes as they existed in the eighteenth century. Though he traced institutional deterioration over the course of German history, he assumed that the eye of the trained contemporary observer could restore an unstained past.

What actually was physical geography for Möser? It presupposed two related assumptions: first, that there was a single, unified cultural entity between the Weser and the Elbe – a Westphalia; and, second, that the local peasant culture was an emanation of the "natural" character of the land. The landscape of the region and its human culture shared the same conceptual contours, contours that blurred the boundaries of the natural and human worlds. As a result, the narrative flowed inevitably from the strictly geographical to the human. The catalog of the environment was itself an explanation. Here we have a demonstration of Möser's view of the world as one seamless landscape – its objects, places, and people, its events and activities, indistinct and uniform in their "objectivity."

Thus, Möser accomplished eminently political purposes by removing politics from the center of the narrative and replacing it with a geopolitical explanation. Although he believed that the Empire was ultimately weakened by the short-sighted destruction of local autonomy and the institutions of mutuality, he nonetheless retained a curious faith in the power of the region to maintain the constitutional pluralism. It cannot be said, consequently, that Möser's interpretive framework was logically clean. He presupposed a struggle between the region and the center that dated back to the Carolingian conquest. But he never explained how the imperial institutions became powerful enough to destroy the Westphalian commons, and yet never become indigenous to the region itself. As we will see in the next section, contemporaries like J. C. Gatterer pointed out this and other fundamental inconsistencies. But from our point of view, Möser's problems with interpretation lie deeper; his commitment to a legal future without change forced him to develop explanatory hypotheses – of primary and secondary social contracts, of original settlement, conquest, and renewed settlement – in order to justify the pattern of land tenure and political authority in the eighteenth century. The "physical history" of Osnabrück became in this way an idealized justification of eighteenth-century social relations, now perceived as the stable remnant of a once flourishing commons. From this point of view, Möser's work became profoundly unhistorical, and, as we will see later in Chapter 6, his theories could not withstand contemporary criticisms.

### THE ENLIGHTENMENT RESPONSE

Möser's attempt to demonstrate the correspondence between the ancient Germanic commonweal and his own Estatist universe generated a surprisingly flat and static

[41] Möser, *SW*, 12/1:139, 140, 146, 147.

history of the bishopric. Meinecke accounted for this character of Möser's work by referring to the "utilitarian view" that survived in his thought.[42] Yet as we have seen, the static structure of the *Osnabrück History* derived less from an explanatory ideal than from the work's political agenda: Möser's commitment to Osnabrück's political institutions prevented him from exploring the implications of his own historical intuitions. I think this is a major reason why Möser never brought the *History* beyond the thirteenth century and why his account settles in the second volume into political narrative, in the manner of the imperial historians. As we will see in Chapter 6, Möser's historical imagination soared only in those occasional essays of the 1770s and 1780s in which he was not constrained to defend the corporate political order.

Möser's political purposes in the *Osnabrück History* did not go unnoticed by his readers. Johann C. Gatterer, for instance, one of the leading figures in historical studies at the University of Göttingen, wrote a long, graciously critical review of the *History* in 1769 soon after it first appeared.[43] He questioned on scholarly grounds the objectivity of Möser's explanatory pattern. He agreed that a history of the nation from the perspective of property holding was an important undertaking, but he was careful to point out that this perspective proved in Möser's treatment to be a "juridical" one, written to explain the evolution of "corporate freedom."[44] It legitimated the present, he implied, but did not necessarily render an adequate account of the past. Gatterer was thus particularly concerned with correcting Möser's view of the "golden age" of Germanic freedom. In the first place, he rejected Möser's efforts to legitimate Osnabrück's legal institutions on the basis of the original settlement. Indeed, he argued, there was no certainty that the freehold system was original in any sense. Gatterer went so far as to maintain that there had never been a period of common freedom and honor. He supposed rather, on the basis of evidence, that authority and dependence had always existed; thus, rights founded on conquest and usurpation had probably always been part of the Germanic past.[45]

In the second place, Gatterer questioned the legitimacy of Tacitus as a source for establishing a golden age of freedom and property. He saw that the society described by Tacitus in the *Germania* was already fully formed and that, as a result, one would need to go even farther back into unrecorded time to establish the legal origins of the Germanic order.[46] He also concluded that Tacitus should not be taken literally, but should be read with his Roman purposes and prejudices in mind; these, in turn, rendered his description of Germanic liberty suspect. Gatterer doubted, for example, the precision of Tacitus's statement that the

---

[42] Meinecke, *Entstehung des Historismus*, 345, 347.
[43] In Johann C. Gatterer, ed., *Allgemeine Historische Bibliothek*, 9 (Halle, 1769), 67–119. For Gatterer, see Peter Hanns Reill, "History and Hermeneutics: The Thought of Johann Christoph Gatterer," *JMH*, 45 (1973):24–51.
[44] Gatterer, *Allgemeine Historische Bibliothek*, 68 and 82, respectively.
[45] Ibid., 73–4, 88–9.
[46] Ibid., 75.

ancient Germans could not tolerate cities; he pointed out that from a Roman perspective, no German hamlet or village could have been considered a city. He argued by implication, in sum, that Tacitus's account was of little use in establishing a legal framework that could demonstrate Möser's claims.[47]

Gatterer's review was important because it undermined the legitimating power of the distant past for the present. Gatterer sought to keep the bishopric's history open to change in the present by rejecting a direct correspondence between the ancient Germanic order and the world of the eighteenth-century Estates. Furthermore, by restoring inequality to the golden age of freedom and property, he refused to accept the regressive utopian vision of the *Osnabrück History* and thereby returned to the present claims for social and political improvement. Hence his criticism of Möser sketches in embryonic form the debate over rights that gathered force in Europe in the 1770s and 1780s and erupted with the outbreak of the French Revolution. Yet it would be inaccurate to overdramatize the rigor and significance of Gatterer's critique. He expressed a great deal of sympathy for corporate institutions in his review, explicitly rejecting republican government. "We do not know republican freedom," he wrote, "but we also do not know republican tumults; and we prefer to leave our well-being in the hands of our princes rather than in the rhetorical arts of an advocate who places himself in danger of losing his head for his people."[48]

From our point of view, then, the *Osnabrück History* was a work that rested on the traditions of humanist historiography and imperial history rather than one that pointed toward the future. But Möser conveyed his oligarchical attitudes within a quasi-republican narrative structure, and this was the principal reason that his book could be read creatively by Herder and others of the *Sturm und Drang*. They recognized his antiabsolutist perspective and linked his vision of an ancient agrarian republic of soldier-freeholders to the utopia of ancient Sparta that attracted Rousseau, among others.[49] In this way, they could ignore the oligarchical elements in the *Osnabrück History* and accept the language of participation in the distinction between nobles and commons. As long as the institutions of the Empire were not threatened in the years before the French Revolution, the full significance of Möser's position did not need to be explored. But once the revolution broke out, Möser's vision in the *Osnabrück History* became untenable. Then the regional perspective became directly allied to an attack on the cosmopolitan values of the Enlightenment. We will see this argument unfold in the next chapters.

---

[47] Ibid., 75–6.

[48] Ibid., 97.

[49] For the image of Sparta as the model of the mixed constitution and its influence on Rousseau, see Elizabeth Rawson, *The Spartan Tradition in European Thought* (Oxford, 1969), esp. 186–201, 231–41. For Heyne's and Herder's approval of the Spartan constitution, see 311–12. For the influence on Rousseau see also Judith Shklar, *Men and Citizens. A Study of Rousseau's Social Theory* (Cambridge, 1969), 3–5, 12–32, 199–200.

# 5

*The party of incremental movement: social and economic reform in Möser's Osnabrück*

Justus Möser entered the regency at a moment when war had brought Osnabrück's economy near collapse. Forced requisitions by the occupying armies had sorely depleted the population of draught and domestic animals. The production of flax and the number of grazing sheep had fallen dramatically. The cottage linen and woolens industry was severely depressed by the lack of raw materials – bleaching agents, wool, flax – and of capital and entrepreneurial skills. Rural indebtedness had increased sharply, since warfare and occupation had made it impossible for most of the rural population to pay rents, taxes, and personal duties. Finally, the administration of the bishopric and the Estates of the Osnabrück Diet were also deeply in debt from forced loans, actually ransoms, paid to each of the occupying armies.[1]

Collapse was the incentive to reform, and Möser played a central part in the reform effort. His preeminence derived from his superior intellectual gifts, which placed him above the other figures within the administration; from the power exercised through his many offices; and from the special constitutional situation of the regency, during which he acted as the pivotal mediator between the Estates and the Hanoverian government. As we have already noted, he served as syndic and secretary to the *Ritterschaft*, arranging its agenda and preparing its policy recommendations. As chief administrator and consultant to the London chancellery, he was able to force compromises on the two resident privy councillors, since he cast the deciding vote in deadlocked situations. In addition, he formulated the memoranda and legislative drafts that were sent to the German chancellery in London to be transformed into law, and often these drafts were copied verbatim into the final decrees.[2] Afterward, moreover, he was responsible for executing these decrees once they were ratified by the Diet.

[1] Joachim Runge, *Justus Mösers Gewerbetheorie und Gewerbepolitik im Fürstentum Osnabrück in der zweiten Hälfte des 18. Jahrhunderts*, in *Schriften zur Wirtschafts- und Sozialgeschichte*, 2 (Berlin, 1966), 21; Alfred Frankenfeld, *Justus Möser als Staatsmann im Siebenjährigen Krieges* (Göttingen, 1922), 231.

[2] Otto Hatzig, *Justus Möser als Staatsmann und Publizist*, in *Quellen und Darstellungen zur Geschichte Niedersachsens*, 27 (Hanover, 1909), 24; with regard to Osnabrück guild decrees, see Runge, *Justus Mösers Gewerbetheorie*, 51–2.

The Osnabrück newspapers, founded by Möser, and his articles in them also had their place in the bishopric's legislative ritual. Both Möser and the London chancellery viewed them as a way to mobilize local support for economic recovery.[3] They attempted to persuade local readers of needed reforms, explain the reasons behind recent decrees, or justify administrative inactivity. By assuming the voices of the various social interests, Möser was able to constitute public debate and thereby to construct an artificial consensus in a society without real parliamentary give and take. Most of his specific reform essays first appeared during the period of economic recovery from 1767 to 1774. They bear witness to the administrative energies unleashed after the war, and they show the long shadow cast by Möser's figure over reform efforts in the bishopric, even where there is no direct archival evidence of his intervention or participation.

The reforms in Osnabrück were thus largely the work of a single architect. This does not mean, however, that they follow a simple line easily identified with a particular ideology, enlightened or otherwise. In the first place, Möser was not a theoretician.[4] His approach was practical; he sought to work within the system of Estates, sacrificing, in the words of Friedrich Nicolai, "dreams" for "effectiveness."[5] This was typical of administrators in the period, for they, in contrast to the more programmatic pamphlet writers, tended to rest in a world of detailed changes and small beginnings. Describing such details, however, often makes it difficult to locate the larger historical pattern. Furthermore, the pattern of Enlightenment reform reveals generally eclectic and inconsistent practices, and many of its policies were continuous with an older tradition of cameralism. This often makes it difficult to locate the boundaries between the older tradition and the newer demands formulated by the Enlightenment.

In the second place, there was very little administrative leverage for reform within Osnabrück. The situation after the Seven Years War demanded measures of two kinds: short term, to alleviate the disruptions of war, and long term, to attack structural problems in the prewar economy. The bishopric's political system, however, prevented fundamental reform. Because of the independence of the city of Osnabrück, for instance, it was impossible for the episcopal administration to intervene there, either to enforce imperial decrees – such as those

---

[3] See the letters from Minister von Behr in London: Möser, *Briefe*, 227–8, 229; Möser, "Nachricht von der osnabrückischen Brodtaxe" [1767], *SW*, 8:83–4. (Note: the articles are undated in Möser's collected works. Dates are given in brackets so that the reader can keep his views in their historical context.)

[4] The eclectic quality of Möser's reforms allowed Wilhelm Roscher to claim Möser as the "greatest German national economist of the eighteenth century." What appealed to Roscher was precisely Möser's acceptance of "realistic" restraints and slow, incremental change; this, according to Roscher, led him away from useless abstractions and toward a more important preoccupation "with the everyday," with the "ordinary of a people's existence," with the "ethnocultural" (*volkstümlich*). See Wilhelm Roscher, *Geschichte der National-Oekonomik in Deutschland* (Munich, 1874), 502. Schumpeter was more accurate when he wrote: "[Möser] was an excellent man, no doubt, but he was no economist at all." See Joseph Schumpeter, *History of Economic Analysis* (New York, 1954), 174n.

[5] Friedrich Nicolai, *Leben Justus Mösers*, in Möser, *W*, 10.

against illegal guild activities – or to institute much needed uniformities in the economic code. It was equally impossible for the episcopal administration to attack the prerogatives of the cathedral canons and the landed Protestant nobility in order to initiate comprehensive land reform. Above all, it was impossible to undertake basic institutional reform during the regency, since the government had not been accepted by the cathedral chapter.

Thus the reforms after the Seven Years War proved to be limited adjustments. They nonetheless reveal the conflict between entrenched corporate interests and the modest social and economic reform program traditionally associated with the Enlightenment in Germany. It is again broadly typical of the German situation that small adjustments were the rule, whereas fundamental reforms tended everywhere to founder in the realization. Many of the ideas brought forth in the 1760s, 1770s, and 1780s, especially those concerning agrarian reform, were not implemented until the revolutions of 1848. Osnabrück was a case in point. Reform there proved to be narrow, avoiding a basic attack on the political and social prerogatives of the Estates, especially those of the local nobility.

Möser's contribution to the reform movement is significant to an understanding of the societal pressures facing administrators during these years, not the least because he wrote with such clarity about those pressures. Using Möser's newspaper essays, his memoranda and briefs, and the eventual decrees, I examine in this chapter material reform in Osnabrück and Möser's commitment to social and economic change. The chapter begins by describing the overall pattern of his reforms and focuses more specifically in the second, third, and fourth sections on the textile industry, on the effects of rural overpopulation on the large class of wage laborers, and on peasant emancipation. In this way, I explore another dimension of the relationship between corporatism and Enlightenment.

## CAMERALISM AND REGIONALISM IN MÖSER'S POLICIES

The Enlightenment penetrated public administration slowly. By the 1760s only rudimentary notions of the public good had emerged in Germany among its professional administrators.[6] Such ideas appeared more feasible in the large and medium-sized states that could be considered functioning nation-states, but even there, older cameralist or mercantilist views continued to prevail. Administrators saw society and economy as belonging to the exclusive legal domain of the prince. Their authority to act continued to be derived from the paternal powers of the monarch and from the corollary that the economy was a form of private property and an extension of the sovereign's household. Reform, accordingly, was perceived in narrow fiscalist terms, as those improvements that increased princely revenues. In this legal context, economic reform was determined by the will of the sovereign,

[6] Hubert C. Johnson, "The Concept of Bureaucracy in Cameralism," *PSQ*, 79 (1964):378–402, esp. 382–3, 388–9; Marc Raeff, "The Well-Ordered Police State and the Development of Modernity in Seventeenth- and Eighteenth-Century Europe," *AHR*, 80 (1975):1222, 1224–9.

the degree of organized resistance by the Estates, and the extremity of the fiscal or economic crisis confronting the state.

It was especially difficult for notions of the public good or for coherent reform to emerge in the ecclesiastical states, even in the midst of crisis, since power was shared between the prince-bishop and the Estates and since the sovereign was not a hereditary ruler who could pass property on to his heirs. Any commitment by rationalizing administrators to long-term reform was, as a result, spotty and irregular. As an anonymous author wrote in Schlözer's *Staatsanzeigen* (1786): "In the ecclesiastical states . . . all other means of improvement are useless, all changes prove to be a mere patchwork, without a total recasting of the basic institutional structure."[7] The reform literature on the ecclesiastical states recognized this problem, often recommending that these states be made hereditary and that professional administrators be recruited.[8]

Osnabrück, however, was a special variant on the pattern of clerical states because of the partly hereditary alternate succession. Although its Catholic bishops had little concerned themselves with economic improvements in the period after 1648, its Protestant bishops were secular princes from one house who eventually wanted to assimilate the bishopric into their Hanoverian domains. Probably for this reason, the yearly subsidies they demanded had traditionally been much smaller than those of the Catholic bishops. Indeed, the decision to confirm the regency of Frederick of York was influenced by the English promise to reduce the yearly subsidy during the regency and to commit the surplus to Osnabrück's economic recovery. By comparison with the Catholic rulers, the Protestant bishops also appear to have become gradually more concerned with improving economic productivity. Under Ernst August I (1661–98) such improvements were minimal: the only reforms were stopgap measures designed to improve the flow of taxes into the episcopal coffers. But Ernst August II (1716–28) began cameralist reforms similar to those initiated elsewhere in the previous century. He founded a saltworks at Rothenfelde in the Iburg district, had marshy areas drained, and instituted a uniform property code that regularized the duties of dependent serfs and laborers to their masters. Such efforts were largely halted under Catholic Clemens August (1728–61), who increased his own subsidies while showing little or no concern with the economic condition of the bishopric.[9]

---

[7] Anonymous, "Freimütige Gedanken veranlasst durch die Fuldaische Preisaufgabe," *Staatsanzeigen*, 9 (1786):401.

[8] See Chapter 3, section 2 and the conclusions of Peter Wende, *Die geistliche Staaten und ihre Auflösung im Urteil der zeitgenössischen Publizistik* (Lübeck, 1966), 34–47.

[9] Reinhard Renger, *Landesherr und Landstände im Hochstift Osnabrück* (Göttingen, 1968), 19–25. The yearly subsidy of Karl von Lothringen (1698–1715) had approached 126,000 Taler, that of Clemens August (1728–61) 108,000 Taler. The yearly subsidy of Ernst August II (1716–28), on the other hand, had been 91,000 Taler, whereas that of the regency government of Frederick of York averaged, over a nineteen-year period from 1764 to 1768, only about 55,000 Taler. Besides pointing to the different conceptions of the Protestant and Catholic bishops, these figures mark a gradual impoverishment of the bishopric over the course of the eighteenth century that appears to have made larger claims untenable. Even so, there was a sharp increase in the subsidy for Clemens August

Under Möser's administration the Hanoverian encouragement of material improvement resumed. His reforms rested on traditional cameralist principles. In legal terms, this meant that Möser subordinated the economy to the political needs of the prince-bishop. Because the regency was only quasi-legitimate, however, the sensitive relations between prince and Estates forced the princely administration to greater cooperation. On this account, a broader notion of the public interest seems to have been encouraged in Osnabrück, unlike other ecclesiastical states, along with traditional cameralist policies. Möser himself was forced to develop a wider view because he acted in the interests of both the Estates and the prince-bishop, but even the ministers in the German chancellery in London adopted a similar attitude, encouraging and supporting Osnabrück's newspaper and Möser's weekly contributions. (This contrasts starkly to the situation in neighboring Münster, where Franz von Fürstenberg found it extremely difficult to overcome the resistance of the Estates to any reform program and even to reducing the enormous indebtedness from the Seven Years War.[10] )

Thus, reform in postwar Osnabrück was a mixture of cameralism and a local patriotism that sought to define the public good. In accordance with traditional cameralist policies, Möser struggled to balance trade by establishing and protecting local industries, controlling imports, and encouraging sacrifice among the poor and disenfranchised. Among other measures, we find him trying to limit the flow of money outside the bishopric. In 1768, for instance, he sent a circular of inquiry to local officials concerning the economic status and potential of each district. He proposed that "all attention be given so that at least those things which are primary necessities . . . might be produced in the country, so that they [need] not be imported and the money for the same be taken out of the country."[11] To this end, financial aid was given throughout the period from 1768 to 1787 for the construction of small-scale pottery factories in order to keep at home "the 4000 Reichstaler which left the bishopric yearly."[12] For similar reasons, Möser supported in 1773–4 the founding of a basket factory that was given the exclusive right to produce and sell reed baskets and sieves (*Wannen*)

compared to that of his predecessor, Ernst August II. The lowered subsidy for Frederick of York was, as noted in the text, greatly influenced by the debts of the bishopric at war's end. See Hatzig, *Justus Möser als Staatsmann und Publizist*, 6, 28–30; and Anlage 3, 194. Concerning the long-term agrarian crisis and economic improvement in the bishopric prior to the regency, see Heinrich Hirschfelder, *Herrschaftsordnung und Bauerntum im Hochstift Osnabrück im 16. und 17. Jahrhundert*, in *Osnabrücker Geschichtsquellen und Forschungen*, 16 (Osnabrück, 1971), 175–90; Klaus Winkler, *Landwirtschaft und Agrarverfassung im Fürstentum Osnabrück nach dem Dreißigjährigen Kriege* (Stuttgart, 1959), 139–40; Runge, *Justus Mösers Gewerbetheorie*, 114; Paul Rohde, "Geschichte der Saline Rothenfelde," *Osn. Mitt.*, 31 (1906):1–59; Klaus Scharpwinkel, *Die Westfälischen Eigentumsordnungen des 17. und 18. Jahrhunderts* (Diss. Jur., Göttingen, 1965), 24–31.

10   See Alwin Hanschmidt, *Franz von Fürstenberg als Staatsmann*, in *Veröffentlichungen der Historischen Kommission Westfalens*, 18 (Münster, 1969), 101–3; and Heinrich Joseph Brühl, "Die Tätigkeit des Ministers Franz von Fürstenberg auf dem Gebiet dur inneren Politik des Fürstbistums Münster 1763–1780," *Westfälische Zeitschrift*, o.s. 63 (1905):167–248.

11   Quoted in Runge, *Justus Mösers Gewerbetheorie*, 54.

12   Each new venture failed; see ibid., 110.

essential in the yearly grain harvest.[13] A local tobacco industry was begun in this period (1766–79), and tobacco in fact became, next to textiles, Osnabrück's most important export commodity.[14] Similarly, the government gave financial support to individual craftsmen who proposed to settle in Osnabrück and supply its needs: the cabinetmaker Ruwen was given 1,000 Reichstaler in 1767 to settle in Osnabrück; the transportation costs of the stockingmaker Buchner were paid in 1775 to enable him to settle in Melle; the sculptor Wessel was given travel money in 1771, 1773, and 1777 to learn his craft in the capitals of Europe, on condition that he ultimately practice in the bishopric.[15]

Möser's public essays after the war supported from the beginning his own administrative effort to tighten cameralist controls. He condemned the introduction of manufactured goods in the countryside as a needless luxury, as destructive of the morals of the rural population, or as contributing to a negative balance of payments (1767).[16] He urged strict controls on the import and consumption of the "coffees, teas, sugars, and wines which are now among a beggar's needs."[17] He opposed the burning of grain for brandy production because it increased the need for grain imports (1771).[18] Typical of Möser's approach is the following from the *Osnabrück Intelligencer* (1772):

In all households a large number of wooden implements are used, such as mugs, buckets, plates, spoons and so forth, that surely are made by cottagers and brought to the market. Now since these come into the bishopric from outside, we desire a complete description of their fabrication and of the woods necessary to it, along with a recommendation how and where, with regard to the desirable woods, the same [industry] can be introduced into the bishopric.[19]

While attempting to expand the production of necessities, Möser also tried to intensify traditional administrative controls. Thus, he sought to revive and enforce the ordinances separating town and country, and thereby eliminate free

---

[13] This factory proved much more successful, and the protective monopoly against neighboring Münster was dropped in 1786. For a discussion of these events, see ibid., 106–9; also Hatzig, *Justus Möser als Staatsmann und Publizist*, 117–18; Möser, "Aufgaben" [1771], *SW*, 8:265.

[14] The extent of Möser's personal involvement is unclear. See Konrad Machens, "Beiträge zur Wirtschaftsgeschichte des Osnabrücker Landes im 17. und 18. Jahrhunderts," *Osn. Mitt.*, 70 (1961):91–96.

[15] Details can be found in Runge, *Justus Mösers Gewerbetheorie*, 60–2.

[16] Möser, "Klage wider die Packenträger" [1767], *SW*, 4:185–7; "Noch etwas gegen die Packen- oder Bundträger" [1767], *SW*, 8:113–20.

[17] Among the many essays, see Möser, "Vereinigung zwischen einem H. Domkapital und der H. Ritterschaft wegen der Trauer" [1766], *SW*, 8:56–7; "Schreiben eines Krämers im Dorfe, den Kaffee betreffend" [1768], *SW*, 8:138–40; "Kurzer Auszug verschiedener eingelaufenen Schreiben, den Rockenkoffee betreffend" [1768], *SW*, 8:141–2; "Hochgeehrster Herr Schwiegervater" [1770], *SW*, 8:228–31. Henri Brunschwig viewed complaints against coffee drinking as a common Enlightenment theme. See his *Enlightenment and Romanticism in Eighteenth-Century Prussia*, trans. Frank Jellinek (Chicago, 1974 [1947]), 75–7. See also J. A. Klöntrup, "Caffee," in his *Handbuch*, 1:206–7.

[18] Möser, "Also ist das Branntwein zu verbieten" [1771], *SW*, 5:131–3.

[19] Möser, "Aufgabe" [1772], *SW*, 9:60.

enterprise in the countryside, where it could not be easily controlled or taxed.[20] Except for the particular requirements of the rural textile industry – and this was an important exception – he tried to force artisans and craftsmen back into the established guilds within Osnabrück and the other towns of the bishopric. He proposed that a two-mile boundary (*Bannmeile*) of exclusive trading rights be given to the cities, outside of which no craftsmen would be allowed to practice (1768).[21] In other essays he tried to restore the urban monopoly of trade by preventing foreign peddlers from selling their wares in the countryside; they tempted the gullible wives and daughters of hard-working peasants to buy inappropriate finery, he argued, and their presence merely contributed to the flow of cash out of Osnabrück. In decrees of 1768–9, peddlers were even prohibited from plying their trade in the monopoly areas of the cities, as well as from traveling off the main highways to isolated farms and from selling articles produced by local craftsmen.[22]

Möser's effort to enforce the restrictions between town and country reflected traditional fiscalist methods of controlling trade and increasing revenues. But his concerns were broader: he also viewed the economy as composed of competing social interests, and his own role as that of balancing these interests. In Osnabrück claims were necessarily unequal; nonetheless the various groups needed to be separated rigidly and protected against the destructiveness of unlimited economic growth. Hence a limited sense of social justice survived in Möser's thought as part of the older moral economy. His lengthy stay in London had caused him to see the future with a certain defensiveness and even dread. We encounter such fears and conclusions directly in one of his longest essays, "On the Causes of the Decline of Crafts in Small Cities" (1768). In it he treated the economic benefits of the division of labor or, in his language, of "simplification" (*Simplifikation*). He recognized that the simplification he had observed in London made it possible to make rapid technological improvement, to produce much higher-quality manufactured goods, and to employ inanimate sources of energy (wind and water). In spite of this, he saw unchecked economic growth occurring at the expense of social stability. Regulated scarcity was far better than unchecked competition, especially in smaller cities such as Osnabrück that lacked sustaining financial resources, large markets, and technical advantages. As he wrote in the essay, "one can easily see that traders, who can obtain better and cheaper goods from

---

[20] See, for instance, the opening paragraphs of Möser, "Von der ehemaligen Schafzucht in der Stadt Osnabrück" [1768], *SW*, 8:130–1.

[21] Möser, "Von dem Verfall des Handwerks in kleinen Städten" [1768], *SW*, 4:165.

[22] Möser, "Klage wider die Packenträger," *SW*, 4:185–9; "Noch etwas gegen die Packen- oder Bundträger," *SW*, 8:113–19. This last essay contains a detailed account of the variety of manufactured goods brought into Osnabrück and estimates of the sums of money that left the bishopric yearly. See also "Schutzrede der Packenträger" [1769], *SW*, 4:189–94; "Urteil über die Packenträger" [1769], *SW*, 4:194–97. Also see Hatzig, *Justus Möser als Staatsmann und Publizist*, 128–30. The decree is published in *Codex Constitutionum Osnabrugensium*, 2 vols. (Osnabrück, 1783–1819), 2, no. 1154.

such large cities [e.g., London or Paris], will rapidly increase in number and thereby crush the [local] artisanate. . . . [A] place which begins to decline in this manner will lose its most valuable citizens, and, since for every ten taler gained by a trader a hundred will be exported, it must fear for its certain decline insofar as it does not have an unusual wealth in raw materials for export."[23] Given this situation, Möser thought that economic improvement could result only from social discipline and group sacrifice induced by administrative pressure. For this reason, he justified the restoration of medieval controls: uniforms for the citizenry, the two-mile boundary, and trading monopolies.[24]

Möser's economic proposals, however, went beyond the confines of a traditional cameralism based on the state and adjusted themselves to the peculiarities of northwestern Germany, where the economy was clearly regional. He was aware that "the small states consist simply of borders."[25] Which borders were to dictate policy? Should trade conducted between imperial estates (Reichsstände) be considered foreign or domestic? Möser saw that the peculiar conditions within Osnabrück forced innovation upon its administrators. He argued in a number of essays that the bishopric's economy could be improved only by conceiving it as part of a regional solution. Möser interpreted a number of the bishopric's problems in regional terms – solving the general decline of trade in the northwestern German cities (1768), creating a regional system of factories for the supply of capital goods (1765), moving grain between the small states, controlling its use in alcohol production (1770), and constructing a common granary on the Weser for times of dearth (1770).[26]

Along with such recommendations for regional solutions, Möser thought about the limits of administrative intervention at the local level. Thus, after the war, he suggested that all regulations on wool imports into the region be removed.[27] During the great dearth of the 1770s, he also proposed that all controls be lifted on the export, pricing, and sale of grain. He saw that state intervention eliminated competition, depressed the grain market, prohibited grain merchants (Kornjuden) from taking the necessary risks for the health of the trade, and encouraged

[23] Möser, "Von dem Verfall des Handwerks in kleinen Städten" [1768], SW, 4:158–9. Also see "Gedanken über dem Verfall der Handlung in den Landstädten [1769], SW, 4:28.
[24] Möser, "Von dem Verfall des Handwerks," 165–72.
[25] Möser, "Vorstellung zu einer Kreisvereinigung, um das Brannteweinsbrennen bei dem zu besorgenden Kornmangel einzustellen" [1770], SW, 4:301.
[26] Möser, "Gedanken von dem Verfall der Handlung in den Landstädten" [1769], SW, 4:15–28; "Vorstellung zu einer Kreisvereinigung, um das Brannteweinsbrennen bei dem zu besorgenden Kornmangel einzustellen" [1770], SW, 4:300–3; "Vorschlag zu einer Korn-Handlungskompagnie auf der Weser" [1770], SW, 4:255–60; "Gedanken über die Anlage einiger Faktorien in einem Schreiben an den Herrn von S." [1765], SW, 8:26. On the question of Westphalian economic intradependence in the eighteenth century, see Peter Schöller, "Die Wirtschaftsräume Westfalens vor Beginn des Industrie Zeitalters," Westfälische Forschungen, 16 (1963):84–6, 96–101; see also the map and discussion in Wilhelm Müller-Wille, Westfalen. Landschaftliche Ordnung und Bindung eines Landes (Münster, 1952), 230 (map), 221–50 (discussion).
[27] Möser, "Zur Beförderung einheimischer Wollenfabriken" [1772], SW, 5:122–6.

speculation and corruption. "It should be an eternal, unchanging law of every state that grain prices should always take their course no matter what the circumstances are."[28]

Hence there is some truth in the view of Möser as a precursor of economic liberalism, since he advocated the development of a regional market and proposed the creation of a regional free trade zone. Yet this free trade zone merely reflected the region's political fragmentation; the cameralist principles behind his policies remained intact. If the economy needed to be regulated at the local level, regional solutions also required the formation of regional institutions that could, in effect, substitute for controls already existing in the large territorial states. Möser proposed in a number of essays that the regional institutions of the Empire, the *Kreisverfassung*, be redirected to the solution of economic problems: "how highly useful it would be," he wrote, "if the imperial Estates in the Westphalian Circle were to unify for the sake of certain public services (*Polizeianstalten*) and begin a correspondence with the neighboring Circle of Lower Saxony."[29] Thus, Möser's economic arguments for free trade were accompanied at every point by a concern for controls, which tempered the laissez-faire components of his trade policies. From his administrator's perspective, each layer of the economy required its institutional checks. As the activities of peddlers in the countryside were to be supervised, so too were those of grain merchants and even the grain trade itself. Lifting controls acted only temporarily to free a dimension of the economy until the scope of the market could be determined.[30]

Regional economic reforms did not take place in Osnabrück during Möser's lifetime. Still, by viewing Osnabrück's economy as enmeshed in systems that were wider than the bishopric's narrow political boundaries, Möser separated the economy from strict questions of political power even as he advocated controls. In trying to solve the question of economic decline he could suggest, for instance, that the cities of northwestern Germany follow the example of the Hanseatic League and reunite.[31] It is in Möser's ability to make this separation that his profounder link to later German economic liberalism is to be found. Regional administration was a substitute for political unification; by adopting this perspective, the economic and administrative planners could bypass the formation of a Westphalian nation-state, which otherwise would have been necessary. Möser, in other words, remained both a critic of political centralization – "despotism," as he called it – and an advocate of regional economic planning.[32] Thus his policy

[28] Möser, "Vorschlag, wie der Teurung des Korns am besten auszuweichen" [1771], *SW*, 5:29–30.
[29] Möser, "Vorstellung zu einer Kreisvereinigung," 301.
[30] When it proved impossible to develop regional institutions, Möser recommended a system of local relief based on the individual parish. See Möser, "Vorschlag, wie der Teurung des Korns," 31. The system of grain distribution that was eventually instituted is described in "Einige Bemerkungen über Ein- und Ausfuhr des Korns bei teuren Zeiten im Stifte Osnabrück" [1773], *SW*, 9:55–9.
[31] Möser, "Also sollen die deutschen Städte sich mit Genehmigung ihrer Landesherrn wiederum zur Handlung vereinigen" [1769], *SW*, 4:215–23.
[32] For a different view, see Ulrike Brünauer, *Justus Möser* (Berlin, 1933), 14–15.

recommendations offered an alternative that continued to preoccupy German liberalism throughout the nineteenth century. At the same time, his actual contribution to policymaking was to isolate the economic systems within the bishopric and to try to abolish the local administrative controls that interfered with their functioning. As we will see next, he brought such a perspective both to the textile trade and to Osnabrück's migratory labor force.

## THE TEXTILE TRADE

Along with the trade in grain and tobacco, Osnabrück's textile industry was the major commercial activity linking the bishopric to the vicissitudes of the Western economy.[33] The industry was of long standing: already important in the fourteenth century, it grew with the power of the German Hansa and survived the Hansa's collapse. Since the seventeenth century Osnabrück had become the center, along with neighboring Tecklenburg, for the production and export of a high-quality coarse linen, sold widely in the colonies to clothe slaves under names such as "true born Osnabrughs," "Osnabrugg's lawn," and "brown Osnabrughs." The bishopric's weavers were also important producers of a linen paint canvas (*Parchent*) for Dutch factories in Enschede; another heavy canvas-like durable cloth made of a mixture of wool and linen, called *Wollaken*, that was valued by the

[33] On the Westphalian textile industry, the basic work with an extensive bibliography is Peter Kriedte, Hans Medick, and Jürgen Schlumbohm, *Industrialisierung vor der Industrialisierung* (Göttingen, 1978). See also Josef Mooser, *Bäuerliche Gesellschaft im Zeitalter der Revolution 1789–1848* (Ph.D. diss., Bielefeld, 1978), 29–122. Other general surveys of value are Bruno Kuske, "Die Textilwirtschaft," in his *Wirtschaftsgeschichte Westfalens in Leistung und Verflechtung mit den Nachbarländern* (2nd ed.; Münster, 1949), 69–96; Edith Schmitz, *Leinengewerbe und Leinenhandel in Nordwestdeutschland, 1650–1850*, in *Schriften zur Rheinisch-Westfälischen Wirtschaftsgeschichte*, 15 (Cologne, 1967), esp. 16–48. Of importance for the quantification but weak in analysis are the series of essays by Stephanie Reekers, "Beiträge zur statistischen Darstellung der gewerblichen Wirtschaft Westfalens um 1800," *Westfälische Forschungen*, 17 (1964), 18 (1965), 19 (1966), 20 (1967); an attempt to develop interpretive guidelines for this material was made by Schöller, "Die Wirtschaftsräume Westfalens," 84–101. For Osnabrück's textile industry, see the two important essays of Jürgen Schlumbohm, "Der saisonale Rhythmus der Leinenproduktion im Osnabrücker Lande während des späten 18. und der ersten Hälfte des 19. Jahrhunderts: Erscheinungsbild, Zusammenhänge und interregionaler Vergleich," *Archiv für Sozialgeschichte*, 19 (1979):263–98; and "Agrarische Besitzklassen und gewerbliche Produktionsverhältnisse: Großbauern, Kleinbesitzer und Landlose als Leinenproduzenten im Umland von Osnabrück und Bielefeld während des frühen 19. Jahrhunderts," in *Mentalitäten und Lebensverhältnisse. Rudolf Vierhaus zum 60. Geburtstag* (Göttingen, 1982), 315–34. See also Hermann Wiemann, "Die Osnabrücker Stadtlegge," *Osn. Mitt.*, 35 (1910):1–76; statistical information in Reekers, "Beiträge," *Westfälische Forschungen*, 17 (1964):90–139 and 19 (1966):41–64; also see Runge, *Justus Mösers Gewerbetheorie*, 66–106; Hatzig, *Justus Möser als Staatsmann und Publizist*, 95–119; Machens, "Die Tuchmacherei des Osnabrücker Landes im 17. und 18. Jahrhundert," *Osn. Mitt.*, 69 (1960):48–61.

Of comparative significance, recently collected as the essays of Herbert Kisch, *Die Hausindustriellen Textilgewerbe am Niederrhein vor der industriellen Revolution*, in *Veröffentlichungen des Max-Planck-Instituts für Geschichte*, 65 (Göttingen, 1981); for Switzerland, the two works by Rudolf Braun, *Industrialisierung und Volksleben* (2nd ed; Göttingen, 1979) and *Sozialer und kultureller Wandel in einem ländlichem Industriegebiet im 19. und 20. Jahrhundert* (Erlenbach-Zurich, 1965); for England, David Levine, *Family Formation in an Age of Nascent Capitalism* (New York, 1977), esp. 1–57.

coastal peoples of Holland and East Frisia; and a number of lesser cloths for local and specialty markets.[34] In addition, Osnabrück exported large quantities of unworked linen thread to the manufacturies of England and Holland. In the decades prior to the Seven Years War, Osnabrück's weaving trade became uncompetitive, its markets declined, and it began to lose its once high reputation. For this reason, it became a special focus of reform in the immediate postwar years.

The linen industry was crucial to Osnabrück's economic recovery not merely because it generated the bishopric's major export commodities but also because cottage weaving, in Osnabrück as elsewhere, was integral to the structure of rural society.[35] Unlike other weaving areas, however, where weaving stood as a completely separate industry and the raw materials had to be imported, in Osnabrück large crops of flax and hemp were grown and sheep were raised for their wool.[36] The activities associated with the cottage textile industry – spinning, carding, combing, weaving, bleaching, and dyeing – thus appeared as labor processes supplemental to the seasonal rhythms of the agricultural cycle and still assumed their meaning as part of the seasonal ritual. Though a large population of wage laborers lived mostly from weaving and seasonal agricultural labor, manufactures never emerged in the bishopric to disrupt the seasonal rhythm. Instead the preparation of the hemp and flax took place from the fall harvest to the early spring, when, until early July, the yarn was woven into finished cloth. In the summer months the finished cloth was taken to various points where it was sold to merchant entrepreneurs.

The Osnabrück weaver thus remained more independent than his counterpart elsewhere, because he was largely able to obtain his own raw materials from personally or locally grown flax, hemp, and sheep's wool. On the other hand, he was forced to sell his finished goods to the merchant entrepreneur who organized the trade with the wider market. At this point in the process, the state had long intervened to protect the local merchant monopoly, oversee the quality of the

---

[34] Möser described the type of cloth made in Osnabrück in "Den Landleuten zum Neujahr" [1773], *SW*, 9:21–5.

[35] Schlumbohm's studies of the Osnabrück weaving trade explore the relations between the rural industry and demographic change that are now also being investigated in other regions. His focus, however, is on the nineteenth century, for which the statistical evidence is more trustworthy, although he has said that he believes the general contours to be the same for the last half of the eighteenth century. See also Kriedtke et al., *Industrialisierung*, 155–93. For comparison, see the works cited in footnote 34; also E. L. Jones, "Agricultural Origins of Industry," *Past and Present*, no. 40 (1968):58–71; Max Barkhausen, "Der Aufstieg der rheinischen Industrie im 18. Jahrhundert und die Entstehung eines industriellen Großbürgertums," *Rheinische Vierteljahrsblätter*, 19 (1954):172; the same author's "Staatliche Wirtschaftslenkung und freies Unternehmertum im westdeutschen und im nord- und südniederländischen Raum bei der Entstehung der neuzeitlichen Industrie im 18. Jahrhundert," *VSWG*, 45 (1958):esp. 216; Franklin F. Mendels, "Proto-Industrialization: The First Phase of the Industrialization Process," *Journal of Economic History*, 32/1 (1972):241–61; Wolfram Fischer, "Rural Industrialization and Population Change," *CSSH*, 15/2 (1973):158–70.

[36] Schlumbohm, "Der saisonale Rhythmus der Leinenproduktion," 282–3.

finished product, and collect revenues through the sale of inspection stamps.[37] When Möser discussed the linen trade in the *Osnabrück History*, therefore, he simply described what had been the traditional concern of the episcopal administration. "[L]inen is the most important object of public concern," he wrote, "and it deserves the attention of those who pass the laws and collect the taxes. . . . The concern that good quality thread is sold, that the yarn is properly wound, that the linen is woven in its proper length in compliance with the regulations of every locale, and that honesty prevails in all matters – these are the rules which the police have to observe. The linen trade can suffer irremediably by a single mistake, because the trade stands in danger even without this [supervision]."[38]

Both the city and state administrations attempted to regulate the linen trade. The city of Osnabrück had created a system of enforced inspection for finished linen by the fourteenth century. Since that time, all goods sold by Osnabrück merchants had been examined by inspection officials – for thickness, density of weave, quality of material, length, and breadth – and then graded and stamped with the seal of the city inspectors that guaranteed its quality. When this system – called the *Leggesystem* – functioned in its ideal form, the state may also have protected the small weaver from abuse by the merchant entrepreneurs,[39] though it probably functioned more to control the trade and generate revenues than to dispense social justice.[40] The state had also long interceded to protect flax growers. In order to produce the highest-quality linen cloth, the flax needed to be harvested before it went to seed; consequently, local seed needed to be renewed with seed imported by the state from the Baltic area and inner Russia. To ensure seed quality, it was decreed, for instance, that local growers had to pay the government for seed only when it grew properly; otherwise the grower had to be repaid for all money spent on seed and labor.[41]

When Möser came to power the entire system of municipal and state control had decayed. Bribery ¿nd corruption among inspectors seem to have been common, seals were falsified, and the cloth itself was often adulterated.[42] The reputation of Osnabrück linen also appears to have suffered seriously with the collapse of the inspection system, though the extent of the suffering is difficult to determine, since complaints about quality were a standard device of the guilds and the state to call for controls that, coincidentally, would eliminate the independence of handloom weavers.

---

[37] Bruno Kuske, *Wirtschaftsgeschichte Westfalens*, 82–3; also Schlumbohm, "Agrarische Besitzklassen und gewerbliche Produktionsverhältnisse."

[38] Möser, *Osnabrückische Geschichte, SW*, 12/1:149.

[39] Wiemann, "Die Osnabrücker Stadtlegge," 5.

[40] See the argument of Schlumbohm in "Agrarische Besitzklassen und gewerbliche Produktionsverhältnisse."

[41] Wiemann, "Die Osnabrücker Stadtlegge," 55.

[42] Ibid., 11–13, 18–19, 27, 47; Möser, "Man sorge auch vor guten Leinsamen, wenn der Leinhandel sich bessern soll" [1767], *SW*, 4:53–8.

Möser, however, clearly thought that control was the answer, and he devoted his first serialized essay in the *Weekly Osnabrück Intelligencer* (Nos. 1–4, 1766) to analyzing the decline of the local linen trade and to suggesting the means to improve it. In this essay he rejected the reasons commonly given for the industry's collapse – the disruptions of war, the restrictive English Stamp Act, growing Scottish and Irish competition, the cheapness of English manufactures – and placed the blame completely on the poor quality of Osnabrück's own finished goods. He reproached Osnabrück's merchants for struggling to protect their ever-dwindling privileges at the expense of the entire trade; he pointed to the massive evasion of the city's inspection system; and he accused both merchants and weavers of selling shoddy goods as if they were of the highest quality. According to Möser, the episcopal administration had to intervene to enforce "(1) good regulation concerning the quality and width of the linen; (2) careful inspection; and (3) to reestablish eroded credit."[43] This program formed the core of Möser's administrative efforts for the next decade.

Over the years that followed the publication of this article, we can see Möser acquiring detailed knowledge of Osnabrück's textile industry at each stage of production and marketing. He wrote essays and memoranda on the growth and improvement of flax and hemp; on the varieties of sheep, their husbandry, and the various methods of shearing; on the technical details of production in the home and the manufactury; and on the intricacies of the overseas trade.[44] In fact, he became so much the expert that the other privy councillors refrained from making decisions that affected the trade when he was away.[45]

Möser's study of the textile trade yielded a series of episcopal decrees that gradually regulated more and more of local production and encroached on the inspection privileges of the city. At first, he attempted to raise the quality of export goods through legislation alone. From approximately 1766 to 1770, decrees were passed that chiefly concerned the technical aspects of production and the desired density, thickness, and breadth of the finished cloth. In the beginning, these decrees were enforced by voluntary inspection, but after 1770 fines and punishments were introduced for evasion and falsification. Even though the trade seems to have flourished after this point, repeated decrees after 1770 indicate that

[43] Möser, "Abhandlung von dem Verfall des osnabrückischen Linnenhandels und den Mitteln, solchen wieder aufzuhelfen," *SW*, 8:38.

[44] See, for instance, Möser, "Man sorge auch vor guten Leinsamen," *SW*, 4:53–8; "Abhandlung von der notwendigen Anlage eines spanischen Wollenvorrats in hiesiger Stadt" [1766], *SW*, 8:46–53; "Schreiben über den Zustand der Bramscher Tuchfabrik" [1770], *SW*, 8:244–9; "Zur Beförderung einheimischer Wollenfabriken" [1772], *SW*, 5:122–6; "Aufgabe, den Linnenpreis betreffend" [1773], *SW*, 9:60–1; "Gedanken eines Beamten über die Wollakenfabrik, von dem Verfall derselben und wie sie solcher aufzuhelfen" [1774], *SW*, 9:64–5; "Also muß der Preis auf die Sortierungen des Linnens keinen Einfluß haben" [1775], *SW*, 9:81–3; "Der unmittelbare Handel hat seine Tücke" [1775], *SW*, 9:84–6; "Ueber die Ursachen des diesjährigen Mißwachses im Lein" [1778], *SW*, 9:116–18; "Was soll aus unserm Garn- und Linnenhandel werden?" [1781], *SW*, 8:152–6.

[45] Runge, *Justus Mösers Gewerbetheorie*, 69.

weavers and merchants continued to evade both inspection fees and quality control.[46]

Expanding the inspection system became a way to assert uniformity and to increase episcopal control throughout the bishopric by circumventing the entrenched power of the city's merchants and textile guilds. An observer wrote in 1784 that "the government encourages trade in the countryside because the city is not directly subservient to the bishop . . . as is the countryside."[47] Since 1580 the city had possessed exclusive rights of inspection; in the seventeenth century the Osnabrück seal brought prices as much as 20 percent higher than those of unstamped goods.[48] During the eighteenth century, however, it clearly lost the ability to enforce its privilege. Merchants from outside the city and the bishopric became accustomed to buying cloth directly in the Osnabrück countryside without seeking the required stamps, and weavers also went directly to neighboring states to sell their cloth. From 1770 on, Möser regulated this trade by expanding the episcopal inspection centers into the countryside. A combined system of inspection fees and episcopal subsidies appears to have made it into a successful independent administration. Although the city remained the most important inspection site, its exclusive monopoly appears to have been broken, and the princely authority seems to have grown.[49]

Under Möser's leadership the episcopal administration intervened in other ways as well. Chronic credit shortages were ended by the creation of a warehouse system. Thus, a private company was formed to operate a warehouse in Bramsche for the purchase of Spanish wool and the sale of the finished cloth.[50] Decrees were passed in 1767 and 1769 to regulate the quality of flax seed, and incentives were offered to both merchants and growers to introduce seed of the highest quality.[51] A special fund was created for the weaving guild in the city of Osnabrück to improve its herds of sheep and the quality of their wool.[52] Incentives were also offered – but never accepted – to encourage the weaving guild in Fürstenau to emancipate its trade in linen paint canvas from Dutch buyers.[53]

---

[46] See the articles in Klöntrup, *Handbuch*, 2: "Garnhandel," 40–2, and "Legge," 253–8; the conclusions of Hatzig, *Justus Möser als Staatsmann und Publizist*, 103–4.

[47] Frhr. von R., "Briefe über Westfalen," *Deutsches Museum*, 1 (1784):236.

[48] Wiemann, "Die Osnabrücker Stadtlegge," 61.

[49] A statistical table of the number of pieces of linen cloth that passed through the Legge appears in Hatzig, *Justus Möser als Staatsmann und Publizist*, 106; reprinted in Runge, *Justus Mösers Gewerbetheorie*, 70; see also Wiemann, "Die Osnabrücker Stadtlegge," 13, 71; Möser, "Was will aus unserm Garn- und Linnenhandel werden?" [1781], *SW*, 8:152–6.

[50] Hatzig, *Justus Möser als Staatsmann und Publizist*, 111–19; Runge, *Justus Mösers Gewerbetheorie*, 82–93; Möser, "Abhandlung von der notwendigen Anlage eines spanischen Wollenvorrats," *SW*, 8:46–53; "Schreiben über den Zustand der Bramscher Tuchfabrik," *SW*, 8:244–9.

[51] Möser, "Man sorge auch vor guten Leinsamen," *SW*, 4:53–8; "Ueber die Ursachen des diesjährigen Miβwachses im Lein" [1778], *SW*, 9:116–18; Hatzig, ibid., 98–9.

[52] See the discussion in ibid., 116; Möser, "Von der ehmaligen Schafzucht in der Stadt Osnabrück" [1768], *SW*, 8:130–4.

[53] Möser, "Vorschlag zu einer Parchentfabrik," [1778], *SW*, 9:115; Runge, *Justus Mösers Gewerbetheorie*, 80–1.

As in other cases already discussed in this chapter, Möser crafted his newspaper articles in the Osnabrück papers to bolster the reform effort in a number of ways. He invented fictitious authors to represent his own views and to caricature those of his opponents. A "merchant from Cadiz" wrote to praise the vast improvement in the quality of goods and to make recommendations on how to lower Osnabrück cloth prices (1771);[54] a "merchant from Lippe" bemoaned the collapse in the demand for Lippe's linen and thereby praised the newfound strength of Osnabrück's own linen trade (1772);[55] an "Osnabrück merchant" complained of the entire inspection system as "inadequate, useless and destructive," undermined his own arguments, and thereby furthered Möser's own reforms (1766);[56] and, in yet another instance, a "shopkeeper" described his own decline and the improved condition of the rural population since the new inspection system was made mandatory (1771).[57]

In articles like his "New Year's Message to My Countrymen," Möser also used the newspaper to float new ideas for reform, proposing that samples of the fine cloths in demand on the Dutch market be posted at every inn so that each weaver could see and compare his own work (1773).[58] On other occasions he composed pieces examining the global political and economic issues affecting the linen trade.[59] Throughout his career, finally, he wrote numerous essays concerning the discipline and encouragement of the rural weaving population. Essays praised thrift and hard work. Women were admonished to learn the weaving trade. In a saccharine idyll, "The Spinning Room: An Osnabrück Tale," a young bridegroom is converted by his wife from modish frivolity to a useful existence. After a year of wasteful living he finally allows her to build her home around the spinning wheel, as she had wanted from the day of their marriage, "and everyone knows that they have both grown to a ripe old age among the spinning wheels and children" (1766).[60]

All of Möser's efforts to revive the linen trade were based upon administrative practices developed in preceding centuries. They remained limited in scope even where – with the attack on the city's exclusive administrative privileges through expansion of the inspection system, for instance – they appear to have gone much further toward reorganizing and controlling the entire distribution system of the textile trade within the bishopric. We cannot measure the effectiveness of these reforms, for the upswing in the local textile industry in the postwar years coincided with the massive increase in the demand for textile goods that affected the entire

[54] Möser, "Schreiben von Cadix, die Errichtung einer Kompagnie zum Linnenhandel betreffend" [1771], *SW*, 8:255–8.

[55] Möser, "Schreiben eines lippischen Kaufmanns an einen osnabrückischen" [1772], *SW*, 8:338.

[56] Möser, "Also sind die Leggen, welche zur Aufnahme des Linnenhandels in vorschlag gebracht werden, unhinlänglich, unnütz und verderblich" [1766], *SW*, 8:61–7.

[57] Möser, "Also soll man keine Kompagnie zum Linnenhandel errichten?" [1771], *SW*, 8:259–64.

[58] Möser, "Den Landleuten zum Neujahr" [1773], *SW*, 9:21–5.

[59] Möser, "Was will aus unserm Garn- und Linnenhandel werden?" *SW*, 7:152–6; also a satirical piece, "Der unmittelbare Handel hat seine Tücke" [1775], *SW*, 9:84–6.

[60] Möser, "Die Spinnstube, eine osnabrückische Geschichte" [1766], *SW*, 4:53.

European textile industry on the eve of industrialization. For this reason, it might be argued that demand, not administrative intervention, bettered the Osnabrück trade: given the high demand, in other words, goods of any quality would have found their way to the market. In any case, the evidence is far too spotty for us to know how significant were Möser's efforts.

## THE RURAL POOR

Reform of the cottage textile industry might also have served to increase the living standard of the spinners, weavers, and their families – people whose dependence on income from textile production often made the difference between meager subsistence and starvation. Here, however, we can discover little effort on Möser's part to ameliorate their harsh existence. The opposite seems to have been the case, for he consciously continued to isolate the working poor from Osnabrück's political institutions while creating greater pressures on them to work in the local textile industry. This pattern should be looked at with greater care, since it constitutes a substantial aspect of Möser's inegalitarian vision.

In Osnabrück as elsewhere in Europe where the textile trade developed in the countryside, the growth of a market-oriented industry gave rise to a population of wage laborers who supported themselves by engaging the entire family in spinning and weaving.[61] Propertyless or propertypoor, the weavers and spinners came in Osnabrück to settle on the fringes of rural society. They existed largely outside the system of legal bondage (*Leibeigenschaft*), outside the system of property ownership, and outside the peasant commune (*Bauerschaft*). Their marginal legal status reflected rigid adherence to a system of landholding frozen since the sixteenth century, when they had emerged as a social and economic group. In Osnabrück, as throughout northwestern Germany, the size of peasant holdings and the legal restrictions concerning the sale and division of estates still mirrored the settlement of the land.[62] The holdings – generally distinguished as divisions of larger parcels, as *Vollerbe*, *Halberbe*, and *Erbkötten* (*Viertelerbe*) – were the key to access to rural society. Only their tenants had legal representation in the commune, rights to the common lands, and legal rights in the local courts.[63]

By the end of the sixteenth century, these original holdings had been filled and subdivided to their legal limits; from then on the so-called latecomers began

[61] See the general description in Levine, *Family Formation*, esp. 9–15; Kriedte et al., *Industrialisierung*, 155–93, 309–20.

[62] For a discussion of the system of land tenure and the size of holdings in Westphalia, see Scharpwinkel, *Westfälische Eigentumsordnungen*, 4–7; Hans Motteck, *Wirtschaftsgeschichte Deutschlands*, 2 vols. (Berlin, 1968–9), 1:325; Heinrich Niehaus, *Das Heuerleutesystem und die Heuerleutebewegung* (Quakenbrück, 1924), 11–14; Heinrich Hirschfelder, *Herrschaftsordnung und Bauerntum im Hochstift Osnabrück im 16. und 17. Jahrhundert*, 54–114; Heinrich Schotte, "Die rechtliche und wirtschaftliche Entwicklung des westfälischen Bauernstandes bis zum Jahre 1815," *Beiträge zur Geschichte des westfälischen Bauernstandes*, ed. Engelbert Freiherr von Kerckerinck (Berlin, 1912), 25–7, 51–4.

[63] Werner Wittich, *Die Grundherrschaft in Nordwestdeutschland* (Leipzig, 1896), 84–116, 121–30.

to settle as lease- and copyholders on common lands, on the lands of wealthier peasants, on portions of some noble estates, and on uncleared wastelands. These later settlers were labeled variously according to where they settled, so that throughout Möser's writings we read of *Markötter, Brinksitzer, Brinkligger*, and *Bagger*. Most commonly these people were referred to by general terms that indicated their negligible legal status: as *Nebenwohner*, those who live on the edge or alongside, and as *Heuerlinge* or *Heuerleute*, those who were propertyless and therefore for hire as wage laborers.[64] The settlers of the commons, the cotters or *Markötter*, appear to have been accepted into the local communes in the seventeenth century in order to help with the enormous feudal burdens, and gradually they received a vote within the commune as its fourth class.[65]

The *Heuerleute* or *Heuerlinge* – the laborers for hire – comprised the largest single group of laboring poor. Although accepted within the economic system of rural society and assessed a household tax (*Rauchschatz*), they never acquired legal rights within the commune. The local historian of Osnabrück's legal and social customs, J. A. Klöntrup, described this legal apartheid in his article on *Heuerleute* (1799): "The *Heuerleute* do not belong to the commune (*Landfolge*) because they do not own land. . . . It can never be demanded of a *Heuermann* that he give his life for the defense of the state; such a sacrifice can only be derived from the property which one possesses in the state. . . . The state has more interest in one landed proprietor (*Erbeständer*) than in ten *Heuerleute* who have nothing to lose."[66] In spite of this legal discrimination, the population of *Heuerleute* continued to grow because, as spinners and weavers, they became invaluable to the cottage textile economy and, as seasonal laborers in the Netherlands, these so-called *Hollandsgänger* were integrated into a larger regional economy. It is clear from the census of 1772 that the *Heuerleute* were distributed unevenly throughout the districts (*Aemter*) and parishes of the bishopric.[67] To some extent, this distribution reflected both the earlier settlement of land and property law restrictions that severely limited the division of estates. Where large farms and estates prevailed, as in some city parishes, there were more *Heuerleute*; where the plots were smaller and the land poorer, as in the Wittlage district, their numbers also declined.

In this way the propertyless and the propertypoor were legally confined to certain parishes in Osnabrück through the enforcement of property and inheritance laws. These people depended on the textile trade, on seasonal migratory labor,

---

[64] For a discussion of *Nebenwohner*, see Hatzig, *Justus Möser als Staatsmann und Publizist*, 147–9; Niehaus, *Heuerleutesystem und Heuerleutebewegung*, 18. At his most ideological, Möser managed to conceive as *Nebenwohner* all "latecomers" who had come to Osnabrück since the "original" Germanic settlement of the area; see his "Von dem Einflusse durch Nebenwohner auf die Gesetzgebung" [1773], *SW*, 5:12; "Gründe, warum sich die alten Sachsen der Bevölkerung widersetzt haben" [1769], *SW*, 4:211–15.

[65] Klöntrup, "Markötter," *Handbuch*, 2:319.

[66] Klöntrup, *Handbuch*, 2:162–4. The quotation is almost an exact transcription of a passage in Möser's "Gedanken über den westfälischen Leibeigentum" [1768], *SW*, 6:231.

[67] Census statistics for the year 1772 are published as Anlage 6 of Hatzig, *Justus Möser als Staatsmann und Publizist*, 199–200; also 149–51.

and on work in local agriculture to survive. Yet they remained chronically underemployed. Constituting more than half of Osnabrück's population, they both taxed the parish poor relief system to its utmost and were the source of the bishopric's wealth. Thus Klöntrup could continue in the same article: "Still at least half of the inhabitants of this bishopric consist of *Heuerleute*. Our industry is largely founded on this [fact]; and should future offers or military conscription drive our *Heuerleute* to neighboring Holland . . . not only would our agriculture suffer but especially our thread and linen trade would cease. Soon Osnabrück would be the poorest province in Westphalia."

Möser's writings show his understanding of the relations between rural industrialization and the growth of the class of wage laborers. His real concern, however, was the way the rural poor seemed to threaten Osnabrück's social and political institutions.[68] He argued, for instance, that labor-intensive spinning and weaving had made it possible for many to make a tenuous living largely independent of normal agriculture. As a consequence, the *Heuerleute* were freed from the controls inherent in serfdom. Along with restrictions on their ownership of real property, such freedom had acted to lift the social restraints on the birth rate. Marriages now occurred at twenty instead of thirty; the birth rate had increased accordingly by as much as one-third; in addition, a higher infant mortality rate and a shorter life expectancy had contributed to a decline in public morals by brutalizing the population. Möser estimated that 4,000 new cotter households had appeared in Osnabrück since the beginning of the century, and even though more than 10 percent of this population failed to return to the bishopric each year from their seasonal migration to the Netherlands, their number continued to grow.[69] Möser wrote of the growing number of *Heuerleute* with considerable alarm. The relative lack of social controls on marriage and childbirth and the scarcity of wider economic opportunities made life unremittingly bleak, thus making them a corrosive social force within estate society.[70]

Möser's administrative decrees after the Seven Years War were intended to prevent the further expansion of the *Heuerleute* and to coerce them into working. They were, for example, the target of harsh poor laws.[71] ("A state with ten thousand farms and two hundred thousand *Heuerleute*," warned Möser, "cannot

---

[68] Möser, "Unvorgreifliche Beantwortung der Frage: ob das häufige Hollandgehen der osnabrückischen Untertanen zu dulden sei?" [1767], *SW*, 4:77–84; "Die Frage: Ist es gut, daß die Untertanen jährlich nach Holland gehen? wird bejahet" [1767], ibid., 84–97; "Antwort an den Herrn Pastor Gildehaus, die Hollandsgänger betreffend" [1768], ibid., 98–101; "Von dem Einflusse der Bevölkerung durch Nebenwohner auf die Gesetzgebung," [1773], *SW*, 5:11–22. Compare with Levine, *Family Formation*, 58–87, and Kriedte et al., *Industrialisierung*, 157–93.

[69] Möser, "Die Frage: Ist es gut," 86–7.

[70] Möser, "Unvorgreifliche Beantwortung der Frage," 81–2. He partly defends the rise in the number of *Heuerleute* in "Die Frage: Ist es gut," 88, although he is again directly critical of their presence in "Von dem Einflusse der Bevölkerung," 12–14, 19–20.

[71] Möser, "Vorschlag zur Beschäftigung der Züchtlinge" [1767], *SW*, 8:122–4; "Etwas zur Verbesserung der Zuchthäuser" [1778], *SW*, 7:121–6; "Oekonomische Aufgabe der Armen betreffend," *SW*, 9:49–50; "Vorschlag wie die gar zu starke Bevölkerung im Stifte einzuschränken" [1771], *SW*, 8:299–300; Hatzig, *Justus Möser als Staatsmann und Publizist*, 164–6.

treat all the poor and sick equally."[72] ) Regulations passed in 1766 limited begging to parishes where one had been born, where one's next of kin by blood lived, or where one had worked "honorably" for ten years or more. In order to enforce this practice, the bishopric's general poor relief fund, which had previously not discriminated by parish, was abolished; instead, 5 percent of the household tax from each parish was to be used in their relief. The poor born outside the bishopric were to be banished from its borders, and able-bodied men, women, and children found begging were to be placed in punitive workhouses. The refusal to continue to distribute poor relief simply on the basis of need brought complaints from the beginning. Nonetheless Möser persisted in arguing that stricter controls could be maintained only if each parish were responsible for its own poor. Overpopulated areas were to be forced to deal with their own population problems. Only through suffering, he argued, would population growth be eventually controlled: "necessity is the best disciplinarian"; "well-being creates new good-for-nothings."[73] Similarly, new decrees tied the poorest spinners and weavers more tightly to local merchants. Foreign jobbers were specifically excluded in the *Wollaken* trade in Bramsche so that spinners and weavers would not be able to acquire ready money to free themselves from the endless credit cycle. As a district official in Bramsche wrote: "Credit has brought the otherwise lazy poor back to work again."[74]

Along with tightened controls on the rural poor went loosened travel restrictions for those who traveled mostly to Holland to perform seasonal labor. Möser appears to have abandoned the prevailing wisdom on this matter. Cameralists had long believed that population growth was a form of wealth and, consequently, had encouraged population growth, new settlements, and restrictions on foreign travel.[75] Möser not only satirized attempts to establish colonies within Westphalia but also argued that it was better to permit migratory labor than to confine wage laborers within a state that could not offer them economic survival.[76] "The only

---

[72] Möser, "Von dem Einflusse der Bevölkerung," 19.

[73] "Es ist eine oft gemißbrauchte Regel: man müsse die Leute drücken, um sie fleißig zu machen: aber die Wahrheit, so darin liegt bleibt allemal richtig, daß die Not der beste Zuchtmeister und es fehlerhaft sei, diese zu erleichtern, wann, so wie bei Handarbeitern allezeit zu besorgen ist, das Wohltun neue Müßigänger macht." From Möser, ibid., 20.

[74] Quoted in Runge, *Justus Mösers Gewerbetheorie*, 79.

[75] The opinion of Frederick II of Prussia was typical: "The first and truest principle which holds good everywhere is that the strength of a state consists in the number of its subjects. To verify this you have only to compare Holland, which is some 40 leagues long and 15 leagues wide at most, with Siberia, which is probably 300 leagues long and perhaps 100 or more leagues wide. You will find that Holland has 3 million industrious inhabitants who pay the republic 15 to 16 million crowns and once assumed the whole weight of the war against its tyrant, Philip II of Spain, wholly on its own. . . . You can see, therefore, that the decisive factor is the number of industrious inhabitants, not the extent of territory." Quoted in Brunschwig, *Enlightenment and Romanticism*, 101. See also Schumpeter, *History of Economic Analysis*, 250; Mark Blaug, *Economic Theory in Retrospect* (rev. ed.; Homewood, Ill., 1968), 61; Friedrich Lütge, *Deutsche Sozial- und Wirtschaftsgeschichte* (3rd ed.; Berlin, 1966), 344; Friedrich-Wilhelm Henning, *Landwirtschaft und ländliche Gesellschaft in Deutschland*, 2 vols. (Paderborn, 1978–9), 1:229–39.

[76] Möser, "Schreiben über ein Project unserer Nachbarn Kolonisten in Westfalen zu ziehen" [1770],

advantage the wage laborer who stays at home has over the migratory laborer (*Hollandsgänger*)," he wrote, "might be the comfort of his womenfolk, his health, and the better upbringing of his children. . . . The man who stays at home, drinks water, and cannot make a living perhaps worries himself to death; instead . . . the migratory laborer works himself to death and dies in an honorable bed."[77] From this passage we can see that Möser had little concern for the emotional well-being of the working poor; instead he conceived of seasonal travel as both a social safety valve and a means to bring more money into the bishopric.[78]

These administrative regulations represented Osnabrück's attempt to confine the effects of population growth to the main textile-producing parishes and, through repressive measures, to force the poor to work. In their utilitarian harshness and abandonment of older ethical notions of social justice, they were certainly not unusual in the eighteenth century and were actually, in that context, "progressive" and even "enlightened."[79] Nevertheless, even Möser's admirers attacked such policies. Winold Stühle, a fellow Osnabrücker and one of Möser's first biographers (1798), wrote, "Even if the wage laborer (*Heuerbewohner*) has no land and often has no material wealth in comparison to other fellow citizens, he still works with them toward common purposes which lead to the well-being and preservation of the entire society. And who would occupy the cottages (*Nebenhäuser*) built by the property owner . . . if there were no wage laborers . . . in the state."[80] Möser, on the other hand, refused to use the language of citizenship with regard to the rural poor, retaining an exclusionary corporate attitude toward the rural weaving population. This attitude was also shared by classical liberal administrators who sought to transform legal relations in the countryside from personal dependence on a landlord to implicit citizenship in the state ("virtual representation"). Möser, on the other hand, refused to enlarge political rights and to separate the political privileges of *Herrschaft* from their medieval legal basis.

Möser accepted, as indicated in Chapter 4, an institutional order artificially frozen in time and maintained by a rigorously enforced property law. He accepted the premises of seventeenth- and eighteenth-century Westphalian property law codifications. These aimed to exclude the newer elements of rural and urban

---

*SW*, 4:285–90; "Am meinen Freund zu Osnabrück, über die Beschwerlichkeiten, Kolonisten anzusetzen" [1770], ibid., 290–5; "Antwort an den Herrn Pastor Gildehaus, die Hollandsgänger betreffend" [1768], ibid., 100.

[77] Möser, "Die Frage: Ist es gut," 87.

[78] See, for instance, "Von dem Einflusse der Bevölkerung," 18, where he argued that the state had to accept the sacrifice of half of its working population in order to produce an industrious artisanate.

[79] Rudolf Endres, "Das Armenproblem im Zeitalter des Absolutismus," *Jahrbuch für fränkische Landesforschung*, 34/35 (1974–5):1010–16, 1020; L. Koch, *Wandlungen der Wohlfahrtspflege im Zeitalter der Aufklärung* (Erlangen, 1933). For a comparison to France, see Olwen Hufton, *The Poor of Eighteenth-Century France, 1750–1789* (London, 1974), esp. 131–244, and Colin Jones, *Charity and Bienfaisance: Treatment of the Poor in the Montpellier Region, 1740–1815* (New York, 1982).

[80] Winold Stühle, *Ueber Möser und dessen Verdienste ums Vaterland, nebst verschiedenen Bemerkungen über Staatsverfassung* (Osnabrück, 1798), 94.

society from the traditional Estate system,[81] and defined the linen trade and the chronically underemployed rural poor who made its expansion possible as exogenous elements who "merely" supplied the material wealth to make Osnabrück's archaic Estate system function. Möser might work to ameliorate the physical suffering of the *Heuerleute* by allowing them to work outside of Osnabrück, but this goal was incidental to the economic needs of the state. To him the possible extension of citizenship to all who lived in Osnabrück signaled the emergence of some vague political "despotism." Even in episcopal Osnabrück he could not conceive of a republican government based on popular sovereignty: "Philosophers then come to exist who write general legal codes and regents who want to introduce the same. And the state is praised where the rights of mankind are most extended or − to speak the truth clearly − where the landed proprietor is robbed of all the dignity he had received from the original contract, and only the regent is raised that much higher above the rest."[82]

In this way, Möser justified maintaining restrictive laws that controlled the potential for unlimited growth in the textile trade and thus deadened its impact on the social and political life of the bishopric. We can see him adopt what become liberal economic reform policies − the emancipation of the textile trade from narrow guild restrictions and the defense of the right of unencumbered travel in search of work − as a means to preserve Osnabrück's political order. He was constantly aware that there were limits to the expansion of the episcopal economy. Reform, as a consequence, always remained a technical adjustment of the historically evolved given. By the same token, his defense of the Westphalian settlement was also a defense of natural inequality and, of course, of the political status quo. Thus he consciously walked the line between economic modernization and political and social stability. We can see the same concerns in his writings on agrarian reform.

### PEASANT EMANCIPATION

Among enlightened publicists the term "peasant emancipation" (*Bauernbefreiung*) emerged in the 1780s and 1790s to imply a radical emancipation on the basis of natural rights − the meaning that became dominant in the nineteenth century. Administrators, on the other hand, referred to peasant emancipation in the later eighteenth century as "settlement" (*Regulierung*), as "redemption" (*Ablösung*), or as "dissolution of the seigneurial system" (*Grundentlaßung*). Thus it was a term linked to the issue of the practical transformation of obligations and dues, and was based on the notion of compensating seigneurs in exchange for the personal

---

[81] Scharpwinkel, *Westfälische Eigentumsordnungen*, 24–31; Klöntrup, "Eigentumsordnung," *Handbuch*, 1:320–1.

[82] Möser, "Von dem Einflusse der Bevölkerung," 14.

freedom of and hereditary land tenure by dependent laborers or serfs.[83] The lord had to be compensated for the rights and services belonging to him as master of a bound serf or *Leibeigener*. The most glaring of such rights surviving in northwestern Germany were death fees (*Sterbefall* ), which could involve the sale of a dead serf's possessions, and rights to the forced labor (*Zwangsdienst*) of a serf's children in the seigneurial household.[84] Seigneurs also needed compensation for lost ground rents and dues when the land was bought or turned into hereditary leaseholds; for the much hated tithe; and, finally, for his patrimonial legal rights (*Patrimonialgerichtsbarkeit*) where they survived within the manoral system of *Gutsherrschaft*, such as in Mecklenburg or Brandenburg-Prussia. Among administrators the discussion of emancipation was also inextricably linked to issues of agricultural productivity. This gave impetus to the enclosure movement and was a fundamental tenet among physiocratic reformers. The failed Josephinian reforms began in the 1780s by surveying the Habsburg lands and attempting to judge their actual and potential productivity.[85] In this activity, the future social and political rights of the peasantry following emancipation were largely left out. Where patrimonial rights were to be eliminated, for instance, a paternalistic state apparatus was to substitute for arbitrary seigneurial rule.[86]

Although Möser attempted to isolate the textile industry and the rural poor from the institutions of landed society, he maintained a more complex position with regard to Osnabrück's peasantry. As chief administrator of an absentee prince, he continued to maintain the fiscal interest inherent in traditional policies of peasant protection (*Bauernschützpolitik*): the intervention of the territorial or central authority in order to maintain the tax base of the state. However, as syndic of the nobility, he was their representative against all reforms that might abridge their collective or individual interests.

We can best appreciate Möser's belief in technical reform by examining the important memorandum he wrote in 1779 to officials of Joseph II in response to a query concerning serfdom in Osnabrück.[87] He states at the beginning that

[83] Friedrich Lütge, "Ueber die Auswirkungen der Bauernbefreiung in Deutschland," in his *Studien zur Sozial- und Wirtschaftsgeschichte. Gesammelte Abhandlungen* (Stuttgart, 1963), 174–6; Jerome Blum, *The End of the Old Order* (Princeton, N.J., 1978), 308–10; Christof Dipper, *Die Bauernbefreiung in Deutschland 1790–1850* (Stuttgart, 1980).

[84] See Hirschfelder, *Herrschaftsordnung und Bauerntum im Hochstift Osnabrück*, esp. 116–74. For a discussion of duties and burdens in Osnabrück and Westphalia in the seventeenth and eighteenth centuries, see Scharpwinkel, *Die westfälischen Eigentumsordnung*, 56–121; also valuable are the individual articles in Klöntrup, *Handbuch*, e.g., 1:8–14 ("Abfindung der Kinder"); 1:58–70 ("Anerbe"); 1:91–6 ("Auffahrt"); 1:101–7 ("Auslobung"); 1:140–3 ("Bettemund"); 1:173–4 ("Blutzehnten"); 1:184–90 ("Brautschatz"); 2:35 ("Fruchtzehnt"); 2:136–8 ("Handdienst"); 2:252–3 ("Lange Fuhr"); 2:264–75 ("Leibzucht"); 3:177–82 ("Spanndienst"); 3:291–5 ("Weinkauf"); 3:327–34 ("Zehnten").

[85] See the argument of Roman Rozdolski, *Die große Steuer- und Agrarreform Josef II* (Warsaw, 1961).

[86] Lütge, "Auswirkungen der Bauernbefreiung," 182–94.

[87] Möser, "Bauernbeschaffenheit in Osnabrück n. 1779," in Osterreichisches Staatsarchiv Wien: Habsburg-Lothringisches Familienarchiv, Poschakten Jüngere Serie; Karton 3; folio pages 406–32. My thanks to William Sheldon for sharing a transcription.

"serfdom (*Leibeigenthum*) is a notion which can be eradicated by a carefully conceived theory or better [which] can be regulated, so that it is beneficial to the state; and I have ventured to eliminate it without either lord or peasant noticing [what was taking place]."[88] Two things allowed Möser to make such an extraordinary statement. In the first place, he was not concerned about dependency as a philosophical or ethical principle; indeed, he was at pains in the memorandum to show that dependency existed throughout society, and he concluded by describing "dependency" (*Hörigkeit*) as "nature itself."[89] (This defense of dependency is important and will concern us in the next chapter.) In the second place, and more significant in the present context, Möser was able to speak of abolishing serfdom without anyone noticing because he felt that serfdom embodied a concrete set of social and economic relationships that could be reformed, after which an independent peasantry would exist regardless of the label. The purpose of his memorandum, accordingly, was to persuade Joseph's officials not to be misled by words but to probe deeper and to reform certain concrete matters: credit and indebtedness by promoting fiscal solvency; the inheritance laws by encouraging the development of economically viable parcels of land; and the legal system by creating an independent system of justice in the countryside.[90]

What made Möser's approach plausible was the particular configuration of legal dependence in Osnabrück and northwestern Germany. This system of dependence, the so-called *Meierrecht*, was a milder and more mediated system than that of East Prussia and Pommerania, Mecklenburg, or neighboring Hesse. (On the other hand, it was certainly more severe than the system in the hereditary Danish lands, where gradual emancipation began in the 1760s and culminated in the emancipation decrees of 1788.)[91] In Osnabrück, land was parceled out in a system of leaseholds – *Vollerbe, Halberbe,* and *Viertelerbe* – that made wealthy peasants only nominally dependent and blurred, as a result, the worst features of legal bondage. Furthermore, these leaseholds were to a large degree already hereditary by the eighteenth century. In addition, the local nobility had never acquired omnipotent legal rights on their estates, as did the Prussian or Mecklenburg nobility. In sum, dependent peasants continued to remain at an enormous disadvantage throughout Möser's lifetime but were not altogether without legal rights. Thus Möser could write with a certain justification that "we have no

---

[88]   Ibid., f. 408.

[89]   Ibid., f. 431.

[90]   Ibid., ff. 409–15, 417–19.

[91]   Besides the works by Lütge, Blum, and Dipper cited in footnote 83, for the history of ideas, see John Gagliardo, *From Parish to Patriot. The Changing Image of the German Peasant 1770–1840* (Lexington, Ky., 1969), esp. 1–57. For Germany see also Motteck, *Wirtschaftsgeschichte Deutschlands*, 1:315–52; Henning, *Landwirtschaft und ländliche Gesellschaft in Deutschland*, 1:250–7; idem, *Dienste und Abgabe der Bauern im 18. Jahrhundert* (Stuttgart, 1969); Hans-Heinrich Müller, *Märkische Landwirtschaft vor den Agrarreformen von 1807* (Potsdam, 1967). For the Danish hereditary lands, see the contemporary pamphlet by Georg Christian Oeder, *Bedenken über die Frage: wie dem Bauernstande Freiheit und Eigenthum in den Ländern, wo ihm beydes fehlt, verschaffet werden könne* (Frankfurt, Leipzig, 1769).

better recruits for serfdom (*Leibeigenschaft*) than the *Heuerleute*. Only these [serfs] are able to leave something to their children or to lease a debt-free piece of land."[92]

Thus Osnabrück saw few dramatic changes in the direction of peasant emancipation and the transformation of the system of land tenure during Möser's lifetime. Only one serf, a wealthy leaseholder named Schulte, is known to have been emancipated, and he purchased his freedom for the large sum of 2,000 Reichstaler.[93] Similarly, there was little movement toward a rationalized agriculture that might have disrupted legal relations. There were few new enclosures, for example: although Möser was a decided advocate of enclosures, only seventeen peasant communes (*Mark*) were divided after 1760, most of those enclosed having already been divided in the period between 1735 and 1746.[94] In addition, although Möser's essays are filled with recommendations for improving the fertilization of crops, introducing newer breeds of sheep and pigs, and preserving local forests, he does not appear to have tried to force improvements in local agriculture.[95]

Instead of focusing on the legal language of emancipation, Möser attempted to expand the regulative prerogatives of the episcopal administration to include the right to intervene in the affairs of local seigneurs, and he did so by developing a limited notion of the good of the state. He argued in various essays that the administration was the guardian of the land and its resources. In "Reflections on the Grounds for Expulsion or Eviction" (1774) he stated that "one can say *there is no property within the state* because, necessarily, the natural proprietors must have abandoned ownership when society began. In a theocracy Moses states: *the earth belongs to the Lord*; and in our constitutions it says: *the earth belongs to the state*."[96] In another place in the essay he stated that "every estate (*reihepflichtige Hof* ) . . . is a possession (*Pfründe*) of the state as a consequence of the original social contract."[97] Seigneurial rights, therefore, were limited by needs arising

---

[92] Möser, "Die Frage: Ist es gut, daβ die Untertanen jährlich nach Holland gehen? wird bejahet" [1767], *SW*, 4:94.

[93] Möser, "Formular eines neuen Kolonatkontrakts, nach welchem einem vormaligen Kammer-Eigenbehörigen nach vorgängiger Freilassung der Hof übergeben worden" [1781], *SW*, 7:273–83; "Formular des hiebei erteilten Freibriefes" [1779], *SW*, 7:284–5; Hatzig, *Justus Möser als Staatsmann und Publizist*, 70–1.

[94] A list of the enclosed communes appears in Hatzig, *Justus Möser als Staatsmann und Publizist*, 163. See also Klöntrup, "Marktheilung," *Handbuch*, 2:328–41. The clearest statement of the advantages of enclosure is in Möser, "Etwas von Teilung unserer Marken" [1777], *SW*, 9:105–11; see also "Der Mahlmann bei seiner ungeteilten Mark" [1770], *SW*, 9:235–7; "Sind die Gemeinheiten nach geschehener Teilung mit Steuern zu belegen oder nicht" [1772], *SW*, 5:165–74.

[95] Of the many essays dealing with local agricultural improvements, see, for instance, "Vom Heide und Moorbrennen" [1767], *SW*, 8:79–83; "Einige Gründe gegen den Plaggendünger" [1768], *SW*, 8:152–6; "Ein Patriot muβ vorsichtig in seinen Klagen bei Landplagen sein" [1771], *SW*, 5:35–6; "Die moralischen Vorteile der Landplagen" [1772], *SW*, 5:37–40; "Vom Hüten der Schweine" [1775], *SW*, 5:178–93. See also Friedrich Herzog, *Das Osnabrücker Land im 18. und 19. Jahrhundert* (Oldenburg, 1938), 30–92.

[96] Möser, "Betrachtungen über die Abäuβerungs- oder Abmeierungsursachen" [1771], *SW*, 6:278.

[97] Ibid., 284. See also the revised edition of the *Osnabrück History* (1780), where he noted: "Der

from the larger political body: "The serf exists in a two-fold bond, the first is based upon the welfare of the state while the second [is based] on the lease contract between him and his lord."[98] The distinction allowed Möser to uphold judicial control by the episcopal administration over the sometimes shortsighted interests of both lord and peasant. Judges should remain independent agents, he wrote, and "not become mere executors of arbitrary seigneurial power." Otherwise tenants for abandoned peasant holdings could not be found, credit would disappear, and "in the end the seigneur carries the burden of supporting every unworthy fellow."[99]

This expanded claim of administrative competence has emerged in a different context in each of the previous chapters and as a constant theme in this one. Here, however, Möser failed to articulate independent or public criteria defining the common good or good of the state that might have given a specific meaning to the notion of possession or the welfare of the state. Without such a definition, these notions became empty fictions justifying existing inequities. Möser's efforts to reform Osnabrück's complex system of land tenure consequently never possessed the utopian power that the call for total emancipation among enlightened publicists had. Rather, he searched for general technical principles within existing property law that, from an administrator's perspective, could regulate the system of dependence more efficiently and thus also reform its worst excesses. Here we discover his typical acceptance of slow change, and this is ultimately the attitude by which he must be judged.

Thus Möser sought to ameliorate the worst symbolic and economic features of serfdom in Osnabrück without attacking the paternalism fundamental to the structure of the property law.[100] Instead he tried to improve specific abuses. After the war, for example, he launched a major effort to stabilize rural property holding by slowing the rate of eviction for chronic indebtedness. In many essays and memoranda he warned that the accelerated rate of eviction for unpaid debts and quick profits from resettlement fees of new leaseholders loosened paternalistic ties between lord and peasant and argued the importance of long-term economic improvement over immediate gain.[101] He attempted, for this reason, to reform

osnabrückische Eigenbehörige wird ohne Mittel des Gutsherrn zu gemeiner Reihe und Runde bestellet, bestrafet und besteuret; und wenn eine allgemeine Rekrutenlieferung geschehen müsste, würde der Gutsherr sich wegen seiner Freibriefe aus Erbe halten müssen und seinen Leibeignen nicht zurückfordern können. Alle gemeinen Landesgleicher Masse; und der Staat sieht von seiner Seite beide als gleich huldige und gewärtige Leute an" (*SW*, 12/2:120).

[98] Möser, "Betrachtungen über die Abäußerungs- oder Abmeierungsursachen," *SW*, 6:280–1.

[99] Möser, "Die Abmeierungen können dem Hofesherrn nicht überlassen werden" [1774], *SW*, 6:271–2; see also Hatzig, *Justus Möser als Staatsmann und Publizist*, 43.

[100] Lütge, following Wittich, argues that this was characteristic in the kingdom of Hanover: peasant emancipation occurred without giving the peasants complete control over their property. See Lütge, "Auswirkungen der Bauernbefreiung," 179, and Wittich, *Grundherrschaft in Nordwestdeutschland*, 451.

[101] Möser, "Also sollte man den Rentekauf für den Zinskontrakt wieder einführen" [1769], *SW*,

the moratorium laws (*Stillestand*) on indebtedness, recommending the use of the episcopal administration to regulate usurious interest rates through the introduction into each parish of general books of indebtedness. All debts were to be listed; only such public debts were to be legally binding; and borrowing could occur only up to a fixed percentage of an estate's total value. Similarly, he attempted to restrict the lender's rights to appropriate movable goods for unpaid debts to those things that would not affect the economic survival of the particular holding. Under this proposed reform neither seed, essential farming implements, basic livestock, nor certain household goods could be claimed for debt, nor could a dependent peasant borrow against them.[102] In the same way, Möser tried to limit the period of indebtedness. In a curious essay on Mosaic law, he recommended that debts that could not be repaid within eight years be forbidden, and after the indenture a debtor should be freed of all obligation.[103] Möser attacked indebtedness from another direction by recommending that all leaseholds – by freemen and serfs alike – should become hereditary. As he stated elsewhere, indebtedness would thereby decline, because each serf would take a more active interest in leaving debt-free property to his heirs. He devoted a great deal of energy to this idea, which, however, was never realized due to the resistance of the nobility.[104]

Möser also sought to persuade the nobility to abolish the worst symbolic features of serfdom. In memoranda and essays he urged that particularly odious customary dues be transformed into a system of fixed payments; he singled out for particular criticism the customs of *Sterbefall*, or death fees, and *Zwangsdienst*.[105] He sought to change other customary duties into a system of payments like those he proposed for indebtedness; these duties were to be recorded publicly and payable in both labor and cash according to the capacity of the dependent peasant.[106]

Möser's own complicated reform views concerning serfdom are crystallized in an essay from 1775, a "letter" from a "*Gutsfrau* to her friend." The *Gutsfrau* is writing to praise the new spirit on the estate since her "husband had finally risked it and given all his serfs their freedom." A liberty tree has been planted

5:88–93; "Gedanken über den Stillestand der Leibeigenen" [1772], *SW*, 6:316–23; "Von dem Konkursprozesse über das Landeigentum" [1778], *SW*, 7:213–21.

[102] Möser, "Von dem hiesigen Provinzialretrakt" [1767], *SW*, 8:89–99; "Vom gläubiger und landsässigen Schuldner" [1768], *SW*, 6:308–16; "Nichts is schädlicher als die überhandnehmende Ausheuerung der Bauernhöfe" [1772], *SW*, 6:238–55.

[103] Möser, "Gedanken über die Mittel, den übermäßigen Schulden der Untertanen zu wehren" [1768], *SW*, 4:119–29; a similar argument without the appeal to Mosaic law is in "Von den Vorzügen des ehmaligen Äußerprozesses vor dem neuern" [1769], *SW*, 8:206–14.

[104] Hatzig, *Justus Möser als Staatsmann und Publizist*, 62; Möser, "Also sind die unbestimmten Leibeigentumsgefälle zu bestimmen" [1770], *SW*, 6:287–93.

[105] Möser, "Also sollte jeder Gutsherr seine Leibeigenen vor Gerichte vertreten und den Zwangdienst mildern" *SW*, 7:285; "Die Abmeierung, eine Erzählung" [1771], *SW*, 5:100–2.

[106] Möser, "Schreiben einer Gutsfrau, die Freilassung ihrer Eigenhörigen betreffend" [1775], *SW*, 6:200.

on the estate, she reports, under which the articles of emancipation are to be read every year. What the articles of emancipation formalize, however, are the existing legal relationships:

> they divide them [serfs] by their real situation into whole, half, and quarter [legal] individuals and also [create] as many classes as necessary for lesser [individuals]; they make the duties of each class as uniform as possible and, for instance, bind the *half individual* (*Halbmann*) to half as much as the *whole* is bound. Then all these duties are written in a public record and read aloud to the gathered freedmen under the oak tree and it is accepted by them as correct. . . . In this way the duties can not easily be disputed; and the requests that my husband might make in certain extreme cases may never become normal and customary duties because the *request* speaks for itself and the instances of extreme need are so carefully limited.[107]

The seigneurial right to rule was transformed in this manner, acquiring a new quasi-rational economic function. But, to anticipate the next chapter, Möser also envisaged that the seigneur would remain the legal protector of his social inferiors. The letter continues:

> They are not allowed to engage in legal disputes before reporting it to us; and, for a certain yearly fee, my husband retains a common lawyer, to whom they must turn and who must render his legal opinion before the matter goes before the court. My husband believes this to be the true and holy duty of every lord and seigneur who enjoys rents and services.[108]

Thus Möser's proposals concerning the local system of serfdom involved a transition from strict legal dependence of the peasantry upon the rural nobility to a more indirect economic and moral dependence in a differently fashioned territorial state. The peasantry would be transformed into a class of hereditary leaseholders with legal guarantees and a rigidly delimited stake in Osnabrück's economic life. The nobility would emerge as a service nobility – one serving both its local population of inferiors and the state. In this way rural society would successfully adapt to the conditions of the modern world under the continued tutelage of the traditional elites.

### ENLIGHTENMENT AND REFORM

The question of reform in the later eighteenth century has too often been over-simplified in favor of an artificial distinction between "progressive" and "tradi-

---

[107] Ibid., 199.
[108] Ibid., 203. See also his "Also sollte jeder Gutsherr seine Leibeignen vor Gerichte vertreten und den Zwangdienst mildern," *SW*, 7:285. There he argues: "[D]ie erste Pflicht der Gutsherrn sei die Verteidigung ihrer Eigenbehörigen vor Gerichte und zu Felde. Hat gleich die letzte aufgehört, nachdem man eine neue Art der Verteidigung zu Felde eingeführet hat und leidet auch gleich die jetzige gerichtliche Verfassung nicht mehr, daß der Gutsherr selbst ins Gerichte gehe, um seinen liebeignen Mann zu vertreten: so bleibt doch für ihn immer eine gewissenhafte Verbindlichkeit zurück, und jeder ehrliche Mann muß für sein Eigentum stehen. Der Herr, der seine Untertanen nicht mehr schützen kann, verliert sein Recht."

tional" economic and social policy. This oversimplification has allowed a recent commentator on Möser's economic policies to claim that "the ideas of the Enlightenment remained without any influence on Möser's intellectual attitude; they were also far too distant from historical reality to awaken in him understanding, affection, or enthusiasm."[109] This judgment is untenable, as we have seen, largely because it lacks a historically adequate definition of Enlightenment administrative behavior. How are we to place Möser's administrative reforms within the broader movement of the Enlightenment in the later eighteenth century? Given Osnabrück's narrow horizon and the inflexible political and social structure within which his reforms were conceived, how are we to separate intentions from results? Can we properly identify any of these reforms as "enlightened"? If so, what criteria should we employ?

To assess what occurred in Osnabrück under Möser's administration, we must understand that this type of limited, unsystematic reform was the rule throughout the Germanies. Older mercantilist and cameralist policies continued to predominate even where the intellectual assumptions of individual monarchs and administrators should have or might have led to liberal or physiocratic economic policies. The problem lay in implementation: The social and economic institutions, the attitudes of administrators and ruler, and the traditional patterns of economic behavior proved much more resistant to change than intellectual assumptions.

Economic historians, as a consequence, have found it difficult to distinguish a particular Enlightenment economic policy from the existing traditions in Germany and in Europe.[110] Many of the elements first identified with the Enlightenment have proven, on closer scrutiny, to be little different from the older modes of cameralist organization and reform. At most there was an intensification of effort rather than a qualitative change. On the level of policy, historians point to impulses toward rational and centralized reform, toward an awareness of a new public sector, and toward a systematic understanding of the economy; but these impulses antedate the Enlightenment in Germany. Moreover, the drive to systematic theoretical understanding – for example, Hume's and Cantillon's contribution to monetary theory[111] – encompassed only certain aspects of economic life and, as we would expect, promoted piecemeal, eclectic reforms within the

---

[109] Runge, *Justus Mösers Gewerbetheorie*, 150.

[110] See, for instance, Friedrich Lütge, *Deutsche Sozial- und Wirtschaftsgeschichte* (3rd ed.; Berlin, 1966), 321. Lütge exaggerates the effects of the Thirty Years War; in his survey, the period from 1648 to 1815 is a transitional one without internal distinction. See also Josef Kulischer, *Allgemeine Wirtschaftsgeschichte des Mittelalters und der Neuzeit*, 2 vols. (Munich, 1928–9), 2:87, 102; Motteck, *Wirtschaftsgeschichte Deutschlands*, 1:245–63, 353–9; 2:1–42; Georg Jahn, "Merkantilismus," *Handwörterbuch der Staatswissenschaften*, 8 vols. (3rd ed.; Jena, 1909–11), 5:573–6; Anton Tautscher, *Staatswirtschaftlehre des Kameralismus* (Bern, 1947). For the view that mercantilism is merely intellectual shorthand for state interventionism, see the caustic criticism of A. V. Judges, "The Idea of a Mercantile State," in D. C. Coleman, ed., *Revisions in Mercantilism* (London, 1969), 58–9.

[111] Schumpeter, *History of Economic Analysis*, 317; Blaug, *Economic Theory in Retrospect*, 17–24.

older economic patterns. For these and other reasons, it is easier to write not of the contributions of the Enlightenment to economic change, but of the emergence of capitalism or industrialization.

Physiocracy, the doctrine Möser called the "expression of our Iroquois philosopher,"[112] was, of course, the radical exception. Quesnay's *Tableau economique* was a total reform program that broke with tradition everywhere. The intellectual components of this theory depended on shared Enlightenment assumptions among certain French *philosophes* – and certain German rulers – and the evanescent reign of the physiocratic movement in the decade of the 1760s reflected a realistic analysis of critical French fiscal and economic problems (tax reform, land distribution, internal tariff policies, monopolies). Nonetheless, physiocratic reforms failed almost completely in France; to the extent that they influenced reforms in the German-speaking areas – in Baden and the Habsburg domains – they were often adapted to preexisting administrative traditions.[113]

Even if we turn to Adam Smith, we find the same difficulty in developing criteria for Enlightenment economic practice. *The Wealth of Nations* was not the work of a historian but of a reformer; for this reason, Smith never accurately characterized earlier economic policy – conflating a variety of approaches and tendencies in the phrase "mercantile system" – and never appreciated the continuities with the older tradition.[114] This imprecision is exacerbated by the lack of systematic unity in his work. Scholars have often pointed out the divergence between his Enlightenment ethical theory in *The Theory of Moral Sentiments* and his liberal economic theory in *The Wealth of Nations*. As he moved away from ethics and toward economic policy, the philosophical underpinnings of his thought became blurred. Furthermore, even within the context of his economic writings, he was eclectic – a man deeply influenced by Grotius, Pufendorf, Shaftesbury, Locke, Montesquieu, and Hume. He possessed great synthetic powers but made few intellectual advances beyond his predecessors.

For these reasons, it is difficult, as with Möser, to locate the originality in Smith's individual proposals. Thus the publication of *The Wealth of Nations* in 1776 is a somewhat arbitrary benchmark for measuring change in economic

[112] Möser, "Wie ist die Drespe im menschlichen Geschlechte am besten zu veredlen?" *SW*, 7:44.
[113] Of the large literature on physiocracy, see Ronald L. Meek, *The Economics of Physiocracy* (Cambridge, Mass., 1963), 15–34, 364–98; Schumpeter, *History of Economic Analysis*, 223–49; Blaug, *Economic Theory in Retrospect*, 24–9; Ernst Hinrichs, "Produit Net, Propriétaire, Cultivateur. Aspekte des sozialen Wandels bei den Physiokraten und Turgot," in *Festschrift für Hermann Heimpel*, 2 vols. (Göttingen, 1971–3), 473–510. Of physiocracy and its impact on German reform, see the older study by Roscher, "Die Physiokratie in Deutschland," *Geschichte der Nationalökonomik in Deutschland*, 480–500. For Baden, see Helen Liebel, *Enlightened Bureaucracy versus Enlightened Despotism in Baden*, in *Transactions of the American Philosophical Society*, 55/5 (Philadelphia, 1965), 49–53; for the Habsburg domains, see the general statement of Hugo Hantsch, *Die Geschichte Oesterreichs*, 2 vols. (2nd ed.; Graz, 1953–9), 1:142; and for the influence of Turgot and physiocracy on Joseph II, see Rozdolski, *Große Steuer- und Agrarreform*, 17 and note 25.
[114] Adam Smith, *Wealth of Nations*, ed. Edwin Cannan (New York, 1965), 4:1, 398–419. For a brief history of the concept, see V. A. Judges, "The Idea of a Mercantile State," 36–40; Lütge, *Deutsche Sozial- und Wirtschaftsgeschichte*, 368.

policy. Smith advocated the elimination of government controls in four main areas: freedom to work through the abolition of guild regulations and settlement laws; free trade in land; internal free trade; and free trade in foreign commerce. Of these proposals, it is clear that certain were already realized, others never to be. At the same time Smith never advocated unbridled competition, allowing for government interference in places where it promoted the general welfare – in the administration of justice, in protection against foreign enemies, and in the construction of public works.[115]

Möser too, as we have seen, presented reform proposals that seem to foreshadow future liberal economic policy; he argued, for instance, for free trade in grain and for the right of seasonal migration for Osnabrück's laboring poor. In other respects, however, his economic thought differed from Smith's in emphasis and approach. Smith, skeptical of the state's competence, accorded to government areas of intervention within a basically free market; Möser, possessing more faith in government regulation and skeptical of unchecked interests, granted to society enclaves of economic freedom within a highly regulated economic system that was subordinated to the needs of the state. This shift in accent was one of the chief characteristics of the older cameralist tradition and remained a distinguishing feature of German liberalism throughout the nineteenth century.[116]

Thus even when we find points of contact between Justus Möser and a man like Adam Smith, it is difficult to feel comfortable about the similarities, particularly if we see them in terms of future liberal theory. It is clear that we must develop a more flexible notion of Enlightenment reform, treating the various elements of Enlightenment thought – its intention and potential theoretical coherence – together with the historical context of its reception and adaptation. In Osnabrück's mixed economy, with its heavy dependence upon the export of workers and linen and its large migratory labor force, neither physiocracy, nascent liberal economic theory, nor a rigid cameralism made sense. Even with these qualifications, it remains difficult to decide whether Möser's own administrative reforms resulted from a commitment to enlightened values, however defined, or whether they prove to be mere accidents of the economic dependence of the small bishopric upon the larger regional economy. Since he believed in concrete, technical reforms and argued for these only indirectly, the answer will remain unclear.

In order to establish the range of economic policy in the decades after the Seven Years War, we can compare Möser's views and reform efforts to the reforms undertaken in the so-called enlightened absolutist states: the Brandenburg-Prussia of Friedrich II, the German-speaking Habsburg domains of Joseph II, and the Baden of Karl Friedrich. In each of these countries, economic policy also stopped

---

[115] The points in this paragraph are based on Jacob Viner, "Adam Smith and Laissez Faire," in his *The Long View and the Short* (Glencoe, Ill., 1958), 221–3, 225, 231–45.

[116] Schumpeter, *History of Economic Analysis*, 172; Liebel, *Enlightened Bureaucracy*, 69–70; see also the argument in Krieger, *The German Idea of Freedom* (Boston, 1957), and Donald Rohr, *The Origins of Social Liberalism in Germany* (Chicago, 1963).

far short of the systematic application of ideas we might like to see as part of a model of Enlightenment reform. In each, reform was continuously adapted to vested social and political interests.[117] In each, the absolutist impulse made mercantilism into a system that subordinated the economy to concerns of politics and power[118] – the "program of an absolute prince ruling in the interest of his feudal patrimony"[119] – and in each, the absolutist impulse weighed as heavily as the enlightened impulse.[120] It is difficult to see how more was accomplished in these states prior to the French Revolution than Möser accomplished in Osnabrück.

In the other ecclesiastical states of northwestern Germany we note even less reform than in Osnabrück. In neighboring Münster, for instance, Franz von Fürstenberg came to power with unlimited authority given to him by archbishop Max Franz in Cologne, and he launched an ambitious effort to rebuild the bishopric after the war. When he failed to link the bishopric more closely to England, he changed to an active cameralism similar to Möser's policies in Osnabrück – limiting imports and encouraging exports through an expansion of the linen trade. He also tried to reduce the large postwar debt, to expand roads and waterways, and to regulate relations between seigneurs and peasants by adopting Osnabrück's property law as his model. Though von Fürstenberg had far more power than Möser, his reforms proved to be relatively insignificant, since he was never able to overcome the resistance of the Estates.[121] In Cologne, Max Franz also tried to bring about similar reforms, but he was never able to go beyond small beginnings or to attack agrarian relations. His significant

---

[117] For Brandenburg-Prussia, see Horst Krüger, *Zur Geschichte der Manufakturen und Manufakturarbeiter* (Berlin, 1958), 101–5 and throughout; for Prussia and the Rhineland, see Herbert Kisch, "The Textile Industries in Silesia and the Rhineland: A Comparative Study in Industrialization," *JEH*, 19 (1959):542–54; also his *Hausindustrielle Textilgewerbe am Niederrhein*; Motteck, *Wirtschaftsgeschichte Deutschlands* 1:333–53; Müller, *Märkische Landwirtschaft*; Hugo Rachel, "Der Merkantilismus in Brandenburg-Preussen," *FBPG*, 40 (1927):238–42, 246, 255. For Baden, see Liebel, *Enlightened Bureaucracy*; for the Habsburg domains, see the older study of Paul von Mitrofanov, *Josef II. Seine politische und kulturelle Tätigkeit*, 2 vols. (Vienna, 1910), vol. 2, and Rozdolski, *Große Steuer- und Agrarreform*.

[118] Viner, "Power versus Plenty as Objectives of Foreign Policy in the 17th and 18th Centuries," in his *The Long View and the Short*, 277–305; D. C. Coleman, "Eli Heckscher and the Idea of Mercantilism," *Revisions in Mercantilism*, 92–117.

[119] Leibel, *Enlightened Bureaucracy*, 9. With this formulation, Liebel attempts to distinguish between mercantilism and a cameralism "which began to stand for the policies of the bourgeois bureaucracy." It does not seem possible, however, to separate intentions and make the political distinction so easily. For the opposite view of cameralism, see Krüger, *Zur Geschichte der Manufakturen*, 67.

[120] Unfortunately, the discussion of enlightened absolutism has rarely examined policies; rather, it has remained in the more rarified air of absolutist sentiment. See the criticisms of George Lefebvre, "Der aufgeklärte Absolutismus," 80–2, and Hans Rosenberg, "Die Ueberwindung der monarchischen Autokratie (Preußen)," 182–7; both are reprinted in *Der aufgeklärte Absolutismus*, ed. Karl Otmar Freiherr von Aretin (Cologne, 1974).

[121] Hanschmidt, *Franz von Fürstenberg*, 2–3, 99–124; Rudolf Vierhaus, "Die Landstände in Nordwestdeutschland im späteren 18. Jahrhundert," in Dietrich Gerhard, ed., *Ständische Vertretungen in Europa im 17. und 18. Jahrhundert*, in *Veröffentlichungen des Max-Planck-Instituts für Geschichte*, 27 (Göttingen, 1969), 86–9.

achievement rested in educational reform with the founding of the university of Cologne and with the general educational code that was promulgated in the 1790s.[122] Farther to the south, in Würzburg or Mainz, for example, there was again little movement except in the area of educational reform. What little occurred, however, was wholly in the spirit of Möser's reforms in Osnabrück.[123]

It is therefore difficult to construct a coherent spectrum of enlightened economic policy in the Germanies in these decades, especially if we base our criteria on administrative practice. Even when liberal economic theory developed from assumptions within the Enlightenment, this theory did not surface as systematic policy until the decades after Möser's death. Moreover, this policy did not become an independent factor in economic change until the pre-March period. As is well known, the earliest influence of Adam Smith's work in Germany appeared in the progressive intellectual environment of Göttingen in the late 1770s, where it had an important influence on professors such as Pütter, Schlözer, Gatterer, Meiners, Beckmann, and later Leuder. But these Göttingen professors were men without administrative powers, and Göttingen was the only locus of "Smithianism" in Germany until the first decades of the nineteenth century, when the students of these men – Hardenberg, Stein, Kraus, Hufeland, Thaer, Thünen – began to promote liberal economic ideas in the Prussian bureaucracy and to disseminate them further in Halle and Königsberg.[124]

The chief issue in Möser's lifetime over which enlightened publicists and administrators differed was peasant emancipation. Here enlightened public opinion became deeply and justifiably aroused. Yet the milder form of Westphalian serfdom made emancipation somewhat more complex than either the sale of mercenary soldiers in Braunschweig or Hesse or the conditions of *Gutsherrschaft* on the large estates of eastern Germany or Mecklenberg. Once again, we need to distinguish between theory and practice. It is typical of Möser's historical position that when peasant emancipation occurred in Germany – in the Rhineland, for instance, during the wars of the French Revolution – it assumed exactly the pattern of Möser's reforms in Osnabrück. There we see the same effort to make technical adjustments while preserving in its totality the political preeminence of the seigneurial class.[125]

In Möser's Germany, then, it is difficult to find an Enlightenment measuring stick by which to gauge Möser's own reforms. In the eighteenth century, the economic and social policies within the individual states were highly eclectic,

---

[122] Max Braubach, *Maria Theresias Jüngster Sohn Max Franz* (Vienna, 1961), 115–73.

[123] T. C. W. Blanning, *Reform and Revolution in Mainz 1743–1803* (Cambridge, 1974), 107–17; Hildegunde Flurschütz, *Die Verwaltung des Hochstifts Würzburg unter Franz Ludwig von Erthal (1779–1795)*, in *Veröffentlichungen der Gesellschaft für fränkische Geschichte*, ser. 9 [*Darstellungen aus der fränkischen Geschichte*, 19] (Würzburg, 1965), 63–172.

[124] Wilhelm Treue, "Adam Smith in Deutschland," in *Deutschland und Europa. Festschrift für Hans Rothfels* (Düsseldorf, 1951), 101–33.

[125] Elizabeth Fehrenbach, *Traditionale Gesellschaft und revolutionäres Recht*, in *Kritische Studien zur Geschichtswissenschaft*, 13 (Göttingen, 1974), 22–8, 36–55, 149.

unsystematic, and continuous with older traditions of administrative centralization and reform. The continuity between economic policymaking and older practices signals a lag between the Enlightenment conceived as a system of ideas – market economy, possessive individualism, civil society – and as a real description of an altering or altered world. In small states like Osnabrück, this lag was intensified. As part of larger economic units, these smaller states were not able to develop economic solutions on a regional scale. Given the intractability of their problems and the slow pace of social and economic change, economic policy had to accept a system of limited wants and inelastic demand. In certain areas, these small economies appear to have imbibed the active spirit of curiosity and experiment we associate with the Enlightenment – in land reclamation, land use and crops, the building of roads and canals, the protectionist support and encouragement of local industry – but these reforms were integrated almost without disruption into the established traditions of mercantile or cameralist exploitation.[126]

For all of these reasons, Möser appears to have been a typical enlightened administrator in the years after the Seven Years War, one who adjusted goals in terms of what he could achieve. From the 1770s on, however, a more self-consciously enlightened public emerged that began to break with the compromises of Möser and his contemporaries. In this changing world, Möser's work began to acquire a different set of meanings. From the 1770s on, the anti- or counter-Enlightenment dimensions in his thought became more prominent, as we will see in the next chapter.

[126] Wilhelm Abel, "Landwirtschaft, 1648–1800," in *Handbuch der deutschen Wirtschafts- und Sozialgeschichte*, ed. Hermann Aubin and Wolfgang Zorn, 2 vols. (Stuttgart, 1971–6), 1:511–13, 519; B. H. Slicher van Bath, *Agrarian History of Western Europe*, trans. Olive Ordish (London, 1966), 239.

# 6

## Möser's social theory: local patriotism and the defense of the estates

In the 1770s Justus Möser acquired national stature as an author, benefiting from an expanding German reading public that became almost insatiable in its consumption of books, newspapers, and journals. The number of writers climbed from an estimated 2,000 in 1770 to 8,000 in 1795, and two-thirds of the roughly 175,000 books published in Germany in the eighteenth century appeared after 1760.[1] The publication of the first three volumes of the *Patriotic Phantasies* in 1774, 1775, and 1778 – the fourth came out in 1786 – were part of this expansion, and their popularity encouraged a second edition in Möser's lifetime; a third edition was published as part of his collected works shortly after his death. Möser's works were popular because, along with novels and belles lettres, the public especially craved historical-political journalism in these years. About 10 percent of all German book production after 1760 fell into the category of history; about 15 percent of all journals specialized in historical subjects. Except for literature, no other category seems to have grown so rapidly.[2] In addition, local reading societies subscribed to a surprisingly large number of historical-political and cameralist journals.[3] The public clearly demanded this type of writing as part of the awakened interest in reform of all kinds; it read such works in order to examine the legitimacy of the existing order and to begin to create a new civil society with its own historical traditions. Consequently, the greatest interest was in history with a contemporary focus: more than 80 percent of the historical journals dealt with contemporary matters. Moreover, like the *Patriotic Phantasies* or the *Osnabrück History,* most of this writing treated provincial affairs.

---

[1] See the statistics reprinted in H. Kiesel and P. Münch, *Gesellschaft und Literatur im 18. Jahrhundert* (Munich, 1977), 181; also Albert Ward, *Book Production, Fiction and the German Reading Public, 1740–1800* (Oxford, 1974).
[2] Otto Dann, "Das historische Interesse in der deutschen Gesellschaft des 18. Jahrhunderts." in Karl Hammer and Jürgen Voss, ed., *Historische Forschung im 18. Jahrhundert* (Bonn, 1976), 392–7; Ingeborg Salzbrunn, *Studien zur deutschen historischen Zeitschriftenwesen von der Göttinger Aufklärung bis zur Herausgabe der Historischen Zeitschrift,* (Ph.D. diss., Münster, 1959), introduction.
[3] Marlies Prüsener, "Lesegesellschaften im 18. Jahrhundert," *Archiv für Geschichte des Buchwesens,* 13 (1973):427–31, 495–504.

145

By 1780 the new public had also become qualitatively different.[4] The traditional carriers of secular culture – the legal profession, the clerical establishment, the university professoriate – were beginning to lose much of their cultural monopoly to writers less clearly attached to official institutions and to the centers of power. The literate classes also began to organize themselves much more intensively into voluntary societies, associations, clubs, and circles – some literary, some practical-economic, some political, and some religious. In these associations, traditional social boundaries started to dissolve; burgers and nobles gathered together to experiment with new forms of sociability.[5] As German society became more politicized, certain of these associations began to take on an esoteric character, seeking to influence policy by secretly controlling well-placed figures. Along with the order of Freemasons, the most famous or notorious were the Illuminati and the Wednesday Society or *Mittwochsgesellschaft* in Berlin.[6]

One chief consequence of the altering civil order was that resistance to the Enlightenment increased as latent generational, intellectual, and political differences within the Enlightenment became manifest in these years. The tendency toward division was accelerated by efforts of the authorities to regain control and stifle opposition: thus the Illuminati, founded in 1776, were banned in Bavaria in 1785. In Berlin after the death of Friedrich II (1786), Friedrich Wilhelm II sought to reverse the religious toleration of his predecessor through a return to orthodoxy and increasing censorship, and, in the Habsburg domains, church, aristocracy, and administration increasingly resisted the Josephinian reform movement.[7]

---

[4] Richard von Dülmen, "Die Aufklärungsgesellschaften als Forschungsproblem," *Francia*, 5 (1977):251–75.

[5] See Lessing's famous dialogue "Ernst und Falk, Gespräche für Freimäurer" (1778), in his *Gesammelte Werke*, ed. Paul Rilla, 10 vols. (2nd ed.; Berlin, 1968), 8:547–89; also Norbert Schindler, "Freimaurerkultur im 18. Jahrhundert. Zur sozialen Funktion des Geheimnisses in der entstefenden bürgerlichen Gesellschaft," in *Klassen und Kultur*, Robert Berdahl, et al., eds. (Frankfurt am Main, 1982), 205–63; and the recent collection *Freimaurer und Geheimbünde im 18. Jahrhundert in Mitteleuropa*, Helmut Reinalter, ed. (Frankfurt am Main, 1983).

[6] Regarding the phenomenon of associations, see Thomas Nipperdey, "Verein als soziale Struktur im späten 18. und frühen 19. Jahrhundert," in *Geschichtswissenschaft und Vereinswesen im 19. Jahrhundert*, ed. Hartmut Boockmann, et al. [*Veröffentlichungen des Max-Planck-Instituts für Geschichte*, 1] (Göttingen, 1972), esp. 5–23; Jürgen Habermas, *Strukturwandel der Oeffentlichkeit* (4th ed., Neuwied, 1969), 38–68; *Deutsche patriotische und gemeinnützige Gesellschaften*, ed. Rudolf Vierhaus [*Wolfenbüttler Forschungen*, 8] (Wolfenbüttel, 1980). For a general survey of the Illuminati and other secret societies see Richard van Dülmen, *Der Geheimbund der Illuminaten* (Stuttgart, 1975); also his "Antijesuitismus und katholische Aufklärung," *Historisches Jahrbuch*, 89/1 (1969):52–80; Klaus Epstein, *The Genesis of German Conservatism* (Princeton, N.J., 1966), 84–111, 354–7. For the Berlin *Mittwochsgesellschaft*, see Adolf Stölzel, "Die Berliner Mittwochsgesellschaft über Aufhebung oder Reform der Universitäten (1795)," in *FBPG*, 2 (1889):201–22; Norbert Hinske, ed., *Was ist Aufklärung? Beiträge aus der Berlinischen Monatsschrift* (Darmstadt, 1973), XXIV–XXXVI; Horst Möller, *Aufklärung in Preußen. Der Verleger, Publizist und Geschichtsschreiber Friedrich Nicolai* (Berlin, 1974), 229–38.

[7] See, for instance, Fritz Valjavec, "Das Woellnersche Religionsedikt und seine geschichtliche Bedeutung," *Historisches Jahrbuch*, 72 (1953):386–400; Ernst Wangermann, *From Joseph II to the Jacobin Trials* (2nd ed.; Oxford, 1969), 5–55.

The new constellation also brought forth intensified intellectual resistance to the chief ideas of the Enlightenment. Such opposition had always existed, deriving its strength from an allegiance to Christian-medieval values and institutions. The church, aristocracy, and corporations continued in these years to resist Enlightenment notions of reform. They defended the system of Estates, absolute monarchy, or the prerogatives of the nobility by attacking younger natural rights doctrines of individual autonomy, freedom, and legal equality.[8] They idealized inequality, hierarchy, prescriptive rights, and social harmony within corporate institutions. But now the Enlightenment more clearly set the terms of the discussion, for the critics began to justify themselves and their threatened world in the language of the Enlightenment itself. Möser was significant to the public debate because he recast estatist or corporatist presuppositions in the language of the Enlightenment and thus served as a link to traditionalist critics.

Some opponents went further than Möser, attempting, like J. G. Hamann (1730–88) and Joseph d'Maistre (1753–1821), to develop a secular philosophical justification of the medieval-Christian order by rejecting both the language and values of the Enlightenment. Hamann's attacks on Enlightenment culture and rationalism were typical of the attempt to construct a counterposition. He praised religious belief over secular humanism, intuition and spirituality over analytical method, the eternal over the fleeting. He argued that all truths were particular, never general; understanding was an immediate mystical communion with God, and poetry and history were direct ways of experiencing a God-filled human reality.[9] In Hamann's work we can see the outline of what would become philosophical irrationalism in the next century: the methodological commitment to intuitionism, hermeneutics, and an aesthetic of "totality"; the presumption of the plurality and uniqueness of cultures; a deep pessimism concerning the perfectability of the species; and an equally profound skepticism concerning the existence and meaning of nature or scientific laws.[10]

Cultural historians and philosophers from the late nineteenth century on have used labels like "irrationalism" or "counter-Enlightenment" to characterize this intellectual resistance; nonetheless, it is dubious whether it ever formed a clear system of ideas.[11] To write of irrationalism as a philosophy or the counter-Enlightenment as a movement, historians have had to project ideal constructs

[8] Fritz Valjavec, *Die Entstehung der politischen Strömungen in Deutschland 1770–1815* (2nd ed.; Düsseldorf, 1978), 39–87; idem., "Die Entstehung des europäischen Konservatismus," reprinted in *Konservatismus*, ed. Hans Gerd Schumann (Cologne, 1974), 138–55; Alfred von Martin, "Weltanschauliche Motiven im altkonservativen Denkin," in *Deutscher Staat und deutsche Parteien. Festschrift für Friedrich Meinecke*, ed. Paul Wentzke (Munich, 1922), 342–84.

[9] Rudolf Unger, *Hamann und die deutsche Aufklärung*, 2 vols. (4th ed.; Darmstadt, 1968), and the valuable translation, introduction and commentary with bibliography by James C. O'Flaherty to *Hamann's Socratic Memorabilia* (Baltimore, 1967).

[10] Isaiah Berlin, "The Counter-Enlightenment," in *Against the Current*, ed. Henry Hardy (New York, 1980), 1–24.

[11] Georg Lukács, *The Destruction of Reason*, trans. Peter Palmer (Atlantic Highlands, N.J., 1981), 96–7, 125.

back onto a more complex and richer reality. They have also had to portray the world view of the Enlightenment as more limited and more coherent than was in fact the case. The Enlightenment appears in this interpretation as a movement of cold rationalists devoid of any appreciation of the sensual, the emotional, and the spiritual, attributes that became the monopoly of the counter-Enlightenment. The historical reality was not so simple, however. Philosophical irrationalism was more a reactive than a constructive movement, a response to specific forms of rationalism and a defense of particular objects and institutions that the Enlightenment attacked. Hence it lacked the drive to be systematic or self-sustaining, receiving its impetus only from the concrete historical debate with rationalism.[12] The counter-Enlightenment developed alongside the Enlightenment and acquired historical significance only in opposition to it. As a movement, the counter-Enlightenment was even broader and less coherent than philosophical irrationalism; most of its spokesmen did not adopt a purely negative stance toward the Enlightenment, as did Hamann or d'Maistre, but compromised with it, accepting some aspects of the Enlightenment vision while rejecting others. The construct of counter-Enlightenment thus proved to be a Procrustean bed; its incumbents fit only if certain basic features of their thought were suppressed or reduced to the status of residue. Figures such as Vico, Herder, or Justus Möser are typical victims of such maneuvers.[13]

The relations between the Enlightenment and the counter-Enlightenment were especially complex in Germany during the years after the Seven Years War. Though there was a clear movement against the Enlightenment, central elements usually identified with the counter-Enlightenment were in fact fundamental to the Enlightenment itself. Hermeneutical method and qualitative analysis, for example, had been part of German university education since the Reformation and were frequently used by academically trained participants in the German Enlightenment movement.[14] Shaftesbury, a figure whom Berlin sees as critical to the development of the counter-Enlightenment, was also clearly significant to individuals such as Lessing, Mendelssohn, Nicolai, and other Enlightenment writers.[15] The political Estates, finally, and corporatism as a system of social

---

[12] The classic statement remains Karl Mannheim, "Conservative Thought," in *Essays on Sociology and Social Psychology*, ed. Paul Kecskemeti (London, 1966), 74–164.

[13] For Herder, see Emil Adler, *Herder und die deutsche Aufklärung* (Wien, 1968), 136–46. Hans Aarsleff has shown persuasively Herder's dependence on Condillac and, in general, how historically doubtful is Berlin's account of Herder. See Aarsleff's discussion and his exchange with Berlin, "Vico and Berlin," *London Review of Books*, 3/20 (1981):6–8, 4/10 (1982):4–5; also Aarsleff, *From Locke to Saussure* (Minneapolis, 1982), esp. 117, 150–1, 195–8, 218–20. For Berlin's views, see "Herder and the Enlightenment," in his *Vico and Herder* (New York, 1976), 143–216, and the views in *Against the Current*. On this general problem, see also Jaroslav Kudrna, "Vico and Herder," *Jahrbuch für Geschichte*, 19 (1979):61–88. On Möser, see Joachim Streisand, *Geschichtliches Denken von der deutschen Frühaufklärung bis zur Klassik* (2nd ed.; Berlin, 1967), 8, 67–72.

[14] Notker Hammerstein, "Der Anteil des 18. Jahrhunderts und der Ausbildung der historischen Schulen des 19. Jahrhunderts" in Hammer and Voss, ed., *Historische Forschung*, 436–42.

[15] Berlin, *Against the Current*, 9. Nicolai recorded how important Shaftesbury was to Lessing, Men-

values were still a vital part of everyday life and a focus of continuing commitment. A radical democratic or egalitarian Enlightenment did not emerge in Germany prior to the outbreak of the French Revolution. Wherever radical democracy had joined with the Enlightenment – in France, England or America – it forced the clarification of political ideals within the inegalitarian Enlightenment, thus causing typically liberal and conservative beliefs to emerge with greater systematic coherence. In Germany, however, political beliefs were not openly articulated clearly until the Napoleonic Wars and even further into the pre-March period.[16]

As a consequence, the complicated, ambivalent attachment to the Enlightenment that we have traced in Justus Möser was far more common to the broad center of the German Enlightenment than is normally assumed. Möser is best understood as part of the moderate reform movement I have labeled the "corporatist Enlightenment," and there is no doubt that his attitudes and concerns were broadly typical of the German Enlightenment in these years. Möser saw himself as progressive in the context of the ecclesiastical states, since he was the figure providing whatever movement was possible in the inflexible institutional world of Osnabrück. He and his fellow administrators undertook technical and limited reforms; their intention was modestly progressive without being revolutionary. They were, in sum, political paternalists committed to the Estates or to absolute monarchy, who sought to adapt the spirit of the Enlightenment to Germany's oligarchical institutions.

The question still remains of how Justus Möser could have become a figure of counter-Enlightenment revolt to later philosophers and historians. In this chapter I have examined those themes related to place, region, and the social and political environments that might link him to chief assumptions of the counter-Enlightenment. I have gathered these loosely connected elements together under the rubric of Möser's social theory. It is important to realize, however, that such themes remained fragmentary in his work; he never treated them with any consistency, and it is therefore difficult to discover a clear pattern of development.

I consider first Möser's struggle to reconcile local and cosmopolitan values. European culture was still swayed by the great theme of regionalism in Möser's day; this had both a universalist and a particularist dimension: the local could be seen both as a deepening and a rejection of the cosmopolitan.[17] In the eighteenth century, "local patriotism" – in the sense of both attachment to and reform and improvement of local conditions – was a key theme within the German Enlightenment; in the nineteenth century, however, localism often became associated with anti-Enlightenment values. Möser's writings toward the end of his life evoked such associations, and he was so read in the nineteenth century.

delssohn, and himself; see Friedrich Nicolai, *Ueber meine gelehrte Bildung* (Berlin, 1799). See also my own comments in the section "Enlightenment in Osnabrück" in Chapter 2.

[16] See the persuasive argument in Valjavec, *Entstehung der politischen Strömungen*.

[17] Dietrich Gerhard, "Regionalismus und ständisches Wesen," in his *Alte und neue Welt in vergleichender Geschichtsbetrachtung*, in *Veröffentlichungen des Max-Planck-Instituts für Geschichte*, 10 (Göttingen, 1962):27, 37.

Second, Möser was not a carrier of urban values. Like James Harrington or John Locke in England, he was attached to agrarian society and had the mentality of a member of the provincial gentry. He defended the political world of the Estates and the social prerogatives of the nobility not only as secretary to the nobility but also from inner conviction. This defense became a rather critical link to late-nineteenth-century German conservatism, which rejected parliamentary institutions and civil liberties. Möser developed these ideas in his inegalitarian social contract theory, his *Aktientheorie*, but he expressed his defense of feudal privileges in enlightened language. It is perhaps for this reason that his ideas appealed predominantly to liberals like Karl Rotteck, Karl Theodor Welcker, and Friedrich List in the pre-March period.[18] It was not until the second half of the century that conservatives began to recognize Möser as one of their own – a fact that reveals more about the evolution of liberalism and conservatism as political ideologies in the nineteenth century than about Möser's own, more ambiguous political views.[19]

Considered last is Möser's historical aesthetic, his theory of "totality" or "total impressions" (*Totaleindrücke*), which he developed in connection with the peasant mentality. Historians have seized on these fragments in order to link Möser to the historicist movement, giving them in the process an importance beyond their worth.[20]

Thus this is a chapter in historical ambiguity and later misreading. In it I examine Möser's social thought in a twofold context: the growing intensification of debate within the Enlightenment from the later 1770s until the end of the century and the nebulous history of philosophical irrationalism and the counter-Enlightenment, which is largely the construct of a later period. Among other things, the chapter shows how weak are the philosophical links between Möser and the counter-Enlightenment. Instead what emerges as central is his defense of the Estates and his rationally argued commitment to inequality. This stance marks a boundary between him and a more egalitarian Enlightenment and at the same time places him within the mainstream of European liberalism in its inegalitarian form.

## LOCALISM AND ANTICOSMOPOLITANISM

The conflict of loyalties between the local and the cosmopolitan has been one of the permanent themes of European history. The view that provincial life is narrow and stultifying is based to an extent on a basic fear of the outsider that survives in local communities. The Enlightenment exacerbated such fears, particularly by

---

[18] See Ernst Hempel, "Justus Mösers Wirkung auf seine Zeitgenossen und auf die deutsche Geschichtsschreibung," *Osn. Mitt.*, 54 (1933):43–8.

[19] Hans Rosenberg, *Politische Denkströmungen im deutschen Vormärz {Kritische Studien zur Geschichtswissenschaft*, 3] (Göttingen, 1974), 20–39.

[20] Hans Baron, "Justus Mösers Individualitätsprinzip in seiner geistesgeschichtlichen Bedeutung," *HZ*, 130 (1924):31–57; Georg Iggers, *The German Conception of History* (2nd ed.; Middletown, Conn., 1984).

threatening patterns of life, church customs, or privileges gained through kinship or inheritance.[21] Yet the German Enlightenment was itself a provincial movement, since every urban center in Germany was part of a particular provincial society with its own linguistic, religious, and social peculiarities. The provincial dimension may have been weaker in the early Enlightenment, which concerned itself with narrower philosophical and technical scientific matters. Once the Enlightenment became a popular movement, however, it was forced to explore the special nature of the national or regional culture in which it existed.

From the Seven Years War on, local patriotism began to pervade the Enlightenment in Germany.[22] This should not be seen as part of the first wave of counter-Enlightenment; rather, it was part of a deepening and differentiation within Enlightenment culture itself. Bodmer and Breitinger in Switzerland, Albrecht von Haller in Göttingen, and the small circle around Lessing and Nicolai in Berlin all began to emphasize German themes as aspects of the Enlightenment. Even J. C. Gottsched, the advocate of French style and standards, called for the study and publication of medieval German poetry. Local patriotism did not prevent reform or change from occurring at home. Rather, it accentuated the traditional debate between localism and cosmopolitanism at the level of public opinion. This debate, however, could be easily misconstrued as a protest against everything contemporary, so that in years after the outbreak of the French Revolution, in the midst of the Romantic revolt, the protective attitude toward one's region could easily by mistaken – and appropriated – as part of an anti-Enlightenment stance.

Möser's attitudes toward the Enlightenment were formed within the context of a defensive Westphalian patriotism. Westphalia (Osnabrück is today part of Lower Saxony) had long been associated with backwardness, ignorance, and superstition.[23] Consider, for example, the character of Baron Thunder-Ten-Tronckh in *Candide* (1759), who "was one of the most powerful lords of Westphalia, for his castle possessed a door and windows." During Möser's lifetime this topos became interwoven with a new Enlightenment debate over cultural advance in the provinces. A tone of defensiveness and criticism runs throughout the domestic travel literature of the period and can be found in the works of

[21] Edward Shils, *Tradition* (Chicago, 1981), 2–6; *Sozialer und kultureller Wandel in der ländlichen Welt des 18. Jahrhunderts*, ed. Ernst Hinrichs and Günter Wiegelmann [Wolfenbüttler Forschungen, 19] (Wolfenbüttel, 1982), 8–10, 45–50.

[22] Friedrich Meinecke, *Weltbürgertum und Nationalstaat* (4th ed.; Stuttgart, 1964); Wolfgang Zorn, "Reichs- und Freiheitsgedanken in der Publizistik des ausgehenden 18. Jahrhunderts (1763–1792)," *Quellen und Darstellungen zur Geschichte des deutschen Freiheitsbewegung*, 2 (1959), esp. 35–49; Hans Erich Bödeker, "Thomas Abbt: Patriot, Bürger und bürgerliches Bewußtsein," in *Bürger und Bürgerlichkeit im Zeitalter der Aufklärung*, ed. Rudolf Vierhaus (Heidelberg, 1981).

[23] For this general problem see Paul Casser, "Das Raum Westfalenbewußtsein im Wandel der Geschichte," in *Der Raum Westfalen*, ed. Hermann Aubin, 4 vols. (Münster, 1931–58), 2:213–94; Friedrich Keinemann, "Zeitgenössische Ansichten über die Entwicklung von Wirtschaft, Gesellschaft und Kultur in den westfälischen Territorien in der zweiten Hälfte des 18. Jahrhunderts," *Westfälische Zeitschrift*, 120 (1970):399–454; Paul Probst, *Westfalen in der Kritik des XVIII. Jahrhunderts* (Ph.D. diss., Münster, 1912).

many of Möser's acquaintances. Georg Ludwig von Bar, Möser's most cultivated noble patron, composed an ode to his Westphalian fatherland in which he accused it of being the land of Swift's Yahoos.[24] Johann Christian Gruner, also a friend of the Möser family, wrote a *Defense of Westphalia*,[25] and Pastor Johann Moritz Schwager of Osnabrück, one of Möser's intellectually eccentric contemporaries, published a marvelously backhanded "Attempt at a Defense of the Westphalians" in the *Berlinische Monatsschrift* (1783) that was noteworthy for the narrowness and provinciality it sought to deny.[26]

Typical of such essays is one by an anonymous author from nearby Göttingen, which recounted in Schlözer's *Staatsanzeigen* (1783) the forms of discrimination Westphalians continued to suffer. King Friedrich II of Prussia, for example, was supposed to have broken off a conversation with Stephen Pütter, the Göttingen professor of law, when he learned Pütter was from Westphalia. The author concluded that "the Westphalians and the Pomeranians from time immemorial have had the special fate among Germans to be the object of various tales and legends and held as incapable of finer cultivation and Enlightenment. . . . Whenever a Westphalian enters another province he is treated as a person requiring care and guidance in manners and culture."[27]

Although Osnabrück and its history as part of Westphalia was at the center of Möser's work, it is significant that we find little Westphalian defensiveness in it. Möser did not concentrate on Westphalian matters for their own sake alone, but used local themes for more universal purposes. His first play, *Arminius* (1748), imitated French tragedy in Germanic costume, adapting the legend of Roman defeat in the local Teutoberg forest by Saxon warriors under Arminius. He made classical heroes of the ancient Germans, keeping the Latin name of Arminius (in place of the German Hermann) and defending their Stoic demeanor and classical cultivation. "I am not of the opinion," he wrote, "that our ancestors were such boobs (*Klötze*) as one normally imagines from the first reading of Tacitus."[28] In the same way, his Latin treatise, "Concerning the Old Germanic and Gallic Theology, Mystical and Popular" (1748) used local ruins of a pre-Christian site

[24] Quoted in Probst, *Westfalen*, 47.

[25] Ibid., 70.

[26] Schwager wrote the following about Osnabrück: "In Osnabrück sind wir schon sehr vorwärts, und wenn ich etwas beklagen soll – so ist es für Osnabrück ein zu großer Grad von Verfeinerung. Dieser Ort steckt voll von Adel und Gelehrten oder Studirten, Protestanten und Catholiken, die meist alle, und selbst die letztern, wenn sie sich nicht der Kirche widmen, nach Göttingen oder Leipzig gehen, und größtentheils nicht leer wiederzurück kommen. In Osnabrück finden sie alle Arten von feinen Vergnügungen, Concerten, Bälle, Pickenicke, Maskeraden, Assembleen, Clubs, mit unter Comödien, Coffeehäuser, in- und außerhalb der Stadt, Buchläden, Leihbibliotheken, Leser- und Journalgesellschaften, u.s.w. Man will behaupten, daß diese Verfeinerung für Verfaßung vieler Theilnehmer zu weit gehe, wenigstens kömmt das Heurathen aus der Mode." In "Versuch einer Schüszchrift für die Westfälinger," *Berlinische Monatsschrift*, 1 (1783):494–5.

[27] Anonymous, "Von dem preußischen Westfalen," *Staatsanzeigen*, 3/11 (1783):353–64. The article is signed "B———e" [Boie?], and the quotation is a composite from 353 and 358. See also similar views in anonymous [Frhr v. R], "Briefe über Westfalen," *Deutsches Museum*, 1 (1784):365.

[28] Möser, *SW*, 2:122.

of worship as the occasion to pursue a typical deistic argument – that the religion of the ancient Germanic peoples comprised both a popular "natural" religion and a mystical one of the priests.[29]

Local issues were, of course, also basic to the *Osnabrück History*. Peter Schmidt has shown that certain of its themes, especially the attempt to glorify the ancient Germans, belong to this tradition of local patriotism.[30] In examining Möser's library, he noted that Möser drew upon a contemporary work of regional piety by Pastor Gottfried Schütze of Altona, *Three Small Apologies for the Ancient Germans* (1746): there we learn that honesty, probity, and modesty were Germanic virtues, that Germans were not cannibals, that they hated lawyers, and that there was no religious strife. ("There was no conflict between theologians and philosophers then because the druids knew how to unite both in one person. Had the famous Wolff lived then, I am absolutely certain that the druids would all have been strict Wolffians.")[31] Möser adopted a similar, if less consciously naive, attitude in his history of Osnabrück when he defended the wisdom of the ancients, idealized their institutions, and interpreted the Carolingian conquest as the loss of a local golden age.

Thus Möser tested and adapted Enlightenment literary forms to Westphalian particularist materials. At the same time, he drew on local patriotism in the service of rhetorical engagement and political myth. In his later writings he adopted various voices that played with the range of attitudes surrounding Westphalian provinciality. In a "Letter of a French Traveller to His Host in Westphalia" (1773), for example, he parodied the values of the cosmopolitan. "I don't understand," the Frenchman wrote, "how people can live in such a place where they do nothing but work, eat, sleep, and are happy."[32] These essays, like those of Franklin's Poor Richard, associated the provincial with virtue and common sense and the cosmopolitan with aridity and frivolity. Yet these essays resemble the others we have examined: the more playful and aware they are, the more difficult it is to find Möser's own voice. A nationalist or racialist reader of Möser might well find a kindred spirit in one of Möser's many personae.

Alongside these light essays, however, which drew on provincial feelings, are others where Möser defended change and local improvement in the cosmopolitan language of the broader Enlightenment. A piece from 1770, "To my friend in Osnabrück", provides a typical example:

---

[29] *De veterum Germanorum et Gallorum Theologia mystica et populari*. See the text in ibid., 266–85; German translation, 393–404. In this treatise Möser acknowledged his direct dependence on the English deists Cudworth and Warburton, and also cited Pierre Bayle with approval. See also Werner Pleister, "Die geistige Entwicklung Justus Mösers," *Osn. Mitt.*, 50 (1929):53–62.

[30] Peter Schmidt, *Studien über Justus Möser als Historiker* (Göppingen, 1975), 11–23.

[31] M. Gottfried Schütze, *Drei kleine Schützschriften für die alten Deutschen* (Leipzig, 1746), quotation on 55.

[32] Möser, "Schreiben eines reisenden Franzosen an seinen Wirt in Westfalen" [1773], *SW*, 5:187–90. See also "Es bleibt beim Alten [1769]," *SW*, 4:183–5. See also "Für die warmen Stuben der Landleute" [1773], *SW*, 5:241–3; "Die Häuser des Landmanns im Osnabrückischen sind in ihrem Plan die besten" [c. 1767], *SW*, 6:127–9.

A native who travels will bring the sciences of many provinces home and introduce nothing of substance. But foreigners who settle down, introduce their customs and the old folks assimilate the good: buckwheat [and] potatoes were brought to us by foreigners – we did not do it ourselves, if I have been properly informed. All successful revolutions in economic life have occurred through wars, emigrations, and transplantations. We have no need of such revolutions – our country is not so crude – but to settle foreigners among our inhabitants is still valuable. There are certain artisanal and agricultural techniques and, along with these, certain implements and machines whose advantages deserve to be imitated. I do not need to speak of the advantages that accrue to the local inhabitants with respect to manners, religion, and public morality. Contact with foreigners makes one gentler and politer, and conquers prejudices peculiar to every nation. These are the advantages for the province.[33]

Here Möser welcomed the outsider, describing the advantages of a broader outlook than narrow provincialism. In other moods, however, he felt called to defend the local at the expense of the cosmopolitan, notably when he felt the world of the Estates and the decentralized institutions of the Empire to be threatened. This allowed him to protect the established local order against change or innovation that might be introduced from outside the region. This position drew on the belief that the productions of historical evolution had their own intelligent – and profounder – logic. This conclusion, in turn, was not far removed from hypostasizing that historical logic – "an experience of more than a hundred years is," as Möser wrote, "an astonishing experiment."[34] As a result, every change introduced from the outside, by invasion or the importation of foreign ideas, could be viewed as a betrayal of a more legitimate historical order. In this manner, the local could come to signify permanence and vitality, the cosmopolitan superficiality and corruption.

## DEFENDING THE ESTATES

At those moments when Möser felt that the independence or future of the bishopric was threatened, he fell back upon corporate attitudes and prejudices that were rooted in Osnabrück's constitutional system and his own administrative responsibilities. To his mind, he was a realist who accepted a society of limited options. In Osnabrück this meant accepting as natural an equilibrium between the legally constituted social forces – the Estates with their political rights and social prerogatives – and the land and its limited resources. Permanent social and political inequities existed because the land and its resources were limited. Reform might take place within these boundaries, but essentially each individual

---

[33] Möser, "An meinen Freund zu Osnabrück, über die Beschwerlichkeiten, Kolonisten anzusetzen" [1770], *SW*, 4:294. See also, for instance, his "Vorschlag zu einer Praktika für das Landvolk" [1772], *SW*, 5:134–7; "Ueber die verfeinerten Begriffe" [1777], *SW*, 6:220–2; "Also soll der handelnde Teil der Menschen nicht wie der spekulierende erzogen werden" [c. 1780], *SW*, 7:26–30.

[34] Möser, "Es bleibt beim Alten" [1769], *SW*, 4:184.

had to adapt to the institutional mechanisms controlling scarcity. In this way, Möser treated politics and institutions as emerging from society and the economy. He assumed a basic continuity between substructure and superstructure. He saw himself as an administrator mediating between legitimate social and economic interests in the name of impartial justice. But the Estates themselves provided the fundamental legal framework and perpetuated the natural equilibrium.

The mere existence of the Estates, however, did not explain why *this* order should have any claims on the living. Möser understood that he also needed to justify the power of the Estates within the context of the German Enlightenment by translating corporate inequality into terms appropriate to the later eighteenth century. He composed the *Osnabrück History* partly for this purpose, but he also cast his defense of the system of Estates in a language more general than that of the *Osnabrück History*. In his theoretical essays he justified existing inequities in two separate languages: that of a traditional corporatism and that of a modified social contract theory. We need to examine the different languages Möser used because they provide the link between the two systems of value.

The survival of corporate language in Möser is encapsulated in his traditional image of the state as a pyramid. The state "can be considered beautiful," he wrote, "when it has its proper proportions, resting on a good base and diminishing toward the top in such a way that the bottom carries the top without the least burden."[35] The three traditional Estates, the ruling, the military, and the commons, were permanent social bodies: each corresponded to the eternal necessities of communal life. Inequality was fundamental to the functioning of society because it promoted the greatest number of benefits for each order. Möser wrote, for example, that "differences between the estates in the world is a useful and necessary matter. Where everything is intertwined and the least [individual] may succeed to the highest posts, there is certainly a great deal of despotism and little incentive to service . . . . It is in the interest of each estate that the estate above it receive the greatest advantages."[36]

To Möser distinction between the orders of society was not simply "useful and necessary"; it was, as he had written to the officials of Joseph II, "part of nature itself."[37] One of his chief concerns, consequently, was to strengthen the bonds of solidarity within each order. Möser seemed to feel it his responsibility to support the dignity and virtue of the individual orders and political Estates, each of which had its particular "honor" and ethos. He articulated such views particularly in the midst of the postwar reforms during the 1760s and 1770s, attempting to bolster the rights and the unique importance of each Estate in order, one suspects, to rally the population around the necessity of continued

[35] Möser, "Der Staat mit einer Pyramide verglichen. Eine erbauliche Betrachtung" [1773], *SW*, 5:214–18. There he speaks of a high *Dienerschaft*, a *Wehrstand*, and a *Nährstand*.
[36] Möser, "Vom Unterschied der Stände," *SW*, 9:64. This fragment is undated and was titled by the editors.
[37] See Chapter 5, footnote 87.

sacrifice. The tone of overt political exhortation is overwhelming in the essays that employ corporate language and defend hereditary inequality. In "No Satires against Entire Estates," for example, Möser described how the magistrate "speaks with veneration of the peasant, even if at the same time, he allows a bad manager to feel the lash of criticism; he makes the artisan into the first patriot in order to stay him from the temptation to become a noxious peddler; and [he] prefers the large merchant to all important and insignificant men, so that he will not demean himself through a patent of nobility or convince his daughter to [enter] a marriage inappropriate to her burgher estate."[38]

Möser also promoted the honor of the various social orders by using historical arguments to trace the formation of the ethos and corporate function of each order or estate. Thus, he produced a series of sketches of each order's most significant moment in the past; these served as iconic types for his readers to admire and imitate. His essay on the feud (*Faustrecht*) served this purpose for the nobility, glorifying the individual combat and feudal warfare of the twelfth and thirteenth centuries. "The age of the feud in Germany appears to me to have been that period when our nation showed the greatest sense of honor, the greatest physical valor, and an individual greatness."[39] In other essays he celebrated the feats of the merchants and commoners of the Hanseatic League, contrasting urban inventiveness to imperial and aristocratic shortsightedness.[40] In still others he idealized the simple life of the peasant in the ancient days of "freedom and property" and praised it over a life of urban affectation or aristocratic decadence.[41]

We must understand that although these essays were cloaked in historical rhetoric, Möser was not concerned with historical explanation. Their purpose was political: to defend Osnabrück's institutional system. It was this purpose that allowed Möser to view each Estate and social order from its own corporate perspective and to praise each at the expense of the others. Möser created individually consistent historical archetypes that situated the rights and prerogatives of each group within the political life of the bishopric. With regard to our example concerning the right of the feud, for instance, Möser adopted a critical urban perspective that condemned feudal warfare, arguing that its abolition was necessary before a society of laws could emerge.[42]

---

[38] Möser, "Keine Satire gegen ganzen Stände," *SW*, 6:109.

[39] Möser, "Der hohe Stil der Kunst under den Deutschen," *SW*, 4:263–8. See also "Und doch reisen unsre Maler nach Italien oder unsre angehenden Gelehrten lernen Griechisch und Latein" [1774], *SW*, 9:71: "Freiheit, Größe und edler Empfindung war gewiß in den sogenannten Ritterzeiten tausendmal mehr in Deutschland als jetzt, seitdem wir durch jene Studien geschwächt worden."

[40] Möser, "Gedanken über den Verfall der Handlung in den Landstädten," *SW* 4:15; "Von den wahren Ursachen des Steigens und Fallens der Hanseatischen Handlung," ibid., 225–32; "Also sollen die deutschen Städte sich mit Genehmigung ihrer Landesherrn wiederum zur Handlung vereinigen," ibid., 215–23.

[41] Möser, "Die Spinnstube, eine osnabrückische Geschichte," *SW*, 4:42; "Es bleibt beim Alten," ibid., 183; also *Osnabrück History*, *SW*, 12/1:160.

[42] See, for instance, "Vorschlag zu einem neuen Plan der deutschen Reichsgeschichte," *SW*, 7:130; and "Der hohe Stil der Kunst under den Deutschen," 263.

Möser's ability to shift perspective from problem to problem and from one social group to another allowed him to understand the legal confusions within Osnabrück's static universe. His perspectivistic style reflected his position as mediator between entrenched interests. These short essays allowed him to gloss over problems of conflict and exploitation, evoking instead an idealized portrait of a Germanic, medieval, or early modern urban culture that would satisfy the craving for a lost harmonious past. At the same time, this format never forced him to resolve contradictions and to decide which explanation had the greater weight. Such a format was also fraught with explanatory confusion, never forcing him to develop a more coherent analytical style.

Möser's writing of this period ultimately seems not only contradictory but inauthentic, because he treated issues of historical development and change within the immutable legal framework of the bishopric. His simple social categories were actually political categories, and this deprived them of empirical force. His essays of social theory make no effort to portray the diversity of social life with the verisimilitude apparent in the many essays on local customs. Every theoretical essay that employed corporate language was concerned with the political purpose of the social group and, consequently, reduced the social to the legal. Möser described and defended the political function of the nobility in the state, for example, always stressing its ethos of honor, but he never analyzed the nobility as a highly differentiated social class.[43] (We glimpse the social and legal diversity among the local nobility only in random comments in letters and essays devoted to other purposes.) In the same manner, he portrayed the peasantry in functional terms, as the "necessary support of the state," and not in terms reflecting the intricacy of rural life.[44] Most telling for a historian living in an ecclesiastical state, he omitted all discussion of the clergy; as an order of resident outsiders, like the rural poor, they did not form part of the political order.

Why did Möser argue so readily in political terms? Apparently he perceived the institutional and social compromise among the Estates in Osnabrück to be exposed and potentially unstable. This anxiety revealed itself as a constant concern about despotism, although his interpretation of the despotic changed and was self-contradictory. He used despotism essentially as a formal category to express his sense that Osnabrück's institutions were inevitably in decay. The honor, ethos, and prerogatives of each order and political Estate had been formed at

---

[43] See, for instance, Möser, "Von der Nationalerziehung der alten Deutschen" [1781], *SW*, 7:19–23; "Ueber die Erziehung des Adels. Von einem Edelmann" [undated], ibid., 23–6; "Warum bildet sich der deutsche Adel nicht nach dem Englischen" [1780], ibid., 203–13; "Ueber die Adelsprobe in Deutschland" [undated], ibid., 221–42; "Wie der Unterschied der Stände auch schon in dem ersten Sozialkontrakt gegründet sein könne" [1793], ibid., 191–4. For a counter view without evidence, see Erich Botzenhart, *Die Staats-und Reformideen des Freiherrn vom Stein* (Tübingen, 1927), 164–7, 182–5.

[44] The closest example we can find of such a view is in a fragment where Möser searches for linguistic equivalents to the term "peasant" (*Bauer*) in other languages; but he is not concerned with social realities, only with distinctions in speech. See the fragment "Das Wort 'Bauer' " [undated], *SW*, 10:107–8.

some point in the past – in the eighth, twelfth, or fifteenth century – and their legal suspension within the Westphalian settlement was necessarily a sign of the deterioration of that past glory. The belief that change means inevitable decay is common in quasi-static societies and perhaps partly explains the psychological power of the myth of a golden age.[45] Whatever the case, Möser often wrote as if any alteration in the bishopric's political institutions would lead to a loss of freedom and generate greater despotism.

It is this anxiety toward political change that attached Möser to the traditions of European and German conservatism. Within corporate Europe, human life was conceived in permanently stratified, holistic terms; new ways of life had to carve out their own place and eliminate or displace preexisting living patterns. In this corporate world, the most infinitesimal innovation thus could be conceived as an attack on the entire order. As we have seen in earlier chapters, Möser did not always write as if he feared slow, incremental change. But he was also capable of veiled hysteria about the future. When in this mood, he linked coffee drinking to moral decay; condemned smallpox vaccinations; defended the torture of prisoners against new standards of gentility; wanted illegitimate children to be stigmatized permanently for their parents' sins; fought to drive peddlers from the countryside for introducing new goods and ideas among the peasantry; and thought the improvement and expansion of roads to be a useless frivolity.[46] Möser was capable of seeing even the smallest innovation as a threat to an entire way of life. "What would it help to have the best hatmaker," he asked, "if the French were to decide all of a sudden to wear hats made of oil cloth? How easily a new fashion robs the best craftsmanship of its fruits. And how far must a state sink if it does not anticipate [these developments] or does not change its craft?"[47]

Thus Möser used his historical studies to combat anxiety about the future by reviving the past. But he was constantly confronted by the contradiction between his historical perceptions and his attachment to corporate Osnabrück. As a historian, he sought to explain change over time, tracing the evolution of social forces to a point where a different political order had to emerge to account for new developments. The theoretical language of corporatism, on the other hand, tied as it was to the idealized political structures and institutions of the *Ständestaat*, prevented him from admitting the political legitimacy of newer social groups. Therefore it could not penetrate the social order as it was constituted in Möser's lifetime. In the end, Möser's use of corporate language heightened his awareness

---

[45] Fritz Redlich, "The Role of Innovation in a Quasi-static World," in his *Steeped in Two Cultures* (New York, 1971), 183–98.

[46] Möser, "Also sollte man die Einimpfung der Blättern ganz verbieten. Schreiben einer jungen Matrone," *SW*, 7:59; "Ueber die zu unsern Zeiten verminderte Schande der Huren und Hurkinder," *SW*, 5:142; "Ueber die Todesstrafen," *SW*, 7:111; "Also ist es ratsamer, die Wege zu flicken als neu zu machen," *SW*, 5:243; "Umgekehrt: Es ist ratsamer, die Wege zu bessern als auszuflicken," ibid., 247; "Erinnerung des Altflickers zum vorigen Stück," ibid., 254; "Klage wider die Packenträger," *SW*, 4:185; "Schutzrede der Packenträger," ibid., 189; "Urteil über die Packenträger," ibid., 194.

[47] Möser, "Von dem Nutzen einer Geschichte der Aemter und Gilden" [1767], *SW*, 4:60.

of social and historical processes while preventing him from pursuing his own insights. He was capable of describing social phenomena in rich detail, but his use of corporate language barred him from transforming his perceptions into a richer understanding of the social life of his own day.

Möser also employed a modified form of social contract theory in his writings. He thought of the state not only as a hierarchical pyramid but also as a joint stock company. This language placed him within the tradition of the Enlightenment – even the image of the joint stock company can be found in Locke's writings.[48] But Möser consciously translated the critical rationality inherent in social contract theory into a view that legitimated hierarchy, inequality, and serfdom as a legal system.[49] In this way, he was able to reconcile corporatism with Enlightenment political theory.

Imagine, he proposed, that the state is similar to a joint stock company and that the stockholders are the original settlers of the land, who banded together to form a land company (*Landaktie*) in order to provide for the common defense. The shares in this company were distributed according to the size of the land-holdings, the shareholders being full, half, or quarter participants in the company or state. With the passage of time, however, the original company of stockholders made room for a second and a third group, who, because they did not have land as collateral security, were given lesser shares according to their individual contributions. City dwellers used money as security (*Geldaktie*), and other later shareholders, those who had neither land nor money, used their bodies (*Leibaktie*) and so became serfs.[50]

Using these three contracts, Möser felt able to derive the entire hierarchy of estate society, from nobility to commons, from freedom to dependency.[51] In this view, the state was not a depository of communal virtue; rather – and here Möser converged with liberal social theory – the contacts created a "negative" institution that functioned merely to preserve property, whether in the form of land, money, body, or soul, under the general rule that the "business of the company be conducted with the least possible sacrifice." Thus "no stockholder pledges himself to more than is demanded by the common need of the state. On this point rests the great supposition for freedom and property."[52] It also followed from this

[48] See, for instance, C. B. Macpherson, *The Political Theory of Possessive Individualism* (Oxford, 1962), 195, 251–3.

[49] In certain fragments, Möser stated such views directly. For instance: "Da jetzt viele Philosophen sich bemühen, den Inhalt des ersten Sozialkontrakts nach Vermutungen und Hypothesen ausfindig zu machen und darauf ein sogenanntes Menschenrecht zu gründen: so scheint es mir wohl der Mühe wert zu sein, in der Geschichte nachzuforschen, wie sich die Menschen bei ihren ersten Verbindungen würklich betragen haben. Ich werde dieses jetzt besonders in der Absicht tun, um zu zeigen, daß sich Menschen als Menschen nicht leicht miteinander verbunden haben." From "Zum ersten Sozialkontrakt" [undated], *SW*, 9:281. See also ibid., 366, 377.

[50] There is a fragment of a story Möser began of that founding. See "Boiocala oder die Verwandlung des Eigentums in Pachtgut" [undated], *SW*, 9:89; also "Kurze Geschichte der Bauernhöfe" [1770], *SW*, 4:269–76.

[51] Möser, "Der Bauernhof als eine Aktie betrachtet" [1774], *SW*, 6:265.

[52] Ibid., 262–3.

assumption that the state was a limited enterprise: The monarch, for instance, was not there for all individuals. "The monarch is actually the *primus familiarum* of the landed proprietors," as Möser wrote in a fragment, "and not of all people gathered in the state."[53] Only those persons and their descendents who had shares in the nation could join the stock company. "Love of humanity and religion cannot make the individual a member of such a society . . . . We make the most transparent mistakes . . . as soon as we confuse stockholders or citizens with men or Christians."[54] After these original social contracts were made, the rights of the individual or citizen were subordinated to the requirements of the land or the company itself – even if, as he admitted, the social contract was only hypothetical or acceded to in silence.[55]

In this way, Möser, like Hobbes, used social contract theory to create an unalterable coercive order. After the original contract was made, consent passed from the consenting individuals to the state. Even though the original consent might have been given in silence or might have been only hypothetical, Möser admitted no mechanism of change. Freedom lay in conformity to a historical evolution that the Estates and property law confirmed. Yet unlike Hobbes, Möser created a coercive institutional structure that was pluralistic and not unitary; he retained the vision of the Estates and not that of monarchical absolutism.

By transforming social contract theory in this manner, Möser felt able to prove that a differential legal system necessarily emerged within the state. Rewards and punishments could be meted out only according to the size and type of share in the state. This theory served, in other words, as the basis for an attack on equality in the name of property and legitimacy. Equality, like truth, was perceived as lying outside the realm of human institutions. In an essay on real and formal law (1780), he contrasted truth to legality, concluding that ultimate truth was for God and the church to decide. What was legal, however, the state decided.[56] He made exactly the same point elsewhere in dealing with civil and Christian marriages: what was legitimate in the eyes of the church may be illegitimate in the eyes of the state (1780).[57]

In Möser's eyes, in other words, no natural rights could force the state to change. In order to interpret equality in corporatist terms, as equality within social groups rather than among individuals, Möser was forced to separate law from natural rights. He argued ceaselessly that it was impossible to create an effective system of law proceeding from the individual. The state is a state of men and not man; accordingly, to each is due his proper rights (1773).[58] By

---

[53] Möser, "Der König der *primus familiarum* der Landeigentümer," *SW*, 9:258–9. This fragment is undated and was titled by the editors.
[54] Möser, "Der Bauernhof als eine Aktie betrachtet" [1774], *SW*, 6:255–6.
[55] Ibid., 259.
[56] Möser, "Von dem wichtigen Unterschiede des würklichen und förmlichen Rechts" [1780], *SW*, 7:99.
[57] Möser, "Ueber den Unterschied einer christlichen und bürgerlichen Ehe" [1780], *SW*, 7:101–5.
[58] Möser, "Von dem Einflusse durch Nebenwohner auf die Gesetzgebung" [1773], *SW*, 5:15–16.

denying legal rights to the individual and maintaining that he must remain a member of a family, corporation, or estate, he rendered necessary social hierarchy, with its gradations of privileges: the nobility required its special legal status and the poor theirs. The death penalty could be demanded of the serf, whose body was his only stake in the nation, but not of the noble, whose land and honor were the basis of his contract.[59]

Möser's attack on equality, in sum, was written from the perspective of political necessity and legitimacy; it buttressed the corporatist perspective, now dressed in the language of the Enlightenment, and it continued to lay claim to a greater realism. Möser was able to join a justification of inequality from a corporatist perspective to the contractual language of the natural rights tradition. This allowed him to appeal to the majority in the Enlightenment who believed in meritocracies or class privilege in some form. In this way he linked two conceptual worlds and helped to perpetuate corporatist arguments in the later Enlightenment and throughout the nineteenth century.

## THE AESTHETIC OF TOTALITY

If attachment to the provincial and a defense of inequality brought Möser into proximity with opponents of the Enlightenment in the years before the outbreak of the French Revolution, so too did the skeptical style we associate with his perspectivism. Isaiah Berlin has argued that such skepticism was basic to the formation of the counter-Enlightenment, buttressing the rejection of Enlightenment assumptions and supporting intuitionist and irrationalist doctrines.[60] Möser's skepticism, however, was not really attached to a philosophical position; he simply rejected all forms of religious or political dogmatism that might require the individual to alter his life. This attitude acquired greater significance in his later years as he gradually developed, from about 1780 on, a fragmentary and somewhat primitive historical aesthetic that he called "total impressions" (*Totaleindrücke*).

The idea of total impressions was the holistic opposite of the analytical language of the social contract. It expressed Möser's feeling that historical and rural life were, in some sense, mysterious, awe-inspiring, and for that reason incapable of rational analysis. Some elements of this view appear in his early writings, but in these the term "total impressions" reflected a concern with finding the proper perspective by which to study a subject or handle a theme. In a comparatively early essay, "Concerning the Moral Perspective" (1767), Möser wrote that "every-

[59] Though the example is from a later period, the views are consistent; from "Ueber das Recht der Menschheit als den Grund der neuen französischen Konstitutions" [1790], *SW*, 9:143.
[60] Berlin, *Against the Current*, 1–3. Skepticism was, of course, a fundamental strand within the Enlightenment itself. Compare Leszek Kolakowski, *The Alienation of Reason*, trans. Norbert Guterman (Garden City, N.Y., 1968), 10–44; Richard Popkin, *The History of Skepticism* (rev. ed.; New York, 1968), esp. 132–54; and J. P. Stern, *Lichtenberg* (Bloomington, Ind., 1959), 75–126.

thing has *its perspective* in which it *alone* is beautiful; as soon as you change it, as soon as you cut into the entrails with an anatomical knife, the previous beauty evaporates with the changed perspective."[61] He also emphasized the importance of the proper perspective in his letters to Thomas Abbt on writing history in the form of an epic.[62]

But from approximately 1780 to 1786, Möser composed a number of essays and letters that bear witness to a more complete articulation of this idea – one in which intellectual fantasy triumphed over the analytical. Writing to the poet Sophie La Roche, he reflected "that it is not such a bad trade to have received a bit more heart than brain. The former contains the sum of all total impressions which nature or the things themselves have made in us. The latter, on the other hand, contains nothing more than we can think or express. The former combines infinite magnitudes with infinite magnitudes, the produces results in our actions which are also infinite."[63] In a letter to Georg H. Hollenberg (1782), he viewed total impressions not merely as sentiment but as a sign of the ineffable in life. "[O]ur words and thoughts are simply certain numbers or signs which are incapable of expressing the infinity of total impressions which [shape] our actions and feelings."[64] In another letter from this period to the educator Rudolf Zacharias Becker (1786), he associated sentiment and mystery with the cultural superiority of the simpler rural life. Total impressions, he wrote, were like the education of the peasant:

No one carries misfortune with greater integrity than the peasant; no one dies more peacefully than he; no one goes to heaven so uprightly as he. And why? Because his virtue rests not on syllables but on total impressions of Creation which he can neither characterize with clear concepts nor with words. Much of the impression of the whole is lost by dissecting the total impressions; and the man who is overwhelmed by the beauty of Creation, falls on his face and is silent, expresses more thankfulness than he who can express his good fortune to the Creator in incomplete finite numbers.[65]

The issue was not to reconcile theory with experience, as he wrote to the philosopher Christian Garve in another formulation, but to experience the impression of the whole.[66]

Thus what began as a form of relativism in Möser became tied to a particular world of arcadian sentimentality. The doctrine of total impressions expressed personal humility about the limits of human understanding and the complexity of human experience among archaic institutions and social habits. There was little pathos in Möser's attitude. He sought to preserve different rules for the everyday and for the agrarian world of the Estates. Nonetheless, this undeveloped

---

[61] Möser, "Von dem moralischen Gesichtspunkte" [1767], *SW*, 4:97.
[62] Möser, *Briefe*, 183, 189.
[63] Ibid., 360.
[64] Ibid., 364–5.
[65] Ibid., 393.
[66] Ibid., 379–80.

aesthetic provided another potential link with nineteenth-century Romantic conservatism. To nineteenth-century readers, Möser's fragmentary comments appeared to express a form of intuitionism and empathetic understanding (*Verstehen*) close to their own; in searching for a kindred spirit, they gave far more substance to such inchoate views than they were worth.

In various ways, then, Möser's commitment to the political and social system of the Estates brought forth attitudes that connected him to classical conservatism and inegalitarian liberalism. With the outbreak of the French Revolution, these ambivalent attitudes crystallized into a final defense of the corporate order, as the final chapter shows.

# 7

~~~~~~~~~~~~~~~~~~~~~~~~~~~~~~~~~~~~~~~~~~~~~~~~~~~~~~~~~~~~~~~~

## *The dialectic of Enlightenment:*
## *the debate over theory and practice*

In the decades before the French Revolution, the "party of reform" accommodated a variety of views: in those years an ambiguous compromise still seemed credible between the head and the heart, between the reform ideals of the Enlightenment and the political realities of corporate society. Reform did not mean revolution, and it was still possible to believe in gradual reform, without subscribing to the disruption of lawfully constituted institutions. But as has often occurred in periods of crisis, the moderate position eroded with the outbreak of revolution.[1] From this point on Enlightenment began to be associated with political revolution, and all reform assumed revolutionary potential. As the cultural meaning of the Enlightenment became radicalized – and reified – so too did the interpretation of corporate society and its political institutions, producing a reasoned and systematic defense of hierarchy, law, and order.

Möser took part in this realignment in the years before his death in January 1794.[2] This required little change in his views. In his last essays, we find the

[1] See the thoughtful review of the historiography by Jörn Garber in his afterword to the new edition of Fritz Valjavec, *Die Entstehung der politischen Strömungen in Deutschland 1770–1815* (Düsseldorf, 1978), 543–92. Of the recent literature, see also Dietfried Krause-Vilmar, "Neuere Literatur zum deutschen Jakobinismus," *Das Argument*, 57 (1970):233–43; Axel Kuhn, "Der schwierige Weg zu den deutschen demokratischen Traditionen," *Neue Politische Literatur*, 18 (1973), esp. 437–8; Claus Träger, ed., *Die Französische Revolution im Spiegel der deutschen Literatur* (Leipzig, 1975), esp. 17–22; Inge Stephan, *Literarischer Jakobinismus in Deutschland* (Stuttgart, 1976); Elisabeth Fehrenbach, "Deutschland und die Französische Revolution," *Geschichte und Gesellschaft*, supplement no. 2 (1976):232–53. Concerning the conservative tradition, see Klaus Epstein, *The Genesis of German Conservatism* (Princeton, N.J., 1966); Jörn Garber, ed., *Kritik der Revolution. Theorien des deutschen Frühkonservatismus 1790–1810*, 1: *Dokumentation* (Kronberg/Ts., 1976); Jacques Godechot, *The Counter-Revolution. Doctrine and Action 1789–1804*, trans. Salvator Attanasio (New York, 1971). For the literature concerning Möser, see Hermann Bausinger, "Konservative Aufklärung – Justus Möser vom Blickpunkt der Gegenwart," *Zeitschrift für Volkskunde*, 68 (1972):161–78.

[2] Möser, "Ueber das Recht der Menschheit als den Grund der neuen französischen Konstitution" [1790]; "Ueber die gänzliche Aufhebung des *Droit d'Aubaine* in Frankreich" [1790]; "Etwas zur Verteidigung des sogenannten Aberglaubens unsrer Vorfahren" [1790]; "Ueber das Recht der Menschheit, insofern es zur Grundlage eines Staates dienen kann" [1791]; "Der arme Freie. Eine Erzählung" [1791]; "Wann und wie mag eine Nation ihre Konstitution verändern?" [1791]; "Ueber die Einwendung des Herrn K. im Februar dieses Jahrs [1792]; "Wie der Unterschied der Stände

themes described in the previous chapter applied almost unchanged to the new revolutionary situation in France. He defended the system of Estates, inherited inequality, and even the historical rationality of serfdom – all in the rationalistic language of contract theory. In this way, his entire ouevre and long public life became a coherent critique of the French Revolution and the radical Enlightenment. Thus, historians have found it easy to see him as a major carrier of conservative opinion even in the prerevolutionary years: is not the defense of the corporate order one of the central components of classical conservatism? However, it is one thing to observe how old views acquire new functions in changed circumstances and another to project these functions backward into the prerevolutionary decades. For this reason, Möser's intellectual biography is similar to a geological map detailing the fissures and fault lines in an area before a large earthquake: we can see what might occur but must project the explanation backward after the fact; moreover, once the earthquake erupts, we must redraw the map.

The German debates in the 1790s over the revolution reveal two main strands. There was, on the one hand, a movement of synthesis and retrospection as individuals of Möser's generation struggled to clarify their beliefs, particularly their commitment to reform within the institutions of the old regime. The French Revolution offered them a chance to disentangle their ideas, but they continued to look back to the world of the Estates. But there was also another group, composed mainly of younger men, who accepted the discontinuity with the prerevolutionary decades as the basis for new intellectual and experiential formations. These individuals recast the old beliefs and set aside the ambivalences of their elders; in the process, they looked forward to the world of the nineteenth century. The historian of the late Enlightenment, therefore, must not conflate the two movements. The 1790s represent a watershed: the debates of the 1790s show the coherence of the Enlightenment in the period between 1763 and 1789 and point toward the new constellation after 1800.

I try to show in this chapter the contours of the summation that occurred in the 1790s among the older generation by examining Möser's late writings and his disagreement with Kant. This disagreement focused on the general theme of theory and practice. The distinction between the theoretical and the practical was in fact the intellectual shorthand Möser and his generation used to characterize their attitude toward Enlightenment values. It allowed them to distinguish between those elements of the Enlightenment that they saw as dangerously and politically radical – elements that they associated with theory – and those that they accepted and approved. Thus, they saw themselves in a defensive pact of corporate intellectuals and practical men against the theoretical passions of the university professoriate represented by the writing of men like Kant or the young Fichte. The debate with Kant found Möser allied with a number of significant

---

auch schon in dem ersten Sozialkontrakt sein könne" [1793]; "Noch etwas über Geburtsrechte" [1794]. All are published in *SW*, 9:140–97.

figures in the intellectual life of these years: administrators such as August W. Rehberg and Friedrich Gentz, the Berlin publisher and writer Friedrich Nicolai, and the popular philosopher Christian Garve. Each in his own way tried to preserve some aspect of the practical Enlightenment against Kantian criticism. Rehberg and Gentz, for instance, tried to employ Kantian concepts in order to defend the independence of the social order against the claims of natural rights theory. Nicolai tried to salvage the lay ideal of the Enlightenment by rejecting Kantian language and philosophical exclusiveness. Garve, the translator of Francis Hutcheson, Adam Ferguson, and Edmund Burke, sought to save the critical moral language of the Scottish Enlightenment. These men, in other words, joined forces to retain the lay, utilitarian tradition in the German Enlightenment.

This chapter examines how Möser participated in the reconceptualization of the Enlightenment after the outbreak of the French Revolution. The first section shows how he adapted corporatist ideas originally conceived with respect to Osnabrück and Westphalia to the revolution in France. The second and third sections take up the debate with Kant. For Möser, on the one side, the intractable world of the Estates and the rights of custom became a counterweight to the emancipatory claims of theory; for Kant, on the other, the revolution in France was an occasion to consider the limits of individual freedom and the right of revolution. By seeing how Kant also compromised with Germany's corporate institutions, we can understand how the corporatist Enlightenment affected another of the fathers of German liberalism.

### MÖSER AND THE FRENCH REVOLUTION

Möser's last essays reveal a decline in intellectual rigor. He felt called on to write about the revolution in France but never completely understood what was taking place there. By 1790 he was seventy and losing his health. In the early 1780s, he had already begun to remove himself both from the daily concerns of the episcopal administration and from his editorial responsibilities for the local newspaper. The letters that survive from his last decade are uncharacteristically given to descriptions of a debilitating nervous disorder that, for years on end, had deprived him of sleep and inner peace.[3] This illness probably accounts for the decrease in his published work during the mid-1780s and for the deterioration in the quality of the *Osnabrück History;* the history began to deviate from the original plan of the general introduction, becoming in the later parts a traditional series of biographical portraits of successive prince-bishops. In addition, Möser's wife died in 1787, loosening his ties to home. In these last years he often visited

---

[3] Möser, *Briefe,* 359, 366–7, 378, 381, 391, 399. A lengthy description of his nervous disorder is printed as a supplement to Nicolai's biography of Möser in *W,* 10:129–32; see also the correspondence of his daughter, Jenny von Voigts, to Princess Luise von Anhalt-Dessau, in William and Ulrike Sheldon, eds., *Im Geist der Empfindsamkeit,* in *Osnabrücker Geschichtsquellen und Forschungen,* 17 (Osnabrück, 1971), 82, 106, 117, 128.

friends, moving between Osnabrück and his daughter's home in Melle and making regular yearly excursions to the spa at Pyrmont, where he met his Berlin companions, men such as J. E. Biester and Friedrich Nicolai.[4]

Möser's last essays show signs not only of his increasing detachment from public life but also of his growing prestige. Although there was neither arrogance nor condescension on his part, he seems to have settled easily into the role of spokesman for the party of order. This made his regular participation in the *Berlinische Monatsschrift* an important confirmation of the journal's credibility in official circles. Biester, the journal's coeditor, clearly encouraged this relationship. Except for a single graceful complaint about Möser's habit of publishing his essays simultaneously in too many journals, Biester was always careful to treat him deferentially.[5] This deference marks Biester's letters, his editorial introductions to Möser's essays, and his published accounts of Möser's retirement celebration and death.[6]

As a leading figure of the German political establishment, Möser felt called on to respond when the revolution broke out in France, but he clearly had only a marginal interest in the events of the first years of revolutionary activity. The creation of the National Assembly, the storming of the Bastille, the abolition of feudal privileges, and the first attempts at legal and financial reorganization appeared only at the edge of his work. He did not discuss them as important historical events in their own right but rather reflected on their legal and political meaning for the world of the small German states. They inspired him in 1790 to weave together and formally connect themes he had once presented much more sketchily. He thus began the process of conscious self-reinterpretation that ended by placing his previously ambivalent attitudes firmly within the camp of order and legitimacy. The result was an attack on the French Revolution that, in its continued appeal to contract theory, was important for its continuity with classical Lockean liberalism. At the same time, however, he sacrificed whatever suppleness and originality existed in his political thought to the demands of systematic presentation, revealing thereby the internal inconsistencies in his thought to critics who once might have refrained from public comment. In this section, then, I examine the themes of Möser's last essays for the survival of corporatist

[4] We have only the tersest of reports of his wife's death: see Möser, *Briefe*, 401 and the correspondence of his daughter, where she writes in Sheldon and Sheldon, *Im Geist der Empfindsamkeit*, 225–6: "Mein gutter vater erträgt diesen Verlust mit einer Größe, die ihm eigen ist." Concerning Möser in these last years, see a letter of Luise Meyer to H. C. Boie in *Ich wohl war Klug, das ich dich fand*, ed. Ilse Schreiber (2nd ed.; Munich, 1963), 189. See also August Rehberg's evaluation of his stay in Osnabrück in his *Sämmtliche Schriften*, 3 vols. (Hanover, 1828–31), 2:20–4; also a letter describing a visit by Caroline Rehberg to the Möser family in Osnabrück and their subsequent trip to Pyrmont in Josef Körner, ed., *Briefe von und an A. W. Schlegel*, 2 vols. (Zurich, 1930), 1:15–18, 2:7–8. See also Sheldon and Sheldon, *Im Geist der Empfindsamkeit*, 86, 253.
[5] Möser, *Briefe*, 375.
[6] Anonymous, "Mösers Tod: am 8 Jaunuar 1794 im 74sten Jahr seines Lebens," *Berlinische Monatsschrift*, 23 (1794):270–83; Johann Friedrich Kleuker, "Noch etwas über Mösers Tod," ibid., 486–97.

values in Enlightenment language and look at the responses of his critics to his defense of inequality and the legitimacy of the corporate order.

Möser's last essays start as commentaries on the French decrees of August 1789 that abolished feudalism and on the October Declaration of the Rights of Man and Citizen. Regardless of the particular occasion, however, each essay had the same end: to prevent natural rights – here specifically perceived as the belief in natural equality and popular sovereignty – from making reformist claims on the traditional political institutions. In this enterprise (as throughout his work), Möser was willing both to argue from theoretical perspectives that he did not completely comprehend and to use almost any argument if it fitted his purpose. As a result, he sought to persuade less by clear analysis than by a rhetorical blurring of the issues. At every opportunity, for instance, he treated natural rights as a one-dimensional, coherent doctrine in order to caricature it or brand it as illusory. "Now, my dear R . . . ," he wrote, "human rights may exist or they may not." Or, "As a joke or also as part of a parade a French duke may well appear with his tailor in the National Guard as one of the unpaid troops and so reveal the right of humanity in a comic form."[7] Similarly, Möser claimed that the doctrine of equality introduced dubious Christian principles into civil society: either equality was a Christian delusion or it should be restricted to "God's church where all men are equal."[8] With such statements, he seems not only to have drawn on the anticlerical beliefs discussed in Chapter 3 but also to have wanted to taint egalitarianism with the odor of religious enthusiasm.

Möser also tried, in all of these late essays, to restrict the normative consequences of theory, which he associated with natural rights. How can a fictional notion like that of equality, the consequence of an inflated "book theory," be accorded the power to alter legitimate existing institutions? This question eventually formed the crux of his disagreement with Kant. But until he read Kant's essay on theory and practice, Möser seems not to have understood how central the point was and to have remained entangled instead in lesser issues and weaker arguments. Previously, he had been willing to give ground on issues surrounding the claims of theory, because, he reasoned, even were such a dubious, abstract doctrine to exist in the minds of naive scholars and priests, the historical record itself was irrefutable: no state had ever been founded according to principles of natural rights; all states, on the contrary, existed to protect property, and the division of property always had been unequal, producing hierarchical differences in rights, privileges, and responsibilities. He doubted, therefore, whether a lasting state could be created from a theory of human rights. Moreover, the logical form of such a state must necessarily be a repugnant type of Christian

---

[7] Möser, "Ueber das Recht der Menschheit als den Grund der neuen französischen Konstitution," 140 and 143, respectively.

[8] Ibid., 141, 144; see also his "Letters from Virginia," "Ueber die allgemeine Toleranz," in *W*, 5:293–315.

communism such as the Jesuits had instituted in Paraguay; "such a system," he wrote, "gives . . . too little room to our noble feelings and serves only for sheep-like men."[9]

To fight against such an abstract, crypto-Christian view of human rights, Möser returned again and again to the "realism" of inequality, to the "necessity" of differential rights, and to the "justice" of laws that restricted individual potential. With the added pressure of the official abolition of feudalism in the French National Assembly, his quasi-historical theory of society as a joint stock company became the vehicle of "realism" for the continued attack on equality. But here his argument became transformed into an unambiguous defense of the legitimacy of the old order.

Möser had originally proposed a view of the state as a legal composite, constructed from various contracts, each of which had been entered into at different historical stages by different kinds of stockholders with differently weighted shares in the state (land, money, or individual labor potential). This image slowly disappeared from his late essays, to be replaced by a doctrine of primary and secondary appropriation in which property became the only basis for rights. Although the state, he argued, had a legal basis that derived from a series of contracts of mutual interest, such contracts further rested on a more fundamental division of the state into owners and leaseholders.[10] Once evolved, this two-step division was, without exception, immutable. "Latecomers," as he called them in the language used for Osnabrück's propertyless and propertypoor, necessarily had to acquiesce to conditions set forth by the first appropriators because these "have a right, on the strength of their first seizure and possession of the land, to exclude all later arrivals or to prescribe terms of them which they have to accept."[11]

In this way Möser shifted the stress from an evolutionary explanation of unequally shared privileges (*Libertät*) to political legitimacy and positive law. His joint stock company theory itself derived, as mentioned in Chapter 6, from Locke, who had used it to deprive the political realm of its sacred underpinnings and to create in its stead a rational genetic explanation for the transfer of power from monarchy and aristocracy to the nonnoble gentry and the monied burgesses in the House of Commons. To a certain extent, Möser shared similar attitudes, as we have seen in Chapters 3 through 6. He demonstrated in his earlier writings both a rational attempt to locate political power in contracts, rather than in the divine or in monarchical absolutism, and a certain recognition of the need to expand legal rights (in contradistinction to political rights). But in these late essays the meaning of the contract changed: the historical contracts that had

---

[9] Möser, "Ueber das Recht der Menschheit, insofern es zur Grundlage eines Staates dienen kann," 158–9. Möser was quite possibly associating himself with beliefs among the conspiracy theorists that the revolution was a Jesuit plot: see Z. P., "Paragui und Paris," *Berlinische Monatsschrift*, 24 (1794):88.

[10] Möser, "Wann und wie mag eine Nation ihre Konstitution verändern," 180.

[11] Möser, "Ueber die Einwendungen des Herrn K. im Februar dieses Jahres," 183.

created the political system of Estates became the basis of a class theory of domination. Consequently, the static legal division of the state into property owners and leaseholders inverted Lock's original intent, and Möser's theory became an unambiguous defense of the property laws of an aristocratically dominated society.

Furthermore, the model of a primary and a secondary appropriation robbed the stock company theory of even its historical veneer, since the original theory was predicated on the gradual expansion and transfer of political rights through the creation of new contracts that continuously subdivided political authority. In its adjusted form, the theory became a naked doctrine of power that ultimately undermined Möser's own arguments for the institutional legitimacy of corporate society. Möser, however, neither recognized the ways in which his position had changed nor acknowledged it as a doctrine in which force decreed law.[12] Instead he saw it simply as a corollary to a stable property law. The consequent inviolability of the institutions and their functional ahistoricity was not a form of tyranny played by the dead on the living but an expression of a state under law. For Möser the tyrannical or despotic was, on the contrary, the doctrine of equality and the self-proclaimed enthronement of the French National Assembly, which perverted history, confiscated property, and destroyed the legal order.

The idea of a primary and a secondary appropriation presupposed a hypothetical beginning point when property relations were first determined and legitimated. Möser himself seems to have realized that this founding could only have occurred at an indefinite point in the past and was, in effect, a necessary legal fiction. (In Chapter 4 we saw Gatterer make exactly this criticism of the *Osnabrück History*.) Nonetheless, Möser never explicitly admitted the hypothetical nature of such contracts, perhaps because he would have been forced, by extension, to admit that the doctrine of natural rights was an equally valid regulative fiction. In these late essays, as a consequence, he treated the historical beginning point of the first contract hypothetically in various tales of a plausible founding – one stemming from the external threat of war, for example, or one arising from a natural catastrophe, as in the case of a community of dike builders who must found a political society with varied rights and privileges in order to repel and defeat the sea. In one of the only places where Möser discussed openly the origins of the state and the continuity of the original contract through all its historical changes, he carefully evaded the issue of continuing legitimation: "it is self-evident," he said, "that the society of property-holders is closed when all the land is divided and still can expand when land remains."[13] Whether the original group of property owners obtained their property legally was of no concern.

---

[12] Möser at one point came close to this view, although it appears to be more rhetorical than serious: "Meiner Meinung nach besteht das Recht der Menschheit in der Befugnis, alles Ledige zu erobern und alles solchergestalt Eroberte zu verteidigen." From his "Ueber das Recht der Menschheit, insofern es zur Grundlage eines Staates dienen kann," 160.

[13] Möser, "Ueber die Einwendungen des Herrn K. im Februar dieses Jahres," 186.

Möser thus rendered the political demands of natural rights theory meaningless by narrowing the political realm to a formal adherence to property boundaries and property law. Elsewhere he circumvented the issue of rights by praising the wisdom of the original founders, by bringing forth historical evolution itself as the force of legitimacy, or by calling upon the lengthy continuity of the law: each of these approaches justified whatever usurpation or act of illegality might have been present at the founding of society. As Möser's contract theory was transformed into a doctrine of legitimacy, it functioned more and more to preserve eternal divisions between haves and have-nots; the distant past and custom were sanctified at the expense of human volition as the rational basis of law in contract.

As Möser's theory of the joint stock company tended toward a clear defense of order, his arguments became less analytical. Although he made custom, contract, property law, and historical origins into pillars of legitimacy, he was no longer capable of using them as tools to explore the lived past. What is curious about the last essays – especially when we consider that he was, at the same time, writing the last volumes of the *Osnabrück History* – is the degree to which he resorted to fictional and hypothetical analogies, instead of historical examples, to support his appeals to history and reality. He "proved" the historical validity of institutional and hereditary inequality through his analogy of the state to a community of dike builders.[14] He defended serfdom, not by a detailed analysis of its function in the eighteenth century, but by thin fictional tales concerning its origin.

When Möser began to rely on fictional tales to demonstrate historical points, his arguments in fact became self-conscious political myths. Indeed, with "The Poor Freeman" (1791–2), he transformed the Enlightenment moral tale into a counterrevolutionary educational tract.[15] In this *Candide*-like story of political naïveté, Jean Le Grand, emancipated by his father at the greatest personal sacrifice, returns home to a village in Burgundy at the news of his father's death. He discovers that he cannot inherit the family leasehold without binding himself again, and though the wise and gentle prior attempts to convince him of the inherent wisdom of serfdom's mildly paternalistic structure, Jean refuses to abandon his personal freedom and chooses instead to wander in an unequal world, preaching and searching for equality. Under this premise, Möser moves poor Jean about, setting him in a variety of contexts – at an exploitive manufactury near Lyon; on the estate of a Mecklenburg noble; in Osnabrück, where "freeman and serf enjoy the same honor"; in Amsterdam among poor, starving dockhands, with a ship's captain who would place him into a seven-year indenture as the price of the trip to America; and in Newgate prison, where he eventually dies

---

[14] The community of dike builders is developed in his "Ueber das Recht der Menschheit, insofern es zur Grundlage eines Staates dienen kann," 156. He had first developed this analogy earlier in "Kurze Geschichte der Bauernhöfe" [1770], *SW*, 4:269. The defense of serfdom occurs in "Ueber die gänzliche Aufhebung des *Droit d'Aubaine* in Frankreich," 145; "Wie der Unterschied der Stände auch schon in dem ersten Sozial Kontrakt gegründet sein könne," 191.

[15] Möser, "Der arme Freie," 162–86.

because of an unpaid five-pound debt. These stations in Jean Le Grand's political education satirized every claim for legal equality and social justice; through them Möser also attempted to show that the paternalistic system of serfdom, at least in its Burgundian and Westphalian forms, was more humane than any capitalist system of economic organization.

Such patently provocative articles exposed Möser to critics who began to dispute his views. It is a sign of the political conservatism of the German Enlightenment that Möser enjoyed the political support of the editors of the *Berlinische Monatsschrift*. Biester, for instance, felt bound to print the opinions of Möser's critics, noting that views should be "illuminated from all sides"; but he also defended Möser's essays in the forewords and afterwords he attached to each published criticism. There is a certain humor in Biester's repetitive attempts at fair play: in each essay he saluted the critic for his love of truth and then proceeded to praise Möser for the shrewdness of his stock company analogy and for his accuracy in separating humanity and natural rights from the "requirements" of civil society.[16]

But to the perceptive minority of Möser's critics, his separation of the moral from the political was a distinctly important issue. Eduard von Clauer, an avowed follower of Kant, formulated the clearest response to Möser's views (1790).[17] Against Möser's caricature, Clauer argued that natural rights were not an "absolute" but a "regulative" fiction. Though imperfectly realized at any one time, they were still the guide toward which society pointed "more or less as was possible." The contract itself was also based implicitly upon natural rights, for the notion of contract implied a universal standard of judgment by which men were able to make binding agreements. These standards, furthermore, must have existed at the time of the first appropriation. If contract theory itself was adopted, in other words, then natural human rights must also have had an existence prior to the first contractual restraints. Natural rights thus did not come from some state of nature; rather, they were norms that "each member of the community and each shareholder, as man, can demand, both from the entire community and from each individual member."[18] In this way Clauer restored moral claims to the notion of contract. Not only was the idea of natural rights a moral concept and an impulse in humanity itself,[19] he continued, but civil society was the

---

[16] J. E. Biester, "Nachschrift," *Berlinische Monatsschrift*, 16 (1790):211: "Recht der Menschheit und bürgerliche Verfassung haben . . . ganz und gar nichts miteinander zuthun. Die letzte beruht auf Verträgen, Einrichtungen, Gesetzen, und beabsichtigt vorzüglich die Sicherstellung des Eigenthums, von welchem allen die blossen Menschheit nichts weiß."

[17] Clauer's two criticisms were "Auch etwas über das Recht der Menschheit," *Berlinische Monatsschrift*, 16 (1790):197–209, and "Noch ein Beitrag über das Recht der Menschheit," ibid., 441–69. His allegiance to Kant is noted in the second article, 445. Of Eduard von Clauer, little is known; see the biographical summary in Ursula Schulz, *Die Berlinische Monatsschrift (1783–1796). Eine Bibliographie* (Bremen, 1968), 103.

[18] Clauer, "Auch etwas über das Recht der Menschheit," 200.

[19] Clauer argued: "Sobald vom Recht des Menschen, also von sittlichen Varhältnissen die Rede ist, verstehe ich unter *Menschen* nicht jene gras fressende zweibeinig aufgerichtet gehende Bestie mit

necessary embodiment of that moral impulse because the laws that structured contract were themselves moral.[20] Speaking in Möser's terms, he stated "that the shares are only the object or the means by which we at first achieve a civil constitution . . . ; but the preservation of our humanity is the purpose."[21]

Clauer also developed a second series of objections to Möser's use of historical evolution in his theory of the joint stock company. He argued, as did Kant in the ethical writings, that history could never be an adequate principle for law, since it prohibited the use of moral standards to judge illegitimate acts. In Möser's view, time and custom must eventually sanctify every act; however, by using history in this fashion, Möser possessed no real measure to protest the events in France, because one day time and custom would legitimate these changes as well. Equally important, Möser's theory was inadequate to historical experience, since his so-called contracts were arbitrary. There had been no first appropriation: historically, human settlement had been uneven. Many areas within France, Clauer noted, were settled or acquired after the various contracts in land, money, and personal labor had long been present. What legal principle, then, justified the continued domination of one type of contract over the others? For the same reason that history was inappropriate to the system of law, historical evolution could never be an adequate principle for the preservation of corporate society because the principle contained in the theory of gradual contracts had to admit of continued change: there must be a point, therefore, when history supplied the proof of a new contract. Clauer wondered, then, whether that time had not arrived, since the merger of land and movable wealth coincided with the disappearance of the grounds for the first contracts.

Möser's other critics never approached Clauer in their willingness to pursue Möser's ideas seriously and systematically; they tended to dwell on specific points or to satirize his basic attitude. Nonetheless, the sum of their criticisms constituted a considerable rejection of his ideas. They explored, like Clauer, the discrepancy between Möser's general appeal to history and his use of historical detail. One anonymous author suggested that Möser prove his theory by using historical

---

einem unersättlichen Instinkt, so wie ihm der Naturkundige uns darstellt; sondern ein sittliches Wesen, von der Natur versehen mit einer Vernunft, vermöge deren er handlungsfähig ist, und die seine unzubefriedigenden Begierden leitet; – und *Menschheit* ist nach meiner Vorstellung das sittliche Verhältnis, in welchem alle Menschen als handelnde Geschöpfe gegen einander stehn. *Recht der Menschheit* heißt demnach ein solcher sittlicher Zustand des Menschen, vermöge dessen unter ihnen als vernünftigen Geschöpfen, kraft der Natur ihrer Existenz, gewisse Rechte und Verbindlichkeiten, ohne Rücksicht auf besondere Verabredungen und derselben Verfügungen, gegen einander ewig obwalten. . . . Dieser mit dem sittlichen Menschen und seiner Existenz unzertrennliche Zustand könnte nun in der bürgerliche Gesellschaft entweder in seinem ganzen Umfang und in allen Fällen noch besonders verabredet, erläutert und erweitert worden sein, oder nur zum Theil: in jenem Fall wäre der Mensch mit dem Bürger aufs genauste verwebt, und man bedürfte sodann den Rücktritt in die bloße Menschheit nicht; in diesem Fall aber träte der bloße Mensch wieder hervor, da, wo die Verabredung schweigt." In "Noch eine Beitrag über das Recht der Menschheit," 433–4.

[20] Ibid., 452.
[21] Ibid., 468.

evidence.[22] The demand for a real historical beginning point to the social contract had been a basic objection to contract theory since the beginning of the eighteenth century, as we can see in Montesquieu's *Spirit of the Laws*.[23] Who were the first appropriators? When was the process of possession actually ended? Who were the descendants of the first owners? How do we know that the system of law evolved from this first appropriation? Because he doubted Möser's ability to answer these questions, this anonymous critic proposed the legend of the Norman yoke in place of the image of the stock company. He rejected the entire argument of a twofold appropriation as a theory of domination that only confirmed the history of inequity, subjection, aristocratic tyranny, and illegitimate rule that had been the common man's lot since the Frankish conquest. Clearly, within Möser's theory, force alone prevented a third, fourth or fifth contract.[24]

MÖSER AND KANT

The essays of Möser and his critics formed one current in a political debate that began to run more swiftly in the years 1791–2 in response to the intensification of the revolution in France. In these first years, as long as the press remained relatively free, discussion continued to expand over the rights of the nobility, hereditary distinctions, secret societies, the legality of the French constitution, property rights, peasant emancipation, and the progress of humanity.[25] Over the course of the decade the debate became more strident, in part because it was accompanied by an increasing sense of crisis and growing official intolerance. Already in the mid-1780s the official mood had altered in the Hohenzollern lands, particularly in Berlin, with the death of Friedrich II and the accession of Friedrich Wilhelm II (1786). Minister Wöllner presided over new decrees enforcing religious orthodoxy, the persecution of the neologists in the consistory, and the suppression of Kant's religious essays, later collected as *Religion within the Limits of Reason Alone*.[26] The expansion of the revolution in France caused

[22] K., "Ueber des Hrn. Geh. Justizraths Möser Behauptungen im November 1791, Nr. 2," *Berlinische Monatsschrift*, 19 (1792):154.

[23] Montesquieu, *The Spirit of the Laws*, trans. Thomas Nugent (New York, 1949), 4; Möser also made this same point in an undated fragment quoted in Chapter 6.

[24] Anonymous, "Sind denn all Menschen wirklich gleich," *Berlinische Monatsschrift*, 18 (1791):560; see also the humorous attack by Samuel Theokrat, "Wie ein Westphälischer Küster das Recht der Nationen, ihre Konstitution zu ändern, ansehe," *Schleswigsches ehemals Braunschweigisches Journal*, 1 (1792):424–54.

[25] Sensitively discussed in Robert R. Palmer, *The Age of Democratic Revolutions*, 2 vols. (Princeton, N.J., 1959–64), 2:426–456; see also Hans Erich Bödeker, "Zur Rezeption der französischen Menschen- und Bürgerrechtserklärung von 1789/1791 in der deutschen Aufklärungsgesellschaft," in *Grund- und Freiheitsrechte im Wandel von Gesellschaft und Geschichte*, ed. Günter Birtsch (Göttingen, 1981), 258–86; and the important older study by Johanna Schultze, *Die Auseinandersetzung zwischen Adel und Bürgertum in den deutschen Zeitschriften der letzten drei Jahrzehnte des 18. Jahrhunderts*, in *Historische Studien*, 163 (Berlin, 1925), 29–46.

[26] Concerning the situation in Berlin, see Martin Philippson, *Geschichte des Preußischen Staatswesens vom Tode Friedrich des Großen bis zu den Freiheitskriegen*, 2 vols (Leipzig, 1880–2), 1:177–380; Fritz Valjevec, "Das Wöllnersche Religionsedikt und seine geschichtliche Bedeutung," *Historisches Jahr-*

German censors to tighten their grip even further, and this gradually altered the form of the political debate in Prussia and southward throughout the Habsburg Empire. We sense a change of tone in the *Berlinische Monatsschrift* in 1793, three years before its suppression, as intensive discussion of epistemological and ethical issues tended to replace whatever treatment of concrete reform had managed earlier to pass by the Prussian censor. Thus discussions of peasant emancipation or the abolition of the nobility disappeared almost completely.

These years saw the beginning of a profound reorientation in German intellectual history toward idealism, romanticism, and classicism. These changes lie beyond the scope of this biography, however. Möser's contribution, moreover, was limited to a posthumously published fragment (1798) of a response he was preparing at the time of his death to Kant's essay in the September 1793 issue of the *Berlinische Monatsschrift*, "On the Common Saying: This May Be True in Theory But It Does Not Apply in Practice."[27] But if Möser's work played only a small part in the shift in direction, Kant's late postcritical writings were pivotal in reshaping the political debate.[28] That Möser felt drawn into a debate with Kant at a level of philosophical abstraction beyond his capacities or real inclination is an indication of the importance he attached to Kant's opinions and a further sign of the change in public mood. A comparison of the two essays shows even more clearly the way in which views concerning political emancipation were blurred among this older generation of the German Enlightenment.

The 1780s and 1790s were the crucial first decades in the articulation and spread of Kant's philosophy. In the years since the publication of the *Critique of Pure Reason* (1781), Kant had been concerned with exploring the implications of his ideas. He had been equally concerned that his general position reach a wider literate public and had used the *Berlinische Monatsschrift* for this purpose. All of his shorter essays on law, history, and ethics appeared there, as well as certain meteorological and anthropological studies. Like most of the other essays after 1785, Kant's essay on theory and practice was written both as a reply to his critics and as an attempt to develop with greater precision the ethical consequences of his critical philosophy. This work was intended to replace the second, third, and fourth essays of *Religion within the Limits of Reason Alone*, denied publication by the Prussian censor. Although Kant touched on the need for freedom of the press, he was probably not responding directly to the scandal over censorship that ensued. The essay seems to have been inspired by recently published crit-

*buch*, 72 (1953):386–400; still valuable concerning censorship in Berlin is Kuno Fischer, *Geschichte der neueren Philosophie* (4th ed.; Heidelberg, 1898), 4/1:87–97; Klaus Epstein, *The Genesis of German Conservatism* (Princeton, N.J., 1966), 352–68.

[27] Reprinted in Kant, Gentz, and Rehberg, *Ueber Theorie und Praxis*, ed. Dieter Henrich (Frankfurt am Main, 1967), 39–87; also in Immanuel Kant, *Werke*, 6 vols. (Darmstadt, 1966–70), 6:127–72; English translation in Hans Reiss, ed., and H. B. Nisbet, trans., *Kant's Political Writings* (Cambridge, 1970), 61–92.

[28] See the important older work by Wilhelm Metzger, *Gesellschaft, Recht und Staat in der Ethik des deutschen Idealismus* (Heidelberg, 1917), 27–44, 193–220.

icisms (1792) of his work by the popular philosopher from Breslau, Christian Garve.[29] Garve was deeply troubled by Kant's separation of morality and the moral law from eudaemonistic and utilitarian explanations. "In my mind," he wrote, "I well understand the separation of ideas [between duty and happiness] but . . . I cannot find this division of wishes and strivings in my heart."[30] This simple demurer appears to have been far more important to Kant than any academic criticism in the Wolffian tradition, since the first layer of his ethics was based on the derivation of the categorical imperative from the common structure of belief, and he hoped with these essays not only to stifle the most hardened ethical skeptic but also to achieve the greatest possible public effect. For this reason, Garve's objections went to the heart of his journalistic efforts, and they became the occasion for a basic restatement of Kant's own views.

The question of the link between theory and practice appears to be only technical. It triggered in Kant's mind a much broader discussion concerning ethical duty, constitutionality, political justice, and the progress of the human species. Thus his essay drew into its domain the prerevolutionary political debates, the revolutionary events in France, and the possibility of the revolutionary change of estate society. It became thereby an examination of the limits of political Enlightenment as understood by Kant and other members of Möser's generation.

Kant's concern was to preserve the normative claims of theory by denying that there were forms of social life impenetrable to reason. He began his essay by stating that all "practice" is the consequence of a theory of some kind. Practice is intentional behavior that complies with certain rules of procedure and results from an act of judgment. Kant admitted that there might be areas of discrepancy between theory and practice, but he argued that these lay not in theory or in practice per se. Instead the function of theory appeared confused only to theoreticians who could not apply theoretical propositions to concrete situations (and thus in Kant's terms lack judgment) and "practical" men – among others, he gave the examples of agriculturalists and economists – who can develop only to a limited degree without proper theoretical training. Kant thus formulated the problem of linking theory and practice either in terms of inadequate or inappropriate theory, or in terms of an individual's improperly developed faculty of judgment. In other words, the difficulty could not be the capacity of theory qua theory to guide men in their actions. Kant further denied that a science could be mastered without both a theoretical and a practical command of the subject.

Whether or not we accept Kant's definitions and restrictions in these preparatory remarks, they were only intended as a means to introduce his criticism of the "common saying": were reason merely to describe and never to legislate, there would be no possibility for moral autonomy. Kant argued, in other words,

[29] See Henrich, "Einleitung," *Ueber Theorie und Praxis*, 10–12, and Günter Schulz, "Christian Garve und Immanuel Kant. Gelehrten-Tugenden im 18. Jahrhundert," *Jahrbuch der Schlesischen Friedrich-Wilhelms-Universität zu Breslau*, 5 (1960):123–88.

[30] Passage reprinted in Henrich, *Ueber Theorie und Praxis*, 134.

that if theory were to be based solely on past experience or the real restrictions of a presently lived experience, it would be wholly inadequate to the critical, constructive capacity of reason. Thus Kant's ultimate goal was to combat the possible demise of a critical ethics and to save the emancipatory potential of reason.

The first part of Kant's essay, his response to Garve, is not crucial to our present concerns.[31] It was only in the section against Hobbes, "On the Relationship of Theory to Practice in Political Right," that Kant directly approached the themes of this chapter. In an extremely compressed and contradictory manner, he developed the assumptions later accepted as basic by nineteenth-century German liberalism, exploring in less than twenty printed pages the formation of civil society; its constitution; and the issues of freedom, equality, the duties of a citizen, and the rights of revolution. He approached each problem analytically in these pages, arguing the logical structure of civil society from one proposition to the next. But what is important to our comparison with Möser is the degree to which the real structures of estate society intruded upon his analysis and constricted an apparently analytical argument. At many points reason brought him, in spite of inclination, surprisingly close to Möser.

Kant began by positing the unique status of the contract that first establishes a civil state or commonwealth. Unlike contracts that create other social groupings, orders, or corporations, where the "principle" or reason lies in some limited, common feature shared by each member, the principle that founds a civil state is an "end in itself" and brings with it an absolute binding duty. This principle, he asserted, is that of law itself. Kant defined law in general as a restriction of individual freedom in such a way that it "harmonizes," as far as possible, with the freedom of everyone else. Public law or "right" is the distinctive quality of the external laws that make this constant harmony possible. Because public law has a different end than the personal ends of individuals, it follows, according to Kant, that this law is restrictive or coercive to the extent that individual freedoms are curtailed. This coercive power is not arbitrary, however, since the system of contract and public law presupposes a "relationship among free men," who retain their freedom among themselves outside or as the ground of such law. From this "requirement of pure reason which legislates a priori" to create the public and private realms, Kant proceeded to derive the formal system of legal equality that is the guarantor of men's freedom: formal equality at birth, the right of personal freedom, equality under the system of justice, and equality of opportunity.

On the surface, Kant's sketch of a society of law differs considerably from Möser's quasi-historical stock company theory in which the state never acquires moral sanctions or absolute sovereignty to intervene in the semiautonomous sphere

---

[31] For an elaboration of these ideas see Richard Saage, "Besitzindividualistische Perspektiven der politischen Theorie Kants," *Neue politische Literatur*, 12 (1972):168–93; idem, *Eigentum, Staat und Gesellschaft bei Immanuel Kant* (Stuttgart, 1973).

of corporate political institutions. Yet we need to read below the surface of their arguments in order to understand the relationship of their ideas. As we have already seen, Möser could set theory aside to argue for just such intervention when required for practical reform. Thus, he supported an independent judiciary to protect against seigneurial exploitation (see Chapter 5) and sought to give powers to the prince-bishop to resolve questions of religious intolerance (see Chapter 2). Kant, on the other hand, claimed in theory absolute autonomy for the state and the inviolability of individual freedom; in practice, however, he was willing to compromise with the coroporate order in areas he thought peripheral. As a consequence, the rationalistic elements in contract theory and the formal appeal to a system of law figured in the works of both and created surprisingly similar difficulties with historical explanation. This issue needs to be examined in greater detail because it produced illiberal consequences for Kant at the level of social reality.

Kant and Möser both adopted a perspective on law and institutional legitimacy that rendered every purely evolutionary or historical argument inadequate, because legitimacy was a product of historical evolution, whereas law and justice were timeless. History sanctifies institutions only until those institutions alter, as Clauer had already indicated; at that point, other justificatory explanations are needed to counter the argument of historical development. There was, as a consequence, a constant struggle over the explanation of political legitimacy in the period prior to the French Revolution: one side stressed law as structure and the other society as the principle of historical development.

Although liberal contract theory is normally considered to be ahistorical, it actually contained mechanisms or an intellectual shorthand for explaining historical phenomena, a shorthand that needed only to be expanded at moments of political crisis. Not only did the idea of contract contain the potential for real historical explanation – for example, Möser could see a correspondence between contract theory and the actual evolution of the Estates – but the theory of popular sovereignty also provided a flexible historical alternative in its distinctions between the private and the public realms and in the idea that sovereignty, invested in the people, could revert to them through their intermediate agents at moments of extreme political crisis. In this way, the people and society became the fictional carriers of historical and legal continuity in the face of political revolution.

Neither Kant nor Möser, however, followed the obvious intellectual path. Faced with the fact that historical explanation becomes problematic at a moment of revolutionary change, Möser began to develop an unambiguous doctrine of social exclusion and political domination. As we have already seen, he increasingly pushed real historical explanation to the periphery in his later essays as he struggled to defend the principle of legitimacy against the revolutionary order. Rather than investing absolute sovereignty in either the state or the people, Möser turned to the glorification of property law: the state was for him a suprapersonal structure of law created to maintain the system of property and property holding.

Legal and political rights as well as social status emanated from the necessity to preserve property law. Moreover, political rights for this purpose resided not in individuals but in the permanent corporate institutions that were the effective guardians of freedom and property. Thus the revolution in France was illegitimate because it destroyed the continuity of the property law that was the foundation of the state and thereby "paved a high road to monarchical or democratic despotism." For Möser, in sum, *property* law served the same function as *public* law for Kant and the sovereign power for Hobbes: it was the highest arbiter of justice and legitimacy.

Kant experienced similar difficulties with the details of the real historical world. It is not that he was deceived, like Möser, by the persuasive force of mythic or pseudohistorical arguments, but rather that he could not account logically for concrete historical phenomena. He argued specifically in the essay on theory and practice that one need not assume the founding contract as historical fact, "for it cannot possibly be so." It is instead "merely an *idea* of reason, which nonetheless has undoubted practical reality." The civil state, then, is an idea of immutable right, which binds men's actions absolutely by its logical and legal imperatives. Since this state is not a historical entity, every commonwealth must lack precise historical limits and qualities even though it has logical and legal closure. Thus, in Kant's theory, real historical explanation was also pushed to the periphery. Public law cannot have a historical substratum or an explanatory dimension; it must be unchanging and external to individual ends, according to Kant, because it regulates and guarantees the freedom of all who have entered into the contract to secure their personal ends. As a consequence, the "preservation of the state from evil is an absolute duty, while the preservation of the individual is merely a relative duty."

Thus Kant wished to preserve for reason its critical and emancipatory functions in the world of politics, and this prevented him from accounting for concrete historical phenomena: for him the civil state was an "idea of reason," not a product of historical evolution. He understood, however, that this idea needed to conform to the particular historical world. This concession forced him to adjust his definitions in order to accommodate the idea of the civil state to the real conditions of Prussian absolutism. For instance, he separated political rights from legal equality in civil society. He denounced paternalistic government as the "greatest possible despotism," yet he preserved absolute monarchy as a requirement of law, arguing that for the same reason public law is immutable, sovereignty cannot be subdivided into corporations or voluntary associations. Thus he deemed notions of popular sovereignty or a general will to be logically impossible, and he likened the monarch to the regulating function of the will of an individual. As the regulator of the commonwealth, the king stood outside the system of law: for the "head of the state is not a member of the commonwealth, but its creator and preserver, and he alone is authorized to coerce others without being subject to any coercive laws himself." Similarly, Kant attacked dependency, arguing that serfdom was illegal, but he limited political rights to those who were independent. Thus, servants were given legal and political representation only through the paternalistic fiction that the "humblest of . . . servants must possess a right of coercion . . . through the head of the state." He also accepted hierarchical arrangements based on wealth: "the welfare of the one depends very much on the will of the other (the poor depending on the rich), the one must obey the other (as the child its parents or the wife her husband), the one serves (the laborer) while the other pays."[32]

Thus Kant's defense of the idea of law over the particular historical case, his acceptance of real inequality, and his willingness to exclude the dependent from a share in the nation made his political sensibilities conform to the degree of political participation current in the Hohenzollern domains. These views also made his real sensibilities, in practice if not in theory, not very different from Möser's own. Civil society was clearly separate from the political; to Kant the political affairs of the state remained the private affair of the monarchy, whereas to Möser the state remained the private domain of the traditional Estates. When we look at these views, we can appreciate Möser's ironic comment in the Kant fragment: "On the spot where the theoretician and the empiricist stand together at this moment, the first is looking toward the *pure* world eastward, the second, however, toward the *real* world westward; and both have turned their backs to each other."

So, too, Kant's critique of the right of rebellion in the essay brings the two men together, for here the permanence required of public law and Kant's unwillingness to accept the fictions of liberal contract theory — majority rule and popular political representation — left no route of resistance to the powers that be. Just as Möser condemned the actions of the French National Assembly, Kant argued that once the state is founded, "the people . . . has no longer any right to judge how the constitution should be administered." Though a people are oppressed or, as he terms it, suffer "unhappiness," they have only the right of obedience. By reducing all specific demands to this empty "unhappiness," Kant made it seem that tyranny was no different from the sum of individual personal discomforts, and he reduced the test of political legitimacy to the theoretical possibility that all men might agree to the law. As long as "it is not self-contradictory to say that an entire people could agree to such a law, however painful it might seem, then the law is in harmony with right." As a necessary

---

[32] Kant demonstrated, as he had in the *Groundwork*, why the pursuit of happiness, although not unimportant to each individual, cannot be an appropriate foundation for ethics; why, instead, the "unselfish" pursuit of the "highest good on earth" is the only acceptable criterion that binds all rational creatures; why finite rational creatures such as men can only be judged according to their intention to pursue this good (duty), and not according to any quantum of good that might result; why the will requires such a purpose; why without a will there is no morality; why the purpose (fulfilling one's duty) must be unselfish to be morally binding; and, returning again to the opening proposition, why the struggle for the good (duty) must be the "goal of all rational creatures." See H. J. Paton, *The Categorical Imperative* (Philadelphia, 1948), 34–77.

consequence, he subscribed to the absolute right of the sovereign to enforce his will and to the *"absolute* prohibition" of all armed protest against the "supreme legislative power." Neither tyranny nor extreme oppression are adequate grounds for protest, "for it is monstrous to suppose that we can have a right to do wrong in the direst (physical) distress." Finally, Kant closed off any possibility of armed resistance by declaring a majority decision to revolt in the name of the whole and the sovereign power to be a logical absurdity that leads to anarchy "with all the terrors it may bring with it."

Confronted with the absolute rigor of his own defense of public law against the right of resistance to the unjust exercise of that authority, Kant was effectively reduced to arguing for the moral autonomy of the individual within a system of political paternalism. "The non-resisting subject must be able to assume that his ruler has no *wish* to do him injustice. . . . Thus the citizen must, with the approval of the ruler, be entitled to make public his opinion on whatever of the ruler's measures seem to him to constitute an injustice against the common-wealth." In other words, Kant separated the political realm from the moral, as Möser had, by narrowing it to the formal system of law. Möser refused to see that moral claims of any kind could force entry into the political system. Con-sequently, he deprived the peasantry and the rural poor of political rights that he invested in corporate bodies linked to the real social and economic systems. Kant, however, invested the same rights in an absolute monarch outside the law. Civil society was even more completely apolitical in Kant's view, because there was no political process by which rights could be amended or protests made. Against the omnipotence of the ruler Kant could only offer palliatives in the rest of the essay: the pressure of public opinion, the power of the pen, freedom of thought, public education, and a belief in the gradual progress of the entire species. Stressing these "civil rights," he argued for gradual justice through law: once the state is constitutional, founded on public law, and once its citizens instill the moral law in themselves, an enlightened public will achieve what revolution cannot.[33]

## PRACTICAL ENLIGHTENMENT

Kant's essay prompted a wide-ranging debate that continued until the end of the century.[34] Of the many responses Kant provoked, those by Möser and the other so-called conservative critics, Friedrich Gentz and August Rehberg, and

---

[33] Concerning this entire interpretation, see Leonard Krieger, *The German Idea of Freedom* (Boston, 1957), 114–24; Karl Vorländer, *Immanuel Kant*, 2 vols. (Berlin, 1924), 2:210–38; Klaus Weyand, *Kants Geschichtsphilosophie*, in *Kantstudien*, supplement 85 (Cologne, 1963), 186–91; Ernst Bloch, *Naturrecht und menschliche Würde* (Frankfurt am Main, 1961), 81–92. Much more favorable to Kant's position is Iring Fetscher, "Immanuel Kants bürgerlicher Reformismus," in *Theory and Politics. Theorie und Politik. Festschrift zum 70. Geburtstag für Carl Joachim Friedrich*, ed. Klaus von Beyme (The Hague, 1971), 70–95.

[34] For the literature see Henrich, *Ueber Theorie und Praxis*, 12–16.

by Friedrich Nicolai, Möser's friend and publisher, are most important here. If Kant's formal description of an enlightened society of law – the cornerstone of nineteenth-century liberalism – could be made to harmonize with empirical aspects of the corporate order, so too could Kant's conservative critics, in commenting on his work, make their own compromise between the corporate order and the Enlightenment. Nicolai's objections, on the other hand, were less directly political; he wanted knowledge suitable for the wide and real world, and he found Kant's formalism disturbing. In lectures to the Berlin Academy of Sciences, and in essays, books, and novels, Nicolai tirelessly defended both common sense (*gesunde Vernunft*) and social utilitarianism against Kant and his followers.

It is noteworthy that Kant refused to respond to the counterarguments of his own students and yet was provoked to write an open letter at the appearance of Möser's fragment in Nicolai's edition of Möser's works (1798).[35] We do not know why Möser's response to Kant remained fragmentary and cannot exclude as reasons either a loss of interest, a realization of its intellectual inferiority, or his death. But Kant's uncharacteristically angry charges in the open letter are largely independent of Möser's particular criticism. Kant thought, probably with reason, that Möser's fragment was published by Nicolai as yet another attempt, in the spirit of Nicolai's previously published satirical novels, to ridicule Kant's philosophical achievement; he drew the conclusion that either Nicolai had written the fragment himself and had planted it in Möser's works or had thought it useful for his own purpose to publish a fragment by a man no longer living and thus no longer responsible for his views. In either case, Kant interpreted Nicolai's action as a piece of duplicitous personal harassment, and he responded with an open condemnation of Nicolai as writer and publisher. Thus Möser's substantive criticisms of the essay on theory and practice, joined in Kant's mind with Nicolai's often bitter caricature of the philosophy "from in front" (*von vorne; a priori*), lost for Kant whatever intellectual validity they might have possessed.

Although Möser and Nicolai shared the common critical attitude of practical men toward university and professorial pretensions, they criticized completely different aspects of Kant's philosophy. Nicolai's anti-Kantianism was directed against Kant's excessively private language and the apparent castelike exclusiveness of Kant's students, particularly Fichte. Above all, he objected to their philosophical rejection of guiding Enlightenment ideas – notions of utility, the common good, and material betterment – that were fundamental to the reforming impulse in the popular Enlightenment. To Nicolai, Kant's emphasis in his ethics on duty and intention was ludicrous for everyday life. Particularly in the *Life and Opinions of Sempronius Gundibert, a German Philosopher* (1798), the publication of which coincided with his edition of Möser's works, he ridiculed Kant's ethical

---

[35] Immanuel Kant, "Ueber die Buchmacherei. Zwei Briefe an Herrn Friedrich Nicolai" [1798], *Gesammelte Werke* (Berlin, 1912), 8:433–8, 519–20.

writings by showing how it made Sempronius Gundibert unfit for survival in a real world where desire had its natural place.[36]

Möser's criticisms, however, were not of the same kind. As a historian he questioned the capacity of theoreticians to describe real historical phenomena, and as an administrator he challenged the adequacy of Kant's theory of public right as a real political theory. The first criticisms, those concerning the limitations of theoreticians, warranted Kant's somewhat disdainful treatment. In each of the five extant beginnings of the essay – of which Nicolai printed only one – Möser questioned whether theory can ever be an adequate distillation of human experience.[37] He tried to argue that there were forms of experience or practice that must be acquired and can never be expressed in theoretical language, and we can hear echoed his notion of total impressions. "Experience is too rich for theory," Möser wrote, "and a theoretician who stays with generalizations and idealizations does not notice a great deal that is open to the eyes of the man of experience."[38] Möser thus misunderstood totally the epistemological problems in Kant's essay, equating theory with inexperience and naïveté and practice with worldly wisdom and the sum of individual experiences. In this form his criticisms were trivial, and they make it impossible to judge how much of Kant's argument he had followed. It is perhaps understandable, then, that Kant, while questioning Nicoiai's integrity as a publisher, referred to this as a spiteful confusion of *Praxis* (practice) with *Praktiken* (homiletic advice).[39]

Möser's second group of criticisms, however, evolved from his own expertise; although they remain in the form of obscure and repetitive fragments, the argument they contain is of considerably more substance. In them Möser juxtaposed his corporate perspective, which placed customary limits on the administrative competence of the central authority, to Kant's view of a civil order that, although legislating legal emancipation and formal equality, possessed unlimited coercive power under an absolute monarch. The pivotal issue for Möser was the problem of judging which is better: real but gradual emancipation in a corporate world or legal emancipation in a despotic political system. On this point he found himself in fundamental disagreement with Kant.

Though the arguments in the various fragments do not cohere among themselves, they show Möser struggling to describe the economic and political reasons for serfdom's original development and its gradually changed function in the late

---

[36] Concerning Nicolai's relationship to Kant, see his *Geschichte eines dicken Mannes*, 2 vols. (Berlin-Stettin, 1794); his *Leben und Meinungen Sempronius Gundiberts, eines deutschen Philosophen* (Berlin-Stettin, 1798); and his *Ueber meine gelehrte Bildung* (Berlin-Stettin, 1799). Also Walter Strauβ, *Friedrich Nicolai und die kritische Philosophie* (Stuttgart, 1927), 23–7; Karl Aner, *Der Aufklärer Friedrich Nicolai* (Gieβen, 1912), 31–8; and Jonathan Knudsen, "Friedrich Nicolai's 'Wirkliche Welt': On Common Sense in the German Enlightenment," in *Mentalitäten und Lebensverhältnisse* (Göttingen, 1982), 86–90.

[37] The other fragments are collected in Möser, "Ueber Theorie und Praxis," *SW*, 10:141–57.

[38] Ibid., 149.

[39] Kant, "Ueber die Buchmacherei," 437.

eighteenth century. Thus, he narrowed his disagreement with Kant to the defense of hereditary inequality. He attempted to trace the emergence of serfdom both from economic "necessity" and from the "natural" forms of "paternal and charismatic authority." He asserted that the system of obligation between lord and servant prevented the misuse of the private sphere by making everything public.[40] In this way Möser declared serfdom to be an all-encompassing system of checks and balances: "kings could be called serfs of the crown." In opposition to Kant's call for a "destructive" legal emancipation in which all became "subjects" of an omnicompetent crown, Möser thus idealized the entire hierarchical system of obligation as the necessary preventive of despotism. Moreover, he argued that individual choice was also incapable of improving upon a political system evolved over centuries of trial and error. Finally, he concluded against Kant that, given a choice, a people will always desire the exercise of paternalistic authority to absolutism.

Given the fragmentary nature of Möser's remarks, it is not surprising that Kant responded to Möser's views only in the midst of his complaints against Nicolai. He dismissed the historical explanation of serfdom as a reactionary defense. "Möser is not simply a royalist," he noted, "but also . . . an aristocrat or a defender of hereditary nobility to the wonder and anger of many recent political thinkers in Germany."[41]

But what was at issue to Möser went deeper than that and can also be seen in the criticisms of August Wilhelm Rehberg (1757–1836) and Friedrich Gentz (1764–1832).[42] Rehberg, from a Hanoverian secretarial family like Möser's in Osnabrück, had studied in Göttingen with the Freiherr vom Stein. Though sent to study medicine, Rehberg had independently come to be a student of Kant and Enlightenment philosophy. After 1783 he went to Osnabrück as secretary to the prince-bishop and there fell under Möser's influence – though not without maintaining a certain critical distance. By 1792 he returned to Hanover as a member of the chancellery (*Geheim Kanzlei*) and began his critical review of the French revolutionary pamphlet literature. Gentz, on the other hand, was from Breslau, the son of a high official in the Prussian mint. Gentz had known Christian Garve in Breslau and had gone to Königsberg on Garve's recommendation to study with Immanuel Kant, becoming a committed Kantian. In 1786 he entered

---

[40] Möser, "Ueber Theorie und Praxis," 153.

[41] Kant, "Ueber die Buchmacherei," 433.

[42] Texts by Rehberg and Gentz printed in Henrich, *Ueber Theorie und Praxis*, 89–130. See also Rehberg, *Sämmtliche Werke*, 1:1–123, 236–8. For the entire complex of ideas see Gerhard Ritter, "Der Freiherr vom Stein und die politischen Reformprogramme des ancien régime in Frankreich," *HZ*, 137 (1928):442–97; 138, (1929):24–46, and Erich Botzenhart, *Die Staats- und Reformideen des Freiherrn vom Stein* (Tübingen, 1927). For Rehberg's biography see Erich Weniger, "Rehberg und Stein," *Niedersächsisches Jahrbuch*, 2 (1925):1–123; Epstein, *Genesis of German Conservtism*, 547–94; and Ursula Vogel, *Konservative Kritik an der Bürgerlichen Revolution* (Neuwied, 1972). For Gentz, see Paul Wittichen, "Zur inneren Geschichte Preußens während der französischen Revolution. Gentz und Humboldt," *FBPG*, 19 (1906):1–33; Golo Mann, *Secretary of Europe* (New Haven, Conn., 1946), 8–10, 19–29.

the Prussian bureaucracy, and while in Prussian service gradually transformed himself from an enthusiast of the French Revolution to a rabid critic.

Thus all three men had varying degrees of understanding of Kant's philosophy and, at the time of the essay on theory and practice, differing attitudes on the revolution itself. Yet all three were also administrators who argued from this perspective for the relative autonomy of the social world. Kant's chief difficulty in the essays was that he had eliminated the practical world from his view. Although he defined "practice" broadly as "those realizations of a particular purpose which are considered to comply with certain generally conceived rules of procedure," he narrowed "purposive action" – and thus the domain of the practical – to what could also be subsumed under scientific knowledge of some formalized kind.[43] Even according to Kant, however, the concern of practitioners was not that they desired scientific confirmation of their endeavors and were disappointed by the inadequacy of theory; on the contrary, they claimed that the criteria and accomplishments of theoretical knowledge were irrelevant to their problems. Although acknowledging the claims of practice, in other words, Kant was unable to invert his own perspective and to ask whether there might be forms of practice that were incapable of theoretical formulation. Kant's argument seems particularly weak with regard to social behavior. It is difficult to see how his analysis applied to custom – a type of purposive, group-instilled behavior that to a certain extent is self-conscious. Möser appears to have had this weakness in mind when he wrote: from "pure" reason nothing but a "pure" result can be achieved.[44]

All three men accepted that theoretical knowledge formed a distinct realm with its own procedures and norms; they attacked the formalism of Kant's arguments and argued instead for the limited penetration of theoretical knowledge in the practical world. Although they formulated their objections differently, they all saw the need for an empirical science of society and the state. Thus what is often seen as a conservative intention in their criticism stemmed from their experiences as working administrators trained in case and property law and actively involved in modest social and economic reform.

Like Möser, Gentz and Rehberg viewed polity and society as inseparable and subject to laws of group interests. Both feared that if such interests were ignored, there would be no mechanisms to enforce the laws of civil society as Kant had described them.[45] Rehberg, like Möser, remained a particularist in defending the Estates and the corporations as the carriers of concrete liberties. He also employed the idea of contract and Kant's own strict separation between the intellectual and the physical to eliminate the emancipatory intent in Kant's

---

[43] Concerning this issue see Robert Paul Wolff, *The Autonomy of Reason* (New York, 1973), 47, 104; Lewis White Beck, *A Commentary on Kant's Critique of Practical Reason* (Chicago, 1960), 29–41; Nicholas Lobkowicz, *Theory and Practice* (Notre Dame, Ind., 1967), 125.

[44] Möser, "Ueber Theorie und Praxis," *SW*, 10:142–3.

[45] Henrich, *Ueber Theorie und Praxis*, 34–5.

theory; man must have moral and intellectual autonomy insofar as he is an intelligent being, he stated, but man is also a physical being, and his physical being is subject to differences in wealth, station, and privilege. Were this distinction between intellectual and material not to be made, then the only society possible, Rehberg concluded, would be one of "true political equality" and the equal distribution of property.[46] Gentz at this point in his career was still more progressive than Rehberg. Against Kant he argued that the social contract was open and evolved with each generation; he maintained that the moral autonomy Kant praised necessarily abolished the political subordination Kant was willing to accept; and he asserted that the right of rebellion was implied in the idea of contract itself.[47]

In these critiques of Kant, we return to the language of theory and practice and to that distinction between man in his cosmopolitan function and man in his social function that remained central to the older generation in the German Enlightenment. Kant's view and those of Möser and Kant's other critics stayed embedded in the world of argument over the social contract that had flourished in seventeenth-century England. As late as the beginning of the French Revolution, these German conservatives used early Enlightenment ideas of social contract against Kant. This illustrates both the real lag in the modernization of German political institutions and the continued flexibility of the older conceptual mechanisms. Enlightenment administrators and publicists of the prerevolutionary decades still dealt in the political values and patterns of explanation from the early Enlightenment, because their institutional world required little else. It took the French Revolution to introduce a new political vocabulary gradually into the German debates, and even then corporatist Enlightenment – as a reforming conservatism and an inegalitarian liberalism – remained the dominant political constellation in the pre-March period.[48]

Thus, by considering Kant's and Möser's areas of implicit agreement as well as those areas of fundamental disagreement, we can see how the Enlightenment vision of political emancipation had a special German temper in the later eighteenth century. Though we would like to see clearly the emergence of modern liberal and conservative positions from the political views of this older Enlightenment generation, the complexity of corporate institutions in Germany prevented that modern political understanding. Limited reform within the corporate structures of the Estates or legal emancipation within absolute monarchy: these were the choices in the later eighteenth century, and the structure of the German Enlightenment was built around this fact.

[46] Ibid., 124.
[47] Ibid., 106.
[48] See the views of Hartwig Brandt, *Landständische Repräsentation im deutschen Vormärz* (Neuwied, 1968), 7; see also Lothar Gall, *Benjamin Constant* (Wiesbaden, 1963); Hans Rosenberg, *Politische Denkströmungen im deutschen Vormärz* (Göttingen, 1972), 20–39.

# Bibliography of cited works

## I. WORKS OF JUSTUS MÖSER

General note: Though two editions of Möser's works and one edition of his letters have been published, none is complete, and each must be supplemented in various ways. The still incomplete edition of his collected works is particularly difficult to use, since fundamental information concerning the date and place of original publication is often missing. For this reason, the reader still needs to consult Wolfgang Hollman's bibliographical study from 1937. The comprehensive edition of Möser's letters by Beins and Pleister is also incomplete, though the work for a new edition has been started by William Sheldon and continues under the auspices of the Herzog Aubust Bibliothek in Wolfenbüttel. Möser's administrative papers, legal briefs, and pamphlets – documents fundamental to his historical place – have never been collected and published. With isolated exceptions, they are located in the Lower Saxon State Archives in Osnabrück.

### A. MANUSCRIPT WORKS IN THE NIEDERSÄCHSISCHES STAATSARCHIV OSNABRÜCK (STA OSN)

1. Dep 58 Hs. A XIX: Möser's Papers
   I. Drafts of literary, philosophical, and critical writings.
   II. Drafts to the *Patriotic Phantasies* and other writings.
   III. Drafts of historical writings.
   IV. Administrative writings.
   V. Miscellaneous.
2. Dep 58 Hs. A XX: Justus Möser's Gutachten und Bedenken über einige die Dienste und Leistungen der landesherrlichen Eigenbehörigen betreffende Fragen. 1781 and 1782.
3. Dep 58 Hs. A XXI: Excerpta juridica sub divini miminis auspicio compilata a Justu Mösero. 1740–c.1769.
4. Erw A 16 Nr. 41: Collectanea.
5. Dep 58 Hs. A XL: Erfordertes rechtliches Gutachten des Hochfürstl. Os-

nabrückschen Raths- und Regierungs-Referendii auch Riterschaftlichen Syndici und Advocati Patriae Justus Möser, ad causam der Eingessessenen zu Eiche, Kirchspiels Melle, in specie der Landesfürstlichen Eigenbehörigen dasselbst appellanten ctra Dom Succentor Krusen als Besitzern der Vicariae Sti Jodoci in Dom appellaten. Das Zehntengeld betreffend.

6. Dep 58 Hs. A LXVI: Letters from Johann Zacharias Möser to Justus Möser (1752–5).
7. Dep 58d A LXXVII: Inventory of the Möser library.
    For this see Horst Meyer, "Bücher im Leben eines Verwaltungsjuristen. Justus Möser und seine Bibliothek." In *Sammler Private und Oeffentliche Bibliotheken im 18. Jahrhundert*, Heidelberg, 1979, 149–58.
8. Dep 58 Hs. LXXXIa: Letters and papers from the Möser family circle.
9. Dep 110 II, Nr 37B. Justus Möser, "Promemoria bzgl. seiner Stellen als Consulent der Regierung." London, February 1764.

### B. OTHER MANUSCRIPT SOURCES

1. Oesterreichisches Staatsarchiv Wien: Habsburg-Lothringisches Familienarchiv, Poschakten Jüngere Serie; Karton 3 ff. 406–32: Bauernbeschaffenheit in Osnabrück n. 1779.

### C. COLLECTED WORKS

*Justus Mösers sämmtliche Werke.* Edited by Bernhard Rudolf Abeken. 10 vols. Berlin, 1842–3. 2nd ed. Berlin, 1858.
*Justus Mösers sämtliche Werke. Historisch-kritische Ausgabe.* Edited by Eberhard Crusius, Paul Göttsching, Werner Kohlschmidt, and Ludwig Schirmeyer. Vols. 1–2, 4–10, 12/1–2, 13, 14/1 to date. Oldenburg, 1943–1981 to date.
*Briefe.* Edited by Ernst Beins and Werner Pleister. Veröffentlichungen der Historischen Kommission für Hannover, Oldenburg, Braunschweig, Schaumburg-Lippe und Bremen, 21. Oldenburg, 1939.

### D. UNCOLLECTED PRINTED MATERIALS

1. PRO-MEMORIA der Chur-Braunschweigischen Comital-Gesandschaft die zwischen Sr. Königl. Majestät von Grosbritannien und Churfürstl. Durchlauchtigkeit von Braunschweig-Lüneburg und dem Dom-Capittel zu Osnabrück entsandene Streitigkeiten. n.p. 1764.
2. Vergleichung und Betrachtung der Bischöflichen Minderjärigkeit zu Regenspurg vom Jahre 1587, mit derjenigen Bischöflichen Minderjährigkeit, welche sich dermahlen beym Stifte Osnabrück bevorthut, und worüber jetzt in Comitiis gehandelt wird. Angestellt von einem Regenspurgischen Rechts-Gelehrten. n.p. 1764.
3. Memorial an eine Hochlöbliche-allgemeine Reichs-Versammlung in Regenspurg, Die Seiner Königlichen Majestät von Groβ-Britannien von dem Dom-Capittel zu Osnabrück Rechts-Friedenschluβ und Reichs-Constitutions-widrige Zumuthungen betreffend. n.p. 1764.

4. Kurze und vorläufige Abfertigung der sowohl in facto irrigen als in jure höchst unbegrundeten, mit verschieden zuwiderlauffenden Sätzen angefüllten, von dem Osnabrückischen Dom-Capitell übergebenen und den 6. Auf. a. c. durch Chur-Mainz ad Dictaturam gebrachten Vorlegung dessen, was im Stift Osnabrück, usw. n.p. 1765.
5. Rechtliche Behauptung derer Gründe worauf die von Sr. Königl. Majest. von Großbritannien und Churfürstl. Durchl. zu Braunschweig und Lüneburg u. a. in Ansehung der Bischofs-Wahl, und der Regierungs-Einrichtungen im Stifte, während der Minderjährigkeit des erwählten Herrn Bischofs Königlicher Hoheit, genommenen Maasregeln gebauet sind, der näheren Capittel zu Osnabrück angestellet worden, entgegen gesetzt. n.p. 1767.
6. Darstellung der Gründe welche seine Königliche Hoheit den Herrn Herzog von York als Bischofen zu Osnabrück bewogen haben das Simultanum zu Fürstenau und Schledehausen einzuführen . . . Osnabrück, n.d. (c. 1790).
7. Reviews of legal literature in the *Auserlesene Bibliothek der neusten Literatur* 4–10. Lemgo, 1773–6. 4: 575–92; 5: 223–36; 9: 243–53; 10: 548–53, 575–7, 578–80, 592–4, 623–5.
8. STA OSN Slg 100 I; Newspapers.

## II. OTHER ARCHIVAL AND MANUSCRIPT SOURCES

A. STA OSN Erw. A 11: Lodtmann papers.
B. STA OSN Dep Hs. A XLVI and XLVII: conditions in the city of Osnabrück.
C. STA OSN Dep 3b VI: Sumptuary laws in the city of Osnabrück.

## III. OTHER PRINTED MATERIALS

Aarsleff, Hans. From Locke to Saussure. Minneapolis, 1982.
———. "Vico and Berlin." *London Review of Books* 3/20 (1981): 6–8; 4/10 (1982): 4–5.
Abbt, Thomas. *Vermischte Schriften.* 6 vols. Frankfurt and Leipzig, 1783.
Abeken, B. R. "Erinnerungen B. R. Abeken." In *Festschrift zur dreihundertjährigen Jubelfeier des Ratsgymnasium zu Osnabrück 1895*, edited by A. Heuermann, 13–18. Osnabrück, 1895.
Adler, Emil. *Herder und die deutsche Aufklärung.* Translated by Irena Fischer. Vienna, 1968.
Altmann, Alexander. "Moses Mendelssohn über Naturrecht und Naturzustand." In *Ich handle mit Vernunft*, edited by Norbert Hinske, 45–84. Hamburg, 1981.
———. *Prinzipien politischer Theorie bei Mendelssohn und Kant.* Trierer Universitätsreden 9. Trier, 1981.
Aner, Karl. *Der Aufklärer Friedrich Nicolai.* Studien zur Geschichte der neueren Protestantismus, 6. Gießen, 1912.
Anonymous. "Von dem preußischen Westfalen." *Staatsanzeigen* 3/11 (1783): 353–64.
Anonymous. [Frhr. v. R.]. "Briefe über Westphalen." *Deutsches Museum* 1 (1784):234–61, 352–69.

Anonymous. "Freimütige Gedanken veranlasst durch die Fuldaische Preisauf-gabe." *Staatsanzeigen* 9 (1786):385–408.

Anonymous. "Sind denn wirklich alle Menschen gleich." *Berlinische Monatsschrift* 18 (1791):541–66.

Anonymous. "Mösers Tod: am 8 Jaunuar 1794 im 74sten Jahr seines Lebens." *Berlinische Monatsschrift* 23 (1794):270–283.

Antoni, Carlo. *Der Kampf Wider die Vernunft. Zur Entstehungsgeschichte des deutschen Freiheitsgedankens.* Translated by Walter Goetz. Stuttgart, 1951.

Aretin, Karl Otmar von. "Die Konfessionen als politische Kräfte am Ausgang des alten Reiches." In *Festgabe Joseph Lortz*, edited by Peter Manns and Erwin Iserloh, 2:181–241. 2 vols. Baden-Baden, 1958.

———. *Heiliges Römisches Reich 1786–1806. Reichsverfassung und Staatssouver-anität.* 2 vols. Veröffentlichungen des Instituts für europäische Geschichte Mainz, 38. Wiesbaden, 1967.

———, ed. *Der aufgeklärte Absolutismus.* Neue Wissenschaftliche Bibliothek, 67. Cologne, 1974.

———. *Bayerns Weg zum souveränen Staat. Landstände und konstitutionelle Mon-archie 1714–1818.* Munich, 1976.

Aubin, Hermann, ed. *Der Raum Westfalen.* 4 vols. Münster, 1931–58.

Aubin, Hermann, and Zorn Wolfgang, eds. *Handbuch der deutschen Wirtschafts-und Sozialgeschichte.* 2 vols. Stuttgart, 1971–6.

Bär, Max. *Abriß einer Verwaltungsgeschichte des Regierungsbezirks Osnabrück.* Quellen und Darstellungen zur Geschichte Niedersachsens, 5. Hanover, 1901.

Bäte, Ludwig. *Justus Möser. Advocatus Patriae.* Frankfurt am Main. 1961.

Bahr, Erhard, ed. *Was ist Aufklärung?* Stuttgart, 1974.

Balet, Leo, and Gerhard, E. *Die Verbürgerlichung der deutschen Kunst, Literatur und Musik im 18. Jahrhundert.* Edited by Gert Mattenklott. Reprint 1936 ed. Frankfurt am Main, 1972.

Barkhausen, Max. "Der Aufstieg der rheinischen Industrie im 18. Jahrhundert und die Entstehung eines industriellen Großbürgertums." *Rheinische Vier-teljahrsblätter* 19 (1954):135–78.

———."Staatliche Wirtschaftslenkung und freies Unternehmertum im west-deutschen und im nord- und südniederländischen Raum bei der Entstehung der neuzeitlichen Industrie im 18. Jahrhundert." *VSWG* 45 (1958):168–241.

Baron, Hans. "Justus Mösers Individualitätsprinzip in seiner geistesgeschicht-lichen Bedeutung." *HZ* 130 (1924):31–57.

Batscha, Zwi. *Studien zur politischen Theorie des deutschen Frühliberalismus.* Frankfurt am Main, 1981.

Bausinger, Hermann. "Konservative Aufklärung – Justus Möser vom Blickpunkt der Gegenwart." *Zeitschrift für Volkskunde* 68 (1972):161–78.

Bazan, H. Banniza von. "Ahnenliste von Justus Möser." *Osn. Mitt.* 66 (1954):181–96.

Becher, Ursula A. J. *Politische Gesellschaft. Studien zur Genese bürgerlicher Oeffent-lichkeit in Deutschland.* Veröffentlichungen des Max-Planck-Instituts für Ges-chichte, 59. Göttingen, 1978.

Beck, Lewis White. *A Commentary on Kant's Critique of Practical Reason.* Chicago, 1960.

————. *Early German Philosophy. Kant and His Predecessors.* Cambridge, 1969.

Beckschäfer, Dr. "Evangelische Domherren in Osnabrücker Domkapitel." *Osn. Mitt.* 52 (1930):177–98.

Behrens, C. B. A. "Government and Society." In *Cambridge Economic History*, edited by M. M. Postan and H. J. Habakkuk, 5:549–620, 676–680. 7 vols. in 9. 2nd ed. London, 1966–78.

Bendix, Reinhard, and Lipset, Seymour Martin, eds. *Class, Status and Power.* Glencoe, Ill., 1953.

Benecke, Gerhard. *Society and Politics in Germany 1500–1750.* London, 1974.

Berding, Helmut, and Ullmann, Peter, eds. *Deutschland zwischen Revolution und Restauration.* Königstein/Ts., 1981.

Berlanstein, Lenard R. *The Barristers of Toulouse in the Eighteenth Century (1740–1793).* Baltimore, 1975.

Berlin, Isaiah. *Vico and Herder.* New York, 1976.

————. *Against the Current.* Edited by Henry Hardy. New York, 1980.

Berney, Arnold. "August Ludwig von Schlözer's Staatsauffassung." *HZ* 132 (1925):43–67.

Blackall, Eric A. *The Emergence of German as a Literary Language.* Cambridge, 1959.

Blanning, T. C. W. *Reform and Revolution in Mainz 1743–1803.* Cambridge, 1974.

Blaug, Mark. *Economic Theory in Retrospect.* Rev. ed. Homewood, Ill., 1968.

Bloch, Ernst. *Naturrecht und menschliche Würde.* Frankfurt am Main, 1961.

Blum, Jerome. *The End of the Old Order in Rural Europe.* Princeton, N.J., 1978.

Bödeker, Hans Erich. "Thomas Abbt: Patriot, Bürger und bürgerliches Bewußtsein." In *Bürger und Bürgerlichkeit im Zeitalter der Aufklärung*, edited by Rudolf Vierhaus, 221–53. Heidelberg, 1981.

————. "Zur Rezeption der französischen Menschen- und Bürgerrechtserklärung von 1789/1791 in der deutschen Aufklärungsgesellschaft." In *Grund- und Freiheitsrechte im Wandel von Gesellschaft und Geschichte*, edited by Günter Birtsch, 258–86. Göttingen, 1981.

Bodi, Leslie. *Tauwetter in Wien. Zur Prosa der österreichischen Aufklärung 1781–1795.* Frankfurt am Main, 1977.

Bonin, Henning von. "Adel und Bürgertum in der höheren Beamtenschaft der preußischen Monarchie 1794–1806." *Jahrbuch für die Geschichte Mittel- und Ostdeutschlands* 15 (1966):139–74.

Borinski, Karl. *Baltasar Gracian und die Hofliteratur in Deutschland.* Halle a. S., 1894.

Borst, Otto. "Zur Verfassung und Staatlichkeit oberdeutscher Reichsstädte am Ende des Alten Reiches." *Esslinger Studien* 10 (1964):106–94.

Bossenbrook, William J. "Justus Möser's Approach to History." In *Medieval and Historiographical Essays in Honor of James Westfall Thompson*, edited by James Lea Cate and Eugene N. Anderson, 397–422. Chicago, 1938.

Botzenhart, Erich. *Die Staats- und Reformideen des Freiherrn vom Stein.* Tübingen, 1927.

Bouwsma, William. "Lawyers and Early Modern Culture." *AHR* 78 (1973):303–27.

Brandi, Karl. *Ausgewählte Aufsätze.* Oldenburg, 1938.

Brandt, Hartwig. *Landständische Repräsentation im deutschen Vormärz: Politisches Denken im Einflußfeld des monarchischen Prinzips.* Neuwied, 1968.

Braubach, Max. *Kurköln. Gestalten und Ereignisse aus zwei Jahrhunderten rheinischer Geschichte.* Münster, 1949.

———. *Maria Theresias Jüngster Sohn Max Franz. Letzter Kurfürst von Köln und Fürstbishof von Münster.* Vienna, 1961.

———. *Diplomatie und geistiges Leben im 17. und 18. Jahrhundert. Gesammelte Abhandlungen.* Bonner Historische Forschungen, 33. Bonn, 1967.

Braun, Rudolf. *Industrialisierung und Volksleben.* 2nd ed. Göttingen, 1979.

———. *Sozialer und kultureller Wandel in einem ländlichem Industriegebiet im 19. und 20. Jahrhundert.* Erlenbach-Zurich, 1965.

Brewer, John. *Party Ideology and Popular Politics at the Accession of George III.* Cambridge, 1976.

Brück, Gertrud. *Die Bedeutung Justus Mösers für das Leben und Denken Thomas Abbts.* Munich, 1937.

Brucker, Gene. *The Civic World of Early Renaissance Florence.* Princeton, N.J., 1977.

Brüggemann, Fritz. "Der Kampf um die bürgerlichen Welt- und Lebensanschauung." *DVLG* 3 (1925):94–127.

———. "Die Entwicklung der Psychologie im bürgerlichen Drama Lessings und seiner Zeit." *Euphorion,* 26 (1925):376–88.

———. "Lessings Bürgerdramen und der Subjektivismus als Problem. Psychogenetische Untersuchungen." *Jahrbuch des Freien Deutschen Hochstifts* (1926):69–110.

Brühl, Heinrich Joseph. "Die Tätigkeit des Ministers Franz von Fürstenberg auf dem Gebiet der inneren Politik des Fürstbistums Münster 1763–1780." *Westfälische Zeitschrift* o.s. 63 (1905):167–248.

Brünauer, Ulrike. *Justus Möser.* Probleme der Staats- und Kultursoziologie, 7. Berlin, 1933.

Bruni, Leonardo. *Panegyric to the City of Florence.* Translated by Benjamin G. Kohl. In *The Earthly Republic,* edited by Benjamin G. Kohl and Ronald G. Witt, 135–175. Philadelphia, 1978.

Brunner, Otto. *Neue Wege der Verfassungs- und Sozialgeschichte.* 2nd rev. ed. Göttingen, 1968.

Brunschwig, Henri. *Enlightenment and Romanticism in Eighteenth-Century Prussia.* Translated by Frank Jellinek. Chicago, [1947] 1974.

Carpenter, Kenneth. *Dialogues in Political Economy. Translations from and into German in the 18th Century.* Boston, 1977.

Chisick, Harvey. *The Limits of Reform in the Enlightenment.* Princeton, N.J., 1980.

Church, William F. "The Decline of the French Jurists as Political Theorists, 1660–1789." *French Historical Studies* 5 (1967):1–40.

Clauer, Eduard von. "Auch etwas über das Recht der Menschheit." *Berlinische Monatsschrift* 16 (1790):197–209.

———. "Noch ein Beitrag über das Recht der Menschheit." *Berlinische Monatsschrift* 16 (1790):441–69.

Clive, John. "The Social Background of the Scottish Renaissance." In *Scotland in the Age of Improvement,* edited by N. T. Phillipson and Rosalind Mitchison, 225–44. Edinburgh, 1970.

*Codex Constitutionum Osnabrugensium oder die Sammlung von Verordnungen, gemeinen Bescheiden, Rescripten und anderen erläuternden Verfügungen, welche das Hochstift Osnabrück betreffen.* 2 vols. Osnabrück, 1783–1819.

Coleman, D. C., ed. *Revisions in Mercantilism.* London, 1969.

Dakin, Douglas. *Turgot and the Ancien Regime in France.* New York, [1939] 1972.

Darnton, Robert. "The High Enlightenment and the Low-Life of Literature in Pre-Revolutionary France." *Past and Present* 51 (1971):81–115.

Dawson, Philip. "The *Bourgeoisie de Robe* in 1789." *French Historical Studies* 4 (1965):1–21.

———. *Provincial Magistrates and Revolutionary Politics in France 1789–1795.* Cambridge, Mass., 1972.

Dilthey, Wilhelm. "Das achtzehnte Jahrhundert und die geschichtliche Welt." In *Gesammelte Schriften*, edited by Paul Ritter et al., 3:210–68. 4th ed. 18 vols. to date. Berlin, New York, Stuttgart, 1914–1977.

Dippel, Horst. *Germany and the American Revolution, 1770–1800.* Chapel Hill, N.C., 1977.

———. *Individuum und Gesellschaft. Soziales Denken zwischen Tradition und Revolution.* Veröffentlichungen des Max-Planck-Instituts für Geschichte, 70. Göttingen, 1981.

Dipper, Christof. *Die Bauernbefreiung in Deutschland 1790–1850.* Stuttgart, 1980.

Dorn, Walter. *Competition for Empire 1740–1763.* Rev. ed. New York, 1963.

Dreyfus, F. G. *Sociétés et Mentalités à Mayence dans la second moitié du dix-huitième siècle.* Paris, 1968.

Dülman, Richard van. "Antijesuitismus und katholische Aufklärung in Deutschland." *Historisches Jahrbuch* 89 (1969):52–80.

———. "Der Geheimbund der Illuminaten." *ZBLG* 36 (1973):793–833.

———. "Zum Strukturwandel der Aufklärung in Bayern." *ZBLG* 36 (1973):662–79.

———. *Der Geheimbund der Illuminaten.* Stuttgart, 1975.

———. "Die Aufklärungsgesellschaften in Deutschland als Forschungsproblem." *Francia* 5 (1977):251–75.

Dufour, Alfred. "Die Ecole romande du droit naturel—ihre deutsche Wurzeln." In *Humanismus und Naturrecht in Berlin-Brandenburg-Preußen*, edited by Hans Thieme, 133–43. Berlin, 1979.

Dzwonek, Ulrich, et al. " 'Bürgerliche Oppositionsliteratur zwischen Revolution und Reformismus.' F. G. Klopstocks *Deutsche Gelehrtenrepublik . . .* " In *Deutsches Bürgertum und literarische Intelligenz 1750–1800*, edited by Bernd Lutz, 277–328. Literaturwissenschaft und Sozialwissenschaften, 3. Stuttgart, 1974.

Eisenbart, Lisolette C. *Kleiderordnungen der deutschen Städte zwischen 1350 und 1770.* Göttingen, 1962.

Elias, Norbert. *Ueber den Prozess der Zivilisation.* 2 vols. 2nd ed. Frankfurt am Main, 1978–9.

Emerson, Roger. "The Enlightenment and Social Structures." In *City and Society in the 18th Century*, edited by Paul Fritz and David Williams, 99–124. Toronto, 1973.

Endres, Rudolf. "Das Armenproblem im Zeitalter des Absolutismus." *Jahrbuch für fränkische Landesforschung* 34/35 (1974–5):1003–20.

Epstein, Klaus. *The Genesis of German Conservatism*. Princeton, N.J., 1966.

Etter, Else-Lilly. *Tacitus in der Geistesgeschichte des 16. und 17. Jahrhunderts*. Basler Beiträge zur Geschichtswissenschaft, 103. Basel, 1966.

Ewald, Johann Ludwig. *Ueber Volksaufklärung; Ihre Gränzen und Vortheile*. Berlin, 1790.

Faber, Karl-Georg. "Strukturprobleme des deutschen Liberalismus im 19. Jahrhundert." *Der Staat* 15 (1975):201–28.

Fabian, Bernhard. "English Books and their Eighteenth-Century German Readers." In *The Widening Circle: Essays on the Circulation of Literature in Eighteenth-Centruy Europe*, edited by Paul Korshin, 117–96. Philadelphia, 1969.

Fehrenbach, Elizabeth. *Traditionale Gesellschaft und revolutionäres Recht*. Kritische Studien zur Geschichtswissenschaft, 13. Göttingen, 1974.

———. "Deutschland und die Französische Revolution." *Geschichte und Gesellschaft* supplement no. 2 (1976):232–53.

Feine, Hans Erich. "Zur Verfassungsentwicklung des Heiligen Römischen Reiches seit dem Westfälischen Friedens." *ZSRG (germ)* 52 (1932):65–133.

Fetscher, Iring "Immanuel Kants bürgerlicher Reformismus." In *Theory and Politics. Theorie und Politik. Festschrift zum 70. Geburtstag für Carl Joachim Friedrich*, edited by Klaus von Beyme, 70–95. The Hague, 1971.

Filmer, Robert. *Patriarcha and Other Political Works*. Edited by Peter Laslett. Oxford, 1949.

Fink, Zera. *The Classical Republicans*. Northwestern University Studies in the Humanities, 9. Evanston, Ill., 1945.

Fischer, Kuno. *Geschichte der neueren Philosophie*. vol. 4/1. 4th ed. Heidelberg, 1898.

Fischer, Wolfram. "Rural Industrialization and Population Change." *CSSH* 15 (1973):158–70.

Flaskamp, Franz. "Reformation und Gegenreformation im Hochstift Osnabrück." *Westfälische Forschungen* 11 (1958):68–74.

Fleischmann, Max. *Christian Thomasius. Leben und Lebenswerk*. Halle, 1931.

Flurschütz, Hildegunde. *Die Verwaltung des Hochstifts Würzburg unter Franz Ludwig von Erthal (1779–1795)*. Veröffentlichungen der Gesellschaft für fränkische Geschichte, ser. 9 [Darstellungen aus der fränkischen Geschichte, 19]. Würzburg, 1965.

Ford, Franklin. "The Enlightenment: Towards a Useful Redefinition." *Studies in the Eighteenth Century*, edited by R. F. Brissenden, 17–29. Toronto, 1968.

Forst, Hermann. "Die Geschichtschreibung im Bistum Osnabrück bis zum Ende des XVII. Jahrhunderts." *Deutsche Geschichtsblätter* 5 (1904):117–27.

François, Etienne. "Die Volksbildung am Mittelrhein im ausgehenden 18. Jahrhundert." *Jahrbuch für westdeutsche Landesgeschichte* 3 (1977):277–304.

Frankenfeld, Alfred. *Justus Möser als Staatsmann und Publizist im Siebenjährigen Kriege und am englischen Hofe*. Ph.D. dissertation, University of Göttingen, 1922.

Freckmann, Johannes. "Die *capitulatio perpetua* und ihre verfassungsgeschichtliche Bedeutung für das Hochstift Osnabrück (1648–50)." *Osn. Mitt.* 31 (1906):129–204.

Friedrich der Groβe. *De la littérature allemande*. Edited by Christoph Gutknecht und Peter Kerner. Hamburg, 1969.

Gagliardo, John. *From Pariah to Patriot. The Changing Image of the German Peasant 1770–1840.* Lexington, Ky., 1969.

Gagliardo, John. *Reich and Nation.* Bloomington, Ind., 1980.

Gall, Lothar. *Benjamin Constant. Seine politische Ideenwelt und der deutsche Vormärz.* Veröffentlichungen des Instituts für europäische Geschichte Mainz, 30. Wiesbaden, 1963.

———. "Liberalismus und 'bürgerliche Gesellschaft'."*HZ* 220 (1975):324–56.

Garber, Jörn, ed. *Kritik der Revolution. Theorien des deutschen Frühkonservatismus 1790–1810,* 1: *Dokumentation.* Kronberg/Ts., 1976.

Gatterer, Johann C., ed., [Review of Justus Möser's "Allgemeine Einleitung" to the *Osnabrückische Geschichte*], *Allgemeine Historische Bibliothek von Mitgliedern des Königlichen Instituts der Historischen Wissenschaften zu Göttingen,* 9:67–119. Halle, 1769.

Gerhard, Dietrich. *Alte und neue Welt in vergleichender Geschichtsbetrachtung.* Veröffentlichungen des Max-Planck-Instituts für Geschichte, 10. Göttingen, 1962.

———, ed. *Ständische Vertretungen in Europa im 17. und 18. Jahrhundert.* Veröffentlichungen des Max-Planck-Instituts für Geschichte, 27. Göttingen, 1969.

Gerth, Hans. *Bürgerliche Intelligenz um 1800.* Kritische Studien zur Geschichtswissenschaft, 19. Göttingen, 1976.

Gillis, John R. "Aristocracy and Bureaucracy in Nineteenth-Century Prussia." *Past and Present* 41 (1968):105–29.

Gösling, R., and Schoeller, Harold. "Zur Ahnenliste Justus Mösers. Ergänzungen." *Osn. Mitt.* 68 (1959):391–97.

Goethe, Johann Wolfgang. *Dichtung und Wahrheit.* vol. 3. In *Werke.* 16 vols. Leipzig, 1912–20.

Göttsching, Paul. "Zwischen Historismus und politischer Geschichtsschreibung." *Osn. Mitt.* 82 (1976):60–80.

———. "Geschichte und Gegenwart bei Justus Möser." *Osn. Mitt.* 83 (1977):94–116.

Goldmann, Lucien. *Der christliche Bürger in der Aufklärung.* Neuwied, 1968.

Gray, Hanna. "Renaissance Humanism: The Pursuit of Eloquence." In *Renaissance Essays,* edited by Paul O. Kristeller and Philip P. Wiener, 199–216. New York, 1968.

Grimminger, Rolf, ed. *Deutsche Aufklärung bis zur Französischen Revolution 1680–1789.* Hansers Sozialgeschichte der deutschen Literatur, vol. 3 in 2 parts. Munich, 1980.

Gross, Hanns. *Empire and Sovereignty. A History of the Public Law Literature 1599–1804.* Chicago, 1973.

Gruner, Justus. *Meine Wallfahrt zur Ruhe und Hoffnung oder Schilderung der sittlichen und bürgerlichen Zustandes Westphalens am Ende des achtzehnten Jahrhunderts.* 2 vols. Frankfurt, 1802–3.

Gulyga, A. W. *Der deutsche Materialismus am Ausgang des 18. Jahrhunderts.* Translated by Ileana Bauer and Gertraud Korf. Berlin, 1966.

Gundling, N. H. *Abriß zu einer rechten Reichshistorie.* Halle, 1708.

Haase, Carl. *Ernst Brandes.* 2 vols. Hildesheim, 1973–4.

Habermas, Jürgen. *Strukturwandel der Oeffentlichkeit.* 4th ed. Neuwied, 1969.

Haferkorn, Hans-Jürgen. "Der freie Schriftsteller. Eine literatursoziologische Studie über seine Entstehung und Lage in Deutschland zwischen 1750–1800." *Archiv für Geschichte des Buchwesens* 5 (1964):523–712.

Hammer, Karl, and Voss, Jürgen, eds. *Historische Forschung im 18. Jahrhundert.* Pariser Historische Studien, 13. Bonn, 1976.

Hammermeyer, Ludwig. "Die Aufklärung in Wissenschaft und Gesellschaft." In *Handbuch der bayerischen Geschichte*, edited by Max Spindler, 2:985–1033. 4 vols. in 6. Munich, 1966–75.

―――. "Staatliche Herrschaftsordunung und altständische Repräsentation." In *Handbuch der bayerischen Geschichte*, edited by Max Spindler, 2:1063–89. 4 vols. in 6. Munich, 1966–75.

Hammerstein, Notker. "Zur Geschichte der deutschen Universität im Zeitalter der Aufklärung." In *Universität und Gelehrtenstand, 1400–1800*, edited by Hellmuth Rössler and Günther Franz, 145–82. Limburg/Lahn, 1970.

―――. "Das politische Denken Friedrich Carl von Moser." *HZ* 212 (1971):316–38.

―――. *Jus und Historie.* Göttingen, 1972.

Hanschmidt, Alwin. *Franz von Fürstenberg als Staatsmann.* Veröffentlichungen der Historischen Kommission Westfalens, 18 [Westfälische Biographien, 5]. Münster, 1969.

Hantsch, Hugo. *Die Geschichte Oesterreichs.* 2 vols. 2nd ed. Graz, 1953–9.

Hatzig, Otto. *Justus Möser als Staatsmann und Publizist.* Quellen und Darstellungen zur Geschichte Niedersachsens, 27. Hanover, 1909.

Hempel, Ernst. "Justus Mösers Wirkung auf seine Zeitgenossen und auf die deutsche Geschichtsschreibung." *Osn. Mitt.* 54 (1933):1–76.

Henning, Friedrich-Wilhelm. *Dienste und Abgabe der Bauern im 18. Jahrhundert.* Stuttgart, 1969.

―――. *Landwirtschaft und ländliche Gesellschaft in Deutschland.* 2 vols. Paderborn, 1978–9.

Herder, Johann Gottfried. *Von deutscher Art und Kunst.* Edited by Edna Purdie. Oxford, 1924.

―――. *Von deutscher Art und Kunst.* Edited by Hans Dietrich Irmscher. Stuttgart, 1968.

Hertz, Frederick. *The Development of the German Public Mind*, vol. 2: *The Age of the Enlightenment.* New York, 1962.

Herzog, Friedrich. *Das Osnabrücker Land im 18. und 19. Jahrhundert.* Schriften zur Wirtschaftswissenschaftlichen Geschichte zum Studium Niedersachsens, series A, no. 40. Oldenburg, 1938.

Hettner, Hermann. *Geschichte der deutschen Literatur im achtzehnten Jahrhundert.* Edited by Georg Witkowski. 4 vols. in 1. Leipzig, 1928.

Hildebrandt, Reinhard. "Die Verfassungskonflikte in den Reichsstädten des 17. und 18. Jahrhunderts." *Zeitschrift für Stadtgeschichte, Stadtsoziologie und Denkmalpflege* 1 (1974):221–41.

Hill, Christopher. *Puritanism and Revolution.* New York, 1958.

Hiller, Lotte. *Die Geschichtswissenschaft an der Universität Jena in der Zeit der*

*Polyhistorie 1674–1763.* Zeitschrift des Vereins für Thüringische Geschichte und Altertumskunde, n.s., supplement 18. Jena, 1937.

Hinrichs, Carl. *Preußentum und Pietismus.* Göttingen, 1971.

Hinrichs, Ernst. "Produit Net, Propriétaire, Cultivateur. Aspekte des sozialen Wandels bei den Physiokraten und Turgot." In *Festschrift für Hermann Heimpel,* 1:473–510. 2 vols. Göttingen, 1971–3.

Hinrichs, Ernst, and Wiegelmann, Günter, eds. *Sozialer und kultureller Wandel in der ländlichen Welt des 18. Jahrhunderts.* Wolfenbüttler Forschungen, 19. Wolfenbüttel, 1982.

Hinske, Norbert, ed. *Was ist Aufklärung? Beiträge aus der Berlinischen Monatsschrift.* Darmstadt, 1973.

Hirschfelder, Heinrich. *Herrschaftsordnung und Bauerntum im Hochstift Osnabrück im 16. und 17. Jahrhundert.* Osnabrücker Geschichtsquellen und Forschungen, 16. Osnabrück, 1971.

Hobsbawm, E. J. *Primitive Rebels.* New York, 1959.

Hoche, J. G. *Reise durch Osnabrück und Neidermünster in das Saterland, Ostfriesland und Groningen.* Bremen, 1800.

Hölzle, Erwin. *Die Idee einer altgermanischen Freiheit vor Montesquieu.* Historische Zeitschrift, supplement 5. Munich, 1925.

Hömberg, Albert K. *Westfälische Landesgeschichte.* Münster, 1967.

Hollman, Wolfgang. *Justus Mösers Zeitungsidee und ihre Verwirklichung.* Zeitung und Leben, 40. Munich, 1937.

Holmes, Geoffrey. *Augustan England. Professions, State and Society 1680–1730.* London, 1982.

Holz, Hans Heinz. *Leibniz.* Stuttgart, 1958.

Huber, Ernst Rudolf. "Reich, Volk und Staat in der Reichsrechtswissenschaft des 17. und 18. Jahrhunderts." *Zeitschrift für die gesamte Staatswissenschaft* 102 (1942):593–627.

Huber, Kurt. *Leibniz.* Edited by Inge Köck; aided by Clara Huber. Munich, 1951.

Hufton, Olwen. *The Poor of Eighteenth-Century France, 1750–1789.* London, 1974.

Iggers, Georg. *The German Conception of History.* 2nd ed. Hartford, Conn., 1984.

Im Hof, Ulrich. *Issak Iselin.* 2 vols. Basel, 1947.

Jäger, Hans Wolf. *Politische Kategorien im Poetik und Rhetorik der zweiten Hälfte des 18. Jahrhunderts.* Stuttgart, 1970.

Jaeger, Julius. *Die Schola Carolina Osnabrugensis.* Osnabrück, 1904.

Jarausch, Konrad. *Students, Society and Politics in Imperial Germany.* Princeton, N.J., 1982.

Jentzsch, Rudolf. *Der deutsch-lateinische Büchermarkt nach den Leipziger Ostermeß-Katalogen von 1740, 1770 und 1800 in seiner Gliederung und Wandlung.* Leipzig, 1912.

Johnson, Hubert C. "The Concept of Bureaucracy in Cameralism." *PSQ* 79 (1964):378–402.

Jones, Colin. *Charity and Bienfaisance: Treatment of the Poor in the Montpellier Region, 1740–1815.* New York, 1982.

Jones, E. L. "Agricultural Origins of Industry." *Past and Present* 40 (1968):58–71.

Judges, A. V. "The Idea of a Mercantile State." In *Revisions in Mercantilism*, edited by D. C. Coleman, 35–60. London, 1969.

K. "Ueber des Hrn. Geh. Justizraths Möser Behauptungen im November 1791, Nr. 2." *Berlinische Monatsschrift* 19 (1792):142–55.

Kagan, Richard. "Law Students and Legal Careers in Eighteenth-Century France," *Past and Present* 68 (1975):38–72.

Kant, Immanuel. "Ueber die Buchmacherei. Zwei Briefe an Herrn Friedrich Nicolai." *Gesammelte Werke*. vol. 8. Berlin, 1912.

―――. *Werke*. Edited by Wilhelm Weischedel. 6 vols. Darmstadt, 1966–70.

―――. *Political Writings*. Edited by Hans Reiss and translated by H. B. Nisbet. Cambridge, 1970.

Kant, Immanuel, Gentz, Friedrich, and Rehberg, August. *Ueber Theorie und Praxis*. Edited by Dieter Henrich. Frankfurt am Main, 1967.

Keinemann, Friedrich. *Das Domkapitel zu Münster im 18. Jahrhundert*. Veröffentlichungen der Historischen Kommission Westfalens, 22 [Geschichtliche Arbeiten zur Westfälische Landesforschung, 11]. Münster, 1967.

―――. "Zeitgenössische Ansichten über die Entwicklung von Wirtschaft, Gesellschaft und Kultur in den westfälischen Territorien in der zweiten Hälfte des 18. Jahrhunderts." *Westfälische Zeitschrift* 120 (1970):399–454.

Kiesel, Helmut, and Münch, Paul. *Gesellschaft und Literatur im 18. Jahrhundert*. Munich, 1977.

Kisch, Herbert. "The Textile Industries in Silesia and the Rhineland: A Comparative Study in Industrialization." *JEH* 19 (1959):541–64.

―――. *Prussian Mercantilism and the Rise of the Krefeld Silk Industry: Variations Upon an Eighteenth-Century Theme*. Transactions of the American Philosophical Association, n.s. 58/7. Philadelphia, 1968.

―――. *Die Hausindustriellen Textilgewerbe am Niederrhein vor der Industriellen Revolution*. Veröffentlichungen des Max-Planck-Instituts für Geschichte, 65. Göttingen, 1981.

Klassen, Peter. *Justus Möser*. Studien zur Geschichte des Staats- und Nationalgedankens, 2. Frankfurt am Main, 1936.

Kleinheyer, Gerd. *Staat und Bürger im Recht. Die Vorträge des Carl Gottlieb Svarez vor dem preußischen Kronprinz (1791–2)*. Bonner Rechtswissenschaftliche Abhandlungen, vol. 47. Bonn, 1959.

Kleinmayr, Johann Franz Thaddäus. *Unpartheyische Abhandlung von dem Staate des hohen Erzstifts Salzburg und dessen Grundverfassung zur rechtlich- und geschichtesmäßigen Prüfung des sogenannten Iuris Regii der Herzoge in Baiern, entworfen, im Jahre 1765*. [Salzburg,] 1770.

Klenk, Ernst von. *Preisfrage . . .* Frankfurt and Leipzig, 1787.

Kleuker, Johann Friedrich. "Noch etwas über Mösers Tod." *Berlinische Monatsschrift* 23 (1794):486–97.

Klippel, Diethelm. *Politische Freiheit und Freiheitsrechte im deutschen Naturrecht des 18. Jahrhunderts*. Rechts- und Staatswissenschaftliche Veröffentlichungen der Görres-Gesellschaft, n.s., vol. 23. Paderborn, 1976.

Klocke, Friedrich von. *Patriziatsproblem und Werler Erbsälzer*. Veröffentlichungen der Historischen Kommission Westfalens 22 [Geschichtliche Arbeiten zur Westfälischen Landesforschung, 7]. Münster, 1965.

Klöntrup, Aegidius. *Alphabetisches Handbuch der besonderen Rechte und Gewohnheiten des Hochstifts Osnabrück mit Rücksicht auf die benachbarten westfälischen Provinzen.* 3 vols. Osnabrück, 1798–1800.

Knudsen, Jonathan. "Friedrich Nicolai's 'wirkliche Welt': On Common Sense in the German Enlightenment." In *Mentalitäten und Lebensverhältnisse. Rudolf Vierhaus zum 60. Geburtstag,* 77–91. Göttingen, 1982.

Koch, Dieter. *Das Göttinger Honoratiorentum vom 17. bis zur Mitte des 19. Jahrhunderts.* Göttingen, 1958.

Koch, Lotte. *Wandlungen der Wohlfahrtspflege im Zeitalter der Aufklärung.* Erlangen, 1933.

Köhler, Johann David. *Kurzgefaβte und gründliche Teutsche Reichshistorie.* Frankfurt, 1737.

Körholz, Leo. *Die Wahl des Prinzen Friedrich von York zum Bischof von Osnabrück und die Regierung des Stiftes während seiner Minderjährigkeit.* Ph.D. dissertation, University of Münster, 1908.

Kohlschmidt, Werner. "Neuere Möser-Literatur." *Göttingsche Gelehrten Anzeigen* 102 (1940):229–47.

Kolakowski, Leszek. *The Alienation of Reason.* Translated by Norbert Guterman. Garden City, N.Y., 1968.

Kopitzsch, Franklin, ed. *Aufklärung, Absolutismus und Bürgertum in Deutschland.* Munich, 1976.

Kopitzsch, Franklin. *Grundzüge einer Sozialgeschichte der Aufklärung in Hamburg und Altona.* Ph.D. dissertation, University of Hamburg, 1978.

Korff, Hermann August. *Geist der Goethezeit.* vol 1: *Sturm und Drang.* 4th ed. Leipzig, 1958.

Körner, Josef, ed. *Briefe von und an A. W. Schlegel.* 2 vols. Zurich, 1930.

Kors, Alan. *D'Holbach's Coterie: An Enlightenment in Paris.* Princeton, N.J., 1976.

Koselleck, Reinhart. *Preußen zwischen Reform und Revolution.* Industrielle Welt, 7. 2nd ed. Stuttgart, 1975.

Kramm, Heinrich. "Besitzschichten und Bildungsschichten der mitteldeutschen Städte im 16. Jahrhundert." *VSWG* 51 (1964):454–91.

Kramnick, Isaac. *Bolingbroke and His Circle.* Cambridge, Mass., 1968.

———. "Republican Revisionism Revisted." *AHR* 87 (1982):629–64.

Krause-Vilmar, Dietfried. "Neuere Literatur zum deutschen Jakobinismus." *Das Argument* 57 (1970):233–43.

Krauss, Werner. *Gracians Lebenslehre.* Frankfurt am Main, 1947.

Krauss, Werner. *Perspektiven und Probleme.* Neuwied, 1965.

Kriedte, Peter, Medick, Hans, and Schlumbohm, Jürgen. *Industrialisierung vor der Industrialisierung.* Göttingen, 1978.

Krieger, Leonard. *The German Idea of Freedom.* Boston, 1957.

Krüger, Horst. *Zur Geschichte der Manufakturen und Manufakturarbeiter.* Berlin, 1958.

Krusch, Bruno. "Justus Möser und die Osnabrücker Gesellschaft." *Osn. Mitt.* 34 (1910):271–81.

Kudrna, Jaroslav. "Vico and Herder." *Jahrbuch für Geschichte* 19 (1979):61–88.

Kuhn, Axel. "Der schwierige Weg zu den deutschen demokratischen Traditionen." *Neue Politische Literatur* 18 (1973):430–52.

Kuhnert, Reinhold P. *Urbanität auf dem Lande. Badereisen nach Pyrmont im 18. Jahrhundert.* Veröffentlichungen des Max-Planck-Instituts für Geschichte, 77. Göttingen, 1984.

Kulischer, Josef. *Allgemeine Wirtschaftsgeschichte des Mittelalters und der Neuzeit.* 2 vols. Munich, 1928–9.

Kuske, Bruno. *Wirtschaftsgeschichte Westfalens in Leistung und Verflechtung mit den Nachbarländern.* 2nd ed. Münster, 1949.

Lampe, Joachim. *Aristokratie, Hofadel und Staatspatriziat in Kurhannover.* Veröffentlichungen der Historischen Kommission für Niedersachsen, 24 [Untersuchungen zur Ständegeschichte, 2]. 2 vols. Göttingen, 1963.

Laski, Harold J. *The Rise of European Liberalism.* London, 1947.

Lessing, Gotthold Ephraim. *Gesammelte Werke.* Edited by Paul Rilla. 10 vols. 2nd ed. Berlin, 1968.

Levine, David. *Family Formation in an Age of Nascent Capitalism.* New York, 1977.

Liebel, Helen. *Enlightened Bureaucracy versus Enlightened Despotism in Baden, 1750–1792.* Transactions of the American Philosophical Society, 55/5. Philadelphia, 1965.

Liermann, Hans. "Die rechtsgelehrten Beamten der fränkischen Fürstentümer Ansbach und Bayreuth im 18. Jahrhundert. Ein Beitrag zur Geschichte des deutschen Beamtentums." *Jahrbuch für fränkische Landesforschung* 8–9 (1943):255–92.

Lindemann, Margot. *Deutsche Presse bis 1815.* Berlin, 1969.

Lobkowicz, Nicholas. *Theory and Practice. History of a Concept from Aristotle to Marx.* Notre Dame, Ind., 1967.

Lorenzen, Brigitte. *Justus Mösers Patriotische Phantasien. Studien zur Erzählkunst.* Ph.D. dissertation, University of Göttingen, 1956.

Lough, John. *The Encyclopédie.* New York, 1971.

―――――. *The Philosophes and Post-Revolutionary France.* Oxford, 1982.

Lucas, Colin. "Nobles, Bourgeois, and the Origins of the French Revolution," *Past and Present* 60 (1973). Reprinted in *French Society and the Revolution*, edited by Douglas Johnson, 88–131. Cambridge, 1976.

Lucas, Paul. "Blackstone and the Reform of the Legal Profession." *English Historical Review* 77 (1962):456–89.

―――――. "A Collective Biography of Students and Barristers of Lincoln's Inn, 1680–1804." *JMH* 46 (1974):227–61.

Ludovici, Carl Günther. *Ausführlicher Entwurf einer vollständigen Historie der Wolffischen Philosophie.* 3 vols. Leipzig, 1737–8.

Lütge, Friedrich. *Studien zur Sozial- und Wirtschaftsgeschichte. Gesammelte Abhandlungen.* Stuttgart, 1963.

―――――. *Deutsche Sozial- und Wirtschaftsgeschichte.* 3rd ed. Berlin, 1966.

Lukács, Georg. *The Destruction of Reason.* Translated by Peter Palmer. Atlantic Highlands, N.J., 1981.

Machens, Konrad. "Die Tuchmacherei des Osnabrücker Landes im 17. und 18. Jahrhundert." *Osn. Mitt.* 69 (1960):48–61.

————. "Beiträge zur Wirtschaftsgeschichte des Osnabrücker Landes im 17. und 18. Jahrhunderts." *Osn. Mitt.* 70 (1961):86–104.

Macpherson, C. B. *The Political Theory of Possessive Individualism*. Oxford, 1962.

Maier, Hans. *Die Aeltere deutsche Staats- und Verwaltungslehre (Polizeiwissenschaft)*. Neuwied, 1966.

————. *Politische Wissenschaft in Deutschland*. Munich, 1969.

Maier, Johann Christian. *Teutsches Geistliches Staatsrecht abgetheilt in Reichs- und Landrecht*. Lemgo, 1773.

Mann, Golo. *Secretary of Europe. The Life of Friedrich Gentz, Enemy of Napoleon*. Translated by William Woglom. New Haven, 1946.

Mannheim, Karl. *Essays on Sociology and Social Psychology*. Edited by Paul Kecskemeti. London, 1966.

Marcard, Heinrich Matthias. *Beschreibung von Pyrmont*. 2 vols. Leipzig, 1784–5.

Martens, Wolfgang. *Die Botschaft der Tugend. Die Aufklärung im Spiegel der deutschen moralischen Wochenschriften*. Stuttgart, 1971.

Martin, Alfred von. "Weltanschauliche Motiven im altkonservativen Denken." In *Deutscher Staat und deutsche Parteien. Festschrift für Friedrich Meinecke*, edited by Paul Wentzke, 342–84. Munich, 1922.

Martin, Kingsley. *French Liberal Thought in the Eighteenth Century*. New York, 1962.

Martines, Lauro. *Lawyers and Statecraft in Renaissance Florence*. Princeton, N.J., 1968.

Mascov, J. J. *Geschichte der Teutschen bis zum Abgang der Merowingischen Könige in sechzehn Büchern verfasset*. 2 vols. 2nd ed. Leipzig, 1750.

Mauthner, Fritz. *Der Atheismus und seine Geschichte im Abendland*. 4 vols. Berlin, 1920–3.

McClelland, Charles E. *State, Society and University in Germany 1700–1914*. Cambridge, 1980.

Meek, Ronald. L. *The Economics of Physiocracy*. Cambridge, Mass., 1963.

Mehring, Franz. *Die Lessing Legende*. Gesammelte Schriften, 9. Berlin, 1963.

Meier, Ernst von. *Hannoversche Verfassungs- und Verwaltungsgeschichte, 1680–1866*. 2 vols. Leipzig, 1898–9.

Meinecke, Friedrich. *Zur Theorie und Philosophie der Geschichte*. Edited by Eberhard Kessel. Stuttgart, 1959.

————. *Die Idee der Staatsräson in der neueren Geschichte*. Edited by Walther Hofer. 3rd ed. Munich, 1963.

————. *Weltbürgertum und Nationalstaat*. 4th ed. Stuttgart, 1964.

————. *Die Entstehung des Historismus*. Edited by Carl Hinrichs. 4th ed. Munich, 1965.

Mendels, Franklin F. "Proto-Industrialization: The First Phase of the Industrialization Process." *Journal of Economic History* 32/1 (1972):241–61.

Mendelssohn, Moses. "Sendschreiben an den Herrn Magister Lessing in Leipzig." *Gesammelte Schriften. Jubiläums Ausgabe*. Edited by Fritz Bamberger et al. vol. 2. Berlin, 1929–1984 to date.

Menschenfreund, Christian Friedrich. *Warum ist, oder war bisher der Wohlstand der Protestantischen Staaten so gar viel grösser als der Katholischen.* Vienna, 1782.

Metzger, Wilhelm. *Gesellschaft, Recht und Staat in der Ethik des deutschen Idealismus.* Heidelberg, 1917.

Meyring, Diethild. *Politische Weltweisheit. Studien zur deutschen politischen Philosophie des 18. Jahrhunderts.* Ph.D. dissertation, University of Münster, 1965.

Mitrofanov, Paul von. *Joseph II. Seine politische und kulturelle Tätigkeit.* 2 vols. Vienna, 1910.

Mittenzwei, Ingrid. "Ueber das Problem des aufgeklärten Absolutismus." *Zeitschrift für Geschichte* 17 (1970):1162–72.

———. *Friedrich II. von Preußen.* Cologne, 1980.

Moeller, Bernd. *Reichstadt und Reformation.* Schriften des Vereins für Reformationsgeschichte 180. Gütersloh, 1962.

Möller, Horst. *Aufklärung in Preußen. Der Verleger, Publizist und Geschichtsschreiber Friedrich Nicolai.* Veröffentlichungen der Historischen Kommission Berlin, 15. Berlin, 1974.

Montesquieu, *The Spirit of the Laws.* Translated by Thomas Nugent. New York, 1949.

Mooser, Josef. *Bäuerliche Gesellschaft im Zeitalter der Revolution 1789–1848.* Ph.D. dissertation, University of Bielefeld, 1978.

Morsey, Rudolf. "Wirtschaftliche und soziale Auswirkungen der Säkularisation in Deutschland." In *Dauer und Wandel der Geschichte*, edited by Rudolf Vierhaus and Manfred Botzenhart, 361–83. Munich, 1966.

Moser, Friedrich Karl von. *Der Herr und der Diener.* Frankfurt, 1762 [1758].

———. *Von dem deutschen Nationalgeist.* n.p., 1765.

———. *Ueber die Regierung der geistlichen Staaten in Deutschland.* Frankfurt, 1787.

Motteck, Hans. *Wirtschaftsgeschichte Deutschlands.* 2 vols. Berlin, 1968–9.

Müller, Detlef K. *Sozialstruktur und Schulsystem. Aspekte zum Strukturwandel des Schulwesens im 19. Jahrhundert.* Göttingen, 1977.

Müller, Hans-Heinrich. *Märkische Landwirtschaft vor den Agrarreformen von 1807.* Potsdam, 1967.

Müller-Wille, Wilhelm. *Westfalen. Landschaftliche Ordnung und Bindung eines Landes.* Münster, 1952.

Narr, Dieter. *Studien zur Spätaufklärung im deutschen Südwesten.* Veröffentlichungen der Kommission für geschichtliche Landeskunde in Baden-Württemberg, series B research, vol. 93. Stuttgart, 1979.

Nicolai, Friedrich. "Einige Nachrichten über Nürnberg." *Berlin Monatsschrift* 1 (1783):79–96.

———. *Beschreibung einer Reise durch Deutschland und die Schweiz im Jahre 1781.* 12 vols. Berlin and Stettin, 1783–96.

———. *Geschichte eines dicken Mannes.* 2 vols. Berlin and Stettin, 1794.

———. *Leben und Meinungen Sempronius Gundiberts, eines deutschen Philosophen.* Berlin and Stettin, 1798.

———. *Ueber meine gelehrte Bildung.* Berlin and Stettin, 1799.

Niehaus, Heinrich. *Das Heuerleutesystem und die Heuerleutebewegung.* Quakenbrück, 1924.

Nipperdey, Thomas. "Verein als Sozialstruktur im späten 18. und frühen 19. Jahrhundert." In *Geschichtswissenschaft und Vereinswesen im 19. Jahrhundert*, edited by Hartmut Boockmann et al, 1–44. Veröffentlichungen des Max-Planck-Institut für Geschichte, 1. Göttingen, 1972.

O'Boyle, Lenore. "Klassische Bildung und Sozialstruktur in Deutschland zwischen 1800 and 1848." *HZ* 207 (1968):584–608.

O'Flaherty, James D., ed. and trans. *Hamann's Socratic Memorabilia*. Baltimore, 1967.

Oeder, Christian. *Bedenken über die Frage: wie dem Bauernstande Freiheit und Eigenthum in den Ländern, wo ihm beydes fehlt, verschaffet werden könne*. Frankfurt and Leipzig, 1769.

Oestreich, Gerhard. *Neostoicism and the Early Modern State*. Edited by Brigitta Oestreich and H. G. Koenigsberger. Translated by David McLintock. Cambridge, 1982.

Oestreich, Gerhard, and Auerbach, I. "Ständische Verfassung." In *Sowjetsystem und Demokratische Gesellschaft*, edited by C. D. Kernig, 6:211–35. 6 vols. Freiburg, 1966–1972.

Palmer, Robert T. *The Age of the Democratic Revolution*. 2 vols. Princeton, N.J., 1959–64.

Pareto, Vilfredo. *The Rise and Fall of the Elites*. Totowa, N.J., 1968.

Parry, Geraint. "Enlightened Government and Its Critics in Eighteenth-Century Germany." *Historical Journal* 6 (1963):178–92.

Pascal, Roy. "The 'Sturm und Drang' Movement." *Modern Language Review* 47 (1952):129–51.

―――. *The German Sturm und Drang*. 2nd ed. Manchester, 1959.

Paton, H. J. *The Categorical Imperative*. Philadelphia, 1948.

Payne, Harry. *The Philosophes and the People*. New Haven, Conn., 1976.

Philippson, Martin. *Geschichte des Preußischen Staatswesens vom Tode Friedrich des Großen bis zu den Freiheitskriegen*. 2 vols. Leipzig, 1880–2.

Phillipson, N. T. "Culture and Society in the 18th-Century Province: The Case of Edinburgh and the Scottish Enlightenment." In *The University in Society*, edited by Lawrence Stone, 2:407–48. 2 vols. Princeton, N.J., 1974.

Phillipson, N. T., and Mitchison, Rosalind. *Scotland in the Age of Improvement*. Edinburgh, 1970.

Pleister, Werner. "Die geistige Entwicklung Justus Mösers." *Osn. Mitt.* 50 (1929):1–89.

Pocock, J. G. A. *The Machiavellian Moment*. Princeton, N.J., 1975.

Pocock, J. G. A., ed. *The Political Works of James Harrington*. Cambridge, 1977.

Pole, J. R. *Political Representation in England and the Origins of the American Republic*. Berkeley, 1966.

Popkin, Richard. *The History of Skepticism*. Rev. ed. New York, 1968.

Porter, Roy, and Teich, Mikuláš, eds. *The Enlightenment in National Context*. Cambridge, 1981.

Preuß, Ulrich K. "Bildung und Bürokratie." *Der Staat* 14 (1975):371–96.

Probst, Paul. *Westfalen in der Kritik des XVIII. Jahrhunderts*. Ph.D. dissertation, University of Münster, 1912.

Prüsener, Marlies. "Lesegesellschaften im 18. Jahrhundert." *Archiv für Geschichte des Buchwesens* 13 (1973):369–594.

Pütter, Johann Stephen. *Selbstbiographie zur dankbaren Jubelfeier seiner 50jährigen Professorstelle zu Göttingen.* 2 vols. Göttingen, 1798.

————. *Vollständiges Handbuch der Teutschen Reichshistorie.* Göttingen, 1762.

Pufendorf, Samuel von [Severinus von Monzambano]. *Ueber die Verfassung des deutschen Reiches.* Edited by Harry Bresslau. Klassiker der Politik, 3. Edited by Friedrich Meinecke and Hermann Oncken. Berlin, 1922.

Raab, Felix. *The English Faces of Machiavelli.* London, 1964.

Raab, Heribert. *Clemens Wenzeslaus von Sachsen und seine Zeit (1739–1812).* 1 vol. to date. Freiburg, 1962.

Rachel, Hugo. "Der Merkantilismus in Brandenburg-Preußen." *FBPG* 40 (1927):221–66.

Raeff, Marc. "The Well-Ordered Police State and the Development of Modernity in Seventeenth and Eighteenth-Century Europe," *AHR* 80 (1975):1221–43.

————. *The Well-Ordered Police State.* New Haven, Conn., 1983.

Raumer, Kurt von. "Absoluter Staat, korporative Libertät, persönliche Freiheit." *HZ* 183 (1957):55–96.

Rawson, Elizabeth. *The Spartan Tradition in European Thought.* Oxford, 1969.

Reden-Dohna, Armgard Von, ed. *Deutschland und Italien im Zeitalter Napoleons.* Wiesbaden, 1979.

Redlich, Fritz. *Steeped in Two Cultures.* New York, 1971.

Reekers, Stephanie. "Beiträge zur statistischen Darstellung der gewerblichen Wirtschaft Westfalens um 1800." *Westfälische Forschungen* 17 (1964):83–176; 18 (1965):75–130; 19 (1966):27–78; 20 (1967):58–108.

Rehberg, August. *Sämmtliche Schriften.* 3 vols. Hanover, 1828–31.

Reichardt, Rolf. "Bevölkerung und Gesellschaft Frankreichs im 18. Jahrhundert: Neue Wege und Ergebnisse der sozialhistorischen Forschung 1950–1976." *ZHF* 4 (1977):154–221.

Reif, Heinz. *Westfälischer Adel 1770–1860.* Kritische Studien zur Geschichtswissenschaft, 35. Göttingen, 1979.

Reill, Peter Hanns. "History and Hermeneutics: The Thought of Johann Christoph Gatterer." *JMH* 45 (1973):24–51.

————. *The German Enlightenment and the Rise of Historicism.* Berkeley, 1975.

Reinalter, Helmut, ed. *Freimaurer und Geheimbünde im 18. Jahrhundert in Mitteleuropa.* Frankfurt am Main, 1983.

Renger, Reinhard. *Landesherr und Landstände im Hochstift Osnabrück in der Mitte des 18. Jahrhunderts.* Veröffentlichungen des Max-Planck-Instituts für Geschichte, 19. Göttingen, 1968.

————. "Justus Mösers amtlicher Wirkungskreis." *Osn. Mitt.* 77 (1970):1–30.

Rieck, Werner. *Johann Christoph Gottsched. Eine kritische Würdigung seines Werkes.* Berlin, 1972.

Riedel, Manfred. *Metaphysik und Metapolitik.* Frankfurt am Main, 1975.

Rinck, Fritz. *Justus Mösers Geschichtsauffassung.* Erfurt, 1908.

Ringer, Fritz. *Education and Society in Modern Europe.* Bloomington, Ind., 1979.

Ritter, Gerhard. "Der Freiherr vom Stein und die politischen Reformprogramme des ancien régime in Frankreich." *HZ* 137 (1928):442–97; 138 (1929):24–46.

———. *Stein.* 3rd ed. Stuttgart, 1958.

Ritter, Moritz. *Die Entwicklung der Geschichtswissenschaft.* Berlin, 1919.

Robson, Robert. *The Attorney in Eighteenth Century England.* Cambridge, 1959.

Roche, Daniel. *Le Siècle des lumières en Province.* 2 vols. Paris, 1978.

Rörig, Fritz. *Wirtschaftskräfte im Mittelalter.* Edited by Paul Kaegbein. Cologne, 1959.

———. *Die europäische Stadt und die Kultur des Bürgertums im Mittelalter.* 4th ed. Göttingen, 1964.

Rohde, Christine. *Beamtenschaft und Territorialstaat. Behördenentwicklung und Sozialstruktur der Beamtenschaft im Hochstift Osnabrück 1550–1800.* 2 parts. Ph.D. dissertation, University of Bochum, 1982.

Rohde, Paul. "Geschichte der Saline Rothenfelde." *Osn. Mitt.* 31 (1906):1–59.

Rohr, Donald. *The Origins of Social Liberalism in Germany.* Chicago, 1963.

Roscher, Wilhelm. *Geschichte der Nationalökonomik in Deutschland.* Munich, 1874.

Rosenberg, Hans. *Bureaucracy, Aristocracy, and Autocracy: The Prussian Experience, 1660–1815.* Boston, 1966.

———. *Politische Denkströmungen im deutschen Vormärz.* Kritische Studien zur Geschichtswissenschaft, 3. Göttingen, 1974.

Rothkrug, Lionel. *Opposition to Louis XIV.* Princeton, N.J., 1965.

Rozdolski, Roman. *Die große Steuer- und Agrarreform Josef II.* Warsaw, 1961.

Rüping, Hinrich. *Die Naturrechtslehre des Christain Thomasius und ihre Fortbildung in der Thomasius Schule.* Bonner Rechtswissenschaftliche Abhandlungen, 81. Bonn, 1968.

Rürup, Reinhard. *Johann Jakob Moser. Pietismus und Reform.* Veröffentlichungen des Instituts für europäische Geschichte Mainz, 35. Wiesbaden, 1968.

Ruggiero, Guido de. "Positivism." In *Encyclopedia of the Social Sciences,* 12:260–65. New York, 1934.

———. *The History of European Liberalism.* Translated by R. G. Collingwood. Boston, 1959.

Runge, Friedrich. *Geschichte des Ratsgymnasiums zu Osnabrück.* Osnabrück, 1895.

Runge, Joachim. *Justus Mösers Gewerbetheorie und Gewerbepolitik um Fürstentum Osnabrück in der zweiten Hälfte des 18. Jahrhunderts.* Schriften zur Wirtschafts- und Sozialgeschichte, 2. Berlin, 1966.

Saage, Richard. "Besitzindividualistische Perspektiven der politischen Theorie Kants." *Neue politische Literatur* (1972):168–193.

———. *Eigentum, Staat und Gesellschaft bei Immanuel Kant.* Stuttgart, 1973.

Salzbrunn, Ingeborg. *Studien zur deutschen historischen Zeitschriftenwesen von der Göttinger Aufklärung bis zur Herausgabe der Historischen Zeitschrift.* Ph.D. dissertation, University of Münster, 1959.

Sartori, Joseph von. *Statistische Abhandlung über die Mängel in der Regierunsverfassung der geistlichen Wahlstaaten und von den Mitteln, solchen abzuhelfen.* Augsburg, 1787.

———. *Geistliches und weltliches Staatsrecht der deutschen, catholischgeistlichen Erz-Hoch- und Ritterstifter,* 2 of 3 parts in 6 vols. Nürnberg, 1788–91.

Sauder, Gerhard. "Verhältnismäßige Aufklärung. Zur bürgerlichen Ideologie am

Ende des 18. Jahrhunderts." *Jahrbuch der Jean Paul Gesellschaft* 9 (1974):102–26.

———. "Aufklärung des Vorurteils – Vorurteil der Aufklärung, *DVLG* 57 (1983): 258–77.

Sauer, Wolfgang, "Das Problem des deutschen Nationalstaates," In *Moderne deutsche Sozialgeschichte*, edited by Hans Ulrich Wehler, 407–36, 544–50. Neue Wissenschaftliche Bibliothek, 10. Cologne, 1966.

Scharpwinkel, Klaus. *Die Westfälischen Eigentumsordnungen des 17. und 18. Jahrhunderts*. Juridical Dissertation, University of Göttingen, 1965.

Scheel, Günter. "Leibniz und die deutsche Geschichtswissenschaft um 1700." In *Historische Forschung im 18. Jahrhundert*, edited by Jürgen Voss and Karl Hammer, 82–101. Bonn, 1976.

Schieder, Theodor. "Partikularismus und nationales Bewuβtsein im Denken des Vormärz." In *Staat und Gesellschaft im deutschen Vormärz*, edited by Werner Conze, 9–38. Industrielle Welt, 1. Stuttgart, 1962.

Schierbaum, Heinrich. "Justus Mösers Stellung in den deutschen Literaturströmungen während der ersten Hälfte des 18. Jahrhunderts." *Osn. Mitt.* 33 (1908):167–216.

———. "Justus Mösers Stellung in der Literaturströmungen des 18. Jahrhunderts. II Teil," *Osn. Mitt.* 34 (1909):1–43.

Schindler, Norbert. "Freimauerkultur im 18. Jahrhundert. Zur sozialen Funktion des Geheimnisses in der entstehenden bürgerlichen Gesellschaft." In *Klassen und Kultur*, edited by Robert Berdahl et al., 205–62. Frankfurt am Main, 1982.

Schirmeyer, Ludwig. "Georg Ludwig von Bar, 'der beste französische Dichters Deutschlands,' ein Vorbild Wielands und Freund Mösers." *Osn. Mitt.* 32 (1907):1–71.

———. "Das Möserbild nach neuen Briefen." *Osn. Mitt.* 59 (1939):57–98.

Schissler, Hanna. *Preuβische Agrargesellschaft im Wandel*. Kritische Studien zur Geschichtswissenschaft, 33. Göttingen, 1978.

Schlechte, Horst *Die Staatsreform in Kursachsens 1762–63*. Berlin, 1958.

Schlie, Ulrich. *Johann Stephen Pütters Reichsbegriff*. Göttinger Rechtswissenschaftliche Studien, 38. Göttingen, 1961.

Schlumbohm, Jürgen. *Freiheit. Die Anfänge des bürgerlichen Emanzipationsbewegung in Deutschland im Spiegel ihres Leitwortes*. Geschichte und Gesellschaft, vol. 12. Düsseldorf, 1975.

———. "Der saisonale Rhythmus der Leinenproduktion im Osnabrücker Lande während des späten 18. und der ersten Hälfte des 19. Jahrhunderts: Erscheinungsbild, Zusammenhänge und interregionaler Vergleich." *Archiv für Sozialgeschichte* 19 (1979):263–98.

———. "Agrarische Besitzklassen und gewerbliche Produktionsverhältnisse: Groβbauern, Kleinbesitzer und Landlose als Leinenproduzenten im Umland von Osnabrück und Bielefeld während des frühen 19. Jahrhunderts." In *Mentalitäten und Lebensverhältnisse. Rudolf Vierhaus zum 60. Gerburtstag*, 315–34. Göttingen, 1982.

Schmauβ, Johann Jakob. *Kurzter Begriff der Reichshistorie*. Leipzig, 1720.

Schmidt, Peter. *Studien über Justus Möser als Historiker.* Göppinger Akademische Beiträge, 93. Göppingen, 1975.

Schmitz, Edith. *Leinengewerbe und Leinenhandel in Nordwestdeutschland, 1650–1850.* Schriften zur Rheinisch-Westfälischen Wirtschaftsgeschichte, 15. Cologne, 1967.

Schnaubert, Andreas Joseph. *Ueber des Freiherrn von Mosers Vorschläge zur Verbesserung der geistlichen Staaten in Deutschland.* Jena, 1788.

Schneiders, Werner. *Die wahre Aufklärung.* Freiburg, 1974.

Schneiders, Werner, ed. *Christian Wolff 1679–1754.* Studien zum achzehnten Jahrhundert, 4. Hamburg, 1983.

Schochet, Gordon J. *Patriarchalism in Political Thought.* New York, 1975.

Schöffler, Herbert. *Deutsches Geistesleben zwischen Reformation und Aufklärung.* 2nd ed. Frankfurt am Main, 1956.

Schöller, Peter. "Die Wirtschaftsräume Westfalens vor Beginn des Industrie Zeitalters." *Westfälische Forschungen* 16 (1963):84–101.

Schopenhauer, Johanna. *Jugendleben und Wanderjahre.* vol. I. Braunschweig, 1839.

Schotte, Heinrich. "Die rechtliche und wirtschaftliche Entwicklung des westfälischen Bauernstandes bis zum Jahre 1815." In *Beiträge zur Geschichte des westfälischen Bauernstandes,* edited by Engelbert Freiherr von Kerckerinck, 3–106. Berlin, 1912.

Schramm, Percy Ernst. *Neun Generationen,* 2 vols. Göttingen, 1963–4.

Schreiber, Ilse, ed. *Ich wohl war klug, das ich dich fand.* 2nd ed. Munich, 1963.

Schütze, M. Gottfried. *Drei kleine Schützschriften für die alten Deutschen.* Leipzig, 1746.

Schultze, Johanna. *Die Auseinandersetzung zwischen Adel und Bürgertum in den deutschen Zeitschriften der letzten drei Jahrzehnte des 18. Jahrhunderts (1773–1806).* Historische Studien, 163. Berlin, 1925.

Schultze, Karl-Egbert. "Zur Ahnenlist Justus Mösers. Ergänzungen." *Osn. Mitt.* 69 (1960):127–8.

Schulz, Günter. "Christian Garve und Immanuel Kant. Gelehrten-Tugenden im 18. Jahrhundert." *Jahrbuch der Schlesischen Friedrich-Wilhelms-Universität zu Breslau* 5 (1960):123–88.

Schulz, Ursula. *Die Berlinische Monatsschrift (1783–1796). Eine Bibliographie.* Bremen, 1968.

Schumann, Hans Gerd, ed. *Konservatismus.* Neue Wissenschaftliche Bibliothek, 68. Cologne, 1974.

Schumpeter, Joseph. *History of Economic Analysis.* New York, 1954.

Schwab, Dieter. "Die Familie als Vertragsgesellschaft im Naturrecht der Aufklärung." *Quaderni fiorentini per la storia del pensiero giuridico moderno* 1 (1972):357–76.

Schwager, Johann Moritz. "Versuch einer Schützschrift für die Westfälinger." *Berlinische Monatsschrift* 1 (1783):487–500.

Seeberg-Elverfeldt, Roland. "Zur Ahnenliste Justus Mösers. Ergänzungen." *Osn. Mitt.* 69 (1960):128–9.

Seliger, Martin. *The Liberal Politics of John Locke.* New York, 1968.

Sheehan, James. "Liberalism and the City in Nineteenth-Century Germany." *Past and Present* 51 (1971):116–37.

Sheldon, Ulrike, and Sheldon, William. *Im Geist der Empfindsamkeit. Freund-schaftsbriefe der Mösertochter Jenny von Voights und die Fürstin Luise von Anhalt-Dessau, 1780–1808*. Osnabrücker Geschichtsquellen und Forschungen, 17. Osnabrück, 1971.

Sheldon, William F. *The Intellectual Development of Justus Möser: The Growth of a German Patriot*. Osnabrücker Geschichtsquellen und Forschungen, 15. Osnabrück, 1970.

Shils, Edward. *Tradition*. Chicago, 1981.

Shklar, Judith. *Men and Citizens. A Study of Rousseau's Social Theory*. London, 1969.

Sidgwick, Henry. *Outlines of the History of Ethics*. London, 1886.

Slicher van Bath, B. H. *Agrarian History of Western Europe*. Translated by Olive Ordish. London, 1966.

Smith, Adam. *Wealth of Nations*. Edited by Edwin Cannan. New York, 1965.

Smith, T. B. "Scots Law and Roman-Dutch Law." *Judicial Review* 6 n.s. (1963):32–52.

Spechter, Olaf. *Die Osnabrücker Oberschicht im 17. und 18. Jahrhundert*. Osnabrücker Geschichtsquellen und Forschungen, 20. Osnabrück, 1975.

Stein, Peter. "Legal Thought in Eighteenth-Century Scotland." *Juridical Review* 1 (1957):1–20.

Steinbicker, Clements. "Das Beamtentum in den geistlichen Fürstentümern Nordwestdeutschlands." *Beamtentum und Pfarrerstand 1400–1800*, edited by Günther Franz, 121–48. Limburg/Lahn, 1972.

Steiner, Gerhard. *Franz Heinrich Ziegenhagen und seine Verhältnislehre*. Berlin, 1962.

Stephan, Inge. *Literarischer Jakobinismus in Deutschland (1789–1806)*. Stuttgart, 1976.

Stephen, Leslie. *History of English Thought in the Eighteenth Century*. 2 vols. Reprint 3rd ed. New York, 1962.

Stern, J. P. *Lichtenberg: A Doctrine of Selected Occasions*. Bloomington, Ind., 1959.

Stintzing, R., and Landsberg, Ernst. *Geschichte der deutschen Rechtswissenschaft*, 3 vols. in 4. Munich, 1880–1910.

Stölzel, Adolf. "Die Berliner Mittwochsgesellschaft über Aufhebung oder Reform der Universitäten (1795)." *FBPG* 2 (1889):201–22.

Stolleis, Michael. *Die Moral in der Politik bei Christian Garve*. Ph.D. dissertation, University of Munich, 1967.

Stone, Lawrence. "Social Mobility in England 1500–1700." *Past and Present* 33 (1966):16–55.

———. "Literacy and Education in England 1640–1900." *Past and Present* 42 (1969):69–139.

Strauss, Gerald. "The Holy Roman Empire Revisited." *CEH* 11 (1978):290–301.

Strauß, Walter. *Friedrich Nicolai und die kritische Philosophie*. Stuttgart, 1927.

Streisand, Joachim. *Geschichtliches Denken von der deutschen Frühaufklärung bis zur Klassik*. 2nd ed. Berlin, 1967.

Struve, Burcard Gotthelf. *Einleitung zur Teutschen Reichs-Historie*. 4th ed. 2 vols. Jena, 1747.

Stühle, Winold. *Ueber Möser und dessen Verdienste ums Vaterland, nebst verschiedenen Bemerkungen über Staatsverfassung.* Osnabrück, 1798.

Stüve, Carl Bertram. *Heinrich David Stüve, Doktor der Rechte und Bürgermeister der Stadt Osnabrück.* Jena, 1827.

Stüve, Johann Eberhard. *Beschreibung und Geschichte des Hochstifts und Fürstenthums Osnabrück.* Osnabrück, 1789.

Tautscher, Anton. *Staatswirtschaftlehre des Kameralismus.* Bern, 1947.

Taylor, George V. "Noncapitalist Wealth and the Origins of the French Revolution." *AHR* 72 (1966–7):469–96.

Theokrat, Samuel. "Wie ein Westphälischer Küster das Recht der Nationen, ihre Konstitution zu ändern, ansehe." *Schleswigisches ehemals Braunschweigisches Journal* 1 (1792):424–54.

Thieme, Hans. "Die Zeit des späteren Naturrechts. Eine privatrechtsgeschichtliche Studie." *ZSRG (germ)* 56 (1936):202–63.

Thieme, Hans, ed. *Humanismus und Naturrecht in Berlin-Brandenburg-Preußen.* Veröffentlichungen der Historischen Kommission zu Berlin, 48. Berlin, 1979.

Thomasius, Christian. *Deutsche Schriften.* Edited by Peter von Düffel. Stuttgart, 1970.

Thompson, E. P. "The Moral Economy of the English Crowd in the Eighteenth Century." *Past and Present* 50 (1971):76–136.

———. "Eighteenth-Century English Society: Class Struggle without Class?" *Social History* 3 (1978):133–65.

Träger, Claus, ed. *Die Französische Revolution im Spiegel der deutschen Literatur.* Leipzig, 1975.

Treue, Wilhelm. "Adam Smith in Deutschland." In *Deutschland und Europa. Festschrift für Hans Rothfels*, 101–133. Edited by Werner Conze. Düsseldorf, 1951.

Trunz, Erich. "Der deutsche Späthumanismus um 1600 als Standeskultur." In *Deutsche Barockforschung*, edited by Richard Alewyn, 147–181. Cologne, 1965.

Unger, Rudolf. *Hamann und die deutsche Aufklärung*, 2 vols. 4th ed. Darmstadt, 1968.

Valjavec, Fritz. *Die Entstehung der politischen Strömungen in Deutschland.* Afterword by Jörn Garber. Reprint 1951 ed. Düsseldorf, 1978.

———. "Das Woellnersche Religionsedikt und seine geschichtliche Bedeutung." *Historisches Jahrbuch*, 72 (1953):386–400.

———. *Ausgewählte Aufsätze.* Edited by Karl August Fischer and Mathias Bernath. Munich, 1963.

Vann, James. *The Swabian Kreis: Institutional Growth in the Holy Roman Empire.* Brussels, 1975.

Vann, James, and Rowan, Steven, eds. *The Old Reich: Essays on German Political Institutions 1495–1806.* Brussels, 1974.

Vierhaus, Rudolf. "Montesquieu in Deutschland." In *Collegium Philosophicum*, ed. Ernst-Wolfgang Böckenförde et al., 403–37. Basel, 1965.

———. "Ständewesen und Staatsverwaltung in Deutschland im späteren 18. Jahrhundert." In *Dauer und Wandel der Geschichte. Festgabe für Kurt von Rau-*

*mer*, edited by Rudolf Vierhaus and Manfred Botzenhart, 337–60. Münster, 1966.

―――. "Politisches Bewußtsein in Deutschland vor 1789." *Der Staat* 6 (1967): 175–96.

―――, ed. *Eigentum und Verfassung. Zur Eigentumsdiskussion im ausgehenden 18. Jahrhundert*. Veröffentlichungen des Max-Planck-Instituts für Geschichte, 37. Göttingen, 1972.

―――. "Absolutism." In *Marxism, Communism and Western Society*, edited by C. D. Kernig, 1:1–12. 8 vols. New York, 1972–3.

―――. "Land, Staat und Reich in der politischen Vorstellungswelt deutscher Landstände im 18. Jahrhundert." *HZ* 223 (1976):40–60.

―――. *Deutschland im Zeitalter des Absolutismus*. Göttingen, 1978.

―――, ed. *Deutsche patriotische und gemeinnützige Gesellschaften*. Wolfenbüttler Forschungen, 8. Munich, 1980.

Viner, Jacob. *The Long View and the Short*. Glencoe, Ill., 1958.

Vogel, Ursula. *Konservative Kritik an der Bürgerlichen Revolution*. Neuwied, 1972.

Voltelini, Hans von. "Die naturrechtlichen Lehren und die Reformen des 18. Jahrhunderts." *HZ* 105 (1910):65–104.

Vorländer, Karl. *Immanuel Kant*. 2 vols. Berlin, 1924.

Walker, Mack. *German Home Towns*. Ithaca, N.Y., 1971.

―――. *Johann Jakob Moser and the Holy Roman Empire of the German Nation*. Chapel Hill, N.C., 1981.

Wallthor, Alfred Hartlieb von. "Die Verfassung in Altwestfalen als Quelle moderner Selbstverwaltung." *Westfälische Forschungen* 9 (1956):26–44.

―――. "Die höheren Schulen Westfalens." *Westfalische Forschungen* 11 (1958):40–51.

Wangermann, Ernst. *From Joseph II to the Jacobin Trials*. 2nd ed. Oxford, 1969.

Ward, Albert. *Book Production, Fiction and the German Reading Public 1740–1800*. Oxford, 1974.

Weber, Max. *Wirtschaft und Gesellschaft*, 2 vols. Edited by Johannes Winckelmann. Cologne, 1964.

Weil, Hans. *Die Entstehung des deutschen Bildungprinzips*. 2nd ed. Bonn, 1967.

Weis, Eberhard. "Ergebnisse eines Vergleichs der grundherrschaftlichen Strukturen Deutschlands und Frankreichs vom 13. bis zum Ausgang des 18. Jahrhunderts." *VSWG* 57 (1970):1–14.

―――. "Absolute Monarchie und Reform in Deutschland des späteren 18. und des frühen 19. Jahrhunderts." In *Aufklärung, Absolutismus und Bürgertum*, edited by Franklin Kopitzsch, 192–219. Munich, 1976.

Weiser, Christian Friedrich. *Shaftesbury und das deutsche Geistesleben*. Leipzig, 1916.

Weiße, Christian Ernst. *Ueber die Säkularisation deutscher geistlicher Reichsländer in Rücksicht auf Geschichte und Staatsrecht*. Leipzig, 1798.

Wende, Peter. *Die geistlichen Staaten und ihre Auflösung im Urteil der Zeitgenössischen Publizistik*. Historische Studien, 396. Lübeck, 1966.

Weniger, Erich. "Rehberg und Stein." *Niedersächsisches Jahrbuch* 2 (1925):1–123.

Weyand, Klaus. *Kants Geschichtsphilosophie*. Kantstudien, supplement 85. Cologne, 1963.

Wieacker, Franz. *Privatrechtsgeschichte der Neuzeit*. 2nd ed. Göttingen, 1967.

Wiemann, Hermann. "Die Osnabrücker Stadtlegge," *Osn. Mitt.* 35 (1910): 1–76.

Winkler, Klaus. *Landwirtschaft und Agrarverfassung im Fürstentum Osnabrück nach dem Dreißigjährigen Kriege*. Stuttgart, 1959.

Winter, Eduard. *Frühaufklärung*. Berlin, 1966.

Wittich, Werner. *Die Grundherrschaft in Nordwestdeutschland*. Leipzig, 1896.

Wittichen, Paul. "Zur inneren Geschichte Preußens während der französischen Revolution. Gentz und Humboldt." *FBPG* 19 (1906):1–33.

Wolf, Erik. "Idee und Wirklichkeit des Reiches im deutschen Rechtsdenken des 16. und 17. Jahrhunderts." In *Reich und Recht in der deutschen Philosophie*, edited by Karl Larenz, 1:93–133. 2 vols. Berlin, 1943.

———. *Große Rechtsdenker*. 4th ed. Tübingen, 1963.

Wolff, Hans M. *Die Weltanschauung der deutschen Aufklärung in geschichtlicher Entwicklung*. 2nd ed. Bern and Munich, 1963.

Wolff, Robert Paul. *The Autonomy of Reason*. New York, 1973.

Wolin, Sheldon. *Politics and Vision*. Boston, 1960.

Wrigley, E. A. "A Simple Model of London's Importance in Changing English Society and Economy 1650–1750." *Past and Present* 37 (1967):44–70.

Wunder, Bernd. "Die Sozialstruktur der Geheimratskollegien in den süddeutschen protestantischen Fürstentümern (1660–1720). Zum Verhältnis von sozialer Mobilität und Briefadel im Absolutismus." *VSWG* 58 (1971):145–220.

———. "Die Entstehung des modernen Staates und des Berufsbeamentums in Deutschland im frühen 19. Jahrhundert." *Leviathan* 2 (1974):459–78.

Wundt, Max. *Die deutsche Schulphilosophie im Zeitalter der Aufklärung*. Heidelberger Abhandlungen zur Philosophie und ihrer Geschichte, 32. Tübingen, 1945.

Zagorin, Perez. *The Court and the Country*. New York, 1970.

Zorn, Wolfgang. "Reichs- und Freiheitsgedanken in der Publizistik des ausgehenden 18. Jahrhunderts (1763–1792)." *Darstellungen und Quellen zur Geschichte der deutschen Einheitsbewegung* 2 (1959):11–66.

# Index

Abbt, Thomas, 31, 52, 97, 102, 106
agriculture, *see* reform; Möser, Justus
anti-Kantianism, *see* Kant, Immanuel
Aristotelianism, links to the Enlightenment of, 13, 99–101, 107–8
*Aufklärung, see* Enlightenment, German

Bar, Georg Ludwig von, 52, 152
Behr, Christian von, 72, 73
Bertling, Ernst August, 44, 55
Biester, Johann Erich, 22, 167, 172
Brandes, Ernst, 44
Buder, Christian Gottlieb, 96
Burke, Edmund, 166
Bussche-Hünnefeld, Klamor von dem, 50, 96, 102
Bussche-Hünnefeld, Johann Friedrich von dem, 51, 59, 60

cameralism, 13, 15, 114–21; *see also* reform
cathedral chapter, *see* Osnabrück: cathedral chapter
Chemnitz, Bogislav, 100
civic republicanism, *see* history
civil society, 8, 9, 18, 29, 86, 87, 143, 172–3, 177, 181; *see also* Kant; liberalism
Clauer, Eduard von, 172–3, 178
Clemens August (Wittelsbach), 36, 44, 67, 68, 69, 75, 115
common sense, 26, 27, 30, 182; *see also* empiricism; practice; theory and practice
conservatism, x, 147–9, 158, 165; *see also* counter-Enlightenment
corporatist Enlightenment, 4, 8–9, 11–19, 29, 149, 167–8; *see also* Enlightenment, German; counter-Enlightenment
counter-Enlightenment, 20, 24, 29, 95, 147–9, 161
Cramer, Johann, 63

Dahlberg, Carl Theodor von, 84
Darjes, Joachim, 63
Diderot, Denis, 53
Dilthey, Wilhelm, 94

economy: cameralist traditions, 13–14, 114–17; moral, 12–13, 118; pattern of reform, 14–16, 113–21; *see also* Möser, Justus; reform
education: Latin, 5–6; in Osnabrück, 55–6; and social mobility, 42–3, 52–4; *see also* humanism
emancipation, peasant, *see* reform: peasant emancipation; society: peasantry
empiricism, 26, 27, 30, 183–6; *see also* practice; theory and practice
Enlightenment, German: attitudes toward Empire, 100; characterized, 25; diffusion, 7–8; economic reform traditions, 138–44; inegalitarianism within, 11–12, 19, 27, 33, 47, 52–4, 56–8, 64, 104–8, 111, 134, 138, 159–61, 163, 168, 178–80, 184; literature regarding, 3n; natural rights tradition, 26, 62–4, 107–8, 160–1, 168, 172–3; pluralism of traditions, x, xi, 6–7, 18–19, 20, 25; relations to European Enlightenment, 3–8, 13, 14, 18, 24; *see also* conservatism; counter-Enlightenment; corporatist Enlightenment; intelligentsia, German; liberalism
Ernst August II (Hanover), 44, 46, 115

Ferguson, Adam, 13
Filmer, Robert, 12
French Revolution, impact on Germany of, 9, 11, 29, 30, 76, 111, 164–8, 169, 174–5
Friedrich II (Hohenzollern), 7, 24, 57, 141, 146, 152, 174
Fritsch, Thomas Freiherr von, 15
Fürstenberg, Franz von, 83, 142–3

213

214                                     *Index*

Garve, Christian, 62, 162, 166, 176, 177, 184
Gatterer, Johann Christoph, 109, 110–11, 143, 170
Gedike, Friedrich, 22
Gentz, Friedrich, 166, 181, 184–6
Gibbon, Edward, 94
Goethe, Johann Wolfgang von, 22, 23, 24, 25
Gottsched, Johann Christoph, 3, 6, 151
Gracian, Balthasar, 57
Grotius, Hugo, 140
Gruner, Johann Christian, 152
Gruner, Justus, 41, 47
Gundling, Nicholas, 101

Haller, Albrecht von, 45
Haller, Carl Ludwig von, 12
Hamann, Johann Georg, 147
Harrington, James, 106, 150
Herder, Johann Gottfried, 23, 27, 103, 111
historicism (*Historismus*), x, 29, 95; *see also* history
history: civic republicanism, 105–6, 107–8, 111; imperial history (*Reichshistorie*), 95–6, 99, 101–2, 105, 111; imperial reform literature (*Reichspublizistik*), 95–6, 99–101; Kant as historian, 29; Latin humanist traditions, 60–2, 95–6, 99, 105; *see also* Aristotelianism; historicism; humanism; Möser, Justus: as historian
Hobbes, Thomas, 160, 179
Hoche, J. G., 41
humanism: Latin, 5–6, 20, 28, 60–1, 94, 106–7, 111; *see also* history: Latin humanist traditions
Hume, David, 13, 28, 30, 77, 106, 139, 140
Hutcheson, Francis, 166

Ickstatt, Johann Adam, 63
Illuminati, 7, 8
inegalitarianism, *see* Enlightenment, German
intelligentsia, German, 4–5, 18–19, 24, 25, 145–6; *see also* lawyers
irrationalism, 147–8; *see also* counter-Enlightenment
Iselin, Isaak, 62

Jesuit order, 7, 24, 55, 169
Joseph II (Habsburg), 15, 74, 133, 141, 155

Kant, Immanuel, 10, 27, 29, 30, 62, 165, 166, 168, 174–86; anti-Kantianism, 23, 30, 166, 181–6
Klein, Ferdinand Ernst, 62
Kleinmayr, Franz Thaddäus von, 99
Klopstock, Friedrich, 54

Köhler, Johann David, 101
Kreittmayr, Wiguläus Xaverius Aloysius Freiherr von, 9

labor, migratory (*Hollandsgänger*), 128–131
lawyers: enlightened cultural values of, 32–4, 60–4; legal notables in Osnabrück, 37, 39–47; social mobility of, 41–2, 49–52
Leibniz, Gottfried Wilhelm, 3, 6
Lenthe, Albrecht von, 70, 71, 72, 73, 97
Lessing, Gotthold Ephraim, 3, 24, 44, 98, 148, 151
liberalism, 27, 28, 120–1, 150, 166, 177; *see also* civil society; social contract theory
Lichtenberg, Georg, 3, 31
localism, *see* particularism
Locke, John, 27, 140, 150, 169; *see also* social contract theory.
Lodtmann, Karl Gerhard Wilhelm, 44, 55, 61, 96
Lodtmann, Justus Friedrich August, 47–8
Ludewig, Johann Peter, 61

Maier, Johann Christian, 88–91
Mascov, Gottfried, 96
Mascov, Johann Jakob, 101
Meinecke, Friedrich, 29, 94, 95, 110
Mendelssohn, Moses, 3, 9–11, 87, 148
Möser, Jenny, 22, 49–50, 56
Möser, Justus: aesthetic of "total impressions," 161–3; anti-Semitism, 87; as critic of the cathedral chapter, 70–3, 78, 80–2; as historian, 22, 23, 27–8, 60–2, 94–109, 156–7, 170–1, 173, 178–9; attitudes: *conservatism*, ix–x, 24, 30; *cultural*, 58–64; *as defender of the political Estates*, 102–111, 154–61, 169–71; *during succession crisis*, 79–83; *toward "freedom and property,"* 24, 29, 103–8, 110, 159–61, 169–71; *toward French Revolution*, 166–9; *hostility to individualism*, 27; *toward peasant emancipation*, 21, 27–8n, 132–8, 171–2, 178; *perspectivism*, 2, 20–1, 157; *toward practice*, 26–7; *religious*, 85–93; *toward rural indebtedness*, 136–7; *toward rural poor*, 129–32; biographical literature, 32n; career as publicist, 20–5, 113; family history, 43–52; offices, 1, 45–6, 48–9, 69–73; political significance in Osnabrück, 1–2, 32, 46–52, 72–3, 83; reform policies after Seven Years War, 114–38, 141; as representative of the *Ritterschaft*, 1, 31, 45, 70, 72–3, 88
Möser, Johann Zacharias [brother], 45, 48
Möser, Johann Zacharias [father], 43–44, 45
Möser, Regina Gertrud (Elverfeld), 44
Möser, Regina Juliana Elisabeth (Bruning), 46, 56